Study for Quiz	Study for Quiz	Study for Quiz	Study for Quiz	Study for Quiz	Study for	Study for Quiz
Study for Quiz	Study for Quiz	Study for Quiz	Study for Quiz	Study for Quiz	for Quiz	for Quiz
Review This	Review This	Review This	Review This	Review This	Review This	Review This
Review This	Review This	Review This	Review This	Review This	Review This	Review This
ASK for HELP	ASK for HELP	ASK for HELP	ASK for HELP	ASK for HELP	ASK for HELP	ASK for HELP
ASK for HELP	ASK for HELP	ASK for HELP	ASK for HELP	ASK for HELP	ASK for HELP	ASK for HELP
Important	Important	Important	Important	Important	Important	Important
Important	Important	Important	Important	Important	Important	Important
Study for Quiz	Study for Quiz	ASK for HELP	ASK for HELP	Review This	Review This	Important

CORNERSTONES
for COMMUNITY
COLLEGE SUCCESS

ROBERT M. SHERFIELD

College of Southern Nevada

PATRICIA G. MOODY

Professor Emerita, University of South Carolina

Boston • Columbus • Indianapolis • New York • San Francisco • Upper Saddle River
Amsterdam • Cape Town • Dubai • London • Madrid • Milan • Munich • Paris • Montreal • Toronto
Delhi • Mexico City • Sao Paulo • Sydney • Hong Kong • Seoul • Singapore • Taipei • Tokyo

Editor-in-Chief: Jodi McPherson
Editorial Assistant: Clara Ciminelli
Development Editor: Jennifer Gessner
Marketing Manager: Amy Judd
Production Editor: Janet Domingo
Editorial Production Service: Omegatype Typography, Inc.
Manufacturing Buyer: Megan Cochran
Electronic Composition: Omegatype Typography, Inc.
Interior Design: Carol Somberg/Omegatype Typography, Inc.
Photo Researcher: Annie Pickert
Cover Designer: Linda Knowles

Library of Congress Cataloging-in-Publication Data

Sherfield, Robert M.
   Cornerstones for community college success / Robert M. Sherfield, Patricia G. Moody.—1st ed.
        p.   cm.
   Includes bibliographical references and index.
   ISBN-13: 978-0-13-707338-2 (pbk.)
   ISBN-10: 0-13-707338-0 (pbk.)
  1. Community colleges—United States.   2. Community college students—United States.   3. Academic achievement—United States.   4. School-to-work transition—United States.   I. Moody, Patricia G.   II. Title.
   LB2328.15.U6S53   2012
   378.1'98—dc22   2010043645

10 9 8 7 6 5 4 3 2 1   WEB   15 14 13 12 11

www.pearsonhighered.com   ISBN 10: 0-13-707344-5
ISBN 13: 978-0-13-707344-3

Robert M. Sherfield, Ph.D.

Robert Sherfield has been teaching public speaking, theater, and student success as well as working with first-year orientation programs for over 25 years. Currently, he is a professor at the College of Southern Nevada, teaching student success, professional communication, public speaking, and drama.

An award-winning educator, Robb was named **Educator of the Year** at the College of Southern Nevada. He twice received the **Distinguished Teacher of the Year Award** from the University of South Carolina at Union and has received numerous other awards and nominations for outstanding classroom instruction and advisement.

Robb's extensive work with student success programs includes experience with the design and implementation of these programs—including one that was presented at the International Conference on the First-Year Experience in Newcastle upon Tyne, England. He has conducted faculty development keynotes and workshops at over 350 institutions of higher education across the United States. He has spoken in 46 states and several foreign countries.

In addition to his co-authorship of *Cornerstone: Opening Doors to Career Success* (Prentice Hall, 2009), he has authored or co-authored *Solving the Professional Development Puzzle: 101 Solutions for Career and Life Planning* (Prentice Hall, 2009), *Cornerstone: Discovering Your Potential, Learning Actively, and Living Well* (Prentice Hall, 2008), *Roadways to Success* (Prentice Hall, 2001), the trade book *365 Things I Learned in College* (Allyn & Bacon, 1996), *Capstone: Succeeding Beyond College* (Prentice Hall, 2001), *Case Studies for the First Year: An Odyssey into Critical Thinking and Problem Solving* (Prentice Hall, 2004), *The Everything Self-Esteem Book* (Adams Media, 2004), and *Cornerstone: Building On Your Best for Career Success* (Prentice Hall, 2006)

Robb's interest in student success began with his own first year in college. Low SAT scores and a dismal high school ranking denied him entrance into college. With the help of a success program, Robb was granted entrance into college and went on to earn five college degrees, including a doctorate. He has always been interested in the social, academic, and cultural development of students and sees this book as his way to help students enter the world of work and establish lasting, rewarding careers. Visit www.robert sherfield.com.

Patricia G. Moody, Ph.D.

Patricia G. Moody is Dean Emerita of the College of Hospitality, Retail and Sport Management at the University of South Carolina, where she has served on the faculty and in administration for over 30 years. An award-winning educator, Pat was honored as **Distinguished Educator of the Year** at her college and as **Collegiate Teacher of the Year** by the National Business Education Association. She was also a top-five finalist for the **Amoco Teaching Award** at the University of South Carolina. She received the prestigious **John Robert Gregg Award,** the highest honor in her field of over 100,000 educators.

Pat has co-authored many texts and simulations, including *Solving the Professional Development Puzzle: 101 Solutions for Career and Life Planning; Cornerstone: Discovering Your Potential, Learning Actively, and Living Well; 365 Things I Learned in College; Capstone: Succeeding Beyond College; Case Studies for the First Year: An Odyssey into Critical Thinking and Problem Solving;* and *Cornerstone: Opening Doors to Career Success.*

A nationally known motivational speaker, consultant, and author, Pat has spoken in most states, has been invited to speak in several foreign countries, and frequently keynotes national and regional conventions. She has presented her signature, motivational keynote address, *"Fly Like an Eagle,"* to tens of thousands of people, from Olympic athletes to corporate executives to high school students.

As the dean of her college, Dr. Moody led international trips to build relationships and establish joint research projects in hospitality. Under her direction, faculty members in her college began a landmark study of Chinese tourists. Pat now travels the country delivering workshops, keynotes, and presentations on topics such as Managing Change, Working in the New Global Community, The Future of the Future, Student Motivation, and Emotional Intelligence. She also serves as a personal coach for business executives.

CONTENTS

ACKNOWLEDGMENTS AND GRATITUDE

Dedication

We would like to dedicate this book to the ***many teachers*** throughout our lives who taught us about life, responsibility, and our role in the world. We carry you with us every day.

Louise Lymas	Neely Beaty	Beverly Jordan
Kitty Carson	Betty Griffin	Dick Smith
Steve Brannon	Frank Jackson	Dr. Harvey Jeffreys
Dr. Marilyn Kameen	Dr. Lars Bjork	Dora T. Martin
Phil Lynn	Dr. Howard Jackson	Dr. Leonard Maiden
Mary Alice Roughton	Dr. Marilyn Neidig	Ann Wenz

We would like to thank the following individuals at the **College of Southern Nevada** for their support:

Dr. Michael Richards, President
Dr. Darren Divine, Vice President for Academic Affairs
Dr. Hyla Winters, Associate Vice President for Academic Affairs
Professor Rose Hawkins, Dean, School of Arts and Letters
Dr. John Ziebell, Department Chair—English
Dr. Levia D. Hayes, Assistant Chair—English
Professor Linda Gannon, Lead Faculty, Academic and Life Strategies

We would also like to thank individuals at the **University of South Carolina,** particularly faculty members in the College of Hospitality, Retail, and Sport Management.

Our fondest gratitude to the following **colleagues and friends** who recommended individuals for the features *How My Community College Changed My Life* and *From Ordinary to Extraordinary: Real People. Real Lives. Real Change:*

Shannon McCasland, Aims Community College
Wistar Withers, Northern Virginia Community College
Amy Baldwin, Pulaski Technical College
Steve Piscitelli, Florida State College at Jacksonville
Sheryl Duquette, Erie Community College
Melanie Deffendall, Delgado Community College
Tina Eliopulos, College of Southern Nevada
Ann A. Cooper, Central Carolina Technical College
Donna J. McCauley, Moraine Valley Community College
Ryan Messatzzia, Wor-Wic Community College
Carol Hedberg, Hawkeye Community College
JoAnne Credle, Northern Virginia Community College
Cheryl Rohrbaugh, Northern Virginia Community College

Charlie Dy, Northern Virginia Community College
Everett Vann Eberhardt, Northern Virginia Community College
Antonette Payne, Pearson Education
Wendy DiLeonardo, Pearson Education

To the **amazing individuals** who shared their life stories with us for the feature *From Ordinary to Extraordinary: Real People. Real Lives. Real Change:*

Bill Clayton
Lydia Hausler Lebovic
Dino Gonzalez, M.D.
Vivian Wong
Dr. Wayne A. Jones
Maureen Riopelle
Odette Smith-Ransome
Sylvia Eberhardt
Luke Bryan
H. P. Rama
Leo G. Borges
Mark Jones

To the **marvellous students (current and former)** who shared their advice and experiences for *How My Community College Changed My Life:*

Brandon Sellers, Aims Community College
Geofferey Kamau, Northern Virginia Community College
Zzavvalynn Orleanski, Pulaski Technical College
Jenna Adams, Florida State College at Jacksonville
Patty Montella, Erie Community College
Alencia Anderson, Delgado Community College
Patricia Walls, College of Southern Nevada
Amy Geddings, Central Carolina Technical College
Mark D. Weber, Moraine Valley Community College
Jeffrey Steele, Wor-Wic Community College
Quenton Richardson, Hawkeye Community College

Our wonderful and insightful reviewers for this and all books in the *Cornerstone* series:

Elvira Johnson, Central Piedmont Community College; Ryan Messatzzia, Wor-Wic Community College; Sarah K. Shutt, J. Sergeant Reynolds Community College; Kristina Leonard, Daytona Beach College; Kim Long, Valencia Community College; Taunya Paul, York Technical College; Charlie L. Dy, Northern Virginia Community College; Gary H. Wanamamker, Houston Community College; Jo Ann Jenkins, Moraine Valley Community College; Judith Lynch, Kansas State University; Timothy J. Quezada, El Paso Community College; Cathy Hall, Indiana University NW; Beverly J. Slaughter, Brevard Community College; Peg Adams, Northern Kentucky University; Sheryl Duquette, Erie Community College; Melanie Deffendall, Delgado Community College; Arthur Webb, Oklahoma State University; Stephanie Young, Butler Community College; Tara Wertz, MTI College; Diana Clennan, College of Southern Nevada; Jennifer Huss-Basquiat, College of Southern Nevada; Wayne A. Jones, Virginia State University; Barbara Auris, Montgomery County Community College, Betty Fortune, Houston Community College; Joel V. McGee, Texas A & M University; Jan Norton, University of Wisconsin–Osh Kosh; Todd Phillips, East Central College; Christian M. Blum, Bryan and Stratton College; James Briski, Katherine Gibbs School; Pela Selene Terry, Art Institute of NYC; Christina Donnelly, York Technical College; Connie Egelman, Nassau Community College; Amy Hickman, Collins College; Beth Humes, Pennsylvania Culinary Institute; Kim Joyce, Art Institute of Philadelphia; Lawrence Ludwig, Sanford-Brown College; Bethany Marcus, ECPI College of Technology; Kate Sawyer, Pittsburgh Technical Institute; Patricia Sell, National College of Business and Technology; Janis Stiewing, PIMA Medical Institute; June Sullivan, Florida Metropolitan University; Fred Amador, Phoenix College; Kathy Bryan, Daytona Beach Community College; Dorothy Chase, Community College of Southern Nevada; JoAnn Credle, Northern Virginia Community College; Betty Fortune, Houston Community College; Doroteo Franco Jr., El Paso Community College; Cynthia Garrard, Massasoit Community College; Joel Jessen, Eastfield College; Peter Johnston, Massasoit Community College; Steve Konowalow, Community College of Southern Nevada; Janet Lindner, Midlands Technical College; Carmen McNeil, Solano College; Joan O'Connor, New York Institute of Technology; Mary Pepe, Valencia Community College; Bennie Perdue, Miami-Dade Community College; Ginny Peterson-Tennant, Miami-Dade Community College; Anna E. Ward, Miami-Dade Community College; Wistar M. Withers, Northern Virginia Community College; Marie Zander, New York Institute of Technology; Joanne Bassett, Shelby State Community College; Sandra M. Bovain-Lowe, Cumberland Community College; Carol Brooks, GMI Engineering and Management Institute; Elaine H. Byrd, Utah Valley State College; Janet Cutshall, Sussex County Community College; Deborah Daiek, Wayne State University; David DeFrain, Central Missouri State University; Leslie L. Duckworth, Florida Community College at Jacksonville; Marnell Hayes, Lake City Community College; Elzora Holland, University of Michigan, Ann Arbor; Earlyn G. Jordan, Fayetteville State University; John Lowry-King, Eastern New Mexico University; Charlene Latimer; Michael Laven, University of Southwestern Louisiana; Judith Lynch, Kansas State University; Susan Magun-Jackson, The University of Memphis; Charles William Martin, California State University, San Bernardino; Jeffrey A. Miller; Ronald W. Johnsrud, Lake City Community College; Joseph R. Krzyzanowski, Albuquerque TVI; Ellen Oppenberg, Glendale Community College; Lee Pelton, Charles S. Mott Community College; Robert Rozelle, Wichita State University; Penny Schempp, Western Iowa Community College; Betty Smith, University of Nebraska at Kearney; James Stepp, University of Maine at Presque Isle; Charles Washington, Indiana University–Purdue University; and Katherine A. Wenen-Nesbit, Chippewa Valley Technical College.

Our Creative and Supportive Team at Pearson

Without the support and encouragement of the following people at Pearson, this book would not be possible. Our sincere thanks to:

Susan Badger   Nancy Forsyth   Jodi McPherson
Amy Judd   Janet Domingo

Your constant belief in us over the years has been a most cherished gift. We are lucky to know you and are better people because of you. Thank you!

We also thank the following friends at Pearson for their support, dedication and exceptional work:

Jenny Gessner, Clara Ciminelli, Antonette Payne, Walt Kirby, Debbie Ogilvie, Alan Hensley, Pam Jeffries, Barbara Donlon, Cathy Bennett, Meredith Chandler, Jeff McIlroy, Matt Mesaros, Connie James, Wendy DiLeonardo, Dave Gessell, Eric Hackanson, Deborah Wilson, Eric Weiss, Julie Morel, Julie Hildabrand, Andrea Iorio, and Richard Rowe.

BEGIN

THE GOAL OF
CORNERSTONES
FOR COMMUNITY
COLLEGE SUCCESS
AND OUR
COMMITMENT
TO YOU

"Talent alone
won't make you a
success. Neither will
being in the right place
at the right time, unless
you are ready. The most
important question is:
'Are you ready?'"

—Johnny Carson

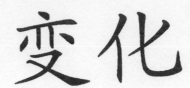

If you look at the figure printed here you will see the Chinese word meaning *"to change."* It is made up of two symbols—the first means *to transform* or to be flexible. The second means *to do or to deliver*. In its purest form, the symbol means to **deliver transformation.** That is what *Cornerstones* is all about, helping you deliver or bring about transformation, positive change if you will, to your life. It is about helping you discover ways to change your thoughts, change your performance, and change your life.

Our goal in writing *Cornerstones* is to help you discover your academic, social, and personal strengths so that you can build on them and to provide **concrete and useful tools** that will help you make the changes that might be necessary for your success. We believe that in helping you identify and transform areas that have challenged you in the past, you can *discover your true potential, learn more actively, and have the career you want and deserve.*

Cornerstones for Community College Success is devoted to three specific areas in which creating positive change can help you become the individual you would like to be:

Changing Your Thoughts
Changing Your Performance
Changing Your Life

Changing Your Thoughts addresses a broad spectrum of topics that begin with a focus on change as it relates to becoming a college student in a different culture and setting than you may have known before. In this section, you will be introduced to tools of self-management as they relate to college life. You will be exposed to a variety of new terms, ideas, and thoughts—all of which begin your journey of change. You will learn to enhance your communication skills, improve your self-concept, and manage conflict, all valuable tools on the road to change. You will also become more adept at critical thinking and problem solving. When you have completed this section, you should notice a difference in the way you approach tasks and think about subjects, challenges, and people.

Changing Your Performance focuses on you and how you physically and mentally manage yourself. You will begin this part of the journey to change by learning to manage your time and control the inherent stress that accompanies being a college student. You will realize that you have a dominant intelligence, learning style, and personality type and will learn how to use them to your advantage. Even though you have been reading for some time, you will be shown strategies to improve both your speed and comprehension because reading is such a major part of college studies. You will be shown several note-taking systems designed to improve your ability to record what your professors are teaching. Finally, you will be taught strategies for empowering your memory, learning to study more effectively, and taking tests with confidence. When you complete this section, you should be able to perform most tasks more effectively and confidently.

Changing Your Life is a culmination of the journey you have embarked on as a first-year student. This section is designed to round out your total personal profile and springboard you to success as you move into a different realm. Many college students do well on the topics covered in the first two sections but fall short when they arrive at this point. To be a complete, successful college student, you need to address all these areas because they are significant to the changes you need to embrace. You will learn to manage your money and your debts wisely. So many college students are burdened with astronomical college debts when they graduate; our desire is for you to have accumulated as little debt as possible at the same time you are taking advantage of all that college has to offer. You will be introduced to techniques for planning your professional career in the face of dramatic global changes. When you finish this section, you should be prepared to move through the next few years of college and beyond with confidence and optimism.

We know that your **time is valuable** and that you are pulled in countless directions with work, family, school, previous obligations, and many other tasks. For this reason, we have tried to provide only the most concrete, useful strategies and ideas to help you succeed in this class and beyond.

We have spent over 55 years collectively gathering the information, advice, suggestions, and activities on the following pages. The ideas and information have come from trial and error, colleagues, former students, instructors across America, and solid research. We hope that you will enjoy discovering the knowledge collected here, learn from it, and most of all, use it to change your life and move closer to your dreams.

Let the journey to positive change begin!

WHY DOES THIS MATTER? IT'S NOT ABOUT WHERE YOU'VE BEEN, IT'S WHERE YOU'RE GOING THAT MATTERS

This book is written especially for community college students. While it follows in the tradition of the *Cornerstone* franchise, the content, examples, and exercises are specifically dedicated to the interests, challenges, and needs of students attending community college.

Features in This Edition

WHERE YOU ARE: THE COMMUNITY COLLEGE FOCUS

▶ This book includes newly developed exercises and examples that relate specifically to the community college population.

▶ **"How My Community College Changed My Life,"** at the beginning of each chapter, tells the stories of successful community college graduates.

▶ **Unique chapters** contain coverage not commonly found in student success textbooks: shaping one's own destiny, understanding and navigating community college culture, transitioning to the university or workplace, and more.

WHY COMMUNITY COLLEGE MATTERS

▶ **"Successful Decisions"** boxes appear in every chapter. They involve students in critical thinking and reflection.

▶ In each chapter, the feature **"From Ordinary to Extraordinary"** showcases real people, real lives, and real change.

▶ **"Creating Your New Reality,"** at the end of each chapter, focuses on envisioning the future and working toward those goals.

WHERE YOU'RE GOING

▶ **Transfer guidance.** Chapter 3 helps students understand what courses to take at the community college level to make the transfer process easier when transitioning to a four-year institution.

▶ **The four-year plan.** Chapter 12 looks ahead to the coursework and other essential steps required to complete a four-year degree plan. This four-year success plan helps students begin planning for the completion of his or her four-year degree from the very first week of the first semester.

Objective listening can be a difficult skill to learn. Have you encountered people with views radically different from your own? How do you respond?

WE HOPE YOU LEARNED YOUR LESSON!

What Is This Thing Called Learning, Anyway?

In its purest and simplest form, learning is a *cognitive mental action* in which new information is acquired or in which you learn to use old information in a new way. Learning can be *conscious* and/or *unconscious*. Do you remember the very day you learned how to walk or talk? Probably not. This learning was more of an unconscious nature. However, you probably do remember learning about the 50 states or subtraction or reading an Edgar Allan Poe poem for the first time. This learning was more conscious in nature. Learning can also be *formal* (schooling) or *informal* ("street knowledge"). Learning can happen in many ways such as through play, trial and error, mistakes, successes, repetition, environmental conditioning, parental discipline, social interactions, media, observation, and, yes, through formal study methods.

Learning is what you do *FOR* yourself; it is not done *TO* you. Parents may discipline you time and time and time again, but try as they might, until YOU learn the lesson trying to be taught, it will NOT be learned. Teachers can preach and talk until they are blue in the face about the 13 original colonies, but until you learn them and commit them to memory, they will NOT be learned. That is what this chapter is all about—helping you discover how you learn, why you learn, and assisting you in finding the best way to learn so that you can DO the learning for yourself on a more effective level.

What Do the Experts Say?

The question still begs: *HOW do we really learn?* By studying a textbook? By reading a newspaper? By looking at pictures? By interviewing someone about a topic? By watching a movie? By trying something to see if it works? Yes, but the process is much more complex than this. Around 300 BC, the great Greek philosopher Socrates introduced his theory of learning. He believed that we learn by asking questions. This is called the **Socratic Method**. His student, **Plato**, expanded on this theory, believing that we learn best by dialogue, called the Dialectic Method,

SQ3R

What Is It and Why Do I Need to Know It?

You may be asking, "*What does SQ3R mean and what could it possibly have to do with me, my text, this course, and my success?*" The answer: **SQ3R (S = Scan, Q = Question, 3R = Read, Recite, Review)** is one of the most successful and widely used learning and study tools ever introduced.

This simple yet highly effective mnemonic (memory trick) asks that **before you actually read the chapter,** you look over the contents, check out the figures and photos, look at section headings, and review any graphs or charts. This is called *scanning*. Step two, *question*, asks that you jot down questions that you think you will need to answer about the chapter's content in order to master the material. These questions might come from charts or figures, but most commonly, they come from the chapter's section headings. Examine the following example taken from a section heading in *Criminal Justice, A Brief Introduction* (6th ed.) by Frank Schmalleger (Prentice Hall, 2006).

---

reported data.[64] Crimes that result from an anomalous event, but which are excluded from reported data, highlight the arbitrary nature of the data-collection process itself.

Special Categories of Crime

crime typology

A classification of crimes along a particular dimension, such as legal categories, offender motivation, victim behavior, or the characteristics of individual offenders.

A **crime typology** is a classification scheme that is useful in the study and description of criminal behavior. All crime typologies have an underlying logic, and the system of classification that derives from any particular typology may be based on legal criteria, offender motivation, victim behavior, the characteristics of individual offenders, or the like. Criminologists Terance D. Miethe and Richard C. McCorkle note that crime typologies "are designed primarily to simplify social reality by identifying homogeneous groups of crime behaviors that are different from other clusters of crime behaviors."[65] Hence one common but simple typology contains only two categories of crime: violent and property. In fact, many crime typologies contain overlapping or nonexclusive categories—just as violent crimes may involve property offenses, and property offenses may lead to violent crimes. Thus no one typology is likely to capture all of the nuances of criminal offending.

---

(1) *What are the categories of crime?*
(2) *Why do they matter?*
(3) *What is crime typology?*
(4) *When are categories of crime most often used?*

After writing these questions from the section heading, a student will read the section and then answer those questions. This technique provides a focus and purpose for reading. Each chapter in *Cornerstones* reflects this method through a feature called **SCAN and QUESTION.** We included this feature in *Cornerstones* to help you become a more active reader with greater comprehension skills in all of your classes. This technique is fully discussed in Chapter 8 of this text.

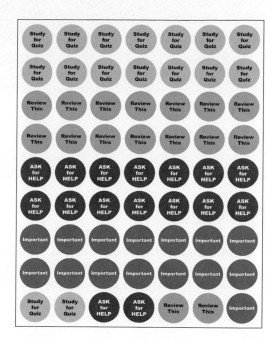

STICKERS for SUCCESS

What Are Those Colorful Stickers in the Front of My Book?

In the front of this text, you will find a sheet of peel-off stickers to help you "tag" pages and content that (1) you need to study for a quiz, (2) review for mastery, (3) seek help with, or (4) mark as important. We encourage you to use them to help you locate information easily.

A WORD ABOUT READING AND USING *CORNERSTONES FOR COMMUNITY COLLEGE SUCCESS*

We encourage you to read this text (and every text) with great care so that you can learn from the ideas presented within its pages. We also encourage you to USE this book by

- Writing in the margins
- Circling important terms
- Highlighting key phrases
- Jotting down word definitions in the margins
- Dog-earing the pages
- Writing questions that you have in the white spaces provided

By treating this book as your basis for creating success, you will begin to see remarkable progress in your study practices, reading comprehension, and learning skills. The example of a "marked up" textbook shows how one student did it.

Supplemental Resources

INSTRUCTOR SUPPORT – Resources to simplify your life and support your students.

Book Specific

Online Instructor's Manual This manual is intended to give professors a framework or blueprint of ideas and suggestions that may assist them in providing their students with activities, journal writing, thought-provoking situations, and group activities. The test bank organized by chapter includes: multiple choice, true/false and short-answer questions that support the key features in the book. This supplement is available for download from the Instructor's Resource Center at www.pearsonhighered.com/irc

Online PowerPoint Presentation A comprehensive set of PowerPoint slides that can be used by instructors for class presentations or by students for lecture preview or review. The presentation includes all the graphs and tables in the textbook. The presentation contains bullet point PowerPoint slides for each chapter. These slides highlight the important points of each chapter to help students understand the concepts within each chapter. Instructors may download these PowerPoint presentations from the Instructor's Resource Center at www.pearsonhighered.com/irc

Online Clicker Questions PowerPoint slides created specifically for use with Clicker systems that can be used by instructors in class lecture situations to assess students' collective knowledge of key concepts through multiple choice questions for each chapter. The presentation includes content from the textbook, with multiple choice assessments in PowerPoint slide format for each chapter. They highlight the important points to help students understand the concepts, and allow instructors to seamlessly use with any Clicker system. Instructors may download these PowerPoint presentations from the Instructor's Resource Center at www.pearsonhighered.com/irc

MyTest Test Bank Pearson MyTest offers instructors a secure online environment and quality assessments to easily create print exams, study guide questions, and quizzes from any computer with an Internet connection.

Premium Assessment Content
- Draw from a rich library of question testbanks that complement the textbook and course learning objectives.
- Edit questions or tests to fit specific teaching needs.

Instructor Friendly Features
- Easily create and store questions, including images, diagrams, and charts using simple drag-and-drop and Word-like controls.
- Use additional information provided by Pearson, such as the question's difficulty level or learning objective, to help quickly build a test.

Time-Saving Enhancements
- Add headers or footers and easily scramble questions and answer choices all from one simple toolbar.
- Quickly create multiple versions of a test or answer key, and when ready, simply save to Word or PDF format and print!
- Export exams for import to Blackboard 6.0, CE (WebCT), or Vista (WebCT)!

Additional information available at www.pearsonmytest.com

MyStudentSuccessLab Are you teaching online, in a hybrid setting, or looking to infuse exciting technology into your classroom for the first time? Then be sure to refer to the MyStudentSuccessLab section included in the coming pages of this Preface to learn more. This online solution is designed to help students build the skills they need to succeed at www.mystudentsuccesslab.com

Other Resources

"Easy access to online, book-specific teaching support is now just a click away!"
Instructor Resource Center - Register. Redeem. Login. Three easy steps that open the door to a variety of print and media resources in downloadable, digital format, available to instructors exclusively through the Pearson/Prentice Hall 'IRC'. www.pearsonhighered.com/irc

"Choose from a wide range of video resources for the classroom!"
Prentice Hall Reference Library: Life Skills Pack (ISBN: 0-13-127079-6). Contains all 4 videos, or they may be requested individually as follows:
- *Learning Styles and Self-Awareness*, 0-13-028502-1
- *Critical and Creative Thinking*, 0-13-028504-8
- *Relating to Others*, 0-13-028511-0
- *Personal Wellness*, 0-13-028514-5

Prentice Hall Reference Library: Study Skills Pack (ISBN: 0-13-127080-X). Contains all 6 videos, or they may be requested individually as follows:
- *Reading Effectively*, 0-13-028505-6
- *Listening and Memory*, 0-13-028506-4
- *Note Taking and Research*, 0-13-028508-0
- *Writing Effectively*, 0-13-028509-9
- *Effective Test Taking*, 0-13-028500-5
- *Goal Setting and Time Management*, 0-13-028503-X

Prentice Hall Reference Library: Career Skills Pack (ISBN: 0-13-118529-2). Contains all 3 videos, or they may be requested individually as follows:
- *Skills for the 21st Century – Technology*, 0-13-028512-9
- *Skills for the 21st Century – Math and Science*, 0-13-028513-7
- *Managing Career and Money*, 0-13-028516-1
  Complete Reference Library - Life/Study Skills/Career Video Pack on DVD (ISBN: 0-13-501095-0).
- Our Reference Library of thirteen popular video resources has now been digitized onto one DVD so students and instructors alike can benefit from the array of video clips. Featuring Life Skills, Study Skills, and Career Skills, they help to reinforce the course content in a more interactive way.

Faculty Video Resources
- Teacher Training Video 1: *Critical Thinking*, ISBN: 0-13-099432-4
- Teacher Training Video 2: *Stress Management & Communication*, ISBN: 0-13-099578-9
- Teacher Training Video 3: *Classroom Tips*, ISBN: 0-13-917205-X
- Student Advice Video, ISBN: 0-13-233206-X
- Study Skills Video, ISBN: 0-13-096095-0

Current Issues Videos
- ABC News Video Series: *Student Success Second Edition*, ISBN: 0-13-031901-5
- ABC News Video Series: *Student Success Third Edition*, ISBN: 0-13-152865-3

MyStudentSuccessLab PH Videos on DVD (ISBN: 0-13-514249-0).
- Our six most popular video resources have been digitized onto one DVD so students and instructors alike can benefit from the array of video clips. Featuring Technology, Math and Science, Managing Money and Career, Learning Styles and Self-Awareness, Study Skills, and Peer Advice, they help to reinforce the course content in a more interactive way. They are also accessible through our MSSL and course management offerings and available on VHS.

"Through partnership opportunities, we offer a variety of assessment options!"
LASSI - The LASSI is a 10-scale, 80-item assessment of students' awareness about and use of learning and study strategies. Addressing skill, will and self-regulation, the focus is on both covert and overt thoughts, behaviors, attitudes and beliefs that relate to successful learning and that can be altered through educational interventions. Available in two formats: Paper ISBN: 0-13-172315-4 or Online ISBN: 0-13-172316-2 (access card).

Noel Levitz/RMS – This retention tool measures Academic Motivation, General Coping Ability, Receptivity to Support Services, PLUS Social Motivation. It helps identify at-risk students, the areas with which they struggle, and their receptiveness to support. Available in paper or online formats, as well as short and long versions. Paper Long Form A: ISBN: 0-13-512066-7; Paper Short Form B: ISBN: 0-13-512065-9; Online Forms A,B & C: ISBN: 0-13-098158-3.

Robbins Self Assessment Library – This compilation teaches students to create a portfolio of skills. S.A.L. is a self-contained, interactive, library of 49 behavioral questionnaires that help students discover new ideas about themselves, their attitudes, and their personal strengths and weaknesses. Available in Paper, CD-Rom, and Online (Access Card) formats.

Readiness for Education at a Distance Indicator(READI) - READI is a web-based tool that assesses the overall likelihood for online learning success. READI generates an immediate score and a diagnostic interpretation of results, including recommendations for successful participation in online courses and potential remediation sources. Please visit www.readi.info for additional information. ISBN: 0-13-188967-2.

Pathway to Student Success CD-ROM
The CD is divided into several categories, each of which focuses on a specific topic that relates to students and provides them with the context, tools and strategies to enhance their educational experience. ISBN: 0-13-239314-X.

The Golden Personality Type Profiler
The Golden Personality Type Profiler™ helps students understand how they make decisions and relate to others. By completing the Golden Personality Type Profiler™ students develop a deeper understanding of their strengths, a clearer picture of how their behavior impacts others, and a better appreciation for the interpersonal style of others and how to interact with them more effectively. Using these results as a guide, students will gain the self awareness that is key to professional development and success. ISBN: 0-13-706654-6.

"For a truly tailored solution that fosters campus connections and increases retention, talk with us about custom publishing."
Pearson Custom Publishing – We are the largest custom provider for print and media shaped to your course's needs. Please visit us at www.pearsoncustom.com to learn more.

STUDENT SUPPORT –
Tools to help make the grade now, and excel in school later.

"Today's students are more inclined than ever to use technology to enhance their learning."
Refer to the **MyStudentSuccessLab** section of this Preface to learn about our revolutionary resource (www.mystudentsuccesslab.com) This online solution is designed to help students build the skills they need to succeed.

"Time management is the #1 challenge students face." We can help.
Prentice Hall Planner – A basic planner that includes a monthly & daily calendar plus other materials to facilitate organization. 8.5x11.
Premier Annual Planner - This specially designed, annual 4-color collegiate planner includes an academic planning/resources section, monthly planning section (2 pages/month), weekly planning section (48 weeks; July start date), which facilitate short-term as well as long-term planning. Spiral bound, 6x9. Customization is available.

"Journaling activities promote self-discovery and self-awareness."
Student Reflection Journal - Through this vehicle, students are encouraged to track their progress and share their insights, thoughts, and concerns. 8 1/2 x 11. 90 pages.

"The Student Orientation Series includes short booklets on specialized topics that facilitate greater student understanding."
S.O.S. Guides help students understand what these opportunities are, how to take advantage of them, and how to learn from their peers while doing so. They include:
 • Connolly: *Learning Communities* ISBN: 0-13-232243-9
 • Hoffman: *Stop Procrastination Now! 10 Simple and SUCCESSFUL Steps for Student Success*, ISBN: 0-13-513056-5
 • Jabr: *English Language Learners* ISBN: 0-13-232242-0
 • Watts: *Service Learning* ISBN: 0-13-232201-0

PEARSON
mystudentsuccesslab™

Succeed in college and beyond!
Connect, practice, and personalize with MyStudentSuccessLab.

www.mystudentsuccesslab.com

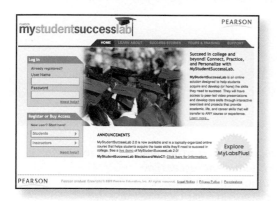

MyStudentSuccessLab is an online solution designed to help students acquire the skills they need to succeed. They will have access to peer-led video presentations and develop core skills through interactive exercises and projects that provide academic, life, and career skills that will transfer to ANY course.

It can accompany any Student Success text, or be sold as a stand-alone course offering. To become successful learners, students must consistently apply techniques to daily activities.

How will MyStudentSuccessLab make a difference?

Is motivation a challenge, and if so, how do you deal with it?
Video Presentation — Experience peer led video 'by students, for students' of all ages and stages.

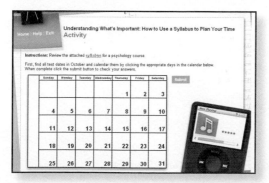

How would better class preparation improve the learning experience?
Practice activities — Practice skills for each topic — beginning, intermediate, and advanced — leveled by Bloom's taxonomy.

What could you gain by building critical thinking and problem-solving skills in this class? **Apply (final project)** – Complete a final project using these skills to create 'personally relevant' resources.

APPLY

Calendaring for the Term

Overview: This "final" activity has students use the syllabus for your course to plan their work in this class for the term. As part of the activity, they're provided a calendar template that can adjust to any start and end date, so no matter what length your course is, this template will work. Then, students are instructed to find all the key dates in your syllabus and calendar sufficient time to complete all assignments or prepare for all tests. Once complete, students submit the calendar to your dropbox for grading.

Grading Rubric Suggestions:

A grade: All important dates are included and clearly specified. Dates should be based on your syllabus but typically include reading assignment due dates, exams and projects to withdrawal dates and extra credit activities. In addition, for each due date, students also calendar adequate time to study, read or otherwise prepare to meet their responsibilities for your course. [Note: To gauge adequate time, estimate 2-3 hours of study for each credit hour. So, for a 3-credit course, students should plan on 6-9 hours of study per week.]

B grade: All but 10-20% of the important dates are included. For each due date on the calendar, sufficient time is allowed for studying, reading, or other preparation and/or 10-20% of the dates have insufficient time for studying, reading, or otherwise preparing.

C grade: Twenty-five percent of the important dates are missing and/or 25% of the dates aren't calendared with sufficient time to prepare for them.

D Grade: Fifty percent of the key dates are missing and/or aren't calendared with sufficient time to prepare for them.

F Grade: Most or all key dates are missing and most or all aren't calendared with sufficient time to prepare for them.

As an instructor, how much easier would it be to assign and use MyStudentSuccessLab if you had an Implementation guide? **Instructor Guide** – Describes each activity, the skills addressed, an estimate of student time on task, and a grading rubric for the final Apply activity.

MyStudentSuccessLab Feature set:

Topic Overview: Module objectives.

Video Presentation - Connect: Real student video interviews on key issues.

Practice: Three skill-building exercises per topic provide interactive experience and practice.

Apply - Personalize: Apply what is learned by creating a personally relevant project and journal.

Resources: Plagiarism Guide, Dictionary, Calculators, and Assessments (Career, Learning Styles, and Personality Styles).

Additional Assignments: Extra suggested activities to use with each topic.

Text-Specific Study Plan (available with select books): Chapter Objectives, Practice Tests, Enrichment activities, and Flashcards.

MyStudentSuccessLab Topic List -

1. Time Management/Planning
2. Values/Goal Setting
3. Learning How You Learn
4. Listening and Taking Class Notes
5. Reading and Annotating
6. Memory and Studying
7. Critical Thinking
8. Problem-Solving
9. Information Literacy
10. Communication
11. Test Prep and Test Taking
12. Stress Management
13. Financial Literacy
14. Majors and Careers

MyStudentSuccessLab Support:

• **Demos, Registration, Log-in** - www.mystudentsuccesslab.com under "Tours and Training" and "Support."

• **Email support** - Send an inquiry to MyStudentSuccessLab@pearson.com

• **Online Training** - Join one of our weekly WebEx training sessions.

• **Peer Training** - Faculty Advocate connection for qualified adoptions.

• **Technical support** - 24 hours a day, seven days a week, at http://247pearsoned.custhelp.com

CORNERSTONES

CHAPTER 1
CREATE

BUILDING YOUR
OWN
SUCCESSFUL
FUTURE

"The greatest reward of an education is to be able to face the world with an open mind, a caring heart, and a willing soul."

—R. M. Sherfield

WHY READ THIS CHAPTER?

What's in it for me?

WHY is it important to know how to create success? WHY is it important to understand the differences between a community/ technical college and a university? WHY is it important to understand the culture of a community college? WHY do I need to know how to write realistic goals?

Why? Because this chapter, indeed this whole book and course in which you are enrolled, is about helping you become the most successful student, thinker, citizen, leader, and lifelong learner that you can possibly be. The information in this chapter is included to help you understand some of the basic truths about community college life and academic survival. Quite simply, this chapter was written to help you learn how to adjust to the culture of a two-year college, discover your potential, build on your strengths, and make positive, intelligent transitions in your life. Understanding your institution and instructors is going to be vastly important to your success.

By carefully reading this chapter and taking the information provided seriously, you will be able to:

▶ Identify and employ the steps to create a successful future.
▶ Understand the culture and basic truths of community colleges.
▶ Identify and discuss the differences between high school, college, and career.
▶ Identify and use the Ten Essential Cornerstones for Success in a Changing World.
▶ Set realistic, attainable goals.

CHAPTER 1 | CREATE

"Though no one can go back and make a brand new start, anyone can start from now and make a brand new ending."

—*Carl Bard*

How my COMMUNITY COLLEGE changed my life

ROBERT M. SHERFIELD
Graduate!
Spartanburg Methodist College, Spartanburg, South Carolina

I am the son of textile workers. Both of my parents worked in a cotton mill for over 30 years. My mom graduated high school but my father only went to the third grade. My hometown is in the rural South about 35 miles from the nearest metropolitan area. I attended a small high school and had never been a good student. Because of my poor performance through the years, working full time, and family commitments, I decided to attend a community college and then transfer to a four-year college. I never imagined how my high school performance would affect my application to college—and indeed the rest of my life. It took me years to overcome the effects of self-defeating behaviors, a horrible academic background, a negative attitude, and terrible study skills. I quickly learned that my success depended on becoming an open-minded person who knew how to set goals, work to achieve them, develop self-motivation, and study effectively. These were not easy steps for me after 12 years of failure and disappointment.

I barely finished high school with a D– average and my SAT scores and class rank were so bad, I was denied entrance to the community college. The college granted me provisional acceptance only if I enrolled in, and successfully completed, a summer preparatory program. I graduated high school on a Friday night and began my college studies the very next Monday morning enrolled in the prep program. I never realized what lay ahead. I never realized how my life was about to change forever.

My first class that semester was English. Professor Brannon walked in, handed out the syllabus, called the roll, and began to lecture. Lord Byron was the topic for the day. My second class was Professor Wilkerson. She entered with a dust storm behind her, went over the syllabus, and before we had a chance to blink, she was involved in the first lecture. *"The cradle of civilization,"* she began, *"was Mesopotamia."* We all scurried to find notebooks and pens to begin taking notes. I could not believe I was already behind on the first day. *"Who teaches on the first day?"* I thought.

One minute before class ended, she closed her book, looked directly at us, and said, *"You are in history now. You elected to take this class and you will follow my rules. You are not to be late, you are to come to this class prepared, and you*

are to do your homework assignments. If you do what I ask you to do, read what I've assigned to you, and do your homework activities, you will learn more about Western civilization than you ever thought possible. If you don't keep up with me, you won't know if you are in Egypt, Mesopotamia, or pure hell! Now get out!"

On the 30-mile trip home, my mind was filled with new thoughts . . . *Lord Byron, Mesopotamia, professors who talked too fast, professors who did not talk at all, tuition, parking, and the size of the library.* I knew that something was different, *something had changed in me.* In one day at my community college, I had tasted something intoxicating, something that was addictive. *I had tasted a new world.* My community college experience changed my life in so many ways, but the number one thing that happened to me was that I learned how to be more comfortable in more places. Because of my experiences at SMC, I began to be as comfortable in New York City at a Broadway play as I was at my job in the cotton mill. I learned to be as comfortable sailing the River Thames past Big Ben and Parliament as I was working at the Buffalo Sewer District. My community college experience taught me to appreciate the joys and wonders of travel, learning, and meeting new people. I had never known this before. This community college experience changed my life, and I will be forever grateful to those professors who opened the door to the world for me.

Over 30 years later as I coauthor your *Cornerstones* text, I am still addicted to that new world I first experienced at my community college. Community college changed my life, and I am still changing—with every day I live, every new book I read, every new class I teach, every new person I meet, and every new place to which I travel, I am changing. I wish the same for you.

THINK ABOUT IT

1. What adversities in your past will you have to work to overcome to persist in your community college studies?
2. What changes and adjustments do you think you are going to have to make in your personal and academic life to reach your goals, graduate, and enter the career you want?

BEFORE YOU READ

SCAN & QUESTION

In the preface of this book (page xiv), you read about the **SQ3R study method.** Right now, take a few moments, **scan this chapter,** and on the SQ3R Mastery Study Sheet on page 25, write **five of your own questions** that you think will be important to your mastery of this material. In addition to the two questions below, you will find five questions from your authors on that study sheet. Use one of your "*Study for Quiz*" stickers to flag this page for easy reference.

EXAMPLES:

▶ What are the steps to creating a successful future? (from page 4)

▶ What are the basic truths about the culture of community colleges? (from page 12)

CREATING YOUR SUCCESS

Can You Really Create Your Future?

Is it really possible to draft a blueprint of your own future? Is it possible to "create success"? The answer is yes. The process of creating success begins with an internal idea that you have the power, the passion, and the capacity to BE successful—to reach your chosen goals. It has been said that those people who are not out there creating their own future will be handed a future over which they have little control. You can be a person who creates the future for yourself and your family. Your college education is vital in this process because your education will give you options and alternatives. It will also help you create opportunities, and, according to Leo Buscaglia, writer and speaker, "the healthiest people in the world are the people with the most alternatives."

"*So, how do I create a successful future with more options?*" you may be asking. The *formula* is simple, but the *action* required may not be as simple—and have no doubt, action **IS required.** The formula consists of four steps:

1. The willingness to set clear, realistic goals and the ability to visualize the results of those goals

2. The ability to recognize your strengths and build on them

3. The ability to recognize your weaknesses or challenges and work to improve them

4. The passion and desire to work at your zenith every single day to make your goals and dreams a reality

iStockPhoto

Simple? The first three are rather simple. Number four is the kicker. Truthfully, most people have little trouble with the first three; it is the work and passion involved with number four that causes most people to give up and never reach their fullest potential—and to be handed a future over which they had little say in creating. You can create your own future, your own success, and your own alternatives.

Coming to the realization that there is no "easy street" and no "roads paved with good intentions" is also important to creating your success. In his landmark book, *Good to Great,* Jim Collins suggests that once you decide to be great, your life will never be easy again. Rid yourself of the notion that there is some easy way out—that college will be a breeze or that college will make your professional life easier. Success requires hard, passionate work on a daily basis. This passionate work may require you to change some of your thoughts, actions, and beliefs. That is what this chapter and indeed this entire course is about—creating success through positive change.

COMMUNITY COLLEGE AND YOU

Why Is It the Partnership of a Lifetime?

What can a community college education do for you? The list will certainly vary depending on whom you ask, but basically, community colleges can help you develop in the areas listed below. As you read through the list, place a checkmark beside the statements that most accurately reflect which skills you hope to gain from attending your community college. If there are other skills that you desire to achieve from your community college experience, write them at the end of the list.

> How can having a positive, healthy attitude help you focus on your future and success?

_____ Grow more self-sufficient and self-confident
_____ Establish and strengthen your personal identity
_____ Understand more about the global world in which you live
_____ Become a more involved citizen in social and political issues
_____ Become more open-minded
_____ Learn to manage your emotions and reactions more effectively
_____ Understand the value of thinking, analyzing, and problem solving
_____ Expand and use your ethical and moral thinking and reasoning skills
_____ Develop commanding computer and information literacy skills
_____ Manage your personal resources such as time and money
_____ Become more proficient at written, oral, and nonverbal communication
_____ Grow more understanding and accepting of different cultures
_____ Become a lifelong learner
_____ Become more financially independent
_____ Acquire credits toward a bachelor's degree
_____ Enter a career field that you enjoy
_____ _____
_____ _____

Scott Cunningham/Merrill

How can your college classes help you grow, change, and prosper?

Which skill is THE most important to you?

_____

_____

Why? _____

_____

What plans will you put into action to hone and master this skill?

_____

_____

_____

CREATING SUCCESS THROUGH POSITIVE CHANGE

How Can You Bring Positive, Lasting Change to Your Daily Life?

Change is quite often met with resistance, not only by the person directly involved in the change, but by those around that person. As you begin to change, grow, and take control of your future, you will notice that your relationships with others may change, too. Change is not easy and the person who initiates it (hopefully you) may not be the most popular person around. People like stability and they like things "the way they have always been." We're creatures of habit, and change creates unfamiliar ground. There will be people along the way who may try to derail your hopes. Some of your friends who have always been comfortable may feel threatened by the differences they see in you. If you are going places, people don't like the idea of being left behind. But remember, there are going to be people pulling for you, too. There are going to be people in your life who support your dreams and goals and want nothing but the very best for you. Your courage and desire and reliance on these people will see you through hard times.

> *"Your time is limited, so don't waste it living someone else's life."*
> —*Steve Jobs*

So why is change so important to you and your future? Quite simply, change that you direct creates opportunities for you to grow and prosper in ways you may have never imagined. It allows you to become and remain competitive. It allows you to actively live in a world that is fluid and unpredictable. There are several things you need to know about creating success in your life through positive change. Consider the following ideas:

1. *Change is a skill.* Change is a LEARNED SKILL that any willing person can accomplish. Period. Public speaking is a skill. Learning how to drive a car is a skill, and just like those activities, learning to change is a skill, too. You'll need to familiarize yourself with the tools to learn this skill.

2. *Change takes time.* Change does not happen immediately at the snap of your fingers. If you've ever taken piano, guitar, or drum lessons, you know it took time to learn how to play because it is a skill—just like change. You did not learn to play overnight just as you won't learn everything about math or history or nursing in one semester. Often, change is a slow, systematic series of events that eventually leads you to your desired end.

3. *Change requires an "attitude adjustment."* A recent contestant on *America's Got Talent* was being interviewed about her chances of success on the show. Queen Emily was an African-American single mother working full time. She had given up her dream of being a professional singer years earlier to raise her children. She stated that before her audition, she stood and looked in the mirror crying. Her only thought was *"My time has passed; this is never going to happen for me. Never!"* Then she looked herself in the eyes and said, *"Why NOT me? I'm talented. I'm good at performing, and I KNOW I can sing.* **WHY NOT ME?"** As corny or hokey as it may sound, her attitude adjustment was the key to her ability to change her life. She auditioned, surpassed thousands of contestants, and was invited to Los Angeles as one of five finalists. She now performs in a major show in Las Vegas, Nevada.

How can surrounding yourself with positive, upbeat, optimistic people help you with personal change?

4. *Change demands action.* Although circumstances and desire may drive the need for change in your life, don't lose sight of the fact that ultimately, change is an action. It is something you must do—mentally, physically, spiritually, and intellectually, just as Queen Emily in the previous example knew that without action by her, her life was not going to change.

5. *Change is about working toward something, not running away from something.* If you want true, lasting, meaningful change in your life, you have to think about it as working toward good, positive, useful results, not as running away from bad, negative, unpleasant circumstances. "Working toward" is **positive and internal.** "Running away from" is **negative and external.** Try to work **toward a goal** and not **run from a problem.**

6. *Change is about letting go and holding on.* As with any new endeavor, you will have to decide what is working in your life and what is not. By doing so, you can decide what you need to hold onto and what you finally need to let go of. You will want to hold onto the positive strengths and talents you have while letting go of the negative, destructive attitudes that you may have held in the past.

THE TIMES . . . THEY ARE A-CHANGIN'

What Is the Relationship Between Your Education and the New World Economy?

Composer, singer, and activist Bob Dylan once wrote, *"The times, they are a-changin'."* Truer words have never been spoken—especially for anyone living at this moment. This is not your daddy's economy. It is not your mama's workplace, and it certainly is not your grandfather's job market. To glide over this simple truth *could be the most costly decision of your life.*

"New world economy," you might say. *"Who cares about a world economy?"*

"China? Who cares about the fluctuating economy in China, Russia, Dubai, or India? I live in Kansas and I'm worried about America's future."

"An iPhone? A BlackBerry? An iPad? Facebooking? Twittering? I can't even afford my bus ticket this month," you may be thinking.

While you may not be alone in thinking *"this does not matter to me,"* you would be very wrong and exceptionally foolish to think that today's world affairs do not concern **you,** your **education,** and your **future.** Yes, it may be true that you are simply trying to get a degree in medical assisting to work in a small doctor's office in Spokane, Washington—or to obtain a degree in criminal justice to work at the local

Corbis RF

> *"When it comes to the future, there are three kinds of people: those who let it happen, those who make it happen, and those who wonder what happened."*
> —John Richardson, Jr.

police department in Union, South Carolina—or to earn a degree in education so that you can teach first grade in Stockton, California. However, no certificate, no degree, no job, and certainly no person will be exempt from the changes and challenges of the new world economy.

"So where does this leave ME?" you might be asking. It leaves you in an exciting, vulnerable, challenging, scary, and wonderful place. We did NOT include this information to scare you or to turn you off, but rather to give you a jolt—to open your eyes to the world in which you live and the workforce for which you are preparing. We included it to encourage you to use ***every tool*** available; ***every resource*** possible; ***every connection*** imaginable; and ***every ethical, moral, and legal means*** feasible to prepare yourself for this ever-changing world in which we live today. The present and the future may not be as rosy as you had hoped for, but it is here, it is real, and it is yours. However, you must know this: If you make the strategic changes in your life now, you can have a much brighter future. No workplace will be immune from the changes facing our world today, and your very survival depends on being prepared and knowing how to quickly adapt and change to a variety of situations.

In *The 2010 Meltdown*, Edward Gordon (2005) writes, "*Simply stated, today in America, there are just too many people trained for the wrong jobs. Many jobs have become unnecessary, technically obsolete . . . or worse yet, the job/career aspirations of too many current and future workers are at serious odds with the changing needs of the U.S. labor market*" (p. 17). However, all is not lost to you or your future. People who possess superb oral and written communication skills, know how to solve problems, have the capacity to change, and can work well with others will *be in high demand* for many years to come.

iStockPhoto

Why is it important to learn as much as possible about technology?

What Employers Are Saying

According to the report *College Learning for the New Global Century* (National Leadership Council for Leadership Education and America's Promise, 2008), "Employers want college graduates to acquire versatile knowledge and skills.... sixty-three percent of employers believe that too many recent college graduates do not have the skills they need to succeed in the global economy and a majority of employers believe that only half or fewer recent graduates have the skills or knowledge needed to advance or to be promoted in their companies." The Association of American Colleges and Universities (2010) cites the following 10 skills as vitally important in today's global economy:

1. The ability to work well in teams—especially with people different from yourself
2. An understanding of science and technology and how these subjects are used in real-world settings
3. The ability to write and speak well
4. The ability to think clearly about complex problems
5. The ability to analyze a problem to develop workable solutions
6. An understanding of the global context in which work is now done
7. The ability to be creative and innovative in solving problems
8. The ability to apply knowledge and skills in new settings
9. The ability to understand numbers and statistics
10. A strong sense of ethics and integrity

Whether we like it or not, a massive transformation is going on all around us in this country, as well as all over the world. Thriving in the coming years is going to be more difficult than in the past and will require certain new and different abilities and attitudes to be successful. You will need to learn and acquire the skills that will make you competitive, give you an edge, and help you master a life filled with changes and challenges. Many of these skills are outlined in the **Ten Essential Cornerstones for Success in a Changing World** (Figure 1.1). These skills will be needed for your success, personal independence, and growth in the new millennium. Study

FIGURE 1.1 *Ten Essential Cornerstones for Success in a Changing World*

PASSION—The ability to show a passion about one's mission and a willingness to align personal goals with education, talents, experiences, and skills. An ability to demonstrate concern not only about personal success, but also about the world and one's surroundings—a commitment to **civic literacy** and seeing oneself as "a citizen of the world."

MOTIVATION—The ability to find the **inner strength and personal drive** to get up each day and face the world with an "I can, I will" attitude. The ability to develop a strong personal value and belief system that motivates you when the going gets tough. The ability to know who you are and never let anyone steal your identity or erode your personal ethics.

KNOWLEDGE—The ability to **become highly skilled in a profession** or craft that will enable you to make a good living for yourself and your family in a rapidly changing workplace and to use lifelong learning to maintain your marketable skill sets. The ability to master important academic information beyond your major field in areas such as math, science, psychology, history, technology, economics, and communication and to practically apply that information in an evolving and highly technical work environment.

RESOURCEFULNESS—The ability to apply **information literacy**—to know WHERE to find information and the resources that will help you be successful in your academic studies and your chosen profession, and HOW to evaluate that information to determine if it is useful and accurate. The ability to look for and to seek new opportunities, options, and outcomes. The ability to imagine, integrate, and implement new ways of solving old problems.

CREATIVITY—The ability to use **creativity and innovation** in solving problems that will enable you to anticipate new and emerging issues, to communicate and use what you know and what you have learned and discovered to answer critical questions and solve complex and demanding problems.

ADAPTABILITY—The ability to make good choices based on future opportunities and a changing workplace and to constantly **reinvent yourself** as change brings about necessity and opportunity. The ability to work effectively in a climate of changing priorities and uncertainty.

OPENMINDEDNESS—The ability to **accept and appreciate a highly diverse workplace** and the inherent differences and cultures that will be commonplace. The ability to listen to others with whom you disagree or with whom you may have little in common and learn from them and their experiences. The ability to learn a new language, even if your mastery is only at a primitive, broken, conversational level. The ability to conduct yourself in a respectable and professional manner.

COMMUNICATION—The ability to develop and maintain healthy, **supportive personal and professional relationships** and to build a solid network of well-connected professionals who can help you and whom YOU can help in return.

ACCOUNTABILITY—The ability to **accept responsibility and be accountable** for all aspects of your future including your psychological well-being, your spiritual well-being, your relationships, your health, your finances, and your overall survival skills. Basically, you must develop a plan for the future that states, "If this fails, I'll do this," or "If this job is phased out, I'll do this," or "If this resource is gone, I'll use this," or "If this person won't help me, this one will."

VISION—The ability to guide your career path in a new global economy and to understand and take advantage of the inherent impact of worldwide competition—even if you live in a small town and work for a small "mom and pop" company. The ability to **"see" what is coming** and prepare for the changes, adapt to circumstances, and grow with grace and style.

them carefully as each one will help you create a positive transition to the university setting or the world of work.

By learning to develop these enduring skills, you will be able to carry them with you on your first job, your tenth job, and well into your future. By learning how to change and reinvent yourself with the times and demands of the world, you will position yourself to become—AND remain competitive.

THE M & M THEORY

What Have Your Money and Your Mama Got to Do with It?

What is the M & M Theory? It is quite simple really. We all pay attention to and try to protect the things that matter most to us. Your "**m**oney and your **m**ama" are symbolic of what you care about. Most people care deeply about what happens to their families, their income, their friends, their careers, and the environment, and most people do care and are concerned about the facts presented regarding our ever-changing world.

However, in the hustle and bustle of finding day care, studying for classes, working a full-time job, cleaning the house, helping the kids with homework, and trying to prepare a meal from time to time, we may lose sight of some of the most important things in our lives. Try to keep this thought in mind: *Your EDUCATION is important, too.* In fact, it is of paramount importance to your future on many levels—culturally, socially, intellectually, and in preparing you for the future. Your education is a part of the M & M Theory because it involves your money—the future financial health for you and your family.

> *"Forget mistakes. Forget failures. Forget everything except what you're going to do now . . . and do it."*
>
> —Will Durant

According to one of the leading research sources in higher education, *The Chronicle of Higher Education* (August 28, 2009, p. 18), first-year students had a variety of thoughts regarding college education and money. Of the 240,580 students who replied to the survey, 76.8 percent noted that *"being very well off financially"* was an essential or very important objective, and 66 percent responded that *"the chief benefit of a college education is that it increases one's earning power."* Another interesting finding was that 79 percent of those responding to the survey stated that they believe that *"through hard work, everybody can succeed in American society."*

The United States Census Bureau's annual report on education and training pay (U.S. Bureau of the Census/ U.S. Bureau of Labor Statistics, 2007) shows that people with college degrees can earn considerably more than those who do not have a degree. For instance, those with a bachelor's degree average approximately $29,000 *more per year* in earnings than those with only a high school education. People with an associate's degree average approximately $10,000 more per year in the earnings than those with only a high school education. For a complete look at the earning power of U.S. citizens 25 and older, look at the figures on annual education, pay, and unemployment in Figure 1.2.

By focusing on money in this section, we do not mean to suggest that the only reason for attending college is to make more money. As a matter of fact, we feel that it is a secondary reason. Many people *without college degrees*

How can your friends, classmates, and peers help you achieve your goals?

Bananastock

FIGURE

1.2 *Education, Pay, and Unemployment Statistics of Full-Time Workers, 25 and Over*

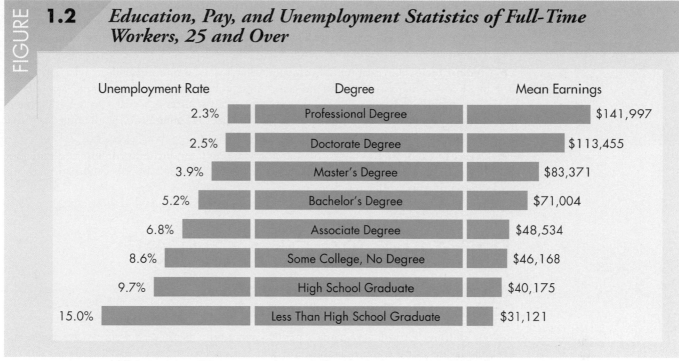

Unemployment Rate	Degree	Mean Earnings
2.3%	Professional Degree	$141,997
2.5%	Doctorate Degree	$113,455
3.9%	Master's Degree	$83,371
5.2%	Bachelor's Degree	$71,004
6.8%	Associate Degree	$48,534
8.6%	Some College, No Degree	$46,168
9.7%	High School Graduate	$40,175
15.0%	Less Than High School Graduate	$31,121

Source: U.S. Bureau of the Census/U.S. Bureau of Labor Statistics, *Education and Training Pay,* 2009.

earn huge salaries each year. However, as the data suggest, traditionally, those with college degrees **earn MORE** money and **experience LESS** unemployment. Basically, college should make the road to financial security easier, but college should also be a place where you learn to make decisions about your values, your character, and your future. The college environment can inspire you to make decisions about the changes that need to occur in your life so that you can effectively manage and prosper in an ever-changing world. College can also be a place where you learn the skills to change and continue to grow long after you graduate.

COMMUNITY COLLEGE VERSUS UNIVERSITY STUDIES

Is There Really a Difference Between the Two?

At first glance, a ***community college*** and ***university*** may look very similar except that you attend one for an associate's degree and the other for a bachelor's, master's, or doctorate degree. However, on further inspection, there are vast differences. Community colleges focus on teaching whereas many universities focus on research, publishing, and grant writing. This is not to say that there are not many, many fine universities that have a teaching focus and that community college faculty do not do research and writing. However, the primary focus of a community college is teaching and learning.

Some other major differences include the following:

▶ **Cost.** Community colleges are most often much less expensive than universities, sometimes by as much as 50 to 75 percent.

▶ **Class size.** Community college classes usually have fewer people enrolled in them. For instance, your community college biology class may have 25 to 30 students whereas a university biology class may have over 200.

▶ **Class make-up.** You will certainly find nontraditional students at a university, but statistically, many more attend community colleges. Over 45 percent of community college students are over 25, 33 percent are female, nearly 90 percent work full or part time, and over 40 percent are the first in their families to attend college.

▶ **Student focus.** Graduation rates are somewhat low at community college, relatively speaking, because many students attend community colleges as "transfer students" with the express intention of moving to a university after a few courses or a year. On the other hand, many students who attend universities do so with the intention of graduating from that institution.

▶ **Degrees.** Community colleges offer a variety of programs, including diplomas, certificates, and associate's degrees. However, some community colleges do offer bachelor's degrees and some universities offer associate degrees.

THE CULTURE OF COLLEGE

What Are the Basic Truths about Community College Success?

In your lifetime, you will have many experiences that influence and alter your views, goals, and livelihood, including travel, relationships, and personal victories or setbacks. However, few events will have a greater influence than your college experience. A community college education and degree can mean hopes realized, dreams fulfilled, and the breaking down of social and economic walls. To get the most from your community college experience and to lay a path to success, it will be important to look at your expectations and the vast differences between high school, jobs you may have held, and the culture of your community college. This section will introduce you to some of the changes you can expect.

Basic Truth 1: Success Is about Choices, Sacrifices, and Making Intelligent Transitions

Life is a series of choices. Hard choices. Easy choices. Right choices. Wrong choices. Nevertheless, the quality of *your life* is determined by the *choices you make* and your willingness to evaluate your life and determine whether transitions are in order. You will have many important and hard choices in the near future, such as deciding whether to devote your time to studying or partying, whether to ask for help in classes that challenge you or give up and drop out, whether to get involved in campus life or "go it alone," and whether to make the sacrifices needed for your future success or take the easy road. Those choices will determine the quality of your future. Some of the choices that you make will force you to step beyond your comfort zone—to move to places that may frighten you or make you uncomfortable. That's OK. That's good. In fact, that's very good.

So what is a *comfort zone?* It sounds cozy doesn't it? Warm and fuzzy. However, do not let the term fool you. A comfort zone is not necessarily a happy and comfortable place. It is simply a place where you are familiar with your surroundings and don't have to work too hard. It is where you feel confident of your abilities, but it is also a place where your growth stops. *It can be a prison, and staying there is a cop-out.* Successful people who have won personal and professional victories know that moving beyond one's comfort zone helps in nurturing change,

> What sacrifices do you think you'll need to make in your personal life to be academically successful?

Patrick White/Merrill

reaching your potential, and creating opportunities for positive growth.

Basic Truth 2: Community College Is a Two-Way Street

Perhaps the first thing that you will notice about higher education is that you have to **give** in order to **receive.** Not only do you have expectations of your community college and instructors, but your community college and instructors have expectations—great expectations of you. To be successful you will need to accept substantially more responsibility for your education than you may have in the past. By attending your college of choice, you have agreed to become a part of its community, values, and policies. You now have the obligation to stand by its code of academic and moral conduct, and you have the responsibility of giving your very best to every class and organization in which you are involved. And you also have a responsibility to YOURSELF of approaching this new world with an open mind and curious enthusiasm. In return, your institution will be responsible for helping you reach your fullest potential and live the life you desire.

So what are your thoughts at the moment? Respond to the following questions honestly and personally.

TIPS FOR PERSONAL SUCCESS

Consider the following tips to help you move beyond your comfort zone:

▶ Take one positive risk per week.

▶ Ask others for help when you need it.

▶ Volunteer for activities and to help others.

▶ Forget past mistakes and setbacks and embrace the future.

List two other tips that would help you move beyond your comfort zone.

1. _____

2. _____

1. Thus far, I think the most rewarding class and instructor this term are going to be _____

_____

2. I believe this because _____

_____

3. To date, I've learned that this instructor expects me to _____

_____

Basic Truth 3: You're in Charge Here—It's All about Self-Motivation and Self-Responsibility

ONE person and ONLY one person has the power to determine your thoughts and the direction of your future. *It is YOU!* You will decide the direction of your future. You are NOT a victim and you will not be treated as a victim at this community college. You will not be allowed to use "victim excuses" or employ the "victim mentality." This is all about you and your desire to change your life. Higher education is not about others doing the work, but rather about finding internal motivation and accepting responsibility for your actions, your decisions, your choices, and yourself. It is not about making excuses and blaming others. *You are in charge here.* This is YOUR education, and no one else will be responsible for acquiring the knowledge and skills you will need to survive and thrive. No one will be able to "give you" personal motivation.

Regardless of your circumstances, that late paper for English is not your husband's fault. That missed lab report is not your child's problem. Your tardiness is not your mother's mistake. That unread chapter is not your partner's liability. Likewise, that 98 you scored on your drug calculation test is yours. That A you got on your paper about the

> *"You gain strength, experience, and confidence by every experience where you stop to look fear in the face. You must do the thing that you think you cannot."*
> —Eleanor Roosevelt

FIGURE

1.3 *Victim and Winner Chart*

The Victim	The Winner
The victim blames others for his or her problems.	The winner accepts responsibility for what happens in his or her life.
The victim procrastinates and makes excuses for not doing a good job.	The winner thinks ahead and plans for success.
The victim sees adversity as a permanent obstacle.	The winner sees adversity as a way to get stronger.
The victim constantly complains and has a negative mentality about most things.	The winner has an optimistic attitude and is pleasant to be with most of the time.
The victim does just enough to get by and is happy with poor grades and mediocre accomplishments.	The winner works hard to raise his or her level of achievement and constantly seeks to improve.
The victim lets life happen without trying to make things happen.	The winner has a plan and sets goals and works every day to make positive things happen.
The victim is always late and often absent and always has an excuse.	The winner is on time, prepared, and rarely ever negligent regarding his or her responsibilities.
The victim hangs out with negative people who are troublemakers and party animals and have low ambition and a poor work ethic.	The winner surrounds himself or herself with people who are working hard to make something of themselves and who are encouraging and motivating.

criminal justice system is yours. That B+ you got on your first math test is yours. This is about YOU! Your life. Your future. Your attitude is going to greatly affect your possibility of success. Consider Figure 1.3's description of the differences between a victim and a winner.

1. Name one person available to you (personally or professionally) who can offer you support, encourage you, and to whom you can turn when things get tough.

   _____

2. Why do you respect or admire this person enough to ask for help?

   _____

   _____

3. Generate a list of three questions you would like to ask about this person's life and how he or she "made it" and overcame adversity.

   1. _____

   2. _____

   3. _____

Basic Truth 4: Self-Management Will Be Your Key to Success

A major transition coming your way involves the workload for your courses and the choices YOU will need to make regarding your schedule and time. You may be assigned a significant amount of reading as homework; in fact, the amount of reading that college classes demand is usually a shock to many students. Although you may have only two or three classes in one day, the basic guideline is that for every hour spent in class, a minimum of two to three hours should be spent in review and preparation for the next class.

Quick math: If you are taking five classes and are in class for 15 hours per week, you need to spend 30 hours studying; this makes a 45-hour week—five hours more than a normal workweek for most people! Not I, you may say, and you may be right. It all depends on how wisely you use your time, how difficult the work is, and the strength of your academic background. We will discuss time management and study techniques later in this text.

Basic Truth 5: This Is Not High School

It sounds so simple, but this is perhaps the most universal and important truth discussed here: College is very different from high school OR the world of work and perhaps one of the most different places you'll ever encounter. High school, college, and work expectations for four different areas are compared in Figure 1.4. Review each area carefully and consider your past experiences as you study the differences.

Basic Truth 6: Eliminating the "This Isn't Harvard" Syndrome Will Be Essential to Your Success

IndexOpen

Some students enter community or technical colleges with little or no perception of how much work is involved or how much effort it is going to take to be successful. They do not think that the local community or technical college could possibly be *"that difficult."* Many even perceive it to be less rigorous than it actually is. *"It's only Brighton Community College"* or *"It's just Trion Technical College,"* some might reason. They do not think that the community or technical college they are attending has the academic standards of a Harvard, a Yale, or a Stanford University. The truth is that your college education is what *YOU make of it.* When you graduate and are interviewing for a job, the name of your institution may hold some weight, but your skills, your passion, experiences, knowledge, and thinking abilities will be the paramount "tipping point."

True, you may not be at Harvard or Yale, but the rigor of your programs, the amount of reading required, the level of math skills needed, and the degree to which critical thinking, communication, and information literacy skills will be demanded may surprise you. We think that it is important to dispel the *"This Isn't Harvard" Syndrome* as quickly as possible so that you can prepare yourself for the coursework and requirements ahead and make the most of your college experience.

You've probably already attended a few of your classes and received syllabi from those classes as you read this. Examine two of your current classes. What has surprised you the most about what is going to be required of you this semester?

What is the most surprising thing you have learned about your institution's curriculum thus far?

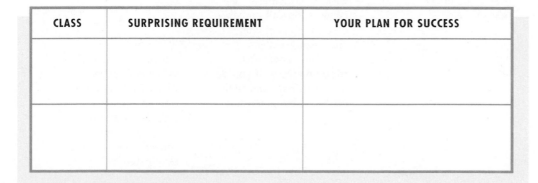

CLASS	SURPRISING REQUIREMENT	YOUR PLAN FOR SUCCESS

By embracing these truths about college life, learning, self-motivation, and education in general, you will have taken some very important steps toward your success.

FIGURE

1.4 *A Guide to Understanding Expectations*

	HIGH SCHOOL	COLLEGE	WORK
Punctuality and Attendance	**Expectations:** • State law requires a certain number of days you must attend • The hours in the day are managed for you • There may be some leeway in project dates **Penalties:** • You may get detention • You may not graduate • You may be considered a truant • Your grades may suffer	**Expectations:** • Attendance and participation in class are strictly enforced by many professors • Most professors will not give you an extension on due dates • You decide your own schedule and plan your own day **Penalties:** • You may not be admitted to class if you are late • You may fail the assignment if it is late • Repeated tardiness is sometimes counted as an absence • Most professors do not take late assignments	**Expectations:** • You are expected to be at work and on time on a daily basis **Penalties:** • Your salary and promotions may depend on your daily attendance and punctuality • You will most likely be fired for abusing either
Teamwork and Participation	**Expectations:** • Most teamwork is assigned and carried out in class • You may be able to choose teams with your friends • Your grade may reflect your participation **Penalties:** • If you don't participate, you may get a poor grade • You may jeopardize the grade of the entire team	**Expectations:** • Many professors require teamwork and cooperative learning teams or learning communities • Your grade will depend on your participation • Your grade may depend on your entire team's performance • You will probably have to work on the project outside of class **Penalties:** • Lack of participation and cooperation will probably cost you a good grade • Your team members will likely report you to the professor if you do not participate and their grades suffer as a result	**Expectations:** • You will be expected to participate fully in any assigned task • You will be expected to rely on coworkers to help solve problems and increase profits • You will be required to attend and participate in meetings and sharing sessions • You will be required to participate in formal teams and possess the ability to work with a diverse workforce **Penalties:** • You will be "tagged" as a nonteam player • Your lack of participation and teamwork will cost you raises and promotions • You will most likely be terminated

FIGURE

1.4 *A Guide to Understanding Expectations (continued)*

	HIGH SCHOOL	COLLEGE	WORK
Personal Responsibility and Attitude	**Expectations:** • Teachers may coach you and try to motivate you • You are required by law to be in high school regardless of your attitude or responsibility level **Penalties:** • You may be reprimanded for certain attitudes • If your attitude prevents you from participating you may fail the class	**Expectations:** • You are responsible for your own learning • Professors will assist you, but there is little "hand holding" or personal coaching for motivation • College did not choose you; you chose it and you will be expected to hold this attitude toward your work **Penalties:** • You may fail the class if your attitude and motivation prevent you from participating	**Expectations:** • You are hired to do certain tasks and the company or institution fully expects this of you • You are expected to be positive and self-motivated • You are expected to model good behavior and uphold the company's work standards **Penalties:** • You will be passed over for promotions and raises • You may be reprimanded • You may be terminated
Ethics and Credibility	**Expectations:** • You are expected to turn in your own work • You are expected to avoid plagiarism • You are expected to write your own papers • Poor ethical decisions in high school may result in detention or suspension **Penalties:** • You may get detention or suspension • You will probably fail the project	**Expectations:** • You are expected to turn in your own work • You are expected to avoid plagiarism • You are expected to write your own papers • You are expected to conduct research and complete projects based on college and societal standards **Penalties:** • Poor ethical decisions may land you in front of a student ethics committee or a faculty ethics committee or result in expulsion from the college • You will fail the project • You will fail the class • You may face deportation if your visa is dependent on your student status	**Expectations:** • You will be required to carry out your job in accordance with company policies, laws, and moral standards • You will be expected to use adult vision and standards **Penalties:** • Poor ethical decisions may cause you to be severely reprimanded, terminated, or in some cases could even result in a prison sentence

SUCCESSFUL DECISIONS: An Activity for Critical Reflection

After the first week of classes, Devon was very disheartened about the difficulty of the classes for which he was registered. He did not think that he was going to have so much reading or homework and he never thought the instructors would be so demanding. He had never been strong in math, but he was just floored at how difficult his beginning math course had become. He failed his first test. He passed his first essay in English, but only with a grade of C. He seriously considered dropping out. It was just too much. It was more than he expected.

Devon knew, however, that he had to succeed. He looked at his current financial situation, his dead-end job, and his desire to work in a health profession. Dropping out would never get him there. Dropping out would never make him a better, more prepared person. Dropping out would never afford him the opportunity to provide a better life for his family. However, Devon felt that he was just too far behind to catch up. He was at a loss as to what to do.

In your own words, what would you suggest that Devon do at this point? Pretend that Devon is enrolled at your institution. List at least two additional approaches that he could take to ensure his success and not drop out. Think about services that are offered and which people might be of assistance to him.

1. _____

2. _____

Basic Truth 7: Avoiding the "Bulldozer" Approach to Education Will Help You Greatly

"Bulldozer approach?" you may be asking. *"What is that?"* The "bulldozer approach" describes taking more classes and engaging in more activities than you can possibly complete successfully. We know that time is money and that many of you may be enrolled to "get in and get out," but try not to engage in more than you can do well. If you have a full-time job, care for children, keep a house, watch out for your elderly parents, and try to take seven classes, most likely it will just be too much. It is much better to slow down and do things well than to cram it all in and do it poorly—or worse yet, fail your classes and put your family in jeopardy. The "bulldozer approach" may sound like a good idea, but you may quickly find that the "turtle approach" is more effective and, in many cases, more enjoyable.

Basic Truth 8: Community and Technical Colleges Help You Prepare for an Exciting Future

You may be attending your two-year college in preparation to transfer to a four-year institution. You may be attending to obtain your degree or certificate to enter the world of work in one of countless exciting professions. Or you may be attending to hone a set of skills that will help you with a promotion and moving up the ranks in your employment. Regardless, research suggests that the benefits of attending community and technical colleges are powerful. From reduced tuition to smaller classes to diverse course offerings to remediation in math and science, two-year colleges help you prepare for a successful future.

People with associate degrees earn on average 20 to 30 percent more than people with only a high school diploma (Bailey et al., 2004). In a recent study profiled in *The Chronicle of Higher Education* (January 29, 2010), one of five Americans who earned a Ph.D. attended a community college at some point. For several minority groups, the proportion was even higher (see Figure 1.5). Allow your community college to help you achieve your goals by participating in the many academic, social, and cultural services provided on campus.

FIGURE **1.5** *From Community College to Ph.D.*

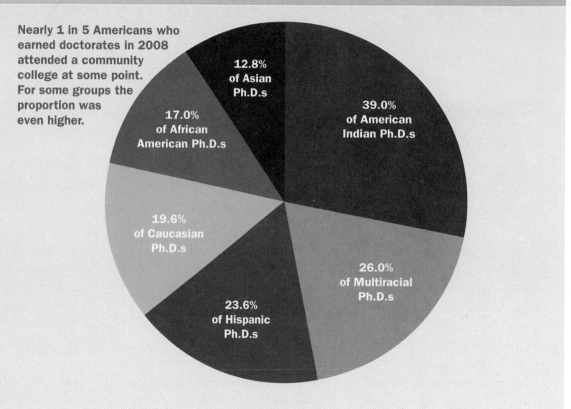

Nearly 1 in 5 Americans who earned doctorates in 2008 attended a community college at some point. For some groups the proportion was even higher.

- 12.8% of Asian Ph.D.s
- 39.0% of American Indian Ph.D.s
- 17.0% of African American Ph.D.s
- 19.6% of Caucasian Ph.D.s
- 26.0% of Multiracial Ph.D.s
- 23.6% of Hispanic Ph.D.s

Source: Adapted from "From Community College to Ph.D." *Chronicle of Higher Education.* (January 29, 2010). Retrieved from http://chronicle.com/article/Chart-From-Community-Colle/63712.

BUILDING A NEW YOU

How Can You Change Your Life Through Goal Setting?

Positive change can be brought about in several ways, but the most effective method is through goal setting and having a "change plan." Think about what you really want or what you need to change in your life. More importantly, think about why you want "this thing" and what it is going to mean to your life. By thinking about what you want, what needs to change, and where you want to be, goals become easier.

Goal setting itself is relatively easy—it is the personal commitment and self-motivation that require detailed attention, hard work, and unbridled passion. The most vital step toward reaching your goal is making a personal commitment to yourself that you are going to achieve it and then committing all of your possible resources toward the completion of that goal.

> *"Decide you want it more than you're afraid of it."*
> —Bill Cosby

Characteristics of Attainable Goals

The following characteristics will help you in your quest to bring about change through effective goal setting. Goals should be:

- ▶ *Reasonable.* Your goal should be a challenge for you, but also within reason based on your abilities.
- ▶ *Believable.* To achieve a goal, you must really believe it is within your capacity to reach it.

From Ordinary to *Extraordinary*

BILL CLAYTON
ACE Certified Personal Trainer / Post-Rehabilitation Specialist
Owner/Operator, Clayton Personal Fitness—Las Vegas, Nevada

"I was . . ." Those are powerful words. For example, *I was* the manager of the gardening department of a major retail chain. *I was* an employee in a shop that prints and mails inserts and flyers. *I was* a rock band drummer for several bands. *I was* a crystal meth addict. Yes . . . *I was!*

It seems strange to write that now, but the term "I was . . ." is impossible to erase. My friends and clients often ask me how I managed to go from the life of a meth addict to a personal trainer. The journey was a strange one and often difficult.

I began playing the drums when I was six years old and by the time I was eight, I had my first "garage band." Writing and playing music were my only passions. They were my life. After high school, I worked many odd jobs, but my love of performing never waned.

In my 20s, I had a band that steadily played gigs and I was living the life of a rocker. We traveled. We sang. We partied. We traveled some more and we partied some more . . . and more. Before I really realized what was happening with me, I had become addicted to meth. It was my life. I hung around people who used with me and they became my family. I met Kathy, the woman I would eventually marry, while performing with my band. She and I hit it off even though she knew of my addiction. One evening after we were married, Kathy and I were talking and she mentioned that she would like to have children one day. I wanted children, too. At that moment, the strangest thing came to my mind. I thought, "If she gets pregnant, I'll stop doing meth." How could I be so messed up that I would work to abolish my addiction for a child not yet born, BUT I would not consider trying to stop *just for ME*? That was my wake-up call. I knew I had to change my life. I was 29 years old.

I was one of the lucky ones. I was able to stop "cold turkey" on my own. I know that others are not so lucky. I began to look at my life and tried to determine what I wanted to do. I had to seriously evaluate every aspect of who and what I was. I knew that I had to set goals to get my life back on track.

> *My friends and clients often ask me how I managed to go from the life of a meth addict to a personal trainer.*

I had been in a life-threatening motorcycle accident years earlier and remembered the great care I received from my physical therapist. So, I began to look at PT programs and that is when I found the Personal Trainer Program at our local college. Something about this was very attractive to me. Again, I was lucky. I happened to find my passion and my life's vocation without much struggle.

Today, after working through my addiction, surviving a divorce, and mourning the death of my mom, I can say without a doubt that I am one of the luckiest people on earth. Because I was willing to change and stay committed to finding a better life, I own my own gym, hold certifications from every major fitness and rehabilitation organization in America, and count each day as a true gift.

EXTRAORDINARY REFLECTION

Read the following statement and respond in your online journal or class notebook.

Mr. Clayton mentions that he was one of the "lucky ones." What role do you think luck plays in one's success? Is there a difference between luck, readiness, and action? If so, what is it?

20

▶ *Measurable.* Your goal needs to be concrete and measurable in some way. Avoid such terms as "earn *a lot*" or "lose *some* weight."

▶ *Adaptable.* Your goals may need to be adapted to changing circumstances that may be happening in your life.

▶ *Controllable.* Your goals should be within your own control; they should not depend on the whims and opinions of anyone else.

▶ *Desirable.* To attain a difficult goal, you must want it passionately. You should never work toward something just because *someone else* wants it.

How to Write Your Goals to Bring about Positive Change

"I will pass my next math test with a B or better" is an example of a short-term goal. *"I will purchase my first home in seven to ten years"* is probably a long-term goal. During college, more of your goals may be short term than long term, but you can certainly begin setting both. Goals can be lofty and soaring, but great goals can also be as simple as *"I will spend two hours at the park with my children tomorrow afternoon."*

Well-written, exciting, and effective goals include:

▶ A goal statement with a target date

▶ Action steps

▶ A narrative statement

▶ An "I deserve" statement

▶ A personal signature

The **goal statement** should be specific and measurable; that is, it should entail some tangible evidence of its achievement and it should have a **target date**—a timeline for accomplishment. Your goal statement MUST also use an action verb. An example of a goal statement with an action verb and target date is *"I will lose 10 pounds in six weeks"* or *"I am going to* join a campus club by the fifth week of this term." This is a much more powerful statement than "I am thinking about joining a club" or "I want to have a new car."

After you write the goal statement, you'll need to create **specific action steps** that explain exactly what you are going to do to reach your goal. There is no certain number of steps; it all depends on your goal and your personal commitment. An example of action steps for weight loss might begin as follows: (1) I WILL join the campus health center, (2) I WILL meet with a personal trainer on campus, (3) I WILL set an appointment with a nutrition counselor in the health center, (4) I WILL . . .

The next step is to write a **narrative statement** about what your goal accomplishment will mean to you and how your life will change because of reaching this goal. For example, if your goal is to lose 30 pounds, paint a "verbal picture" of how your life is going to look once this goal has been reached. Your verbal picture may include statements such as "I'll be able to wear nicer clothes," "I'll feel better," "I'll be able to ride my bicycle again," or "My self-esteem will be stronger." If your goals don't offer you significant rewards, you are not likely to stick to your plan.

Next, write two reasons why you deserve this goal. This is called your **"I deserve it" statement.** It may seem simple, but this is a complex question. Many people do not follow through on their goals because deep down, they don't feel worthy of them. The narrative statement helps you understand how your life will look once the goal is met but your "I deserve" statement asks you to consider *why* you merit this goal.

What exactly is it going to take to achieve your biggest, most important goals?

Shutterstock

FIGURE

1.6 *Goal Sheet*

My Personal Goal

To help you get started, use this goal-setting sheet as a template for this and future goals.

Name _____

Goal Statement (with action verb and target date) _____

_____

_____

Action Steps (concrete things you plan to do to reach your goal)

1. _____
2. _____
3. _____
4. _____
5. _____

Narrative Statement (how your life will look when you reach your goal) _____

_____

_____

_____

What **obstacles** will you need to overcome to reach this goal?_____

_____

_____

I deserve this goal because:

1. _____

_____

2. _____

_____

I hereby make this commitment to myself.

_____   _____

My Signature   Date

Finally, **sign your goal statement.** This is an imperative step in that *your signature* shows that you are making a personal commitment to see this goal to fruition. This is your name. Use it with pride. The goal sheet in Figure 1.6 shows how to build your goals.

ONE LAST, IMPORTANT WORD ABOUT YOUR GOALS

What Happens When Aspirations and Behavior Collide?

Earlier in the chapter you read about how to bring about a positive change in your life. One of the ideas discussed was the process by which *"change demands action."* Your goals demand action, too. Many students are dismayed when they realize that goals don't just happen. Dreams and plans and aspirations are fine, but the ending can be quite painful if you don't put forth the effort to bring them to fruition. To reach your goals and meet your aspirations, you may have to work harder than you've ever worked in the past. You may have to change the way you approach things. You may have to adjust the way you think about involvement and most importantly, you may have to change the level of action that you put toward your goals.

The point at which many students leave college is the point at which their aspirations and behaviors collide. They realize that monumental changes are going to have to occur before their aspirations are met and they are simply not ready, willing, or able to make these adjustments. Begin work today on employing healthy study habits, getting involved in campus life, forging relationships with professors and counselors, working with advisors, and reaching out to people across campus who can help you. Build on your strengths and work tirelessly to overcome your challenges. These steps will help you reach your goals and make your future aspirations a reality.

REFLECTIONS ON CHANGE AND GOAL SETTING

The transition from one place to another is seldom easy, even when the change is what you want. Entering college has given you the opportunity to assume new roles, develop new friendships, meet new people, work under different circumstances, and create a bountiful future. It is an opportunity to improve on who you are at this moment or to build an entirely new person if you choose to do so. Going to college gives you the opportunity to reflect on your strengths and consider areas where you might need to change. These changes form the very essence of the college experience; they create wonderful new experiences and help you discover who you really are and what you have to offer the world.

As you reflect on this chapter, keep the following pointers in mind:

▶ Evaluate your reason(s) for attending college and what it means to your life.

▶ Understand and use the Ten Essential Cornerstones for Success.

▶ Work hard to be a winner, not a victim.

▶ Use goal setting to help you direct changes in your life.

▶ Don't just let change happen; get involved in your own life and learning.

CREATE
SUCCESS
Your Journey to University, Career, and Life Beyond College

CONNECTING Think about the people on your college campus. With whom can you make a connection to learn more about **the power of goal setting?** (Example: counselor, advisor, retention specialist, etc.) Why and how will this connection be important?	
READING Find one brief, relevant article (in print or online) relating to **community college success.** After you have read the article, write a brief summary of the additional facts you have learned.	
E-LEARNING Using any search engine, find one piece of valid, reliable information about **how to bring positive change into your life.** Briefly explain what you learned and why you think it is important.	
ANALYZING Choose one main idea or topic from this chapter. After exploring and researching this idea further, determine how this information can help you succeed in other classes.	
TRANSITIONING How will you use the content found in this chapter to help you create a successful transition plan to your next semester and beyond?	
EMPOWERING Thinking about the entire spectrum of your life (college, family, friends, finances, career, etc.), how can you empower yourself to be more successful through the information found in this chapter?	

SQ3R *Mastery* Study Sheet

EXAMPLE QUESTION *(from page 4)* What are the steps to creating a successful future?	**ANSWER:**
EXAMPLE QUESTION *(from page 12)* What are the basic truths about the culture of community colleges?	**ANSWER:**
AUTHOR QUESTION *(from page 7)* What is the relationship between you and the world economy?	**ANSWER:**
AUTHOR QUESTION *(from page 9)* Identify the Ten Essential Cornerstones.	**ANSWER:**
AUTHOR QUESTION *(from page 10)* What is the M & M Theory and how is it used?	**ANSWER:**
AUTHOR QUESTION *(from page 11)* What are the major differences between community college and university studies?	**ANSWER:**
AUTHOR QUESTION *(from page 19)* What are the characteristics of attainable goals?	**ANSWER:**
YOUR QUESTION *(from page ____)*	**ANSWER:**
YOUR QUESTION *(from page ____)*	**ANSWER:**
YOUR QUESTION *(from page ____)*	**ANSWER:**
YOUR QUESTION *(from page ____)*	**ANSWER:**
YOUR QUESTION *(from page ____)*	**ANSWER:**

Finally, after answering these questions, recite this chapter's major points in your mind. Consider the following general questions to help you master this material:

▶ What was it about?
▶ What does it mean?
▶ What was the most important thing I learned? Why?
▶ What were the key points to remember?

CHAPTER 2
ENGAGE

DEVELOPING
YOUR
PERSONAL
AND
ACADEMIC
MOTIVATION

"To be successful you need to find something to hold on to, something to motivate you, something to inspire you."

—Tony Dorsett

PART ONE CHANGING YOUR THOUGHTS

WHY READ THIS CHAPTER?

What's in it for me?

WHY is personal motivation so vital to my success? *WHY* is overcoming doubts and fears important to my personal success in college and later? *WHY* is self-esteem important to my personal motivation? *WHY* does visualization contribute to what I accomplish?

Why? Because your success depends, to a great extent, on personal motivation and learned optimism. First, you have to decide what you want in life, learn to grow from past failures, put challenges aside, and focus on who you are becoming. You have to physically, mentally, and emotionally engage in motivating yourself to accomplish your goals and dreams. No one can do that for you. Right now—and for the next few years of college—you are literally laying the foundation for the person you will become. You are deciding to excel or to just get by. You are deciding to pay the price to graduate with a college degree or to become a dropout. You are deciding to either take control of your life or let life control you. Developing a passion for learning and personal development can be a critical tool for expanding your internal motivation and drive.

By carefully reading this chapter and taking the information provided seriously, you will be able to:

▶ Understand the difference between internal and external motivation.

▶ Discuss the relationships between internal motivation and Maslow's Hierarchy of Basic Needs.

▶ Define, discuss, and use the Cornerstones of Personal and Professional Success.

▶ Identify your values and use them to develop a strong and enduring "Guiding Life Statement."

▶ Build healthier self-esteem and understand the impact of self-esteem on your values, motivation, and attitude.

CHAPTER 2 | ENGAGE

"The moment you begin to do what you really want to do, your life becomes a totally different kind of life."

—B. Fuller

BRANDON SELLERS
Graduate!
*Aims Community College,
Greeley, Colorado*

How my
COMMUNITY
COLLEGE
changed my life

An interview conducted and
written by
SHANNON McCASLAND
*Assistant Director of
Student Life, Aims
Community College*

Brandon's unplanned journey to college began when he dropped out of the seventh grade in order to get a job to help his single mother pay the bills. Fifteen years and several construction jobs later, a disabling injury brought Brandon to the stark reality that at age 29, he didn't have a plan for taking care of his two children. Construction was all he knew.

"I didn't think I could afford college," said Brandon. "I also knew I wasn't smart enough since I only had a seventh-grade education."

I met Brandon at new student orientation at Aims Community College where he learned about various financial aid opportunities. That was when he realized that if he managed his money right, he could do this *"college thing."*

But three weeks into the semester, Brandon came close to calling the whole thing off. He had gotten his first test grade: 73 percent. He had studied very hard for this history test. The grade sent him over the edge—sitting at home crying like a baby.

"I was thinking: is this what I have to look forward to? Is this my future in college? I felt like I had let myself and my kids down. If I can't be successful at this, what the heck am I going to do?"

For many students, this would have been the end of the story—but not for Brandon. He met with his history professor and immediately knew this man cared about his future.

"The personal attention my professor extended to me that day is THE driving force for why I stayed in college," said Brandon. *"I wasn't just a number. I was somebody to a college professor!"* That was Brandon's turning point.

"Every nontraditional student will hit a bump in the road somewhere during their first semester. It's a decision point. It's critical that someone is there to help the student navigate the challenges," said Brandon. *"My history professor did that for me."*

Brandon decided that to he 100 percent successful, he needed to give college everything he had; he was going to treat it like a job. This included classes and extracurricular involvement.

As Brandon's student government advisor, I watched him meet his goals both inside and outside of the classroom walls. I watched his history professor give him the coveted Aims Distinguished Scholar Award. It was one of the happiest moments in my professional career when I got to place a call to Brandon for the college president inviting him to be the commencement speaker. His story echoed in my mind as he told the graduating class they could be anything they wanted to be. It was no longer a cliché to him.

"I was totally humbled speaking at graduation," said Brandon. *"I was remembering that day I went home crying. I was remembering how close I came to giving up."*

"Aims has really helped me believe that. I've always heard that but never believed it. Coming away from Aims, I know that it actually is true: I CAN be whatever I want to be. Before I came to college, I felt it was for people who

have money and a high school education. But it doesn't matter what your background is. If you want to succeed, the tools are there."

Many doors have opened to Brandon since his graduation from Aims. He is transferring to the University of Northern Colorado with several scholarships.

"We've been given a unique opportunity to go to school—Aims Community College showed me that. Now it's my responsibility to share that with others."

BEFORE YOU READ

SCAN & QUESTION

In the preface of this book (page xiv), you read about the **SQ3R study method**. Right now, take a few moments, **scan this chapter,** and on the SQ3R Mastery Study Sheet on page 51, write **five of your own questions** that you think will be important to your mastery of this material. In addition to the two questions below, you will find five questions from your authors on that study sheet. Use one of your **"Study for Quiz"** stickers to flag this page for easy reference.

EXAMPLES:

▶ What is the difference between internal and external motivation? (from page 30)

▶ How can overcoming self-defeating behaviors help you become a better student? (from page 36)

THE POWER AND PASSION OF MOTIVATION

What Is the Difference Between Internal and External Motivation?

Motivation can change your life! *Read that statement again. Motivation can change your life!* Ask any successful businessperson. Ask your favorite athlete or actor. Ask your classmates who pass every exam, project, or paper with an A. It is their burning desire—their aspiration to succeed, to live an exceptional life, and reach their goals—that changed their lives and got them to where they are today. Motivation is a force that can transform your attitude, alter the course of your performance, intensify your actions, and illuminate your future. Motivation can help you live a life that reflects your true potential. Motivation can help you live a life beyond your grandest dreams.

If you have a need or desire to change your motivation level or attitude toward personal and academic success, there are steps you can take to help you with this goal. Some of the steps described in this chapter will be easy to implement *and* others will greatly challenge you, but taken seriously, each step can assist you in discovering who you really are and what you want in life, and help you find the motivation you need to change. No one can do this for you.

There are two types of motivation: **external and internal.** *External motivation* is the weaker of the two because, as the term suggests, *external forces or people* are causing you to do something. You do not own it. External motivators may be things or people such as your parents, spouse, or partner pushing you to complete your degree; your supervisor telling you to do "x, y, or z" or you will be fired; or even your professors giving you an exam to make sure you have read Chapter 2. You may do the things asked of you, but your reason for doing them is external. You did not necessarily choose to do them on your own.

Internal motivation, on the other hand, is uniquely yours. It is *energy* inside of you—pushing YOU to go after what YOU want. Internal motivation is a strong and driving force because you own it. There are no external forces or people telling you that you must do something—the motivation comes from your desire *to be something, to have something, to attain a goal that you truly desire,* or *to solve a problem.* Successful people live in the world of internal motivation or find ways to convert external motivation into internal motivation.

A simple example of this conversion may be that your current degree requires you to take classes for which you cannot understand the value or purpose. You may ask yourself, *"Why would a theater major have to take two classes in college algebra?"* The class is hard, math is not your thing, the chapters are frustrating and difficult to read, and math has little to do with your interests, career goals, or overall life plan. The challenge for you is to find an internal reason to move forward—a rationale for how math is going to help you, now and in the future. This is called ***internalizing.*** Perhaps you want to own your own theater, which is a business and which will require the use of math. Internalizing the content of this math class and its requirements can motivate you to do well.

Bananastock

How can doing something you love and enjoy increase your motivation level?

By converting this external motivation (a requirement for your degree) into internal motivation (something that can help you run your business), the math class will become easier and more relevant because you have found a way to link it to your success, your goals, your money, your health, your family, or your overall life plan.

By internalizing, you see that good math skills can help you land a work-study job in the theater scene shop. You find that good math skills can help you create an effective personal budget and help you save money. You find that the more you learn about the logic and process of math, the easier it is to solve problems and think more critically, thus helping you perform better in other classes. By silencing your negative self-talk about math (*"I hate math," "Math is so stupid," "I'm going to fail this class"*), you are able to internalize the rewards of the class and own the outcome. You have made a conversion. Consider the exercise in Figure 2.1.

FIGURE

2.1   *Seeing the Importance*

Think about a class required for your degree that seems to have no relevance to you or your career field. (You may have to look at your college catalog to check your degree requirements.) What courses do you think you are going to have to work hard to convert? One example is given below. We have also provided space for you to do several conversions, too.

MY MAJOR IS THEATER/ACTING	HOW CAN THIS CLASS HELP ME IN MY CHOSEN PROFESSION?
Seemingly irrelevant **Class 1** **HISTORY**	✓ A class in history can help me understand the historical and social context in which the plays I'm studying were written. ✓ A class in history can help me understand more about scene design and period costumes.
MY MAJOR IS _____ **Seemingly irrelevant** **Class 1** _____ **Seemingly irrelevant** **Class 2** _____	HOW CAN THIS CLASS HELP ME IN MY CHOSEN PROFESSION? _____ _____ _____ _____

THE NEED TO BE MORE

What Is the Relationship Between Motivation and Maslow?

One important way to think about motivation is to consider the work of Abraham Maslow, a renowned psychologist who in 1943 introduced the ***Hierarchy of Basic Needs*** in his landmark paper, ***A Theory of Human Motivation.*** His basic premise is that EVERY human being is motivated by a set of basic needs and that we will do whatever it takes to have these things in our lives. The bottom four levels are what he calls deficiency needs, and they include things such as food, air, water, security, family, health, sexual intimacy, self-esteem, achievement, and respect from others. The top level is called a psychological need, and it involves self-actualization, personal growth, and fulfillment. See Figure 2.2.

Self-actualization, the top level, is perhaps the most obscure and abstract to understand, but it is the most important when it comes to motivation. Maslow suggests that we all have a basic, driving desire to matter, to have a life in which we are doing what we were meant to do. Self-actualization can also be described as living at our "peak" and being fully ourselves. The renowned psychologist, author, and speaker Dr. Wayne Dyer describes self-actualization as meaning ***"You MUST be what you CAN be."*** By this he suggests that if you know you are living a life that is "less" than the life you know you are capable of living, true happiness will never be yours.

If, indeed, self-actualization is a basic need in us all, then the theory holds that we all have a burning desire to do our best work, to live a life that matters, and to reach our fullest

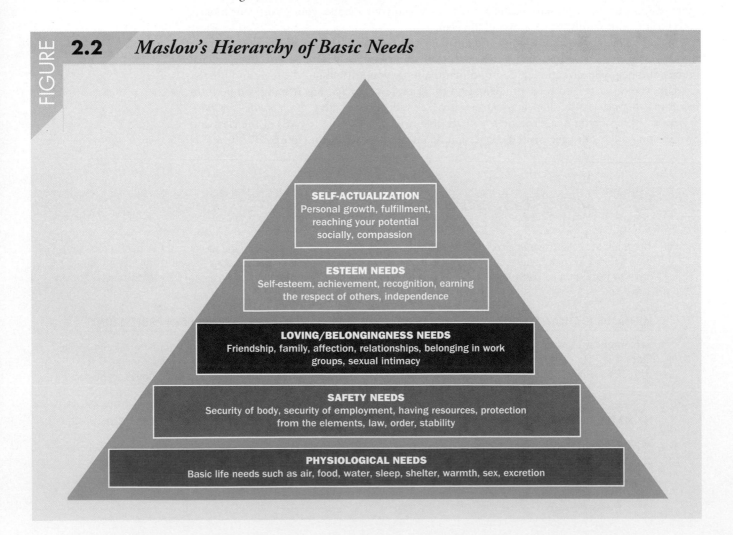

FIGURE

2.2 *Maslow's Hierarchy of Basic Needs*

SELF-ACTUALIZATION
Personal growth, fulfillment, reaching your potential socially, compassion

ESTEEM NEEDS
Self-esteem, achievement, recognition, earning the respect of others, independence

LOVING/BELONGINGNESS NEEDS
Friendship, family, affection, relationships, belonging in work groups, sexual intimacy

SAFETY NEEDS
Security of body, security of employment, having resources, protection from the elements, law, order, stability

PHYSIOLOGICAL NEEDS
Basic life needs such as air, food, water, sleep, shelter, warmth, sex, excretion

potential—"to be what we can be." It means that we want to be fulfilled in our lives and experience personal growth. For example, if you are taking a class that you do not really enjoy and don't know why you have to take, you may not be putting your best "self" forward. Doing this may seem to be OK, but deep down inside, you know that you could, and SHOULD, do better. You know that you are not living up to your full potential or fulfilling your purpose in class, at college, or in life. You know in your heart that you are not living at your peak, and this will begin to gnaw at you until it affects other areas of your life.

THE "FIRST-GENERATION" GAP

How Do You Make It When You're the First in the Family?

Many community college students are **first-generation students,** meaning that their parents' highest level of graduation was a high school diploma or less. This may not seem like such a big deal, but it can be on many levels. If you are a first-generation student, you may not have the support and understanding of family members who know firsthand the pressures of what you're going through. It may seem as if they are not supportive. This could be true, but more than likely, they are unaware how to offer support because "college" is new for them, too. Therefore, it is so very important that you find support beyond what your family may be able to offer. You will encounter many people at your college who are first generation and they can help guide you. Many non-first-generation students, faculty, staff, and personal friends will be able to offer you support, too.

In a personal survey, first-generation students responded that their reasons for attending college were to be well off financially and provide their children with better opportunities than they had. Statistics from years of research with first-generation students also show that many are more likely to have a family of their own (spouse and children), are more likely to be older (30+), come from families with lower incomes, work more full-time hours off campus, enroll part time, be less academically prepared, and attend community colleges. It was also found that first-generation students drop out more frequently than non-first-generation students (U.S. Department of Education, 1998).

Don't despair, however. These statistics do not have to predict your future, who you are, or where you are going. You are not tied to what "others" have or have not done. This is your life, your future, your beginning. Being a first-generation student can have many rewards, such as increased self-esteem from one's sense of accomplishment, the opportunity to serve as a mentor for family and friends, and the ability to increase one's socioeconomic status.

As you begin your studies, however, you may find that you face resistance from some friends and family members. You may even find that some relationships suffer or end because of your pursuit of self-improvement and higher education. Don't let this discourage you. Again, this is one of the many changes that may occur in your personal life as you embark on your college journey. Before ending a relationship, try talking to the other person to give assurances of your continued friendship, while holding fast to the notion that your own life and your own future are of great importance, too. You may find that some people leave you. You may also find that you have to leave some people. Some friends may not be able to rejoice in the fact that you are going to college because they feel that you are leaving them behind; others will simply be jealous of the fact that you are bettering yourself and they are not. If those around you do not support you and your dreams and they cannot be reasoned with, you may have to part company for the sake of growth and future security.

As you begin your studies, let yourself undergo the whole spectrum of the college experience. Try to attend social, sporting,

> What support groups exist on your campus to help first-generation students?

Shutterstock

and cultural events. Use college resources to best advantage. Establish meaningful relationships, and enjoy the ride. Yes, you may face challenges on a day-to-day basis, but growth and change include challenges. It only means you are moving. Expanding! Growing!

If you are a first-generation student, you can do many things to help ensure your success and graduation.

▶ Deal with family conflicts and misunderstandings early and quickly. Talk with them about your plans, daily schedules, and college culture. Keep family members involved so they don't feel left out or that you are abandoning them.

▶ Don't let feelings of guilt or "selling out" derail your goals and plans. Yes, you may be the first in your family to attend college, but with your guidance and mentoring, you will not be the last. You can be a positive influence on others.

▶ Work hard to find a support group, advisor, counselor, peer, or professor who understands your situation and can offer advice. Talk to people. Make friends. Associate.

▶ Try to meet people who have been at your institution for at least one semester or one year so that you can learn "survival tips" from them.

▶ Immerse yourself socially and academically in the campus culture. Make use of every source of academic, financial, career, and cultural assistance possible.

▶ Find a healthy balance between work, family, and your college studies. Remember, this is your future. One way to look at this is to ask yourself, "Is my current job my future? Is it my destiny?"

▶ Involve your family and friends in your education as much as possible. Ask them to attend events with you. Encourage them to begin their studies, too.

▶ Don't be ashamed of what you are doing and for trying to improve your station in life. Dimming your own light does nothing to help others see more clearly. This is a major step forward, and you should be proud of yourself for taking it.

▶ Have an open mind and enjoy the process. This is the time to learn, grow, explore, and prosper.

ACHIEVING YOUR POTENTIAL AND INCREASING YOUR MOTIVATION

What Are the Cornerstones of Personal and Professional Success?

> *"Watch your thoughts, they become words. Watch your words, they become actions. Watch your actions, they become habits. Watch your habits, they become character. Watch your character, it becomes your destiny."*
> —*Frank Outlaw*

"I am a winner."
"I fail at everything I do."

"I am a dedicated person."
"I don't really care about anything."

"I can't wait for my day to start."
"I hate getting up in the morning."

As you can see by the two different perspectives in each set, your attitude and perspective on how you approach life, relationships, problems, and goals can mean the difference between being a motivated, inspired, and successful person and being a weary, frightened, and unsuccessful person.

The reason that we have included the following Nine-Point Plan in this chapter is to help you see that by focusing on you—by becoming a person who knows where you're going, what you want, and what you have to offer—your motivation and passion for learning and growing will flourish. By knowing more about yourself, you can then establish a clearer vision of your true potential. Take your time and read each point carefully. Consider the questions asked and complete the chapter activities to assist you with your motivation plan.

Point 1: Develop a New Attitude

Your attitude—new or old, good or bad—belongs to you. As you learned in Chapter 1, change and growth may require a shift in attitude and actions. If your attitude needs changing, no one else can change it for you. Now is the perfect time to begin changing your attitude if it needs an adjustment because small changes in the way you approach life can mean major changes to your success throughout your college career and beyond.

Just as some people embrace the attitude of *learned helplessness* (i.e., letting your past and the people in your family or personal community and their failures dictate your future), you can just as easily embrace the attitude of learned optimism. A *pessimist* finds bad news in most situations; he or she lives in a world that has a cloud overhead all the time. *Optimists,* on the other hand, can handle bad news and difficult challenges because they have a positive way of viewing the world. Optimists learn how to determine why things "went wrong" and can adjust and fix the underlying problem.

People actually create their own success, reach their goals, and become successful by embracing a positive outlook on life. Conversely, a great deal of personal misery and failure is caused by adopting a bad attitude and by embracing negative feelings and *self-defeating behaviors.* Take the assessment in Figure 2.3 to determine your current attitudes. Afterward select one of the self-defeating habits that you checked. On the lines below, state exactly what your behavior is and why you think you are experiencing this problem.

Do you think that surrounding yourself with optimistic, motivated people will help you succeed? Why or why not?

_____

_____

_____

Develop five action steps to help you change your attitude and overcome this self-defeating behavior.

1. _____
2. _____
3. _____
4. _____
5. _____

Point 2: Make Excellence a Habit

As you work to change some of your habits and to become a highly motivated person, one practice you need to embrace is excellence in everything you do. The average person is happy doing just enough to get by. Those who excel and succeed demand excellence from themselves at all times. If you don't think excellence matters, consider these points: Would you want a doctor who cheated his or her way through medical school to operate on you or your child? Would you want a pilot who hadn't performed very well on the simulated crash test to fly your plane? Would you want to

"NEVER leave well enough alone. If it ain't broke, fix it; take fast and make it faster; take smart and make it smarter; take good and make it great."
—Cigna Advertisement

2.3   *Is My Behavior Self-Defeating?*

Review the checklist below of typical self-defeating habits that can be changed by adopting the right attitude. Place a check by the ones that relate to you and your behavior:

- ☐ I am frequently depressed, lonely, sad, frustrated, worried, or frightened.
- ☐ I spend a lot of time with people who aren't very motivated to excel.
- ☐ I waste a lot of time watching TV, playing video games, texting, scanning Facebook, and so on.
- ☐ I get very uptight and negative when I have to take a test.
- ☐ I am more worried about associating with friends than I am about my grades.
- ☐ I spend money that I shouldn't spend and charge things on my credit card that I can't afford.
- ☐ I eat too much junk food when I get stressed.
- ☐ I don't exercise properly.
- ☐ I procrastinate a lot and I lose my temper quickly when I am under pressure.
- ☐ I tend to give up easily when things get hard.
- ☐ I am having trouble with my living arrangement.
- ☐ I have trouble making it through the day without some form of stimulant such as coffee, cigarettes, drugs, or alcohol.
- ☐ I daydream in some of my classes.
- ☐ I turn in my assignments late and make up excuses as to why.
- ☐ I seem to daydream a lot about how things used to be.
- ☐ I cut class when I feel depressed or unprepared.
- ☐ I don't feel comfortable talking to my advisor and professors.
- ☐ I don't feel like I am making many friends here and I often feel lonely and discouraged.
- ☐ I do not participate in any co- or extracurricular activities.
- ☐ I spend a lot of my time doing nothing.
- ☐ I hate my job.
- ☐ Some of my classes suck and I cut them often.

If you checked off five or more statements on this chart, you may be experiencing self-defeating behavior. You will need to consider carefully how to eliminate these behaviors from your life as you work on a personal attitude adjustment.

cross a bridge every day that was designed by an engineer who cheated his way through design class? ***Excellence matters!***

Figure 2.4 illustrates the importance of excellence in several real-life situations.

Point 3: Overcome Your Doubts and Fears

"People BECOME who they are. Even Beethoven BECAME Beethoven."
—Randy Newman

Success is a great motivator, but so is fear. Actually, fear probably motivates more people than anything else. Unfortunately, fear motivates most people to hold back, to doubt themselves, to stay in their comfort zones, and to accomplish much less than they could without the fear.

Your own personal fears may be some of the biggest obstacles to reaching your potential. If you are afraid, you are not alone; everyone has fears. Isn't it interesting that *our fears are learned?* As an infant, you had only **two fears:** a fear of falling and a fear of loud noises. As you got older, you added to your list of fears. And if you are like most people, you may have let your fears dominate parts of your life, saying things to yourself like: *"What if I try and fail?" "What if people laugh at me for thinking I can do this?"* or *"What if someone finds out that this is my dream?"* You have two choices where fear is concerned: You can let fear dominate your

FIGURE

2.4   *Is 99.9 Percent Good Enough?*

If 99.9 percent were good enough, then:

- 12 newborns would be given to the wrong parents in the United States every day.
- 7 people would be buried in the WRONG graves or cremated incorrectly daily in the United States.
- 292 book titles published in the United States would be shipped with the wrong covers on them this year.
- 400 entries in *Webster's Dictionary* would be misspelled.
- 1,200,000 credit cards held in the United States would have incorrect cardholder information on the black magnetic strip on the back of the card.
- 79,000 drug prescriptions would be written incorrectly this year in the United States.
- 32,000 of the Library of Congress's books would be filed on the shelves incorrectly.

EXCELLENCE MATTERS!

life, or you can focus on those things you really want to accomplish, put your fears behind you, and *"go for it."*

Dr. Robert Schuller, minister, motivational speaker, and author, once asked, ***"What would you attempt to do if you could not fail?"*** This is an important question for anyone, especially someone who is trying to increase his or her motivation level. In the spaces below, work through this idea by answering the questions truthfully. We have adapted and expanded this question for the purpose of this exercise.

1. What would you attempt to do or what would your college major be if you could not fail?

   _____

   _____

   _____

2. Beyond the answers, *"I'm afraid"* or *"Fear,"* WHY are you not doing this "thing"?_____

   _____

   _____

   _____

3. If you did this "thing" and were successful at "it," how would your life change? Be specific.

   _____

   _____

   _____

Consider using the goal sheet in Chapter 1 (Figure 1.6) as a template to develop an entire goal strategy to bring this "thing" to fruition in your life.

Point 4: Put Adversity and Failure into Perspective

Thomas Edison was once asked how it felt to fail over 1,000 times at making the light bulb work. He responded, *"I have NEVER failed at making the light bulb work. I successfully identified over 1000 ways that it would not work."* Edison looked on his unsuccessful attempts to create the electric light bulb positively. He saw them as eliminating ways that would not

"If you fall down or if you're knocked down, try to land on your back because if you can LOOK up, you can GET up."

—Les Brown

Bob Daemmrich Photography

When faced with adversity, what techniques have you used in the past to survive and "move on"?

work, not as failure. Failure is just a temporary by-product of the success that lies ahead if you persevere. A part of being motivated is learning to deal with failure and setbacks. Most people compile a string of failures before they have great success.

Have you ever given up on something too quickly, or gotten discouraged and quit? That feeling is quite different from the feeling you have after completing a goal and getting an adrenaline rush from success. Can you think of a time when you were unfair to yourself because you didn't stay with something long enough? Completing a goal feels much different than giving up. Have you ever stopped doing something you really loved because somebody laughed at you or teased you about it? Doing what brings you joy in the face of adversity gives you a feeling much different than the one you have after caving in to peer pressure. Overcoming failure and learning from mistakes make victory much more rewarding. Motivated people know that losing and making mistakes are necessary aspects of winning: The difference between winning and losing is the ability to get up, stand tall, and try again. Winning is getting up one more time than you are knocked down. A successful person is successful because he or she hung on *just one moment longer* than the person who gave up.

Point 5: Eliminate Negative Self-Talk and the "I CAN'T" Syndrome

Try as you might, sometimes harmful emotions, fear of the unknown, and that nagging little voice inside your head (negative self-talk) can cause problems. Negative self-talk usually appears when you are afraid, uneasy, hurt, angry, depressed, or lonely, feelings most people have experienced. When you undergo change, your body, mind, and soul typically go through a process of physical and emotional change as well. Learning to recognize these symptoms in order to control them can help you handle the stress that can accompany change. You may have to develop a new attitude.

Your attitude is yours. It belongs to you. You own it. Good or bad, happy or sad, optimistic or pessimistic, it is yours and you are responsible for it. However, your attitude is greatly influenced by situations in your life and by the people with whom you associate. Developing a winning, optimistic attitude can be hard yet extremely rewarding work and beneficial to the change process. Motivated and successful people have learned that one's attitude is the mirror to one's soul.

Listen to yourself for a few days. Are you more of an optimist or a pessimist? Do you hear yourself whining, complaining, griping, and finding fault with everything and everybody around you? Do you blame others for things that are wrong in your life? Do you blame your bad grades on your professors? Is someone else responsible for your unhappiness? If these thoughts or comments are in your head, you are suffering from the *"I CAN'T" Syndrome* (**I**rritated, **C**ontaminated, **A**ngry, **N**egative **T**houghts). This pessimistic condition can negatively influence every aspect of your life, from self-esteem to motivation level to academic performance, from relationships to career success.

If you want to eliminate *I CAN'T* from your life, consider the following tips:

▶ Think about the many positive aspects of your life and show gratitude for them.

▶ Work every day to find the good in people, places, and things.

▶ Eliminate negative thoughts that enter your mind before you begin your day.

▶ Discover what is holding you back and what you need to push you forward.

▶ Visualize your success—visualize yourself actually being who and what you want to be.

▶ Locate and observe positive, optimistic people and situations in your life.

▶ Make a list of people who help you, support you, and encourage you to feel positive—then make a point to be around them more.

▶ Take responsibility for your own actions and their consequences.

▶ Force yourself to find five positive things a day for which to be thankful.

You've seen the difference between an optimist and a pessimist. They are both found everywhere—at work, at school, and maybe in your own family. Think of the optimist for a moment. You've probably sat next to a positive person in one of your classes or seen him or her at work—always seeming to be happy, motivated, bubbling with personality, organized, and ready for whatever comes along. Optimists greet people as they enter the room, they respond in class, they volunteer for projects, and they have a presence about them that is positive and lively. You may even look at him or her out of the corner of your eye and ask, "What is this person on?"

Positive, upbeat, and motivated people are easy to spot. You can basically see their attitude in the way they walk, the way they carry themselves, the way they approach people, and the way they treat others.

Be wary, however, of *"the others."* The ones you need to avoid. Whiners. Degraders. Attackers. Manipulators. Pessimists. Backstabbers. Abusers. Cowards. Two-faced racists, sexists, ageists, homophobes, ethnocentrists. These people carry around an aura so negative that it can almost be seen as a dark cloud above them. They degrade others because they do not like themselves. They find fault with everything because their own lives are a mess. They do nothing and then attack you for being motivated and trying to improve your life. We call them **contaminated people.** Unhappy with who they are, contaminated people make themselves feel better by trying to tear down those who take the opposite approach. They belittle your positive actions and try to make your life as miserable as theirs.

Sure, everyone has bad days and bad stretches in their lives. This is *not* who we are talking about here. With contaminated people, being negative and trying to bring others down is epidemic to their lives. It is the way they operate all the time. It is constant. Having a bad day and complaining is normal for some people at various times, but contaminated people see life (and you) as negative and bad on an hourly and daily basis.

Point 6: Identify and Clarify What You Value in Life

If you have been highly motivated to accomplish a goal in the past, this achievement was probably tied to something you valued a great deal. Because most of what you do in life centers on what is truly important to you, you need to identify and then clarify what you value in your life— what really matters to you.

Values, self-esteem, motivation, and goal setting are all mixed up together, making it difficult to separate one from the others. The goals you work to accomplish are directly connected to what you value. Therefore, your ATTITUDE and ACTIONS are tied to your VALUES. If you value an attitude or belief, your actions will be centered on these ideals. If you love to spend time with your friends and this is valuable to you, then you will make the time for this on a regular basis. Why? Because your friendships are a fundamental part of your value system. You like spending time with your friends and get pleasure from it, so you are motivated by it and you do it. It is that simple. Our values influence our actions. It is, once again, tied to Maslow's Hierarchy of Basic Needs.

"Our souls are not hungry for fame, comfort, wealth, or power. These rewards create almost as many problems as they solve. Our souls are hungry for meaning, for the sense that we have figured out a way to live so that our lives matter."

—H. Kushner

Many of our values are in our unconscious mind. They were put there by ideas we've heard, items we've read, music we've listened to, TV shows we've watched, and actions we've seen others do. We may not even know that we value something until it is threatened or removed. Until you clarify what it is that YOU really value, you may be working to accomplish goals or pursuing career choices that someone else values, not you. By having vague or poorly clarified values, you may be working toward something, believing in something, or acting in a way that is not really who you are. This can cause you to wander aimlessly and become frustrated, eventually destroying your motivation level and self-esteem. Values bring direction to your life and help you stay motivated.

Below, you will find a wide and varied list of items. Read them over carefully and circle the ones you truly value. Be careful and selective. DO NOT just randomly circle words. As a criterion for each word you circle, ask yourself, "Can I defend why *I value* this in my life?" and "Is this truly something I value or something I was told to value and have never questioned why?" If you value something that is not on the list, add it in the spaces at the bottom.

Honesty	Affection	Punctuality	Respect
Frankness	Open-Mindedness	Reliability	Trustworthiness
Sincerity	Wit/Humor	Spontaneity	Devotion
Frugality	Justice	Creativity	Caring
Spirituality	Friendliness	Energy	Intellect
Attentiveness	Conversation	Money	Security
Fine Dining	Beauty	Devotion	Enthusiasm
Positivism	Commitment	Foresightedness	Giving
Organization	Learning	Listening	Success
Control	Comfort	Knowledge	Courage
Athletic Ability	Thoughtfulness	Independence	Partying
Safety	Fun	Excitement	Speaking
Love	Friendship	Writing	Teamwork
Reading	Family	Dependability	Walks
Time Alone	Time w/Friends	Phone Calls	Integrity
Exercise	Problem Solving	Empowerment	Tolerance
Service to Others	Modesty	Strength	Power
Imagination	Self-Esteem	Food	Change
Winning	Goals	Risk Taking	Optimism
Self-Improvement	Forgiveness	Fairness	Direction in Life
Successful Career	Motivation	Trust	Mentoring
Working	Hobbies	Books	Stability

_____ _____ _____ _____

_____ _____ _____ _____

_____ _____ _____ _____

_____ _____ _____ _____

Now that you have circled or written what you value, choose the five items that you value the most. In other words, if you were allowed to value ONLY five things in life, what five would you list below? In the space to the right of each value, rank them from 1 to 5 (1 being the most important to you, your life, your relationships, your actions, your education, and your career).

Take your time and give serious consideration to this activity, as you will need to refer to this exercise later in this chapter.

SUCCESSFUL
DECISIONS: **An Activity for Critical Reflection**

Your friend Jamal is struggling with staying motivated during his first semester at college. He didn't have to study much in high school and still pulled good grades, but he has been overwhelmed with the amount of work his college professors are assigning. He knows he is not doing his best work, but he can't seem to get motivated to excel. You know he is capable because he participated in your study group several times before he stopped coming.

Lately, Jamal tells you he has been waking up during the night very stressed out and afraid that he is going to flunk out. His parents will be devastated if this happens because he is a first-generation college student, and they have sacrificed so much to send him to college. His fears gnaw at him all the time.

Sometimes he can see himself going home and telling his parents that he is failing. He visualizes how embarrassed he would be telling them and his friends that he has failed. One of his professors has told him that he has a bad attitude. He spent a long time this afternoon talking to you about his lack of motivation and how he is thinking of dropping out.

What advice and motivational tips would you offer Jamal to help him get on the right track?

1. _____

2. _____

LIST   **RANK**

▶ _____   _____

▶ _____   _____

▶ _____   _____

▶ _____   _____

▶ _____   _____

Now, look at YOUR first item. Where did this value originate?

_____

_____

_____

Defend why this is the one thing you value more in life than anything else.

_____

_____

_____

How does this one value motivate you?

_____

_____

_____

> *"Your character is determined by how you treat people who can do you no good and how you treat people who can't fight back."*
> —Abigail Van Buren

Point 7: Take Pride in Your Name and Personal Character

"My name?" you may ask. *"What does my name have to do with anything?"* The answer: At the end of the day, the end of the month, the end of your career, and the end of your life, your name and your character are all that you have. Taking pride in developing your character and protecting your good name can be a powerful motivational force.

Imagine for a moment that you are working with a group of students on a project for your psychology class. The project is to receive a major grade, and you and your group will present your findings to 300 psychology students at a campus forum. Your group works hard and when you present the project, your group receives a standing ovation and earns an A. The name of each individual group member is read aloud as you stand to be recognized. Your name and project are also posted in a showcase. You are proud. Your hard work paid off. Your name now carries weight in the psychology department, with your peers, and among the psychology faculty. It feels good.

Bananastock

Conversely, imagine that your group slacks off; the project is poorly prepared and received by the audience and your professor. Your team earns an F on the project. Your name is associated with this project, and your name and grade are posted with every other group's. Your group is the only group to receive an F. It doesn't feel good.

Basically, it comes down to this: Every time you make a choice, every time you complete a project, and every time you encounter another person, your actions define your character and your name. People admire and respect you when you make an honorable and moral choice, especially if it is a difficult decision. Both your character and your name are exclusively yours, and you are responsible for their well-being. When you care passionately about your reputation and character, your life is governed by protecting your name. Your actions, beliefs, and decisions are all tied to this one belief: "My name and my reputation matter and I will do nothing to bring shame or embarrassment to my name."

What negative effects can damage to your name and reputation have on your overall success?

Point 8: Develop a Strong, Personal "Guiding Statement"

You're wearing a T-shirt to class. It is not your normal, run-of-the-mill T-shirt, however. No, you designed this T-shirt for everyone to see and read. It is white with bright red letters. On the front of the T-shirt is written your ***personal guiding statement***—the words by which you live—the words that govern your life. What would your T-shirt say? Perhaps you would use the golden rule, "Do unto others . . . ." It might be an adaptation of the Nike slogan, "Just Do It," or it might be something more profound such as "I live my life to serve others and to try to make others' lives better" or "Be a blessing" or "Live, Love, Laugh."

Whatever your guiding statement, it must be yours. It can't be your parents' or your professor's or your best friend's statement. It must be based on something you value and it must be strong enough to motivate you in hard, tough times. Your guiding statement must be so powerful that it will literally "guide you" when you are ethically challenged, broke, alone, angry, hurt, sad, or feeling vindictive. It is a statement that will guide you in relationships with family, friends, spouses, partners, or would-be love interests. It is a statement that gives direction to your DAILY actions. Think about how different your life would be if you woke up each morning and LIVED your guiding statement to the fullest.

One of the best places to start working on your guiding statement is to look back at those things you circled as valuable to you on page 40 of this chapter. If you value something, it may appear in your guiding statement. For example, if you circled the words *Respect, Giving*, and *Optimism* among those you value, this is a basis for your statement. A guiding statement based on these words might read:

"I will live my life as a positive, upbeat, motivated person who respects others and enjoys giving to others on a daily basis."

If your circled words included *Integrity, Honesty*, and *Fairness*, your statement may read:

"My integrity is the most important thing in my life and I will never act in any way that compromises my integrity. I will be truthful, fair, and honest in all my endeavors."

More simply, your guiding statement may read something like:

"Be reliable," "Live optimistically," or ***"Never give up."***

In the space below, transfer the most important words from the values list on page 40 and then work to develop your guiding statement.

The most important values were:

_____   _____   _____

_____   _____   _____

_____   _____   _____

Using these words, draft your guiding statement. (Take your time and be sincere.)

_____
_____
_____
_____
_____

HOW YOUR GUIDING STATEMENT WILL HELP. Now that you have developed your guiding life statement, discuss how this statement would guide you . . .

If you have a disagreement with your supervisor at work _____
_____
_____
_____

TIPS FOR PERSONAL SUCCESS

Assume you are 90 years old and on your deathbed. You are thinking back over your life. Most likely you would think about certain people and events that have transpired. Perhaps you might want people to say or write the following about you:

▶ She was kind to people.

▶ He spent quality time with his children.

▶ She was a wonderful friend.

▶ He was always a giving person.

Now it is your turn. Create a list of at least three things that you hope to have people say or write about you upon your death.

1. _____

2. _____

3. _____

If your class paper or project receives a failing grade from your professor

_____

_____

_____

_____

If you are having a disagreement with someone for whom you care deeply (friend, spouse, partner, parent, work associate, etc.)

_____

_____

_____

If you see that someone is struggling and having a hard time "making it"

_____

_____

_____

_____

Point 9: Make a Commitment to Strengthen Your Self-Esteem

If you were asked to name all the areas of your life that are impacted by self-esteem, what would you say? The correct answer is "Everything." Every area of your life is affected by your self-esteem.

Self-esteem and self-understanding are two of the most important components of your personal makeup! To be truly motivated, you have to know yourself and love yourself! Many people who are in therapy are there simply because they cannot accept the fact that they are OK. Self-esteem is a powerful force in your life and is the source of your joy, your productivity, and your ability to have good relationships with others.

You might think of self-esteem as a photograph of yourself that you keep locked in your mind. It is a collective product—the culmination of everyone with whom you have associated, everywhere you've traveled, and all of the experiences you have had. William James, the first major psychologist to study self-esteem, defined it as "*the sum total of all a person can call their own:* the *Material Me* (all that you have), the *Social Me* (recognition and acceptance from others), and the *Spiritual Me* (your innermost thoughts and desires)."

Stanley Coopersmith, noted psychologist and developer of the most widely used self-esteem inventory in America, defined self-esteem as "*a personal judgment of worthiness.*" Psychologist and author Nathanial Branden defines self-esteem as "*confidence in our ability to cope with the basic challenges of life.*" And finally, psychologist Charles Cooley called it "*the look-*

ing glass." Perhaps in everyday terms, we can define healthy self-esteem as "I know who I am, I accept who I am, I am OK, and I'm going to make it."

Self-esteem has five basic characteristics based on Maslow's Hierarchy of Basic Needs.

▶ A sense of **security** (I am safe and have the basics of life, food, water, etc.)
▶ A sense of **identity** (I know who I am and where I'm going.)
▶ A sense of **belonging** (I know how to love and I am loved.)
▶ A sense of **purpose** (I know why I'm here and what I am going to do with my life.)
▶ A sense of **personal competence** (I have the ability to achieve my goals and grow.)

These characteristics are considered key to a person's ability to approach life with motivation, confidence, self-direction, and the desire to achieve outstanding accomplishments.

Tips to Enhance Your Self-Esteem

TAKE CONTROL OF YOUR OWN LIFE. If you let other people rule your life, you will always have unhealthy self-esteem. Get involved in the decisions that shape your life. Seize control—don't let life just happen to you!

ADOPT THE IDEA THAT YOU ARE RESPONSIBLE FOR YOU. The day you take responsibility for yourself and for what happens to you is the day you start to develop healthier self-esteem. When you can admit your mistakes and celebrate your successes knowing you did it your way, loving and respecting yourself become much easier.

REFUSE TO ALLOW FRIENDS AND FAMILY TO TEAR YOU DOWN. Combat negativity by admitting your mistakes and shortcomings to yourself (without dwelling on them) and by making up your mind that you are going to overcome them. By doing this, you are taking negative power away from anyone who would use your mistakes to hurt you.

CONTROL WHAT YOU SAY TO YOURSELF. "Self-talk" is important to your self-esteem and to your ability to motivate yourself positively. If you allow negative self-talk into your life, it will rule your self-esteem. Think positive thoughts and surround yourself with positive, upbeat, motivated, happy people.

TAKE CALCULATED RISKS. If you are going to grow to your fullest potential, you will have to learn to take some calculated risks and step out of your comfort zone. Although you should never take foolhardy risks that might endanger your life or risk everything you have, you must constantly be willing to push yourself.

STOP COMPARING YOURSELF TO OTHER PEOPLE. You may never be able to "beat" some people at certain things. Does it really matter? You only have to "beat yourself" to get better. If you constantly tell yourself that you are not "as handsome as Bill" or "as smart as Mary" or "as athletic as Jack," your inner voice will begin to believe these statements, and your

Image 100 Ltd.

How can actively participating in class help build your self-esteem?

"To every person there comes that special moment when he is tapped on the shoulder to do a very special thing unique to him. What a tragedy if that moment finds him unprepared for the work that would be his finest hour."
—*Winston Churchill*

From Ordinary to *Extraordinary*

REAL PEOPLE | REAL LIVES | REAL CHANGE

LYDIA HAUSLER LEBOVIC
Jewish Holocaust Survivor
Auschwitz Concentration/Extermination Camp
Auschwitz, Poland, 1944

"Sweet Sixteen." Isn't that the moment of joy for so many female teens today? It is a milestone date when childhood passes and young adulthood arrives. One can legally drive and in many states, "Sweet Sixteen" signifies the age of consent.

My "Sweet Sixteen" was very different. Yes, I was dating, had a somewhat rebellious relationship with my mother, and socialized with friends, but in the countryside around me, World War II raged. In 1944 when I was 16, my family and I were ordered to pack 20 pounds of personal belongings and told that we were being taken to "the Ghetto," a holding area for Jews in my hometown of Uzhorod, Czechoslovakia, now a part of Ukraine. I understood that the situation was not good and that things were changing, but I had no real idea of how my life would forever be altered in the coming weeks, months, and years.

After two weeks in "the Ghetto," my family, friends, neighbors, and I were ordered onto cattle cars—60 to 80 per car—and told that we were being taken to Hungary to work in the corn and wheat fields. So there, in the darkness of night, our journey began—young, old, weak, strong, nursing mothers, and babies—all in the same cattle car with no water and only two buckets to use for a bathroom.

After two days of travel, the train stopped and the doors of the cattle car opened. My mother recognized that we were not in southern Hungary, but rather on the Hungary/Poland border in the north. She took us aside in the car and told us of her suspicion—that we were being taken to Auschwitz concentration camp. After another two days on the train, we arrived at Auschwitz in the early dawn hours.

The doors of the cattle cars opened and the men were quickly separated from the women and the children from the adults. We were put into lines of five and marched forward. In front of every line was an SS officer. Quickly, I was pushed to the right and my mother and sister were pushed to the left. Little did I know at that point that those shoved to the right would be put to work and those shoved to the left would be dead by the evening. I never saw my mother or sister again after that moment. I never said goodbye. I was "Sweet Sixteen."

After the separation, my group was taken to a very large building and told to undress. We were completely shaven, sponged from head to toe with

> *Little did I know at that point that those shoved to the right would be put to work and those shoved to the left would be dead by the evening.*

46

a bleach-like substance, showered, and given a uniform. We were then marched to the barracks where we would sleep 12–14 to a bed with 600 to 800 people per barrack. The black and white photo was taken as we marched toward the barracks from the shower facility and now hangs in the National Holocaust Museum in Washington, D.C.

Some of the Jewish girls who had been in the camp for a while were considered "foremen." I remember approaching one such female. I asked her, "When do I get to see my mother and my sister?"

She took me by the arm and pointed me toward the billowing chimney of the crematory. *"You see that smoke? You see that ash? You smell that flesh burning? That's your mother. That's your sister."* She walked away. I did not believe her at the time, but she was absolutely right. This realization remains the most distressing of all events in my life—past and present—that my mother and sister died in such a horrific manner. Gassed and cremated.

I remained in Auschwitz until I was shipped to the labor camp, Bergen-Belsen, in Germany. We were liberated on April 15, 1945. Upon liberation, I began working for the British Red Cross. Later that year, I was reunited with a friend of my brother and we were married in November of 1945. We moved to Chile in 1947 and then to Los Angeles, California, in 1963.

I now travel the nation speaking about the events of my life and delivering the message, "NEVER AGAIN." I write this essay to you for many reasons, but specifically to let you know this: The Holocaust did not ruin me. They did not destroy me. They did not destroy my belief in love. They did not destroy my faith in people. They did not destroy my religion or values. The events made me a stronger, more compassionate person. I went on to become a loving wife and mother, a successful businesswoman, and eventually a devoted grandmother. *I refused to be ruined.* I encourage you to use the adversity in your life to make you stronger, more compassionate, more caring, and more helpful to mankind.

EXTRAORDINARY REFLECTION

Read the following statement and respond in your online journal or class notebook.

Mrs. Lebovic suffered the death of family members during the Holocaust, but she makes the statement, *"The Holocaust did not ruin me. They did not destroy me. They did not destroy my belief in love. . . . I refused to be ruined."* How can adversity in your life, like that in Mrs. Lebovic's, make you a stronger and more motivated person?

motivation and self-esteem will suffer. Everyone has certain strengths and talents to offer to the world.

KEEP YOUR PROMISES AND BE LOYAL TO FRIENDS, FAMILY, AND YOURSELF. If you have ever had someone break a promise to you, you know how it feels to have your loyalty betrayed. The most outstanding feature of your character is your ability to be loyal, to keep your promises, and to do what you have agreed to do. Few things can make you feel better about yourself than being loyal and keeping your word.

WIN WITH GRACE—LOSE WITH CLASS. Everyone loves a winner, but everyone also loves a person who can lose with class and dignity. On the other hand, no one loves a bragging winner or a moaning loser. If you are engaged in sports, debate, acting, art shows, or academic competitions, you will encounter winning and losing. Remember, whether you win or lose, *if you're involved and active,* you're already in the top 10 percent of the population. You're already more of a winner than most because you showed up and participated.

BE A GIVER. Author, speaker, and teacher Leo Buscaglia states: *"You want to make yourself the most brilliant, the most talented, the most fabulous person that you can possibly be so that you can give it all away. The only reason we have anything is to be able to give it away."* By giving to other people and sharing your talents and strengths, you begin to live on a level where kindness, selflessness, and others' needs gently collide. Whatever you want in this life, give it away and it will come back to you.

REFLECTIONS ON MOTIVATION AND SELF-ESTEEM

Motivation can change your life. Healthy self-esteem can change your life. *You* can change your life. This chapter has been about self-discovery and defining what you value, what role your attitude plays in your motivation, and how to surround yourself with positive, optimistic people. By focusing on YOU and determining what is important to your college studies, your career, your relationships, and your personal life, you can develop a vision of your future. If you can see your future, *really see it*, then you are more likely to be motivated to achieve it. Remember, we are motivated by what we value. As you continue on in the semester and work toward personal and professional motivation, consider the following ideas:

▶ Convert external motivators into internal motivation.
▶ Use the power of positive thinking and surround yourself with positive people.
▶ Step outside your comfort zone.
▶ Use your values to drive your life statement.
▶ Clear up your past by forgiving those who may have hurt you.
▶ Do one thing every day to strengthen your self-esteem.
▶ Turn negative thoughts into positive energy.
▶ Don't give in to defeat.

▶ View adversity as a stepping stone to strength.

▶ Picture yourself as optimistic and motivated.

Good luck to you as you begin developing the motivation and positive attitude you need to be successful in your studies and beyond.

"*The thing always happens that you believe in; and the belief in a thing makes it happen.*"

—*Frank Lloyd Wright*

CREATE SUCCESS
Your Journey to University, Career, and Life Beyond College

CONNECTING Think about the people on your college campus. With whom can you make a connection to learn more about **personal motivation?** (Example: counselor, advisor, retention specialist, etc.) Why and how will this connection be important?	
READING Find one brief, relevant article (in print or online) relating to **internal motivation and Maslow's Basic Needs.** After you have read the article, write a brief summary of the additional facts you have learned.	
E-LEARNING Using any search engine, find one piece of valid, reliable information about **increasing internal motivation.** Briefly explain what you learned and why you think it is important.	
ANALYZING Choose one main idea or topic from this chapter. After exploring and researching this idea further, determine how this information can help you succeed in other classes.	
TRANSITIONING How will you use the content found in this chapter to help you create a successful transition plan to your next semester and beyond?	
EMPOWERING Thinking about the entire spectrum of your life (college, family, friends, finances, career, etc.), how can you empower yourself to be more successful through the information found in this chapter?	

SQ3R *Mastery* Study Sheet

EXAMPLE QUESTION *(from page 30)* What is the difference between internal and external motivation?		**ANSWER:**
EXAMPLE QUESTION *(from page 36)* How can overcoming self-defeating behaviors help you become a better student?		**ANSWER:**
AUTHOR QUESTION *(from page 35)* Why does striving for excellence matter?		**ANSWER:**
AUTHOR QUESTION *(from page 39)* How can identifying your values help you stay motivated?		**ANSWER:**
AUTHOR QUESTION *(from page 42)* Discuss how "character" plays a role in your motivation level.		**ANSWER:**
AUTHOR QUESTION *(from page 44)* Explain how self-esteem plays a role in one's motivation.		**ANSWER:**
AUTHOR QUESTION *(from page 48)* Why is loyalty important to self-esteem?		**ANSWER:**
YOUR QUESTION *(from page _____)*		**ANSWER:**
YOUR QUESTION *(from page _____)*		**ANSWER:**
YOUR QUESTION *(from page _____)*		**ANSWER:**
YOUR QUESTION *(from page _____)*		**ANSWER:**
YOUR QUESTION *(from page _____)*		**ANSWER:**

Finally, after answering these questions, recite this chapter's major points in your mind. Consider the following general questions to help you master this material.

► What was it about?
► What does it mean?
► What was the most important thing I learned? Why?
► What were the key points to remember?

CHAPTER 3
EXPLORE

UNDERSTAND YOUR INSTITUTION AND THE CULTURE OF COLLEGE

"I know the price
of success:
dedication, hard
work, and
constant devotion
to the things you
want to see
happen."

—Frank Lloyd
Wright

WHY READ THIS CHAPTER?

What's in it for me?

WHY is it important to know how to work with my professors, advisors, and counselors? WHY will information on campus resources be of importance to me? WHY do I need to know anything about the success centers on my campus? WHY do I need to know how to stay in college?

Why? Because dropping out of college is a very common event! But this doesn't mean that you and your future have to become casualties. Over 40 percent of the people who begin college never complete their degrees. Many leave because they made serious and irreparable mistakes early in their first year. Some students leave because they did not know how to manage their time. Some leave because they could not manage their money and didn't know how to look for scholarships and other funding sources. Some leave because they couldn't get along with their professors. And still others leave because they simply could not figure out how "the system" works and frustration, anger, disappointment, and fear got the better of them. DON'T be led to believe that you have to be one of these students. You do not! The information shared in this chapter **will help you** maneuver through college with greater ease.

By carefully reading this chapter and taking the information provided seriously, you will be able to:

▶ Understand the differences between the AA, AS, and AAS degrees.

▶ Find and use academic, cultural, campus, and personal success centers.

▶ Define personal responsibility and your role in the grading process.

▶ Develop a strong relationship with your advisor and/or counselor.

▶ Understand the demands of taking an online (distance education) class.

CHAPTER 3 | EXPLORE

"It is difficult to discover new oceans unless you lose sight of the shore."

—Andre Gide

How my COMMUNITY COLLEGE changed my life

GEOFFREY KAMAU, RN
Graduate!
Northern Virginia Community College and Marymount University, Virginia

An interview conducted and written by
WISTAR WITHERS
Associate Professor/ Counselor, Northern Virginia Community College, Annandale, Virginia

Geoffrey Kamau, an honors graduate of Northern Virginia Community College and a native of Nairobi, Kenya, received special honors and recognition in May 2009 as he graduated from Marymount University in Arlington, Virginia, with a bachelor of science degree in nursing. He was one of two students who received the Bishop Ireton Award for "the graduating student who has had the greatest influence of good on his companions and is selected by his peers in the graduating class." At Marymount, Geoffrey was well known throughout the main campus and held numerous leadership positions, including resident assistant, orientation leader, admissions ambassador, and president of the International Club.

He shared with me the fact that his experiences at Northern Virginia Community College (NOVA) gave him the opportunity to enhance his leadership abilities and to improve his study habits; he also learned how to navigate the academic system and excel in obtaining the resources needed to succeed both inside and outside the classroom. As one of the students who founded the African Student Association (ASA) on the Annandale Campus, Geoffrey learned how to assert himself, market his unique abilities, promote his cause, and gain the respect and support of his peers, campus faculty, and college administrators. In addition to being the president of the ASA for two years, he was selected to serve as a student ambassador and inducted into the Phi Theta Kappa Honor Society.

As a foreign student coming from a different culture and educational system, he recalls, *"I experienced culture shock upon arriving on this campus. I enrolled in my student success course, which is for students from different cultures whose first language is not English. As one of my out-of-class projects I assumed the responsibility of organizing the ASA. To this end, I had to find advisors, create a marketing strategy for members, recruit members, establish functioning committees to develop a constitution and by-laws, and have the organization achieve recognition status by the campus administration."*

In addition to his hard work and persistence, what I remember most about Geoffrey's untiring effort to get the organization off the ground was his cheerful disposition. He was al-ways charming and got along well with everybody; I never saw him angry or unpleasant with anyone or anything, including the unexpected death of his father in Africa during the final exam period at the end of his first year. He could not return home during this time for fear of jeopardizing his visa status.

Through my student success course and the community college setting, Geoffrey was able to become acclimated to the American system of education and gain a better understanding of the environment. *"By attending the community college first, I believe that the greatest advantage for me was learning how to adapt and to interact with students and faculty from many different ethnic and diverse backgrounds. I would encourage attending the community college first because it's affordable, has a good teacher/student ratio, has professors who are attentive and really care about the students' progress, offers challenging courses, and prepares students for university studies."*

THINK ABOUT IT

1. What advantages do you think you gain by attending a community college? Why?
2. Geoffrey was involved in many aspects of student life. What opportunities does your community college offer to help you get involved in college activities?

In the preface of this book (page xiv), you read about the **SQ3R study method.** Right now, take a few moments, **scan this chapter,** and on the SQ3R Mastery Study Sheet on page 81, write **five of your own questions** that you think will be important to your mastery of this material. In addition to the two questions below, you will find five questions from your authors on that study sheet. Use one of your *"Study for Quiz"* stickers to flag this page for easy reference.

EXAMPLE:

▶ What are the differences between a degree, diploma, and certificate? (from page 56)

▶ What are the differences between the AA, AS, and AAS degrees? (from page 57)

I WANT A DEGREE! (I THINK)

Should I Work Toward a Diploma, Certificate, or Degree?

As always, the choice is yours, but you need to consider your options when looking at your future, and it is advisable to consult an advisor or counselor at your institution as soon as possible. Students seeking a diploma are usually those who did not graduate from high school and are attending a community college to get a GED. If you want to obtain a degree to enter the workforce or transfer to a university, you may consider an associate's degree. If you already have a degree or simply need to become certified in a specific area, you may want to consider a certificate.

Now, here is where it can get *a little confusing.* There are major differences among the **AA** (Associate of Arts), **AS** (Associate of Science), and **AAS** (Associate of Applied Science) degrees. *"WHAT? They're really that different?"* you may be asking. *Yes, they are quite different* and knowing the difference could save you years of time, thousands of dollars, and countless headaches. If you plan to transfer to a university, you should enroll in either the AA or AS *transfer degree* program. Why? Because these courses are designed to transfer into a bachelor's degree and are taught by faculty with at least a master's degree. If you plan to get your two-year degree and enter the world of work, you should enroll in the AAS degree program. Why? Because these courses are designed for the world of work and may be taught by faculty who are experts in their field but may not have a college degree. To learn more, refer to Figure 3.1.

TRANSFERRING

What Are the Biggest Issues Related to Moving On?

Many students enroll with the notion that they will one day transfer to another institution, perhaps after a semester, a year, or after earning a two-year degree. First, you need to know that your "Survival Guide for Transfer" is the college catalog—not only the catalog from your community college, but also the catalog from the college or university to which you plan to transfer. They are both helpful, but you need to be as mindful of the *receiving college's requirements* and policies as those of your current college. A qualified, informed transfer advisor can assist you with this endeavor.

FIGURE

3.1   *The Differences Between the AA, AS, and AAS Degrees*

Degree	Definition	Emphasis / Purpose
AA	The associate of arts degree consists of around 60–63 semester hours and most universities accept these credits as a part of your bachelor's degree.	The emphasis of the AA degree is the liberal and performing arts, history, English, literature, international languages, psychology, sociology, education, the humanities, and communication. This is a ***transfer degree.***
AS	The associate of science degree consists of around 60–65 semester hours and most universities accept these credits as a part of your bachelor's degree.	The emphasis of the AS degree is math, the sciences (biology, chemistry, physics, geology, geography, astronomy), economics, and accounting. This is a ***transfer degree.***
AAS	The associate of applied science degree consists of around 60–65 semester hours and many of these credits do NOT transfer as university credit.	The emphasis of the AAS degree is employment. Students who want to get a two-year degree and ***then enter the workforce*** in areas such as criminal justice, nursing, dental assisting, graphic design, computers, building technologies, office technology, and medical laboratory work should seek the AAS degree.

By acquiring a catalog from the institution to which you hope to transfer, you can work to take classes at your community/technical college that will count toward your associate's degree ***and*** your bachelor's degree. For example, if English 101, Introductory Composition, is required at Elm Community College and also at Success University, it would be beneficial for you to take this course at your community college. However, if you plan to take English 200, British Literature, at Elm Community College and Success University will only accept English 289, American Literature, for transfer into your selected bachelor's degree program, it would be important to determine if American Literature will work for you at Elm as well. Therefore, you've taken a literature class that counts toward both your associate's and bachelor's degrees.

Course numberings are also important to understand. Some states have common course numberings between two- and four-year colleges, but many do not. If Elm Community College is in Michigan and you plan to transfer to Success University in Michigan AND they have common course numberings, you can be fairly safe that your classes will transfer with relative ease. Example: English 289, American Literature, is the same at Elm Community College as it is at Success University.

However, if the state does not have a common course numbering system and/or a strong transfer or articulation agreement (an agreement to transfer courses between institutions), you will want to consult your advisor at both institutions to save you time and money. For example, you register for English 289, American Literature (a sophomore-level class), at Elm Community College BUT Success University requires English 340, Studies in American Literature, a junior-level course. They seem to be the same, BUT the course from Elm Community College MAY NOT transfer because of content differences and the level of the course (a 200+ level course vs. a 300+ level course). This is especially tricky when you register for many classes in professional fields such as accounting, finance, psychology, education, and so on. Working with your advisors on BOTH campuses can help you navigate the sometimes difficult waters of transferring from one institution to another.

Figure 3.2 provides a basic framework for discussion and examples of transfer options. The requirements at YOUR institution will most likely differ from the classes in the example. As you study Figure 3.2, you will begin to see the importance of working with a transfer counselor at both your two-year and four-year institutions.

You also need to be aware that most colleges WILL NOT accept grades below a C (2.0) from any institution. Also, you will find that your future college DOES NOT transfer your grade point

3.2 *Example of Requirements and Transfers*

Elm Community College Requirement	Success University Requirement	Transfer Notes	Options and Advice
English 101—Composition I	English 101—Composition I	Will likely transfer	Take this class with approval
English 102—Composition II	English 102—Composition II	Will likely transfer	Take this class with approval
Literature (choose from American, British, or World)	English 270—Survey of World Literature	Will likely transfer	Find out if Elm CC offers a world literature class that will count toward your associate degree. This class will likely meet the requirement at both institutions.
Accounting 101—Basic Accounting	Accounting 101—Basic Accounting	Will likely transfer	Take this class with approval
Accounting 200—Accounting and Spreadsheets	Accounting 420—Spreadsheets	Will likely NOT transfer for the spreadsheets course	Take Accounting 200 at Elm CC and WAIT to take 420 at university
Speech 101—Public Speaking	Communication 101—Interpersonal Communication	Will likely NOT transfer as the required interpersonal communication course.	Find out if you can take Interpersonal Communication as the requirement at Elm CC. If not, try to take both at Elm CC to save money and use Interpersonal Communication as an elective if possible.
Social Science (choose from Psychology, Sociology, Anthropology, Philosophy)	Psychology 101—Introductory Psychology	Will likely transfer	Take Psychology 101 because this class will count at both colleges.
Science (7 Credits from Chemistry, Biology, Physical Science, Geology)	Biology 101 with lab	Will likely transfer	Take Biology I with a lab and Biology II to meet the requirements at Elm CC and SU
Math 110—College Algebra I and Math 111—College Algebra II (or higher)	Math 120—College Algebra and Math 121—Intermediate Algebra	Both will likely transfer. Developmental classes (lower than 100) will not transfer.	Take College Algebra at Elm CC on approval from your advisors at both institutions.

average (GPA). When you transfer to your future college, your GPA will start anew. This can be a double-edged sword. If you have a 4.0 at your current college, sadly, you must start again at the future college. However, if you had a 2.0, you get to start over at your future college. GPAs are explained later in this chapter. Also, if you plan to transfer to a four-year institution, you will need to find out what GPA is required to be accepted into your chosen institution.

KNOWING THE RULES UP FRONT

Why Do I Need to Explore My Community College Surroundings?

Policies and procedures vary from institution to institution, but regardless, it is your responsibility to know what you can expect from your community college and what your community college expects from you. These policies can be found in the college catalog (traditional and online), your student handbook, or your schedule of classes, depending on your institution.

Some community college policies are universal:

> *"The very first step toward success in any endeavor is to become interested in it."*
> —William Osler

▶ Students must meet certain residence requirements for a degree (even if you transfer into the two-year college).

▶ All students are subject to the Federal Privacy Act of 1974 (this ensures your privacy, even from your parents).

▶ Most institutions require placement tests (these are different from admission tests). They are used to properly advise you into the correct English, math, foreign language, reading, and/or vocabulary classes.

▶ Most community colleges adhere to a strict drop/add date. Always check your schedule of classes for this information.

▶ Most community colleges have an attendance policy for classroom instruction.

▶ Most community colleges have a strict refund policy.

▶ Many community colleges will not allow you to take more than a certain number of credit hours per semester (18 semester hours is usually the upper limit).

Community colleges do not put these policies and procedures in place to punish you or to make things harder; rather, they are designed to ensure that all students are treated fairly and equitably. Some of the policies are also mandated by the federal government in order for the college to be allowed to receive federal monies. By reviewing your community college's catalog, schedule of classes, or student handbook, you can familiarize yourself with your institution's specific guidelines. Use these documents to complete the **Policy Guide for Your Institution** (Figure 3.3).

FIGURE **3.3** *Understanding College Policy*

Policy Question	Response
What is the last day to drop a class without penalty?	
What is the grade appeal policy for your institution?	
What is your college's refund policy?	
What is your college's academic credit limit policy?	
What is your college's grade appeal policy?	
What is your college's policy regarding religious holidays?	
What is your college's policy for placement in math and English courses?	
What is your college's audit policy?	
What is your college's policy on academic probation?	

By reading your college catalog, website, class schedule, and student handbook, you can learn a great deal about your institution and how to adapt to its policies and regulations.

CREATING A COMMUNITY AS A COMMUTER STUDENT

How Can I Avoid the "Drive by" College Experience?

Going to a community college has countless advantages. Smaller classes, reduced costs, and more personalized attention can be life-altering as you begin your studies. However, one of the biggest complaints among students and faculty is the lack of involvement by students on a commuter campus. When students do not live on campus, they tend to go to class, maybe spend some time in the library or computer center, grab a bite to eat, and then leave. You need to know that there is so much more available to you OR so much more you could create to enhance your community college experience.

"If you're not actively involved in getting what you want, then you don't really want it."
—Peter McWilliams

Check out the number of clubs, organizations, and activities available on your campus. From writing for the campus newspaper to joining the student chapter of the National Nursing Association to starting a debate club, your community college experience is, in a large part, going to be what you make of it. Take a moment and go to your college's website and select at least three clubs, organizations, preprofessional associations, or other activities that you might enjoy taking part in. If there are none listed that interest you, list three that you would consider starting.

1. _____
2. _____
3. _____

CAMPUS RESOURCES

Can Success Centers, Support Services, and College Resources Really Help?

Most colleges offer you assistance for academic, social, cultural, spiritual, and physical enrichment outside the classroom. Your tuition or student activities fee may fund many of the centers on your campus such as the centers and services mentioned in Figure 3.4. You've paid for them; you should take full advantage of their services. Some college services are easier to find than others, but most are usually listed in your student handbook, college catalog, or schedule of classes. When in doubt, don't be afraid to ask your professor, advisor, or counselor if a particular service exists. It could save you time, effort, and in many cases, money.

GREAT EXPECTATIONS

What Do Community College Instructors Really Want?

Many of your community college professors attended college for 7 to over 12 years preparing to teach you. Community college professors, for the most part, must have at least a master's degree in their field, but many have a doctorate. A professor who has obtained a master's or a doctorate may have spent as many as 12 or more years in college. Others will have spent years and years working

FIGURE

3.4 *Conduct Your Own Orientation*

Campus/ Community Service	How It Can Help You	Phone Number and Location on Your Campus
Academic advice/ career centers	Assists in choosing classes for each semester and offers career assessments and advice on careers.	
Computer labs	Offers students the use of e-mail, Internet services, and other on-line applications, usually free of charge. These centers are also usually staffed with trained professionals who can help you with problematic programming issues.	
Writing centers	Offers assistance with your writing skills. They will not rewrite your paper for you, but they can give you advice on how to strengthen your project, properly document information, and add to the overall quality of your work.	
Math centers	Offers help with complex math problems, one-on-one or group tutoring, and study sessions. Traditionally, math is the single most difficult course for first-year students—even for those students who did well in high school math.	
Tutoring or mastery learning centers	Usually staffed by student tutors. Offers assistance in almost any subject matter. Many colleges offer this service free of charge (or for a very nominal fee), whereas an outside tutor may charge $30 to $45 per hour.	
Language labs	Offers assistance with international languages or sign language. There may be "live" tutors to assist you or, more traditionally, there are computer-based tutorials that drill you in the respective language.	
Libraries	The rumor of their death is greatly exaggerated. Your college library can be the hub of your learning experience from printed materials to Internet usage to computer-assisted tutorials. Your library and librarians are vital to helping you become information literate.	
Veteran affairs	Offers assistance to veterans, especially with government paperwork and financial aid.	
Re-entry or adult learning centers	Assists adult students who are returning to school after many years absence. They also offer advice and services on child care, financial aid, and sometimes, text lending programs.	
Health services	Some campuses offer student health services complete with a nurse or physician's assistant. This service is usually free of charge or offered at a greatly reduced rate.	
International student services	Assists international students with admissions, housing, cultural adjustment, and language barriers.	
Minority student services	Offers services and programming for minority students on campus. These services can range from programs on diversity to advice on race-related issues.	
Financial aid office	Assists students with federal, state, and local paperwork to apply for financial aid and scholarships. They are especially helpful in assisting with your FAFSA form each year.	

(continued)

FIGURE

3.4 *Conduct Your Own Orientation (continued)*

Campus/ Community Service	How It Can Help You	Phone Number and Location on Your Campus
Mental/emotional health services	Many colleges now offer mental health services for students who suffer from depression, anxiety, loneliness, and a host of other emotional issues.	
Student activities	Usually run by student government or student affairs, the Student Activity Office offers a wide variety of programming in social and cultural activities.	
Transfer centers	These are centers that help you develop a transfer plan to a four-year institution.	
Disabled student services	If you have a documented disability, colleges and universities across America are required by law to offer you "reasonable accommodations" to ensure your success (Americans with Disabilities Act, Sec. 504). Some of these accommodations include: ▶ Handicapped parking ▶ Special testing centers ▶ Extended time on tests and timed projects ▶ Textbook translations and conversions ▶ Interpreters ▶ Note-taking services ▶ TTY/TDD services ▶ Closed captioning If you feel that you qualify for one of these services, DO NOT hesitate to stop by the disability office. They are not on campus to judge you or make things harder for you, but to offer you advice, support, and help you achieve your educational goals.	
Human services agencies	Many agencies within your community can also assist you with your educational plans. Many human service agencies offer services off campus such as: ▶ Child care ▶ Transportation ▶ Financial assistance ▶ Abuse issues Check your local phone book under Health and Human Services. Your advisor may be able to help you locate many community services, too.	

in their fields as experts in hospitals, car dealerships, hotels, technology companies, and police departments, to name just a few. Basically, your community college professors have spent a lifetime preparing to do what they do at your institution.

The Freedom to Teach and Learn

Professors are entitled to *academic freedom.* Most high school teachers do not have this privilege. Academic freedom means that a professor has the right to teach controversial issues, topics, subjects, pieces of literature, scientific theories, religious tenets, and political points of view *without* the threat of termination. However, this does not mean that a faculty member has the right to push a personal agenda. Teaching information that is related to the course is different from spending an hour talking about his or her political or religious agenda.

You may not have been able to read Mart Crawley's *The Boys in the Band* in your high school drama class because of its homosexual content, but you would be able to study it uncensored in a college literature or drama class. You may have never engaged in a discussion on the "existence of God" in high school, but this may very well be a topic of debate in your logic, religion, sociology, or critical thinking class. This is the right of the college professor—to teach and guide in an unobstructed atmosphere free from parental, administrative, trustee, religious, political, or public pressure.

Shutterstock

Why is it important to establish a positive relationship with your instructors?

I CAN'T BELIEVE YOU GAVE ME AN "F"

What Is *Your Role* in the Grading Process?

There will be times when you are disappointed with a grade that *you earn* from a professor. And yes, you do *earn an A or an F*; professors *do not give A's or F's*. What do you do? Threaten? Sue? Become argumentative? Those techniques usually cost you more than they gain.

First, remember that the grade assigned by a professor is seldom changeable. If you made a less than satisfactory grade, there are several things that you need to do. First, be truthful with yourself and examine the amount of time you spent on the project.

Review the requirements for the assignment. Ask yourself:

▶ Did I miss something?

▶ Did I take an improper or completely wrong focus?

▶ Did I omit some aspect of the project?

▶ Did I turn the project in late?

▶ Did I document my sources correctly?

▶ Did I really give it my very best?

Answering these important questions and the ones listed in Figure 3.5 can help you determine the extent of your personal responsibility and preparation for success.

CLASSROOM CHALLENGES

When the Professor's First Language Is Not Your Language

Yes, you may have professors whose first language is not your first language, be it English or Spanish or Arabic. Community and technical colleges often hire

3.5 *Do I Practice Personal Responsibility?*

Think about a grade or project on which you scored lower than you would have liked or expected. Answer these questions truthfully to determine your role in the grading process. Place a check mark beside the questions that truly reflect your effort. If you have not yet turned in a project or taken an exam, consider these questions as a "check list" to success.

- ☐ I attend class regularly.
- ☐ I participate in class discussions and group work.
- ☐ I ask pointed and direct questions in class.
- ☐ I read my assignments, do my homework, and come to class prepared.
- ☐ I work with a study group.
- ☐ I have all of the supplies I need to be successful in this class (text, workbook, calculator, highlighters, etc.).
- ☐ I visit my professor during office hours to ask questions and seek clarification.
- ☐ I use the academic support services on my campus (tutorial services, math lab, writing centers, communication lab, language lab, science lab, etc.)
- ☐ I use the library as a resource for greater understanding.
- ☐ I practice academic integrity.
- ☐ I bring my best to the class every time we meet.

Being able to answer these personal responsibility questions positively can mean the difference between success and failure with a project, assessment, or a class. If you are truly concerned about the grade, talk to the professor about the assignment. Ask the professor to describe the most apparent problem with your assignment and ask how you might improve your studying or how best to prepare for the *next* assignment.

professors from around the world because of their expertise in their subjects. You may find that it is difficult to understand a professor's dialect or pronunciation from time to time. If you have a professor who is difficult to understand, remember these hints:

- ▶ Sit near the front of the room.
- ▶ Watch the professor's mouth when you can.
- ▶ Follow the professor's nonverbal communication patterns.
- ▶ Use a tape recorder or MP3 device if allowed.
- ▶ Read the material beforehand so that you will have a general understanding of what is being discussed.
- ▶ Ask questions when you do not understand the material.

When You and Your Professor(s) Have a Disagreement

There may be times when you clash with your professor. It may be over a grade, an assigned project, a topic of discussion, a misunderstanding, or a personality issue.

Above all, don't get into a verbal argument or physical confrontation. This will only make matters worse for everyone involved. If you have a disagreement, make sure that *the professor is your first point of contact.* Unless you have spoken with him or her *first* and exhausted all options in that regard, approaching the department chair, the dean, the vice president, or the president will more than likely result in your being sent directly back to the professor.

THE GOLDEN RULE—OR JUST A CROCK

Do Classroom Etiquette and Personal Decorum Affect Success?

You may be surprised, but the way you act in (and out) of class can mean as much to your success as what you know. No one can make you do anything or act in any way that you do not want. The following tips are provided from years of research and actual conversations with hundreds of community college professors teaching across America. You have to be the one who chooses whether or not to use this advice.

> *"Respect your efforts, respect yourself. Self-respect leads to self-discipline. When you have both firmly under your belt, that's real power."*
> —Clint Eastwood

- ▶ If you are late for class, enter quietly, DO NOT walk in front of the professor, don't let the door slam, don't talk on your way in, and take the seat nearest the door. Make every effort not to be late to class.

- ▶ Never carry on a conversation with another student while the professor or another student is talking.

- ▶ Don't ask your professor to "break the rules" just for you. The rules in your class syllabus are provided to everyone so that all students will be treated fairly. If you have a true, legitimate reason to ask for an extension or some other exception, talk to your professor **beforehand.** Please know that if you have an impeccable classroom record (turning in your materials on time, perfect attendance, classroom participation, etc.), your professor is more likely to take your request seriously.

- ▶ Do not sleep in class. If you are having problems staying awake, you should consider dropping the class and taking it at another time next semester. If you have to work too many hours, you might consider taking a reduced course load.

- ▶ If for any reason you must leave during class, do so quietly and quickly. It is customary to inform the professor that you will be leaving early before class begins.

- ▶ If you don't know how to address your professor—that is, by Mr., Mrs., Miss., Ms., or Dr.—ask them which they prefer, or simply call them "Professor _____."

- ▶ You should not wear sunglasses, oversized hats, strong cologne or perfume, or earphones to class.

- ▶ Turn off your iPod, iPhone, BlackBerry, cell phone, beeper, buzzer, tweeter, and other devices. Even if the unit is off, take your earplugs out of your ears. Leaving them on is disrespectful.

- ▶ Be respectful of other students. Profanity and obscene language may offend some people. You can have strong, conflicting views without being offensive.

- ▶ Visit professors during office hours. The time before and after class may not be the most appropriate time for you or the professor. Your professor may have back-to-back classes and may be unable to assist you.

- ▶ If you act like an adult (which you are), you'll be treated as one.

Remember that respect for others on your part will afford you the opportunity to establish relationships that otherwise you might never have had. Respect begets respect.

SELF-MANAGEMENT, ETHICS, AND YOUR FUTURE

Who Are You When No One Is Looking?

> *"Have the courage to say no. Have the courage to face the truth. Do the right thing because it is right. These are the magic keys to living your life with integrity."*
>
> —Clement Stone

Think about these questions: What if there were no rules or laws to govern your behavior? What if there were no consequences or ramifications for any of your actions? Let's pretend for a moment that you could never go to jail or face fines or be shunned for your words, actions, behaviors, or thoughts. What would your life—or the lives of those you love—look like? This is one of the best ways to offer a practical definition of ethics. Basically, ethics is the *accepted* moral code or standard by which we all live, and that code is communicated in many ways, including through our relationships with others. Codes of ethics vary from culture to culture, country to country, college to college, and group to group, but each carry with them certain "rules" that members of the culture, country, college, or group are expected to follow.

Making professional or personal ethical decisions usually involves three factors or levels as shown in Figure 3.6. They include the ***law, fair-***

FIGURE 3.6 *Six Levels of Ethical Decision Making*

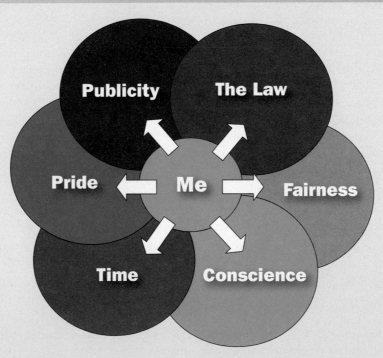

▶ Is it legal?

▶ Is it fair to me and others?

▶ Can I live with my decision?

▶ Is this decision in my long-term best interest?

▶ Could I tell my mama about it and be proud?

▶ How would I feel if this showed up on the front page of the newspaper tomorrow morning?

If you can respond positively to all six statements, most likely, this decision would be in your best interest and the best interest of those around you.

ness, and your *conscience* (Anderson & Bolt, 2008). You might also consider adding three other levels: *time, pride,* and *publicity.*

What Is the Importance of Academic and Personal Integrity?

As a college student, you will be faced with temptations that require you to make hard choices. You have probably already been forced to make decisions based on ethics. Do I cheat and make a higher grade so I can compete with top students? Will cheating help me earn higher grades so I get a better job? Do I copy this paper from the Internet? Who will know? Why shouldn't I buy one of the term papers floating around? What if I just copy someone's homework and not cheat on a test? What if I lie to the instructor and say I was sick so I can get more time on a test for which I am not prepared? What if I let someone look on my paper during a test; I'm not cheating, am I? These are all ethical questions that require you to use your personal integrity to make mature decisions.

Integrity is purely and simply making decisions about what is right and wrong according to your personal code of ethics and accepted social behavior. What will you do when nobody knows but you? It is also making decisions about what is right and wrong according to your institution's standards. As a college student, you will see many people do things that you think are not right. You have to decide what is right for you and follow your values no matter what others may be doing. Just because "everyone is doing it" doesn't make it right, and certainly it doesn't make it right for you.

Even if you cheat and don't get caught, you lose. You lose respect for yourself, your self-esteem is likely to decline, and you cheat yourself of the knowledge for which you are paying. You also lose because you damage your character and the person you hope to become. Cheating can cause you to feel guilty and stressed because you are afraid someone might find out.

> *"No one will question your integrity if your integrity is not questionable."*
> —*Nathaniel Bronner, Jr.*

What Do You Need to Know about Academic Misconduct?

It is important to know what constitutes dishonesty in an academic setting. Following is a list of offenses that most colleges consider academic misconduct.

- ▶ Looking on another person's test paper for answers.
- ▶ Giving another student answers on tests, homework, or lab projects.
- ▶ Using any kind of "cheat sheets" on a test or project.
- ▶ Using a computer, calculator, dictionary, or notes when not approved.
- ▶ Discussing exam questions with students who are taking the same class at another time.
- ▶ Plagiarism or using the words or works of others without giving proper credit. This includes material from the Internet!
- ▶ Stealing another student's class notes.
- ▶ Using an annotated instructor's edition of a text.
- ▶ Having tutors do your homework for you.
- ▶ Copying files from a lab computer.
- ▶ Bribing a student for answers or academic work such as papers or projects.
- ▶ Buying or acquiring papers from individuals or the Internet.
- ▶ Assisting others with dishonest acts.
- ▶ Lying about reasons you missed a test or a class.

From Ordinary to *Extraordinary*

REAL PEOPLE | REAL LIVES | REAL CHANGE

DINO J. GONZALEZ, M.D.

Board-Certified Internal Medicine and AAHIVM Certified HIV Specialist
University Medical Center Wellness Center, Las Vegas, Nevada

Can one person make a difference in your life? Can one person change the course of your destiny? The answer is yes! Most definitely, yes! The person who altered the course of my future was my third-grade teacher, Mrs. Allison. She was a strong African American lady who pushed us to do our best and would not let us fail. She was hard and demanded the best from us, but she was fair and an awesome teacher. She made us bring a toothbrush from home so that we could brush our teeth after lunch. She corrected our grammar and let us know that "street English" would not fly in her classroom. She even made us do Jazzercise after lunch to teach us how to take care of our bodies. I was lucky to be under her tutelage again in the fifth grade.

Why was she so dynamic? Why did she mean so much to my life? Well, I had always been a good student in school, earning mostly A's. However, my home life was another story. I was born in 1970 in a HUD housing project in Las Vegas, Nevada, in the gang-infested 28th Street area. My mother, two brothers, and I lived in poverty. By the time I was three, my mother was bedridden and on disability due to chronic obstructive pulmonary disease, caused by a three-pack-a-day smoking habit.

I was born ... in a HUD housing project in Las Vegas, Nevada, in the gang-infested 28th Street area.

We were on welfare, food stamps, and the free lunch program.

As it turned out, my father never married my mother or helped support us because he was already married to another woman with children of their own. My mother did not know this until after my birth. So basically, we were on our own. Often, I felt alone in my community because I looked different. My father was Hispanic, but my mother was a blond, light-skinned Norwegian. I was not brown. I was not white. I felt like I did not have a real place in my community or in school. Mrs. Allison helped change all of that.

Because of her and a few close friends, I began to see the positive aspect of school and getting an education. I managed to stay away from the heavy gang influence that had engulfed my brothers. By the time I began high school, one of my brothers was already in prison because of drugs and gang activity. Because of Mrs. Allison's influence, I began to surround myself with people who were positive and worked hard. I wanted to be around people who *wanted something*—who had a wider view of the world than I had.

The harder I worked and studied, the better I did. I excelled in junior high and high school and by the time I graduated, I did so with honors. I became the first person in my family to attend college. I was offered four scholarships and they paid for everything, even giving me some spare money to live on. I had been working anywhere from 20 to 30 hours per week since I was 14 years old, but I continued to work full time while attending college.

I had always loved science and the study of the human body, so I decided to major in chemistry and education. I began to develop a keen interest in infec-tious diseases and viruses. By the time I was a junior in college, I had decided to become a doctor, so I dropped my education major and focused on biology. After graduation, I applied to medical school and was accepted into the University of Nevada School of Medicine. I completed my studies, did a three-year residency, and decided to open my own practice. I became board certified in internal medicine and as an HIV specialist. Six years later, my practice is hugely successful and I enjoy days filled with helping people maintain or regain their health. My dream of doing something real and help-ing others is now an everyday occurrence in my life.

My advice to you as a first-year college student is this: You have the power to make your dreams come true. *YOU can CHANGE* your life if you truly know what you want and do the work that comes with making dreams come true.

Surround yourself with upbeat, positive, smart, giving, open-minded people from whom you can learn and grow. Mrs. Allison was my inspiration. Yours is out there, too.

EXTRAORDINARY REFLECTION

Read the following statement and respond in your online journal or class notebook.

Dr. Gonzalez talks about his teacher, Mrs. Allison, and how she challenged him and changed his life. What teacher(s) can you think of who dramatically altered the course of your life?

How Can Plagiarizing Affect Your Future?

Plagiarism is a serious offense, and you should not take it lightly—your professors do not! You have no doubt already heard your professors discuss plagiarism and the ramifications of using someone else's work without proper documentation. You should strongly consider their advice and take this topic seriously so you do not find yourself in trouble. Some college students seem to think plagiarism is merely copying someone else's work or borrowing an original idea and claiming it as their own work, and of course, these acts are included in the definition, but that terminology may not adequately reflect what a serious offense this act can be. Plagiarism includes fraud, stealing, and lying. People who would never take someone's wallet or personal identity information may carelessly "borrow" another person's words and ideas without properly documenting them, which is just as wrong as stealing someone's money.

Plagiarism is often defined as using another's words or ideas as your own without permission. Turnitin.com (2008) provides a solution to avoiding plagiarism: "Most cases of plagiarism can be avoided by citing sources. Simply acknowledging that certain material has been borrowed, and providing your audience with the information necessary to find that source, is usually enough to prevent plagiarism." Citing sources just takes a little more effort, but it saves you a great many problems.

> *"I would prefer to fail with honor than to win by cheating."*
> —Sophocles

TIPS FOR PERSONAL SUCCESS

Consider the following tips for making the most of your relationships with professors, advisors, and counselors:

▶ Make an effort to get to know your professors, advisor, or counselors on a personal basis. Don't avoid these important persons.

▶ When you visit your professor, advisor, or counselor, have a prepared list of questions ready to ask.

▶ Volunteer for projects that allow you to work closely with your professor, advisor, or counselor.

Now, it is your turn. Create a list of at least three more tips that you would offer to assist a fellow student in building positive relationships with professors, advisors, and counselors.

1. _____

2. _____

3. _____

YOUR ADVISOR/ COUNSELOR RELATIONSHIPS

May I Give You a Piece of Advice?

Your academic advisor can be of enormous assistance to you throughout your college career. An advisor is usually assigned to you although a few colleges allow students to select their own advisors. Your advisor will help you select courses for the completion of your degree. However, you are the person most responsible for registering for classes that will count toward graduation. You should know as much as your advisor about your degree.

If you do not know why you have to take certain courses or in what sequence courses should be taken, don't leave your advisor's office until you find out. Lack of understanding of your course sequence, your college catalog, or the requirements for graduation could mean the difference between a two-year degree and a six-year degree, or could mean getting no college degree at all.

Academic advisors are not usually psychological counselors. They are assigned to assist students in completing their academic programs of study. They may offer advice on personal or career matters, but they may not be trained to assist with psychological and emotional matters. However, if you are having problems not related to your academic studies, your academic advisor may be able to direct you to the professional on campus who can best help you address certain issues and problems. Your academic advisor may be the first person to contact in times of crisis.

THE COLLEGE CATALOG

Where Is It Written?

Every college in the nation has a catalog and they are all somewhat different. Your college catalog is one of the most important publications you will read during your college years. It describes the rules, regulations, policies, procedures, and requirements of the college and your academic degree. It is imperative for you to keep the college catalog that was issued during your first year because college degree requirements can change from year to year. Most colleges require that you graduate under the rules and requirements stated in the catalog under which you entered the college. This policy is sometimes referred to as the *grandfather clause*.

Patrick White/Merrill

The college catalog includes information about adding and dropping classes, auditing, probation, plagiarism, attendance, honors, course descriptions, graduation requirements, faculty credentials, and college accreditation, and usually includes a campus map. It is an important tool.

Do you think establishing a positive relationship with your advisor or counselor is really all that important? Why or why not?

THE DEGREE SHEET: YOUR ROADMAP TO GRADUATION

Why Do I Need to Know How to Read a Degree Sheet? Isn't That What an Advisor Is For?

Yes, advisors are here to help you learn what classes need to be taken and in which order to take them. However, you, too, will need to know how to read the degree sheet, self-advise, and work through your degree on your own. Consider the example of a degree sheet shown in Figure 3.7.

After reviewing the degree sheet, list five questions that you need to ask regarding this (*and your*) degree requirements. Who can help you answer the questions about your degree sheet?

Question   **Who Can Help**

1. _____   _____

2. _____   _____

3. _____   _____

4. _____   _____

5. _____   _____

DEVELOPMENTAL/REMEDIAL CLASSES

Why Is It Important to Get the Basics First?

Yes, you may need to take a developmental or remedial class. "What is that?" you may ask. A class in developmental/remedial education is a class that offers basic skills in areas such as math, English, vocabulary, and spelling. Most students who take these classes are directed into them by the college's placement tests. It is true that most of these classes DO NOT carry academic

3.7 *Degree Sheet*

Associate of Applied Science Degree Building Technology Concentration	Credit Hours	Notes about This Degree Requirement Sheet
Communications COM 101, 102, 215, ENG 102, 107, 113, 201, 202, JOUR 101	3	One class from the courses listed (3 credit hours is the usual number of credits for college courses with the exception of some math, science, and international language courses)
English ENG 101	3	English 101 is your only option (you need to determine if a placement test or prerequisite classes are required)
Human Relations ANTH 101, 102, 210, HIST 101, 102, 201, 202, 210, 220, PHIL 101, 102, PSC 200, 201, 202, SOC 101, 102, 103, 110	3	One class from the courses listed
Mathematics Math 110 or above (except Math 120–121)	3	One class in Math 110 or higher. NOTICE that Math 120–121 MAY NOT be used for this requirement. Find out if there is a placement test to enroll.
Science (two classes from) AST 101, BIO 101, 102, 110, 111, CHEM 101, 102, 201, 202, EVN 110, GEOG 103, 104, PHYS 101, 102, 103	7	Two classes (NOTE that 7 hours are required. This usually means two classes and one LAB. Try to take the lab during the same semester that you take the course.)
Fine Arts/Humanities ART 101, 120, 125, THE 101, 103, 110, COM 101, 102, DAN 101, 102, HIST 101, 102, 201, 202, 220, 221, SPN 101, 102, FRN 101, 102, CHI 101, 102	3	One class from the courses listed. (Choose a class that will help you in your field. If you plan to work in an area that has a large Latino population and you don't speak Spanish, you may consider using SPN 101 as your required class. ART 101, 120, or 125 may help you understand blueprints and architecture better.)
Social Sciences ECON 101, 102, 110, 111, SOC 101, 102, 201, 202, PSYC 101, 110, 210, 211, BUS 101, 102	6	TWO classes from the courses listed (if you plan to own your own building/construction business, you might consider taking BUS 101 and 102 to help you start your own business)
Political Science PSC 101	3	This is the ONLY option for this requirement
TOTAL EDUCATION CORE	**31**	
BULD 101—Urban Planning	3	This is the ONLY option for this requirement
BULD 102—Building Codes	3	This is the ONLY option for this requirement
BULD 110—Electrical Codes	3	This is the ONLY option for this requirement
BULD 220—Plumbing Codes	3	This is the ONLY option for this requirement
BULD 221—Mechanical Codes	3	This is the ONLY option for this requirement
BULD 222—Fire Codes	3	This is the ONLY option for this requirement
BULD 223—Blueprint Reading I and II	8	These are the ONLY options for this requirement (NOTICE the credit hour difference—each course is 4 credits, not 3)
CONS 101—Materials or CONS 102—Science of Foundations	4	You can take one or the other
CONS 101—Structural Inspections	3	This is the ONLY option for this requirement
TOTAL MAJOR CORE	**33**	
TOTAL CREDIT HOURS REQUIRED for DEGREE	**64**	You must have at least 64 hours in the required courses (as described above) to receive your degree.

credit, do not count toward graduation, do not transfer, and still cost the same amount as "credit" classes. Because of this, many students try very hard to avoid these classes. This can be a huge mistake on your part.

If you tested and placed in a developmental English or math class, TAKE IT! The assessments were put into place for your well-being, not to punish you. College-level English and math classes are difficult and if you do not know the basics, you will not do well in these and many other classes. For example, many college texts are written on the thirteenth- and fourteenth-grade levels. If you are reading and spelling on the seventh- or even tenth-grade level, you're going to be in trouble. Therefore, do yourself a favor and take the class into which you placed. You'll save yourself money, time, and a great deal of heartache! Trust us on this one.

> "It is better to take many small steps in the right direction than to make a great leap forward only to stumble backward."
> —Chinese Proverb

HOW TO CALCULATE YOUR GRADE POINT AVERAGE

Does 1 + 1 Really = 2?

The grade point average (GPA) is the numerical grading system used by almost every college in the nation. GPAs determine whether a student is eligible for continued enrollment, financial aid, or honors. Most colleges operate under a 4.0 system.

Each A earned is worth 4 quality points
Each B is worth 3 points
Each C is worth 2 points
Each D is worth 1 point
Each F is worth 0 points

For each course, the number of quality points earned is multiplied by the number of credit hours carried by the course. For example, if you are taking

English 101 for 3 semester hours of credit
Speech 101 for 3 semester hours of credit
History 201 for 3 semester hours of credit
Psychology 101 for 3 semester hours of credit
Spanish 112 for 4 semester hours of credit

then you are enrolled for 16 hours of academic credit. Your calculation would look like Figure 3.8. Using Figure 3.8 as a guideline, calculate the GPA in Figure 3.9. Pay close attention to the credit hours and grades assigned.

FIGURE **3.8** *Calculating a GPA*

	Grade	Semester Credit		Quality Points		Total Points
ENG 101	A	3 hours	×	4	=	12 points
SPC 101	C	3 hours	×	2	=	6 points
HIS 201	B	3 hours	×	3	=	9 points
PSY 101	D	3 hours	×	1	=	3 points
SPN 112	B	4 hours	×	3	=	12 points
		16 hours				42 Total Points

42 total points divided by 16 semester hours equals a GPA of 2.62 (or C+ average).

3.9 *Give It a Try–Calculating Bennie's GPA*

Using the information provided below, calculate Bennie's GPA.

English 101	**3 credits**	**Grade = A**	Quality points ____	Total ____
History 210	**3 credits**	**Grade = C**	Quality points ____	Total ____
Art Lab 100	**1 credit**	**Grade = A**	Quality points ____	Total ____
Math 110	**4 credits**	**Grade = B**	Quality points ____	Total ____
French 101	**3 credits**	**Grade = D**	Quality points ____	Total ____
Speech 101	**3 credits**	**Grade = B**	Quality points ____	Total ____
Total	____ **credits**		Quality points ____	Total ____

Bennie's Grade Point Average = _____

GOING BACK AS AN ADULT STUDENT

Is Learning Now Really So Different Than When I Was Younger?

Surprisingly, yes, but that is ***not*** a bad thing. Learning as an adult can certainly have its challenges, such as child care, tending to an elderly parent, working full time, managing a household, self-esteem issues, time management constraints, and trying to maintain healthy relationships. Take heart, however—you are not alone. The ERIC Digest (2010) suggests that almost 50 percent of today's college students are classified as adult or nontraditional. Learning as an adult can also have many advantages:

▶ More focus, drive, and motivation

▶ Increased career focus

▶ Enhanced world and life experiences

▶ Workplace skills and experiences

As someone who may be returning to school after a break of a few years or 30 years, keep the following tips in mind as you begin your incredible journey:

▶ Use the whole campus: tutorial services, career counseling, library, computer centers, student activities, math and language labs. You PAID for these services; don't let them go to waste.

▶ Quickly discover your learning style, dominant intelligence, and personality type (see Chapter 7) so that you can work to adapt your learning style to various teaching styles. Basically, you will need to learn how to process information in a timely, accurate, and compelling way.

▶ Don't be afraid of technology. You won't "blow-up" the computer or the lab and there are people on campus to help you with your technological needs. Technology is now going to be a major part of your life.

▶ NEVER be afraid to ask for help from your professors, staff members, and fellow students.

▶ Don't let your feelings and emotions ruin your future. Yes, you may be challenged, befuddled, afraid, and even intimidated. Everyone is regardless of age. Don't let one professor or one experience strip you of your dreams.

▶ LEARN TO DELEGATE. You'll learn more about this in Chapter 6, but it is of utmost importance that students with jobs, families, responsibilities, and relationships learn to let others do some of the work that you may have been doing for years. Delegate. Delegate. Delegate.

▶ Don't let the "process" ruin your dreams. Yes, there may be times when you simply don't understand why you have to take certain classes or complete certain projects. The process is a means to an end and if you use the process well, you'll learn a great deal. Yes, you have real-world experiences, but you can still learn many valuable things from your professors, peers, and surroundings.

iStockPhoto

THE FAST, EVER-CHANGING FACE OF TECHNOLOGY

Can Anyone Keep Up?

What qualities do nontraditional students bring to the college setting?

You've probably heard the old expression, *"It's like a train wreck . . . you can't look at it and you can't look away."* Some people view today's technological changes and advances as something you can't look at, but if you look away for even a moment, you're lost. Among the tools of Twitter, dimdim, Jing, Bing, Voice Thread, Facebook, Blackboard, Angel, Course Compass, streaming video, Hulu, YouTube, i-Speak, and countless other programs and services, it is vital that you know the basics of these tools as faculty may use them in class or require you to use them beyond the classroom. At the very least, it is important to know they exist and how to find help in using these new, ever-changing learning approaches.

In today's technologically driven education environment, colleges have classes, entire degree programs, schedules, course listings, and other pertinent information and programs online. Office hours with faculty members are held via a learning management program or a social networking tool. Cooperative learning activities take place though programs such as dimdim, WebEx, Go-to-Meeting, or E-lluminate. Often, students are required to research or network with people outside their own institution—many times internationally. We have truly become a global society through technology. This is one reason why we all need to learn as much about new and emerging technologies as possible. You can't be successful in college today without being literate in these areas. Push yourself to learn everything you can about emerging technology and software.

With that said, we all must remind ourselves of the fact that education is, in and of itself, grounded in people, connections, relationships, interpersonal encounters, face-to-face interaction, human trial and error, and yes, even uncertainty in research and relationships. Technology in education is not a cure-all nor is it a means to an easy end. Yes, you can earn an entire degree online, but when it comes to the workplace and dealing with other people, you must possess human relations skills, too. Communication skills such as writing, spelling, grammar, and speaking are consistently rated as essential to success in today's workplace (Steen, 2010). Ironically, communication skill was also ranked as the number ***ONE*** skill most lacking in college graduates. It is for this reason that we, as your authors, have included information on technology to help you create a healthy balance between the raging world of technology and the traditional world of face-to-face, personal interaction and communication. If you can master both, you are truly ahead of the curve.

"Striving for success without hard work is like trying to harvest where you have not planted."
—David Bly

How Can Technology Help in Your Classes?

Regardless of the class, you are probably going to be required to use some type of technology in almost every class you take. From research to editing to communication, the use of technology in today's college classroom is almost inescapable. Consider the following classes found in the "Core of Classes" for many community colleges. List at least two ways that technology could help you in each of these classes. In Figure 3.10, one example is given to you in each category.

FIGURE **3.10** *Ways Technology Can Help in Your Classes*

Core Class	Two Ways Technology Can Help You Be Successful
English	**Example:** Research the proper use of a semicolon. 1. 2.
History	**Example:** Based in research and real-world timelines, create a real World War II air battle scene using avatars. 1. 2.
Hard sciences such as Biology, Chemistry, Physics	**Example:** Watch the virtual dissection of a pig for your anatomy class. 1. 2.
International language such as Arabic, Spanish, French, Russian, Chinese, etc.	**Example:** Initiate a Skype conversation with someone from Russia and ask to converse in his or her native language for practice. 1. 2.
Fine arts such as Theater, Art, Music, Dance	**Example:** Watch a video snip of a Broadway play or dance concert. 1. 2.
Literature	**Example:** Research the life, times, and works of Tennessee Williams. Watch a brief scene of his play *Cat on a Hot Tin Roof*. 1. 2.
Social sciences such as Psychology, Sociology, Anthropology	**Example:** Research the population trends in Africa, plot them on a map, and discuss what those trends mean. 1. 2.
Computer Science	**Example:** Research how to create an Excel spreadsheet. Watch a YouTube video for examples. 1. 2.
Mathematics	**Example:** Watch a YouTube video on how to divide fractions and then practice what you have learned. 1. 2.
One class in **YOUR major** field of study	1. 2.

ON THE GO AND GOING ONLINE

How Do You Succeed in Distance-Education Courses?

Distance-learning classes can be great for students who may live far from campus, have transportation issues, work full time, or care for families and small children. These courses have flexible hours and few, if any, class meetings. Most online classes allow you to work at your own pace, but most still have stringent deadlines for assignment submission.

Do not let anyone try to tell you that these courses are easier than regular classroom offerings; they are not. Distance-learning courses are usually more difficult for the average student. Some colleges reserve distance-learning courses for students with GPAs of 3.0 or higher. You need to be a self-starter and highly motivated to complete and do well in these courses. Take the assessment in Figure 3.11 to determine if an online class is right for you.

FIGURE 3.11 *Distance-Education Readiness Assessment*

Please answer each question truthfully to determine your readiness for online learning.

1.	Do you own your own computer?	Yes	No
2.	Is your computer relatively new (enough memory, CD-Rom, graphics card, wireless Internet, etc.)?	Yes	No
3.	Can you type (NOT text, but type)?	Yes	No
4.	Are you comfortable using a computer and web technology?	Yes	No
5.	Do you have the technical requirements for online learning (Internet access, Internet browser, Adobe, Word or compatible program, PowerPoint)?	Yes	No
6.	Are you highly organized?	Yes	No
7.	Are you a good manager of time?	Yes	No
8.	Are you highly motivated: a self-starter?	Yes	No
9.	If you work full or part time, do you feel you have at least 6–8 hours per week to spend working with each of your online classes?	Yes	No
10.	If you have family issues that require a great deal of your time, do you have family support?	Yes	No
11.	Do you have "down time" to spend working on your online classes?	Yes	No
12.	Can you get to campus if necessary?	Yes	No
13.	Do you feel comfortable chatting online with unknown persons?	Yes	No
14.	Do you think you can "relate" to others in an online relationship?	Yes	No
15.	Do you consider yourself as a good reader with high-level comprehension?	Yes	No
16.	Can you concentrate on your work even with online distractions (e-mail, friends, etc.)?	Yes	No
17.	Do you feel comfortable calling your professor during his or her office hours if you need to do so?	Yes	No
18.	Do you think you will be able to take notes during an online chat or class session?	Yes	No
19.	Are you comfortable with online terminology such as URL, listserv, portal, streaming video, etc.?	Yes	No
20.	Are you excited about taking an online class?	Yes	No

If you answered NO to more than five of these questions, you should reconsider taking an online class at this time. To prepare for future classes, you may also want to spend time researching and becoming more familiar with the questions that you marked "NO." You can also speak with your advisor or professor about your possibility for success in his or her course. Your campus probably offers an online orientation from which you might benefit.

© Robert M. Sherfield, Ph.D., 2009

If you decide to take an online class, consider the following advice:

▶ If at all possible, review the course material before you register. This may help you in making the decision to enroll. Often, professors' syllabi are accessible online.

▶ Begin before the beginning! If at all possible, obtain the distance-learning materials (or at least the text) before the semester begins.

▶ Know whether your class is totally online or a hybrid course: it makes a huge difference.

▶ Make an appointment to meet the professor as soon as possible. Some colleges will schedule a meeting for you. If it is not possible to meet, at least phone the professor and introduce yourself.

▶ Log in on a daily basis even if nothing is due. Important messages may be posted.

▶ LEARN the required technology and software programs to be successful and make sure you have access to these programs.

▶ Develop a schedule for completing each assignment and stick to it! Don't let time steal away from you. This is the biggest problem with online classes.

▶ Keep a copy of all work mailed, e-mailed, or delivered to the professor.

▶ Always mail, e-mail, or deliver your assignment on time—early if possible.

▶ Take full advantage of any online orientation or training sessions.

▶ Participate in class, chats, and in your groups (if you are assigned a group).

▶ If you have computer failure, be prepared with a back-up plan.

▶ Alert your professor immediately if you have family, computer, or personal problems that would prevent you from completing an assignment on time.

▶ Work ahead if possible.

▶ Find out where to go or whom to call on campus should you encounter technical problems with the learning platform or getting online.

▶ NEVER be afraid to knock on your instructor's digital office door. Many instructors hold office hours online and welcome your comments and questions.

SPENDING TIME ONLINE

Are You Searching, Perching, or Lurking?

You get online with a purpose—a real purpose—and before you know it, hours have passed and you find that you've piddled and diddled and nothing has been accomplished. This is not an uncommon occurrence. You may have had the best of intentions to go online and work or research a project, but before you know it, you've checked e-mail, watched a YouTube video, IM-ed three friends, and checked your Twitter messages. How can we spend quality time online?

Consider the following tips when going online to work or complete a school assignment:

▶ Use your favorite e-tools (Twitter, Facebook, etc.) as a REWARD for getting your work done. Work first, then socialize.

▶ Have a plan and a timeline before you go online. If you have a topic to research, allow yourself enough time to do your work and later check your messages and network with friends.

▶ When going online, do not sign into Facebook or Twitter or Friendster until you have completed your work. Don't tempt yourself.

▶ Treat your time online as you would treat your time at work. Divide your time into "work time" and "break time" and put your breaks after work.

▶ Allow yourself enough time during the day to do all of the things online that you love to do, such as network, search iTunes or Rhapsody, Google, or play games. There is nothing wrong with enjoying technology if your studies have been completed.

▶ Let your e-friends know when you'll be online for work and when you'll be online for socializing. Don't cross or blur the lines.

SUCCESSFUL DECISIONS: An Activity for Critical Reflection

JoAnne was a very shy lady who had been out of school for 27 years. When she entered her first class, she was stunned to see so many younger people and to learn that everyone seemed to have more in-depth computer skills than she did.

Horrified that her first assignment was to include a chart created in Microsoft Excel, she thought about dropping the class. *"How am I going to ever learn how to turn data into a chart and insert it into a document by next week?"* she thought. She even heard a classmate grumbling about dropping the class, too. Determined

that she was not going to be beaten, JoAnne decided to go to the computer lab and ask for help. Within an hour, she had learned how to make a simple chart and paste it into a document.

In your own words, what advice would you give to someone who is nervous about being in school (or back in school)? List at least two things that your classmate could do to ensure his or her overall success.

1. _____

2. _____

REFLECTIONS ON EXPLORING YOUR INSTITUTION

College is an exciting and wonderful place. You're meeting new people, being exposed to innovative ideas, and learning interesting concepts. There has never been a time when the old saying "knowledge is power" was more true. By participating in your own learning, engaging in the art of self-management, and taking initiative to learn about your institution, you are potentially avoiding mistakes that could jeopardize your education. Good for you!

Simply taking the time to familiarize yourself with the workings of your college can eliminate many of the hassles that first-year students face. By doing this, you can enjoy your experience with more energy, excitement, and optimism. As you continue on in the semester and work toward self-management, consider the following ideas:

▶ Determine what it is going to take for you to persist and succeed in college.

▶ Guard your ethics and integrity and use civility and personal decorum on campus.

▶ Know the policies and rules of your college.

▶ Establish a *relationship* with your professors, advisors, and counselors.

▶ Join a *campus club* and get involved.

▶ Determine if you have the time to take an online class.

▶ Make use of *student services*.

Practicing self-management can help you not only in your classes, but as you enter the world of work. Strive to become a person who is accountable and responsible for your own life and learning.

> *"There is no secret to success. It is the result of preparation, hard work, and learning from failure."*
> —*General Colin Powell*

CREATE SUCCESS
Your Journey to University, Career, and Life Beyond College

CONNECTING Think about the people on your college campus. With whom can you make a connection to learn more about *taking an online course?* (Example: counselor, advisor, retention specialist, etc.) Why and how will this connection be important?	
READING Find one brief, relevant article (in print or online) relating to *the benefits of getting involved with activities on your college campus.* After you have read the article, write a brief summary of the additional facts you have learned.	
E-LEARNING Using any search engine, find one piece of valid, reliable information about *what college instructors really want from students.* Briefly explain what you learned and why you think it is important.	
ANALYZING Choose one main idea or topic from this chapter. After exploring and researching this idea further, determine how this information can help you succeed in other classes.	
TRANSITIONING How will you use the content found in this chapter to help you create a successful transition plan to your next semester and beyond?	
EMPOWERING Thinking about the entire spectrum of your life (college, family, friends, finances, career, etc.), how can you empower yourself to be more successful through the information found in this chapter?	

SQ3R *Mastery* Study Sheet

EXAMPLE QUESTION *(from page 56)* What are the differences between a degree, diploma, and certificate?		**ANSWER:**
EXAMPLE QUESTION *(from page 57)* What are the differences between the AA, AS, and AAS degrees?		**ANSWER:**
AUTHOR QUESTION *(from page 59)* Why must you understand your college's polices?		**ANSWER:**
AUTHOR QUESTION *(from page 61)* List and discuss at least three student success centers.		**ANSWER:**
AUTHOR QUESTION *(from page 71)* What is a degree sheet?		**ANSWER:**
AUTHOR QUESTION *(from page 72)* What is a credit hour?		**ANSWER:**
AUTHOR QUESTION *(from page 77)* Discuss three ways that you know you are ready to take an online class.		**ANSWER:**
YOUR QUESTION *(from page ____)*		**ANSWER:**
YOUR QUESTION *(from page ____)*		**ANSWER:**
YOUR QUESTION *(from page ____)*		**ANSWER:**
YOUR QUESTION *(from page ____)*		**ANSWER:**
YOUR QUESTION *(from page ____)*		**ANSWER:**

Finally, after answering these questions, recite this chapter's major points in your mind. Consider the following general questions to help you master this material.

▶ What was it about?
▶ What does it mean?
▶ What was the most important thing I learned? Why?
▶ What were the key points to remember?

CHAPTER 4
COMMUNICATE

IMPROVING
PERSONAL
COMMUNICATION,
CULTIVATING
RELATIONSHIPS,
AND MANAGING
CONFLICT

"Words can destroy relationships. What we call each other ultimately becomes what we think about each other, and what we think about each other matters."

—Jeanne J. Kirkpatrick

PART ONE CHANGING YOUR THOUGHTS

WHY READ THIS CHAPTER?

What's in it for me?

WHY will interpersonal communication be important to my life and career? WHY is it important to understand computer mediated communication? WHY does managing conflict really matter at this point in my life? WHY is it important to understand diverse relationships?

Why? Because people simply do not live alone. We are constantly communicating and relating to others even when we think we may not be and even when we are not trying to do so. The ability to know yourself and how to communicate with others—to understand them, to work with them, and to manage conflicts that may arise are some of THE MOST valuable tools you will ever learn. Effective communication determines so much about the nature and quality of your life, including aspects of your education, your relationships, your romances, your career, your future, your friends, your values, your ethics, and, indeed, your character. Also, these qualities are important because most employers name interpersonal communication skills as one of the top attributes that any potential employee should possess.

By carefully reading this chapter and taking the information provided seriously, you will be able to:

▶ Identify the elements and power of the communication process.

▶ Define the concept of interpersonal communication and learn the associated essential skills.

▶ Discuss computer mediated communication as it relates to interpersonal communication.

▶ Define and discuss the role of nonverbal communication.

▶ Navigate and learn how to manage conflict more effectively.

CHAPTER 4 | COMMUNICATE

"I see communication as a huge umbrella that covers and affects all that goes on between human beings."

—*Joseph Adler*

ZZAVVALYNN ORLEANSKI
Graduate!

*Pulaski Technical College,
Little Rock, Arkansas*

How my
COMMUNITY
COLLEGE
changed my life

*An interview conducted and
written by*
AMY BALDWIN
*Instructor of English and
Student Success, Pulaski
Technical College*

I first met Zzavvalynn Orleanski when she stepped into my student success course one fall day. I knew I would remember her for a long time because she had one of the most unusual names I had ever seen, and I enjoyed writing the double letters when I would take attendance. I didn't realize until I got to know her that I would remember her long after she was in my class not just because of her name, but because she possesses one of the most inspiring and infectious attitudes about herself and her future.

It didn't take Zzavvalynn long to share her story with me and the rest of class. *"I flunked out the first time I went to college,"* she said, *"in part because I didn't think I could do it. I felt overwhelmed by everything."* But when she came back the next year, the year I had her in my class, she had decided that she was going to be successful because of her children. ZZavvalynn has three special-needs children, and as a single parent, she is the only one who has the daily responsibility for raising them. *"My children and our future,"* she said, *"are my motivation for going back and doing it right."*

"As I started my classes, I began to feel more comfortable with learning. I had a student success course that taught me strategies for putting together a study plan. My biology instructor always encouraged and reassured me that I was doing well. He even taught me study techniques that he used when he was a first-year student. I can point to other professors who helped me believe in myself."

Zzavvalynn is proud of the fact that she made the dean's list that fall semester. *"I even surprised myself,"* she said. She discovered that her hard work paid off and that gave her even more self-confidence.

Her experience at Pulaski Technical College not only gave her the assurance that she can achieve, but she recalls, *"It was a haven for me while I dealt with the drama in my life. It was a place that made me fulfilled,"* she said, *"because I knew I could do this and could continue on my journey."*

Her advice to other community college students is simple: *"Don't give up!"* What she doesn't reveal, though, is that another part of her success strategy was to develop strong relationships with her instructors and to have a persistent positive attitude. She always made a positive impression on her instructors at Pulaski Tech because she took charge of her situation, despite the numerous challenges she faced each semester, and she made the most of the time she had at her community college.

Now, ZZavvalynn is on her way to becoming what she has dreamt about: a special education teacher. She wants to help others who have challenges in learning—just as she found help at her community college and within herself to be a true success.

THINK ABOUT IT

1. Zzavvalynn states that she was overwhelmed at times. What is the most overwhelming thing that you have faced since beginning college? How are you dealing with this issue?
2. Zzavvalynn called her college "a haven . . . a place that made me fulfilled." What sentence would you use to describe your college experience thus far? Why?

In the preface of this book (page xiv), you read about the **SQ3R study method.** Right now, take a few moments, **scan this chapter,** and on the SQ3R Mastery Study Sheet on page 111, write **five of your own questions** that you think will be important to your mastery of this material. In addition to the two questions below, you will find five questions from your authors on that study sheet. Use one of your *"Study for Quiz"* stickers to flag this page for easy reference.

EXAMPLES:

▶ What are the six elements of the communication process? (from page 86)

▶ What is self-disclosure and why is it important for healthy relationships? (from page 92)

THE COMMUNICATION PROCESS

How Does Communication Work?

Communication is not something we do *to people;* rather, it is something that is done *between people.* Communication can take on a variety of forms such as oral speech, the written word, body movements, electronic messages, and even yawns. All of these actions communicate something to another person. As you begin thinking about communication, it is paramount that you know this: If you are in the presence of another person, communication cannot be stopped.

Basically, the communication process involves **SIX ELEMENTS:** the source, the message, the channel, the receiver, barriers, and feedback. Consider Figure 4.1.

Barriers (represented by the lines in Figure 4.1) are factors that can interfere with the source, the message, the channel, or the receiver. Barriers can occur anywhere within the com-

FIGURE **4.1** *Six Elements of Communication*

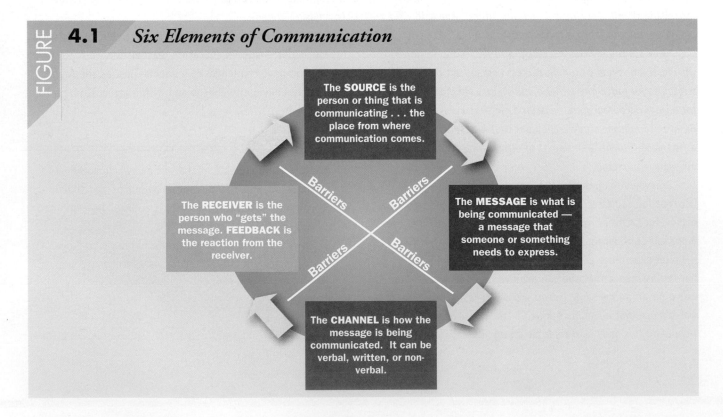

The **SOURCE** is the person or thing that is communicating . . . the place from where communication comes.

The **RECEIVER** is the person who "gets" the message. **FEEDBACK** is the reaction from the receiver.

The **MESSAGE** is what is being communicated — a message that someone or something needs to express.

The **CHANNEL** is how the message is being communicated. It can be verbal, written, or non-verbal.

Barriers

munication process and can include external noise (others talking, cell phones, and traffic), internal noise (self-talk, doubt, and questioning), interference, and poor communication habits. Your emotions, past experiences, social norms, communication expectations, and prejudices can also be barriers to effective communication. Think about a time when your feelings for someone interfered with your ability to listen to that person objectively. This would be a perfect example of a barrier. **Feedback** is the verbal and nonverbal responses the receiver gives you.

What Is the Role of Interpersonal Communication in Everyday Life?

Interpersonal communication is a part of the greater communication spectrum. It is "a dynamic form of communication between two (or more) people in which the messages exchanged significantly influence their thoughts, emotions, behaviors, and relationships" (McCornack, 2007). The messages in interpersonal communication are not necessarily static like the words in a book, a written letter, or a text message; they are fluid and constantly changing, potentially causing your relationships to change along with them. Texting and e-mails are components of interpersonal communication as well as computer mediated communication, which we will discuss later in this chapter.

Steven McCornack, in his book *Reflect and Relate* (2007), suggests that there are three Interpersonal Communication Goals, as shown in Figure 4.2: *Self-presentation, Instrumental,* and *Relationship Goals.*

FIGURE 4.2 *Interpersonal Communication Goals*

Type of Goal	Explanation	Example
Self-Presentation Goals	Goals that help us present ourselves to others in a particular fashion and help others see us as we wish to be seen.	If you want a new acquaintance or love interest to see you as a caring, compassionate person, you will use words and actions that reveal yourself as caring, trustworthy, honest, and compassionate.
Instrumental Goals	Goals that help us present information in a way that we get what we want or need from another person; to possibly win approval	If you wanted to borrow your best friend's laptop computer, you would remind him or her that you are always careful and respect others' property.
Relationship Goals	Goals that help us build meaningful, lasting, effective relationships with other people.	If your friend loaned you her computer, you might write a thank you note or buy a small gift as a token of your appreciation.

Take a moment and identify one way that you could use each of the interpersonal communication goals to help you succeed in college and establish strong relationships.

Self-Presentation Goal   I can use this to _____

_____

Instrumental Goal   I can use this to _____

_____

Relationship Goal   I can use this to _____

_____

Later in this chapter, we will discuss how to use interpersonal communication to your best advantage in understanding and learning from others, building lasting relationships, and dealing with inevitable conflicts both in person and through technology.

Why Is Interpersonal Communication Important?

You do NOT have a choice. If you are in the presence of another human being, you are communicating. Period! Smiling is communication. Reading a newspaper is communication. Turning your back to the wall and hiding your face from everyone is communication. Silence is communication. It is just the law of nature—if you are around one or more people, you are communicating with them. With that said, understanding the impact of your communication is paramount.

Consider this: Nothing in your life is more important than effective communication. Nothing! Your family is not. Your friends are not. Your career is not. Your religion is not. Your money is not. *"Why?"* you may ask. *"That's a harsh, drastic statement."* We make this assertion because without effective communication, you would not have a relationship with your family and friends. You would not have a career or money or even religious beliefs. Communication is that important. In fact, it is so important that communication gives us our identity. That's right. Without communication and interaction, ***we would not even know that we are human beings.***

Take into account the true story of the Wild Boy of Aveyron. It may sound like this story was taken from *The National Enquirer,* but it was not. This story has been documented in many science, psychology, sociology, and communication texts over the years. In January of 1800, a gardener in Aveyron, France, went out one morning to collect vegetables for the day. To his surprise, he heard an unusual moaning and groaning sound. Upon further inspection, he found a "wild boy" squatting in the garden eating vegetables as an animal might do. This boy showed no signs or behaviors associated with human beings. He appeared to be 12–14 years old, but stood just a little more than four feet tall. He had scars and burns on his body and his face showed traces of smallpox. His teeth were brown and yellow and his gums were receding. It can only be assumed that when he was an infant, he was abandoned in the woods and left to die. It has also been suggested, based on the long scar across his trachea, that someone may have tried to kill him as an infant (Lane, 1976).

When he was found in 1800, he could not speak and barely stood erect. **"He had no sense of being a human in the world. He had no sense of himself as a person related to other persons"** (Shattuck, 1980). Because of his lack of communication and contact with other humans, he had no identity, no language, no self-concept, and no idea that he was even a human being in a world of human beings. Of course, he had no religious beliefs or relationships with other human beings. That is how **powerful** communication is in our world today—it gives us our identity. It lets us know we are HUMAN! It helps establish our place and purpose in the world.

The Sapir-Whorf Hypothesis

Much work has been done on the topic of identity, communication, and personal actions, but perhaps the most widely cited research comes from the ***Sapir-Whorf Hypothesis*** (1956). Edward Sapir and Benjamin Whorf researched the relationships between language, culture, and thought. Basically, their theory suggests that the language we know, hear, and speak ***determines the way we interpret and understand*** the world. Just as the Wild Boy of Aveyron had never heard human language, his actions suggested that he did not know he was human. The theory also suggests that as humans, we are ***unconscious*** of this language/action situation and live our lives accordingly, without any choice in the matter. At its core, the Sapir-Whorf Hypothesis suggests that because of the language we hear, our "realities" and interpretations of the world around us vary from culture to culture and person to person.

Consider this example: In the Native American culture, there are no words for *"to own the earth."* The concept of land ownership does not exist because they do not believe that the earth can be "owned" by human beings. Think about that for a moment. If you have no concept of what it means "to own the earth," then your actions and beliefs about the earth differ greatly from those who think they can and do own the earth. Language, in this and many other cases, determines our thoughts and actions.

Another example comes from the Civil Rights Movement of the 1960s. We've all seen the photos of fire hoses being used to "control" African Americans who were marching for equal rights. According to the Sapir-Whorf Hypothesis, if you were raised where segregation was normal and natural and African Americans were considered second-class citizens, this footage may not have affected you at all. In fact, you may have even thought that the police who used the hoses were justified. You may have seen the photos and thought, "They deserved it." If the only language to which you have ever been exposed consists of bigotry and prejudice, then you might naturally believe that supremacy is OK, and your thoughts and actions would mirror this.

On the other hand, if you were reared in an atmosphere where you were taught that everyone is equal and racial prejudice is shameful and disgraceful, you would see these fire hose photos as barbaric and horrific. The language we hear and live with on a daily basis determines how we think and how we act. THAT is the important lesson of the power of language and communication. It gives us our identity. It defines us. It determines our actions. AND, perhaps most importantly, language can help us grow, change, and overcome negative influences, people, and events that might have shaped our backgrounds and held us back. Even if we were raised with language that may well be harmful, language can also be the driving force that teaches us to live in a more positive, optimistic space.

The Role of Nonverbal Behavior in Interpersonal Communication

Nonverbal communication is any and all communication other than with words—and it is ever-constant. We cannot escape our body language or the body language of others. Why is it important to study nonverbal communication? Because there can be so many interpretations of a single nonverbal clue, we must understand that not every action is equal or carries the same message. We must consider everything from cultural traditions to unconscious acts in order to fully grasp what may be intended by a look, a smile, a touch, or how close we stand to someone. We must consider that many of our own nonverbal clues are unintentional. Think about how many interpretations there can be of a pat on the shoulder. It could mean "Congratulations," or "Welcome back," or "Way to go," or "I'm sorry," or "Hey, friend" (Lane, 2008).

Nonverbal clues mean different things to different people and cultures and can be interpreted in vastly different ways. One's facial expressions are perhaps one of the, if not THE, most telling of our nonverbal clues. "One research team found that some facial expressions such as those conveying happiness, sadness, anger, disgust, and surprise were the same in 68 to 92 percent of all cultures examined" (Beebe et al., 2008).

Proximity is also a strong nonverbal clue. Maybe you are not overly fond of a person who has approached you and you decide to keep your distance from him or her. Conversely, when a person that you consider to be your friend and confidant approaches you, you may move closer to him or her. The rules surely vary from culture to culture, but consider the diagram in Figure 4.3, The Classification of Spatial Zones, as described by interpersonal expert Edward T. Hall (1966).

Consider the nonverbal communication chart describing more common nonverbal clues. As you study each action and example in Figure 4.4, try to determine what it would mean to YOU based on your thoughts and cultural traditions.

Understanding nonverbal communication and the cultural clues that can accompany it can greatly enhance your ability to establish effective interpersonal relationships and avoid conflicts caused by misunderstanding. As you grow in your ability to communicate effectively, work hard to hear the verbal message and learn to decode the nonverbal clues in conjunction with the verbal message. This will help you establish a rich, rewarding communication environment.

FIGURE

4.3   *The Classification of Spatial Zones*

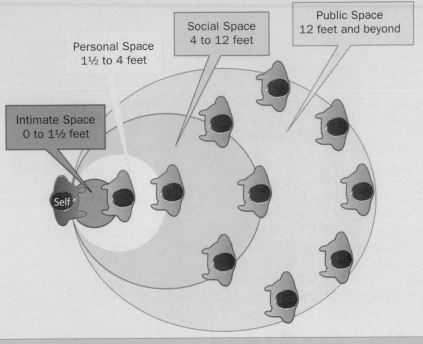

	Distance from Individaul	Example
Zone 1	0 feet–1½ feet	Communicatinig with our most intimate acquaintances
Zone 2	1½ feet–4 feet	Conversing with good friends and family members
Zone 3	4 feet–12 feet	Working in small groups and professional situations
Zone 4	12 feet and beyond	Public speaking situations

COMPUTER MEDIATED COMMUNICATION

R U OTT (Are You Over the Top)?

Believe it or not, there was a time not too long ago when there was no such term as computer mediated communication (CMC). There were no e-mails, BlackBerries, iPhones, text messages, blogs, twittering, Facebook, MySpace, or instant messaging. OMG, YKM! No, we're not kidding you. As a matter of fact, it was not until a few years ago that the study of interpersonal communication even mentioned CMC. It was not considered to be a part of interpersonal communication at all, as it was believed that interpersonal communication had to take place *in person*.

Today, it is widely considered that CMC is a vital subcategory of interpersonal communication studies. "There is some evidence that those wishing to communicate a message to someone, such as a message ending a relationship, may select a less-rich communication message—they may be more likely to send a letter or an e-mail rather than share the bad news face-to-face" (Beebe et al., 2008). Technology has become an integral part of our communication strategies.

Some may ask whether CMC can really be considered "interpersonal" when we are not meeting face-to-face with another person. The answer is yes. Why? Because in today's rich CMC environment, we can ***infer or imply emotions*** as we send and receive electronic com-

FIGURE **4.4** *Nonverbal Communication*

Nonverbal Action	Examples	What They Could Mean
Eye Contact	Looking directly at someone Avoiding eye contact Fixed gaze	_____ _____ _____
Posture	Slumping Standing very erect Leans forward when seated	_____ _____ _____
Facial Expressions	Smiling/frowning Squinted eyes Blank stare	_____ _____ _____
Clothing/Emblems	Well dressed and pressed Wrinkled and sloppy Smelly	_____ _____ _____
Artifacts	Jewelry Tattoos Body/facial piercings	_____ _____ _____
Gestures	Waving arms Fingers pointed toward person Crossed arms	_____ _____ _____
Touch	Patting someone on the back Firm handshake Weak handshake	_____ _____ _____

munication. For example, we use symbols such as ☺ to indicate happiness or humor or others that show sadness or upset. We use abbreviations such as LOL (for "laugh out loud"). We even SCREAM AT OTHERS or SPEAK WITH EMPHASIS when we use all capital letters in our communication. Additionally, many people have cameras connected to their computers, allowing the sender and receiver to see each other's facial expressions on the screen. Therefore, emotions can be conveyed through CMC, although there are not as many nonverbal clues to view and interpret as in face-to-face communication (Lane, 2008). Because we cannot see all the nonverbal clues that are associated with face-to-face communications, we are more likely to misunderstand the message when using CMC.

The fact that we are not face-to-face does not seem to negatively affect our communication efforts via technology. Several studies suggest that CMC relationships differ very little from relationships that involve face-to-face meetings. Further research also suggests that CMC relationships may even be stronger than face-to-face relationships because people using CMC ask more pointed and direct questions, reveal more about themselves, and communicate more frequently (Tidwell and Walther, 2002; Walther and Burgoon, 1992). Think about the last time you revealed something online that you may have never revealed to that person face-to-face.

"The information superhighway is clearly not just a road for moving data from one place to another, but a roadside where people can pass each other, occasionally meet, and decide to travel together."

—Beebe, Beebe, and Redmond

TIPS FOR PERSONAL SUCCESS

Consider the following tips for using CMC (e-mails, text, and instant messaging, etc.):

▶ Never send an electronic message that you would not want the public to see. They are not private and quite difficult, if not impossible, to destroy. If you put things in writing that attack or libel other people, you could be sued for damaging someone else's reputation.

▶ When using CMC, choose your words carefully, as you cannot change them once you have pressed the "send" button.

▶ Never send CMC when you are angry, frustrated, or stressed. If you write a message when you're angry, wait at least 24–48 hours before you consider sending it.

Now, it is your turn. Create a list of at least three more tips that you would offer a fellow classmate to assist him or her with using CMC more effectively.

1. _____

2. _____

3. _____

"Confiding a secret to an unworthy person is like carrying grain in a bag with a hole in it."

—Ethiopian proverb

There is a downside to CMC, however. For years, communication experts have worried about the effects of electronic communication on the entire communication process, especially traditional interpersonal communication. In today's technologically advanced world, we do not have to speak to anyone if we don't want to. We purchase gasoline at the pump, pay for groceries at self-checkout, use automated tellers to get money, go to Amazon.com or iTunes to purchase our music and books, search eBay for sale items, and e-mail others rather than pick up the phone or visit them. Social isolation is a major concern, and you have to work hard to guard against becoming a **technological recluse.**

SELF-DISCLOSURE AND INTERPERSONAL COMMUNICATION

Are You Willing to Let Others into Your Life?

Self-disclosure is how much you are willing to share with others about your life, your goals, your dreams, your fears, and your setbacks. Often, self-disclosure determines the *quality* of your interpersonal relationships. The level of self-disclosure is up to you, and it can vary from *insignificant* facts ("I had dinner at O'Toole's last night" or "I'm a Leo") to *informational* facts ("I'm majoring in history" or "I have two children") to *highly significant* facts ("I'm fighting ovarian cancer" or "I'm going through a divorce"). True self-disclosure must present new information about the parties involved.

Irwin Altman and Dalmas Taylor (1973) state that self-disclosure is "showing ourselves to others on a conscious and unconscious level." They use the analogy of an onion and suggest that you think of your life as having multiple layers. As you know, an onion has layer after layer, each hidden beneath another layer. The outer layer is different from the inner layers and is only the covering of what lies inside—much like our clothes are a covering for what is inside us. The skin of an onion is easily peeled away. The further you peel into the onion, the smaller it becomes and the more protected those inner layers are. We too have many layers and we can choose to "peel" them away or keep them all intact.

Consider Figure 4.5. What would you be willing to reveal (peel away) about yourself and to whom would you feel comfortable revealing this information?

Everyone has more than three layers, but this figure gives you a good example of how you can peel away layers to let others know you more intimately. By self-disclosing and getting past your outer layers, you can enrich the quality of your relationships with others and also strengthen your own self-concept. You must, however, self-disclose (tell the truth) to yourself before you can ever self-disclose to others. Without personal and interpersonal self-disclosure, you cannot have mature, intimate, well-developed, sincere interpersonal relationships because your inner life will remain hidden.

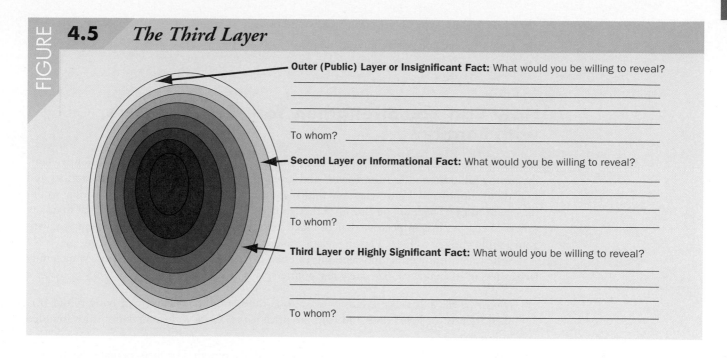

FIGURE 4.5   *The Third Layer*

Outer (Public) Layer or Insignificant Fact: What would you be willing to reveal?

To whom? _____

Second Layer or Informational Fact: What would you be willing to reveal?

To whom? _____

Third Layer or Highly Significant Fact: What would you be willing to reveal?

To whom? _____

THE TIES THAT BIND

How Can You Strengthen Your Relationships with Friends?

Think about your best friend. How did you meet? In class? Through another person? By chance? What was the force that brought you together, and more importantly, what is the "glue" that holds you together? If you compare your relationships with your closest friends, you will probably recognize that honest communication, self-disclosure, and trust are paramount in these relationships. You can't choose your family, but you can, and do, choose your friends.

> *"The worst solitude is to be destitute of sincere friendship."*
> —*Francis Bacon*

So why are friendships important? Friendships can bring a plethora of joys including comfort, understanding, a loyal confidant, and a listening ear. A friend gives you someone to talk with about happiness and sorrow and someone to laugh with when things are funny. You can share your hopes, dreams, and fears with good friends. Take a moment and list the qualities that you like in your close friends. Consider the emotional, intellectual, spiritual, and physical aspects of friendship.

_____

_____

_____

As a new college student, you are in the process of building a community of friends and associates. When making new friends, consider adding people to your life who:

▶ Treat you kindly, fairly, and equally.

▶ Bring new and different ideas and experiences to your life.

▶ May be very different from friends you have had in the past.

▶ Have ambition and courage and are outgoing and adventurous.

▶ Have healthy work habits, strong ethics, and pride in character.

▶ Enjoy college and learning new things.

▶ Have found their goals and mission in life.

How Can You Strengthen Your Relationships with Family?

Almost everyone has a family in one form or another, be it a biological family, an adoptive family, or one pulled together from friends and loved ones. Many people enjoy their families and find them supportive. However, some find that families are not as "functional" as they would like them to be. There are no promises that your family will be any more functional than any other. Therefore, it is imperative that you take steps to communicate openly and honestly with your family and try to forge a lasting relationship that is beneficial to you and them.

When communicating and working to establish a positive relationship with your family (regardless of its makeup), here are a few pointers:

▶ *Honesty is the best policy.* Many of us, at one time or another, have tried lying to our parents, friends, or loved ones and paid the price for it. Work to build relationships founded in honesty.

▶ *Talk things out.* Remember, you have two ears and one mouth. Use them in that proportion.

▶ *Words spoken cannot be unspoken.* This is not to say you won't be forgiven, but forgiving is different from forgetting. The wounds your words cause may last a lifetime, so choose them carefully and give some thought to the message you want to convey before you speak.

▶ *Family is forever, whether it's the one you were born into or the one you have chosen.* Your connections are powerful and should not be taken lightly or abused because of a whim or a passing bad mood.

What role does respect play in love relationships?

Shutterstock

How Can You Strengthen Love Relationships?

There are many types and degrees of love relationships. The love between two old friends differs tremendously from the passion of two lovers. Love can be as relaxing and comfortable as an easy chair or as tumultuous and exhilarating as a rollercoaster ride. The way love is manifested in a relationship does not necessarily attest to the degree or intensity of the love.

Loving someone means caring about that person's happiness, trying to understand and to be understood by that person, and giving as well as receiving emotional support. Most love relationships involve intimacy to some degree. Intimacy is not synonymous with sex; it may or may not involve sexual relations. Intimacy refers to the emotional openness that usually develops over time between two people who love each other. Intimacy allows people to share hopes and dreams as well as pain and sorrows.

To strengthen your love relationships, consider the following tips:

▶ *Respect your partner in both words and actions.* Respect begets respect.

▶ *Don't depend on your partner for your every need.* Healthy relationships need to have two healthy individuals in order to function well. You each need your own interests, friends, and life in addition to that special segment you share only with each other.

▶ *Talk and share your feelings, ideas, frustrations, joys, and sorrows.* Your partner is your life-mate and sharing is an important part of a healthy relationship.

▶ *Don't let things fester and boil over.* If something is wrong, bad, or troubling you, talk about it when it happens, not when it becomes unbearable. Early intervention is the key to solving problems in relationships.

▶ *Accept that no one is perfect, not even you or your partner.* Don't expect perfection and you won't be disappointed when you don't get it.

▶ *Practice the art of compromise.* You can't always have your way. Learn to give in and go with the flow of the relationship. Work together instead of always trying to be "best" or right.

▶ *Make time for your relationship.* Strong, healthy relationships require nurturing, time, and commitment to make them grow and last.

If "Love" Goes Wrong

Every relationship, whether it is a friendship or love relationship, has its period of exhilaration when nothing the other person does is wrong. Everything in the world is brighter because this person is in your life. However, after a while, these feelings may taper off. After the newness of a relationship wears off, you discover whether or not it will continue to be part of your life. This is the ordinary cycle of a relationship. If the relationship blossoms and grows, you begin to settle into a rhythm that works for both of you; if not, hopefully you part ways in a friendly manner that hurts no one.

Unfortunately, there are times when this is not possible, when one or both parties hang on to each other because they are not emotionally prepared to go it alone. Often, this leads to a very **toxic relationship.** What does a toxic relationship look like? You may have seen one or even participated in one. Here are some warning signs:

▶ One person's inability to function apart from the other.

▶ Blaming each other (or perhaps just one of you) for everything that is going wrong in your lives (life).

▶ Using abusive language and/or trying to control through intimidation.

▶ Using intimate knowledge of your weaknesses to hurt you or someone else.

▶ Using intimate knowledge to manipulate you or someone else.

▶ The use of physical violence or any controlling technique.

▶ Another type of toxic relationship may be when sexual harassment is involved.

Domestic Abuse and Violence

We never think abuse, battery, or violence can to happen to us. *"We loved. We talked. We shared. We trusted. We had a family,"* you might be saying to yourself. It is hard to get our minds around the fact that abuse and violence can happen with a person we once held so close—a person we loved and to whom we trusted our thoughts and hearts. But it happens every day, in every part of the world, on every socioeconomic level, with people from every walk of life. The U.S. Department of Justice (2000) states that one in four women will experience domestic abuse in her lifetime. Think about that: If you are sitting in a class with 16 female students, statistically speaking, FOUR of them have been, are, or will be in an abusive relationship.

According to the National Domestic Violence Hotline (2010), "abuse is a pattern of coercive control that one person exercises over another. Battering is a behavior that physically harms, arouses fear, prevents a partner from doing what they wish, or forces them to behave in

> *"There is no greater hatred than the hatred between two people who once loved."*
> —Sophocles from Antigone

ways they do not want." Battering can include the use of physical violence, rape, threats and intimidation, stalking, isolation, emotional abuse, and economic deprivation. According to the Domestic Violence Resource Center, over TEN million women and men are physically and/or sexually assaulted by an intimate partner in the United States each year! The DVRC also states that over five million children witness some form of domestic violence annually.

Many things can contribute to domestic violence including interpersonal incompatibility, being raised in an abusive environment, troubled finances, the need to control others, mental illness, substance abuse, unhealthy self-esteem, and sometimes, surprisingly, religious beliefs. KNOW, however, that there is never a reason for abuse. Some of the signs that you are in an abusive relationship include the following:

► Feeling afraid of your partner

► Having your life threatened by your partner

► Feeling helpless and that you can't do anything correctly

► Constantly being humiliated and criticized by your partner

► Fearing association with others when you're with your partner

► Believing that you are the one to blame for your partner's violence

► Wondering when your partner is going to lose his or her temper and "go off" on you

► Having restrictions placed on your actions and movements

► Being forced to do things sexually against your will

► Having your belongings destroyed

If you are in an abusive relationship, know that nothing you do or say will make the abuser change his or her behavior. Only the abuser can make the necessary changes. All is not lost, however. There are things you can do for yourself if you find yourself in an abusive situation. The choices may seem limited and frightening to you at the moment, but there are ways to escape this life and begin anew.

The first step is to know that you can change your life. You do not have to live in violence. The second step is to locate local resources that can help you make the tough decisions to regain your life. Go online and search websites that guide you toward assistance in your community. The first place to start can be the website of the **National Domestic Violence Hotline** at www.ndvh.org/get-help/help-in-your-area. Check your phone book for local associations or call 1-800-799-SAFE for a referral. If your college has a counseling or health center, make an appointment immediately to speak with a professional. Your counselor may have information that can help you today.

The most important thing to remember is that you do not have to subject yourself to continued abuse and life-threatening situations. Act today to begin the recovery process.

LIVING IN A DIVERSE WORLD AND COMMUNICATING WITH OTHERS

How Can You Strengthen Your Relationships with People of Diverse Backgrounds?

A few pages back, you read about the rule of communication suggesting that if you are in the presence of another person, *you are communicating.* It is inescapable. Well, it is also inescapable that we all live in a diverse world with people from different socioeconomic, cultural, religious, and ideological backgrounds. U.S. culture is one of the most diverse of any on earth! We are a nation of immigrants that still welcomes people from all over the world to our shores.

This fact is one of our greatest strengths because in this country, ideas from all over the world come together in an environment that allows anyone to pursue his or her dreams and ambitions. On the other hand, all this diversity is accompanied by the problem of throwing so many people from diverse cultures together and expecting them to function together as one society. In a society such as ours, it is almost inevitable that prejudice will arise. However, by understanding what it means to live in a diverse society, we can learn how to communicate more effectively and, hopefully, learn more about the cultures and traditions of others.

> *"We don't see things as THEY are, we see things as WE are."*
> —*Anais Nin*

What Are Ethnocentrism and Xenocentrism?

Many people truly believe that they are not prejudiced against any group and that they have no stereotypes in their thought processes about certain groups of people. If we dig deep enough, however, we would find that most of us have some kind of prejudice and that we all discriminate in some ways. Because most of us have lived in rather homogeneous neighborhoods and have primarily hung out with people like us, we may be *ethnocentric,* believing that our particular ethnic background is superior and tending to stay with our own kind.

Ethnocentrism suggests that we tend to fear people from other ethnic backgrounds or that we lump them together and view them *as a group* rather than *as individuals.* We don't think that their culture, religion, or race could possibly be as important or worthwhile as our own. Think about the ramifications to your *own* life if you were judged by "your group" of people instead of as an individual—if everyone judged you *as a woman* and not as Suzanne; if everyone judged you *as a Northerner* and not as Joe; if everyone judged you *as a Pentecostal* and not as Raymond; if everyone judged you *as a lesbian* and not as Sandra.

iStockPhoto

Think about the negative terms many people use to describe practices from other cultures:

"People in England drive on the **WRONG** side of the road."
"The Arabic language is written and read **BACKWARD.**"
"Europeans use the **WRONG KIND** of money."
"Africans dress **FUNNY.**"
"Asians eat **WEIRD** things."
"Indians listen to **STRANGE** music."

Have you ever made a snap judgment about something unfamiliar to you?

Ask yourself this: "Is it really wrong?" "Is it really backward?" "Is it really weird?" or are these customs simply *different* from your own? You know the true answer.

Xenocentrism is the opposite of ethnocentrism in that one believes that other cultures are superior to one's own and that one's own culture has very little or no value to offer. Some people use xenocentrism as an "overcorrection" for their ethnocentrism. Xenocentrism can be just as dangerous as ethnocentrism because once again, we cut ourselves off from learning from everyone and everything we encounter. All people, places, cultures, religions, races, genders, and orientations have something to offer. This does not mean that we have to accept and embrace every idea or characteristic of every person or every culture, but being an educated citizen does mean learning to listen, evaluate, analyze, and then make our decisions.

What Are the Dimensions of Diversity?

Among the kinds of diversity you might encounter are race, religion, gender, age, ethnic group, nationality, culture, sexual orientation, social class, geographic region, and physical challenge (see Figure 4.6). It is important for you to become open to individuals in all dimensions of

FIGURE **4.6**   *Dimensions of Diversity Wheel*

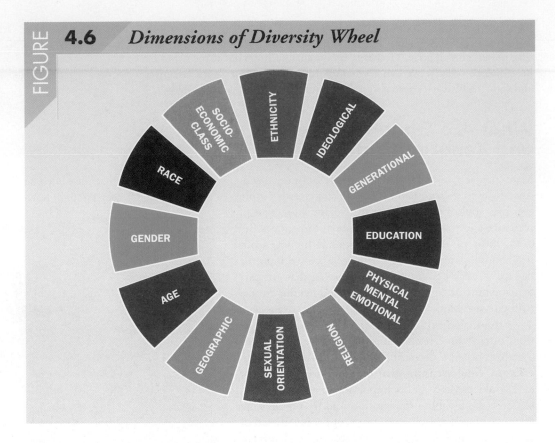

diversity. The most significant thing you can do is to think of people who have more diverse backgrounds than you as individuals, not as belonging to a certain group. Some people need to make bigger changes in their overall belief systems than others; it all depends on what kind of background you come from and what experiences you have had. An explanation of some major dimensions of diversity follows.

RACIAL DIVERSITY. Racism is a prejudicial feeling that exists when an individual has a negative attitude about any racial or ethnic group. Racism can be institutionalized in actions such as racial profiling or refusing to hire people of certain races except for menial manual labor. It can also mean that certain races are charged higher interest rates when borrowing money or have to pay more for an automobile than another race. Racist language usually implies that one group of people or an individual is inferior in some way to others. In many cases, races that are discriminated against have been relegated to inferior positions in society due to economic and political oppression.

RELIGIOUS DIVERSITY. Many types of religions are practiced in this country and around the world. Ranging from orthodox practices that have been in place for hundreds of years to newly formed "cults," people who practice each of these forms of worship are sensitive to unkind remarks about their beliefs. There are actually three major beliefs about other religions: *exclusivism, inclusivism,* and *pluralism.* Those who believe in exclusivism think that other faiths are in grave error and often view them as opponents. Those who practice inclusivism believe that other faiths have some truth to them but are only partially developed. Finally, those who believe in pluralism think that all faiths are legitimate and valid, when viewed from within their particular cultures.

GENDER DIVERSITY. Since the 1960s and the Women's Rights Movement, women in this country have made steady gains toward being treated as well as men, although there are still biases to be found among some institutions and, certainly, among some individuals. The fact that Hillary Clinton was a strong contender for the 2008 Democratic Party presidential nomination and that Sarah Palin was named the Republican vice presidential candidate highlights the fact that women have made significant gains. There are still a large number of **men and women,** however, who will make the statement, "I just can't vote for a woman for president."

AGE DIVERSITY. In your college classes, you are likely to find people of all ages, ranging from 16 to 90. In fact, a large percentage of college students today are nontraditional students (24 and older), as many adults continue their educations and return to college to study an entirely new field. Large numbers of older people return to college to take classes simply for enjoyment after they retire. You might very well find an older person on one of your teams. Certainly, when you enter the workforce, you will immediately be thrust into a community with people of all ages.

ETHNIC DIVERSITY. The word *ethnic* is derived from the Greek word *ethnos,* which means "nation," and some people refer to ethnic groups simply by the country from which they originated. Scholars don't always agree on exactly what constitutes an ethnic group. Some consider an ethnic group to be a social group that is typically distinguished by race, religion, or national origin. These groups may be marked or identified by distinguishing features and physical characteristics. But in some cases, they can be identified by their religion or language even when physical differences do not exist. To others, ethnicity might simply mean national origin. According to Feagin and Feagin (2008), an ethnic group is "a group socially distinguished or set apart, by others or by itself, primarily on the basis of cultural or national-origin characteristics."

SEXUAL ORIENTATION. According to the American Psychological Association, sexual orientation "refers to an enduring pattern of emotional, romantic, and/or sexual attractions to men, women, or both sexes. Sexual orientation also refers to a person's sense of identity based on those attractions, related behaviors, and a membership in a community of others who share those attractions. . . . There is no consensus among scientists about the exact reasons that an individual develops a heterosexual, bisexual, gay, or lesbian orientation. Some think that both nature and nurture both play complex roles" (2008). The conclusion, however, is that most people experience little or no sense of choice about their sexual orientation: "Most scientific thinking holds that one's sexuality is genetically determined rather than being a matter of choice" (DeVito, 2007).

SOCIAL CLASS DIVERSITY. Socioeconomic status or social class can be defined using the parameters of a person's income, education level, type of work he or she does, and family heritage. Someone may have social status because his grandfather was a U.S. senator, but that social status doesn't necessarily mean that he has great wealth. When class is discussed in this country, the terminology generally used describes *upper class* (wealthy), *middle class* (people who have jobs requiring a considerable amount of education or who own businesses that afford them a certain level of income), and *lower class* (people who are unemployed or hold very low-level jobs that do not provide them with a good standard of living).

GENERATIONAL DIVERSITY. Although you may have heard of many different types of diversity, you are less likely to have been informed about generational diversity. More than likely, you know that different generations have been labeled with names such as "Traditionals," "Boomers," "Generation X," and the current generation, which is referred to as the "Millennials." For the first time, four distinctly different generations, each with its own loyalties, priorities, and expectations, are working side by side in the workplace (Glenn, 2007). Naturally, with such a wide range of ages, there are conflicts over how work should be processed, what constitutes company loyalty, how many hours one should work after closing time, and how best to communicate.

GEOGRAPHIC REGION DIVERSITY. As strange as it may seem, there are some who are prejudiced against people from certain geographic regions in this country. It is true that there are people in all parts of our country who have very different ideas from those of the masses; however, we should not label an entire section of the country based on the actions of a few. In the case of geographic regions, as in all cases, one should determine the characteristics of an individual rather than assume that that person's characteristics are based on his or her membership in a particular group. You might find that a friend from California could open up all kinds of new ideas and thinking for you, or that a friend from the South could show you beautiful beaches and golf courses, or that a friend from New York could introduce you to Broadway and Central Park. As you expand your personal community of friends, make a special effort to get to know people from other regions of the country and learn to consider their character rather than where they come from.

PHYSICAL, MENTAL, AND EMOTIONAL DIVERSITY. You will encounter a number of students who deal with physical, mental, and emotional challenges. They could be visually impaired or deaf or confined to a wheelchair. Quite a few college students suffer from depression and others battle bipolar disorders. Research shows that 49.2 percent of all students experience some kind of learning disability such as dyslexia. We tend to assume that students who are labeled legally blind cannot see, when, in fact, 80 percent can read large- or regular-print books. They may have a problem in only one eye. Truthfully, these students are just like everyone else except that they have a physical or mental condition that makes life a little more difficult. They have feelings just like the rest of us; they want to be included in social life and activities; and they don't won't to be treated as disabled, different, and unable to participate.

IDEOLOGICAL DIVERSITY. The fact that we all have different opinions and ideas that are rooted in our family backgrounds, socioeconomic status, religious beliefs, cultural experiences, political beliefs, educational levels, and travel experiences creates great diversity and can cause difficulties between individuals and groups of people. "Individuals tend to come to more extreme views if they deliberate a given issue with like-minded people" (Kallock, 2009). In other words, internal diversity among individuals tends to be squelched by the forces of group polarization. People tend to remain moderate in expressing their beliefs until they are confident that others agree with them, and then they tend to become more extreme in their beliefs. These personal beliefs create diversity in thoughts, reasoning, ideas, and creativity. Political beliefs, for example, can be quite polarizing between individuals and groups. As an educated, enlightened individual, you will need to practice patience and understanding of other people's viewpoints and why they believe them even when you are diametrically opposed to those beliefs.

SEEING THE WORLD WITH CLEAR EYES

Why Is Having an Open Mind So Powerful?

As you seek to develop an open mind and become an educated citizen, you need to be aware of the terms *discrimination* and *prejudice*. If you discriminate against someone, you make a distinction in favor of or against a person on the basis of the group or class to which the person belongs rather than according to merit. For example, you might discriminate against a person who is highly qualified for a job because he is of a certain race or religion rather than on his qualifications. Prejudice, on the other hand, is an unreasonable opinion or feeling formed beforehand or without knowledge, thought, or reason; it is a preconceived opinion of a hostile nature regarding a racial, religious, or national group (*Webster's College Dictionary*, 1995).

If you discriminate against someone, it is because you are prejudiced based on preconceived ideas derived from insufficient knowledge, irrational feelings, or inaccurate stereotypes. As you can see, prejudice is usually not based on reason or knowledge but on opinions most likely shaped by someone who influenced you or a region of the country where you grew up. Finally, prejudice is not an illegal act, whereas discrimination in many cases is. Discrimination is illegal in employment, housing, loans, and many other areas outlined in the Civil Rights Act of 1964.

To experience other people and to receive the benefits of knowing someone, you need to enter all relationships with an open mind. If you have a derogatory mindset toward a race, an ethnic group, a sexual orientation, or a religion, for example, you have internal barriers that can keep you from getting to know who a person really is.

Distinguish between prejudice and discrimination by giving examples of each in the space below:

_____

_____

_____

_____

CONFLICT IN RELATIONSHIPS

Why Is It Important to Learn How You Deal with Conflict?

Many people intensely dislike conflict and will go to extreme measures to avoid it. On the other hand, some people seem to thrive on conflict and enjoy creating situations that put people at odds with each other. While in college, you certainly will not be sheltered from conflicts. In fact, on a college campus where a very diverse population lives and learns together, conflict is likely to arise on a regular basis. The simple truth is that conflict is pervasive throughout our culture, and you simply cannot avoid having some confrontations with other people. Therefore, you should not try to avoid conflict; rather, you can use it to create better relationships by exploring workable solutions—hopefully, win-win solutions.

Consider the Chinese symbol for **conflict** in Figure 4.7. You can see that it is made up of two different symbols: **Danger** and **Hidden Opportunity.** Why? Because when you are engaged in a conflict, you have the potential to enter into *dangerous* territory. Violence, alienation, and irreparable damage could be caused. However, you also have the *hidden opportunity* to grow, learn, and strengthen your relationships. Just because conflict in relationships is inevitable does not mean that it has to be permanent, dangerous, or destructive. Conflict can occur in any relationship, whether it is with your parents, your girlfriend or boyfriend, your best friend, a roommate, a spouse or partner, your children, or a total stranger.

Some of the causes of *relationship tensions* include:

Jealousy	Honesty	Emotions
Dependency	Culture	Sexual orientation
Outside commitments	Opinions, values, beliefs	Perceptions
Personality traits or flaws	Affiliations	

FIGURE 4.7   *Chinese Figure for Conflict*

Danger   Hidden Opportunity

From Ordinary
to *Extraordinary*

VIVIAN WONG
Founder
Global Trading Consortium, Greenville, South Carolina

In the early 1960s, I was a very young woman and a new wife when my husband began talking about coming to America. We dreamed of living in our own house with a yard rather than a flat as we did in China. We were working as front desk clerks in a Hong Kong hotel, when fate intervened in the person of Robert Wilson, who was in China marketing his Barbeque King grills. We told him about our dream, and he decided to help us. Many people would have never followed through, but Mr. Wilson gave us $100 and told us to get photos made and to acquire passports. He promised to work on a visa for us. It took a year for us to finally be granted a trainee visa, and we headed to Greenville, South Carolina, to work for Mr. Wilson, leaving our little girl behind with her grandparents.

In South Carolina we trained and learned to sell Barbeque King grills in China. After about ten months, we were very homesick for China so we went home. We realized after we got to Hong Kong that our hearts were really in America because now we were homesick for Greenville. Without even realizing it, Greenville and America had become our home. Mr. Wilson brought us back and this time, we brought our little girl.

In 1967 we were blessed with twin girls, and in 1968 we were given a permanent visa and U.S. citizenship. I often say, "We spent the first twenty years in America simply trying to earn a meager living and put food on the table." We began to look around to try to figure out what kind of edge we had that we could use to start our own business in Greenville because we didn't want to work for other people the rest of our lives. In 1970, with Mr. Wilson as a partner, we opened our first business, a Chinese restaurant, after my husband had spent two years in Washington, D.C., training for restaurant owner-

> *We spent the first twenty years in America simply trying to earn a meager living and put food on the table.*

ship. We opened other restaurants in 1975, 1976, and 1988. By now, I could put food on the table, and I wanted to do something other than sell egg rolls.

I became very interested in commercial real estate and began to learn everything I could and branched out into real estate. Today I own several hotels in America, and I am starting a chain in China with my brother. This chain will be called Hotel Carolina and is aimed at business travelers. We found a niche that had not been tapped—a clean, reasonable, three-star hotel for business travelers who can't afford five-star accommodations. We also own and operate a large business park and foreign trade zone in Greenville, South Carolina. We are partners and franchisees of the Medicine Shoppe, China's first American pharmacy.

I am also a partner in three banks located in Greenville, Atlanta, and Myrtle Beach. People ask me how I know how to own and manage such a disparate collection of businesses. My answer is simple: "I know how to connect the dots; this is what I do best." I also believe strongly in networking and communicating with partners and people who know how to get things done. I have partners all over the world in a great variety of businesses. I have developed the vision, action plans, and good teams to make things happen. I take nothing for granted!

We have been very blessed to live in America and now to open businesses in our native land. In this wonderful country, we have succeeded beyond our wildest dreams! So can you!

EXTRAORDINARY REFLECTION

Read the following statement and respond in your online journal or class notebook.

Mrs. Wong mentions how important it is to establish relationships, communicate, and network with other people. How can communication, networking, and strong relationships help you in your chosen field?

DEALING WITH CONFLICT. Conflict does not happen in just one form. Conflict can be personal or situational. There are several ways that people deal with issues.

- ▶ *Blowing your lid.* This involves screaming, uncontrolled anger, hurling insults, and an unwillingness to listen.
- ▶ *Shunning.* This involves shutting the other person out and being unwilling to engage in any type of communication or resolution.
- ▶ *Sarcasm.* This involves using stinging remarks to make the other person feel small, unimportant, insignificant, or stupid.
- ▶ *Mocking.* This involves using past experiences or words to "mock" or ridicule the other person; laughing at him or her; or poking fun at him or her or the situation.
- ▶ *Civility.* This involves sitting down and logically, rationally discussing the issues or problems and trying to come to a win-win solution. (Baxter, 1993)

DID YOU KNOW

Michael Nagle/
Getty Images

DITH PRAN was born in 1942 in Cambodia. He learned English and French and worked for the U.S. government as a translator, then for a British film crew, and then as a hotel receptionist. In 1975, after meeting a *New York Times* reporter, he taught himself how to take pictures.

After U.S. forces left Cambodia, he stayed behind to cover the fall of Phnom Penh to the communist Khmer Rouge. Having stayed behind, he was forced to remain in Cambodia while foreign reporters were allowed to leave. From this point, Dith witnessed many atrocities and had to hide the fact that he was educated or knew any Americans. He pretended to be a taxicab driver.

Cambodians were forced to work in labor camps, and Dith was not immune from this. He endured four years of starvation and torture before Vietnam overthrew the Khmer Rouge and he was able to escape the labor camp. He coined the term "the Killing Fields" because of the number of dead bodies he encountered during his escape. He later learned that his three brothers and 50 members of his family had been killed during the genocide.

Dith escaped to Thailand in 1979, fearing for his life because of his association with Americans and his knowledge of what had happened. He moved to America in 1980. In 1984, the movie *The Killing Fields* was released, detailing the horrors and triumphs of his life. He died of pancreatic cancer in 2008.

THE FACES OF CONFLICT

Uggggg! How Do I Deal with Negative, Nasty, Difficult People?

We've all encountered them from time to time: DIFFICULT people who are negative, angry, unhappy, destructive, argumentative, sad, depressed, and/or judgmental. They are people who seem to walk around with a black cloud above their heads and seem to enjoy causing interpersonal conflict—like the negative people discussed in Chapter 1. They are likely to pop up everywhere—at work, in class, in traffic, in restaurants, and even in places of worship. They cannot be avoided. Figure 4.8 profiles the most common types of negative, difficult people. Perhaps you recognize some of them. Read the descriptions and try to develop at least two or three strategies to effectively deal with each type of difficult person. In developing your strategies, you may have to rely on others in your class for assistance, pull from your past experiences (what worked and what did not), and do some research on your own.

Learning to manage conflict and work with difficult people is a very important step in developing sound communication practices and healthy relationships. If you can learn to stay calm, put yourself in the other person's shoes, and try to find mutually beneficial solutions, you will gain admiration and respect from your friends, family, peers, and colleagues. As you consider conflicts in your life and relationships, take a moment to complete the Conflict Management Assessment (Figure 4.9, p. 106) to determine your awareness of issues related to conflict and managing conflict.

Standards for Dealing with Difficult People and Managing Conflict

- ▶ Check your own behavior before doing anything else. Don't become the same type of difficult person as the people with whom you are dealing. Fighting fire with fire will only make the flame hotter. Learn to be the "cool" one.
- ▶ Don't take the other person's attitude or words personally. Most of the time, he or she doesn't know you or your life.
- ▶ AVOID physical contact with others at all expense.
- ▶ If you must give criticism, do so with a positive tone and attitude.
- ▶ Remember that all people are sensitive about themselves and their situations. Avoid language that will set someone off.
- ▶ Do not verbally attack the other person; simply state your case and your ideas.

FIGURE **4.8** *Types of Difficult Behaviors and People*

Types of Difficult Behaviors by Difficult People	Description	What Can You Do to Effectively Deal with Them?
Gossiping	They don't do a lot of work and would rather spread rumors and untruths about others to make themselves feel better.	
Manipulating	They constantly try to negotiate every aspect of life. "I'll do this for you if you do this for me."	
Showing Off	They usually talk more than they work. They know everything about every subject and are not willing to listen to anything or anybody new.	
Goofing Off	They usually do very little and what they do is incorrect. They pretend to be involved, but spend more time looking busy than actually being busy.	
Standing By	They do not get involved in anything or any cause but then complain because something did not go their way.	
Complaining	They may produce work and be involved, but complain about everything and everybody and seem to exist under a rain cloud. Nothing is ever good enough.	
Dooming and Glooming	They are so negative they make death look like a joy ride. They are constantly thinking about the "worst-case" scenario and don't mind voicing it.	

SUCCESSFUL DECISIONS: An Activity for Critical Reflection

In a student leadership council meeting, John suggested that the council sponsor a fundraiser to secure funds for sending the officers to a leadership retreat. His suggestion included having all members of the council participate in raising the funds even though only the officers would get to attend the retreat. This suggestion set Barry off, and he began to talk very animatedly in a loud, intimidating voice about how this would be unfair to everyone who worked and didn't get to attend the retreat. He stood up and towered over John and continued to use abusive language.

Rather than fuel Barry's argument, John remained calm, and in a very quiet, controlled, but firm voice,

said, "Barry, I understand your feelings, but what you need to realize is that next year you will be an officer, and all of us will be working to send you and your team. Why don't we move on to another agenda item and come back to this one after we have all had time to collect our thoughts."

In your own words, what two suggestions would you give John to help him further control the situation at hand?

1. _____

2. _____

FIGURE

4.9 *Conflict Management Assessment*

Read the following questions carefully and respond according to the key below. Take your time and be honest with yourself.

1 = NEVER typical of the way I address conflict
2 = SOMETIMES typical of the way I address conflict
3 = OFTEN typical of the way I address conflict
4 = ALMOST ALWAYS typical of the way I address conflict

1.	When someone verbally attacks me, I can let it go and move on.	1	2	3	4
2.	I would rather resolve an issue than have to "be right" about it.	1	2	3	4
3.	I try to avoid arguments and verbal confrontations at all costs.	1	2	3	4
4.	Once I've had a conflict with someone, I can forget it and get along with that person just fine.	1	2	3	4
5.	I look at conflicts in my relationships as positive growth opportunities.	1	2	3	4
6.	When I'm in a conflict, I will try many ways to resolve it.	1	2	3	4
7.	When I'm in a conflict, I try not to verbally attack or abuse the other person.	1	2	3	4
8.	When I'm in a conflict, I try never to blame the other person; rather, I look at every side.	1	2	3	4
9.	When I'm in a conflict, I try not to avoid the other person.	1	2	3	4
10.	When I'm in a conflict, I try to talk through the issue with the other person.	1	2	3	4
11.	When I'm in a conflict, I often feel empathy for the other person.	1	2	3	4
12.	When I'm in a conflict, I do not try to manipulate the other person.	1	2	3	4
13.	When I'm in a conflict, I try never to withhold my love or affection for that person.	1	2	3	4
14.	When I'm in a conflict, I try never to attack the person; I concentrate on their actions.	1	2	3	4
15.	When I'm in a conflict, I try to never insult the other person.	1	2	3	4
16.	I believe in "give and take" when trying to resolve a conflict.	1	2	3	4
17.	I understand AND USE the concept that kindness can solve more conflicts than cruelty.	1	2	3	4
18.	I am able to control my defensive attitude when I'm in a conflict.	1	2	3	4
19.	I keep my temper in check and do not yell and scream during conflicts.	1	2	3	4
20.	I am able to accept "defeat" at the end of a conflict.	1	2	3	4

Number of 1s _____   Number of 2s _____   Number of 3s _____   Number of 4s _____

If you have more 1s, you do not handle conflict very well and have few tools for conflict management. You have a tendency to anger quickly and lose your temper during the conflict. If you have more 2s, you have a tendency to want to work through conflict, but you lack the skills to carry this tendency through. You can hold your anger and temper for a while, but eventually, it gets the best of you. If you have more 3s, you have some helpful skills in handling conflict. You tend to work very hard for a peaceful and mutually beneficial outcome for all parties. If you have more 4s, you are very adept at handling conflict and do well with mediation, negotiation, and anger management. You are approachable; people turn to you for advice about conflicts and resolutions.

© Robert M. Sherfield, Ph.D.

▶ Allow the other person to save face. Give the person a way to escape embarrassment. People may forgive you for stepping on their toes, but they will never forgive you for stepping on their feelings.

▶ If you have a problem with someone or someone's actions, be specific and let the person know before it gets out of hand. He or she can't read your mind.

▶ If someone shows signs of becoming physically aggressive toward you, get help early, stay calm, talk slowly and calmly to the other person, and, if necessary, walk away to safety.

▶ Allow the other person to vent fully before you begin any negotiation or resolution.

- ▶ Try to create "win-win" situations in which everyone can walk away having gained something.
- ▶ Determine whether the conflict is a "person" conflict or a "situation" conflict.
- ▶ Ask the other person what he or she needs. Try to understand the situation.
- ▶ Realize that *you* may very well be "in the wrong."
- ▶ When dealing with conflict and other people, ask yourself, *"If this were my last action on earth, would I be proud of how I acted?"*

I THINK I WOULD . . .
AN EXERCISE IN
UNDERSTANDING DIVERSITY

Read and respond to each scenario honestly. As you read, think about how the situation makes you feel and what you would do if you happened to be one of the persons depicted. What might you do or say to improve the situation for everyone involved? Each scenario is based on a TRUE story.

You may be asked by the instructor to discuss your responses to these scenarios in class or online. If so, be mindful that these scenarios contain information sensitive to some of your classmates, perhaps to you. Although the purpose of the discussion will be to help everyone understand different perspectives, each person in the class should be aware of others' feelings, life experiences, and personal challenges.

SCENARIO 1. You and Jack, a friend from high school, are attending the same college. Jack has a physical disability that requires him to use a wheelchair. He was an outstanding basketball player and swimmer prior to a diving accident that left him a paraplegic. Jack is an honor roll student. He is an avid basketball fan, attends all the games, and plays on a wheelchair team. He has a great sense of humor. He dealt with his personal situation long ago and now he even jokes about it. Jack is one of your favorite people.

Since you and Jack have been in class together, you have been noticing that people tend to treat him differently from others. Sometimes people talk loudly when talking to Jack, as if he can't hear. Because getting to and from classes is difficult, Jack has someone to help him maneuver around campus. One day you overhear a student talking to the person who is helping Jack as if Jack weren't there. "What happened to him? Can he use his arms?" Although Jack is handsome, friendly, and personable, he is usually left out of the many social activities in which other classmates participate. You know that your classmates would like and admire Jack if they got to know him.

- ▶ How do you think Jack feels when people treat him as though he doesn't exist?
- ▶ Why do you think some people have difficulty relating to people who have physical disabilities?
- ▶ What could you say to classmates that might help them understand how to relate to Jack better and might make them and him feel more comfortable?

SCENARIO 2. Douglas met Andy on the first day of class. Douglas struck up a conversation with Andy because he saw a tennis racket in Andy's gym bag—a welcome sight. Douglas had not found anyone to play tennis with since his arrival on campus. The two decided to get together later in the afternoon to play a game. When the game was over, each knew that he had found a friend. They discovered that they lived in the same residence hall, had the same professor for English, only at different times, and both loved to play tennis. As the semester progressed, Douglas and Andy became very close friends; they studied history together, went to parties together, ate together when their schedules permitted, and double-dated once or twice.

Douglas and Andy enjoyed many of the same sports and movies and had similar tastes in music. Douglas felt that he had met a true soul mate, and Andy could not have been happier to have Douglas to talk to and hang around with. Andy knew, however, that things could soon change. He had made a serious decision; before the Christmas break, he would tell Douglas that he was gay.

Exams ended on Wednesday. Andy decided to break the news to Douglas on Tuesday night. They talked and laughed sitting on a bench outside the athletic center; then the conversation grew still, and Andy chose his words carefully. He told Douglas that he was gay and that he had been involved with someone at home for almost a year.

▶ If you were Douglas, how would you react to the situation?

▶ Should Andy have told Douglas about his sexual orientation? If so, should he have told him sooner? Why or why not?

▶ Does being gay still carry a cultural or social stigma? Why or why not?

SCENARIO 3. Tonya was a first-year student at a major research university. She had an excellent academic background. She had always loved science and math and was seriously considering a major that would allow her to incorporate her love of these subjects into a career. In her second semester at the university, she enrolled in a calculus class taught by Dr. Ralph Bartlett. This class was especially important to Tonya for two reasons. First, Dr. Bartlett was the department chair for the program she was considering pursuing, and second, the course was her first college math course, so she wanted to start off strong.

On the first day of class, Dr. Bartlett made some disparaging jokes about women in the field of science. Although these comments made Tonya uncomfortable, she thought perhaps she was being oversensitive. As the semester progressed, so did Dr. Bartlett's derogatory asides about women. Nonetheless, Tonya loved the course; she was earning A's and she felt that she had found her niche. She decided to major in this area. Tonya made an appointment to discuss possible career opportunities with Dr. Bartlett. Shortly into the appointment, Dr. Bartlett made it clear to Tonya that he didn't think she could cut it and suggested that she look for another program.

▶ How would you feel if you were in Tonya's shoes?

▶ Should you allow one person's assessment of your abilities to dictate your course in life?

▶ How would you feel if you were a male in Tonya's class?

▶ Why do you think women face discrimination in higher education? In the workforce?

SCENARIO 4. Rebecca is a nontraditional student who is 48 years old. She is a single parent with two children. Although she is not a college graduate, she has been promoted through the ranks to a responsible position at a major bank. Because she has now reached the highest level she can achieve without a college degree, she has returned to school. Rebecca has developed excellent computer skills from her on-the-job experience. Working full time, parenting two children alone, and going back to school constitute a heavy load for Rebecca.

You notice that Rebecca comes into class at the last possible moment because she must rush to school from work and find a parking place. As soon as class is over, she makes a dash for her car so she can get back to work. Her classmates have very little time to get to know her and she tends to get left out of discussions.

You and Rebecca have been assigned to a team that has to work together to complete a group project. All of the team members except Rebecca are traditional students. At the first meeting, your group discusses times to meet, and most agree that 1:30 on Tuesday afternoons meets your schedules. When Rebecca tells the group that she can only meet at night because of her job and only on Wednesday nights when her mother can take care of her children, one of the team members makes the following hostile remark to Rebecca: "Well, perhaps you will have to find a way to meet when the rest of us want to since you are the only one causing a problem."

▶ How can you use the conflict resolution techniques discussed earlier in this chapter to immediately ease the tension between team members?

▶ If Rebecca is unable to attend meetings held during her work hours, how can you help her catch up on what she needs to do to be an effective member of your team?

▶ What special skills and attributes can traditional students learn from a nontraditional student like Rebecca?

SCENARIO 5. Jermal, an 18-year-old student of African American and Asian heritage, often feels left out because he doesn't seem to belong to either race. African Americans seem to feel that he is white and Asian Americans believe he is African American. Although he has friends of different races, he is sometimes the brunt of ignorant remarks. Jermal often feels lonely and sometimes scared. He fears that he might become the victim of a hate crime.

While returning to his apartment one evening after a study meeting, Jermal is frightened when a pickup truck slows to match his pace as he walks along the sidewalk. One of the two young men in the truck leans out the window and yells racial slurs at him and spits in his direction before the truck speeds away.

On reaching his apartment entrance, Jermal notices the same truck, now empty, parked outside the building. As he nears the front door, Jermal again hears loud racial slurs being yelled at him from a third-story window directly above the entrance. Clearly, the people are very drunk and obnoxious. As Jermal enters the door, the slurs become mixed with threats to urinate on him. He enters the apartment just as drops of liquid fall around him. Angry and frightened, Jermal rushes to his room and locks the door.

▶ How would you feel if you were Jermal?

▶ What action, if any, do you think Jermal should take?

▶ Do you think racial discrimination and intolerance is a problem on college campuses?

REFLECTIONS ON INTERPERSONAL COMMUNICATION AND CONFLICT MANAGEMENT

In today's fast-paced, ever-changing, cell phone–addicted, text message–crazy, pay-at-the-pump, "don't have to talk to anyone unless I want to," action-packed world, it is easy to forget that communication is paramount in so many areas of your life. From building healthy and meaningful relationships with your fellow students to talking to your instructors to managing conflict, few tools will give you the power to bring about change more than effective interpersonal communication skills will.

By working to improve your interpersonal communication skills, your appreciation of diversity, and your conflict management abilities, you will begin to see how the relationships in your life begin to change and improve. Properly nourished and cultivated relationships will change from superficial, insignificant encounters to powerful, meaningful bonds in which trust, honesty, and maturity are commonplace. As you continue on in your studies and work toward personal and professional growth, consider the following ideas related to interpersonal communication and conflict management:

▶ Work every day to strengthen your interpersonal communication skills.
▶ Use computer mediated communication in conjunction with face-to-face communication.
▶ Strive to let people into your life by "turning off" technology from time to time.
▶ Work hard to understand all aspects of your own life and to develop a positive sense of self.
▶ Peel away "layers" and let people into your life through self-disclosure.
▶ Develop and welcome relationships with people from a variety of backgrounds.
▶ Maintain close friendships through honesty and loyalty.
▶ Learn to manage conflict instead of ignoring or running from it.

"Everything we shut our eyes to, everything we run away from, everything we deny, denigrate or despise, serves to defeat us in the end. What seems nasty, painful, and evil, can become a source of beauty, joy, and strength, if faced with an open mind."

—Henry Miller

CREATE
SUCCESS
Your Journey to University, Career, and Life Beyond College

# **C**ONNECTING Think about the people on your college campus. With whom can you make a connection to learn more about *managing conflict in your life?* (Example: counselor, advisor, retention specialist, etc.) Why and how will this connection be important?	
# **R**EADING Find one brief, relevant article (in print or online) relating to *nonverbal communication.* After you have read the article, write a brief summary of the additional facts you have learned.	
# **E**-LEARNING Review all the types of diversity under the heading, "What Are the Dimensions of Diversity?" Using YouTube, access, view, and study a video that features how to deal with a diverse population in the workplace. Identify two tips that will help you communicate better with people who have different backgrounds from you.	
# **A**NALYZING Choose one main idea or topic from this chapter. After exploring and researching this idea further, determine how this information can help you succeed in other classes.	
# **T**RANSITIONING How will you use the content found in this chapter to help you create a successful transition plan to your next semester and beyond?	
# **E**MPOWERING Thinking about the entire spectrum of your life (college, family, friends, finances, career, etc.), how can you empower yourself to be more successful through the information found in this chapter?	

SQ3R *Mastery* Study Sheet

EXAMPLE QUESTION *(from page 86)* What are the six elements of the communication process?	**ANSWER:**	
EXAMPLE QUESTION *(from page 92)* What is self-disclosure and why is it important for healthy relationships?	**ANSWER:**	
AUTHOR QUESTION *(from page 88)* Why is interpersonal communication important to your professional growth?	**ANSWER:**	
AUTHOR QUESTION *(from page 90)* What is computer mediated communication (CMC)?	**ANSWER:**	
AUTHOR QUESTION *(from page 92)* In your own words, define "technological recluse."	**ANSWER:**	
AUTHOR QUESTION *(from page 97)* Discuss three dimensions of diversity.	**ANSWER:**	
AUTHOR QUESTION *(from page 101)* Discuss at least two strategies for managing conflict.	**ANSWER:**	
YOUR QUESTION *(from page ____)*	**ANSWER:**	
YOUR QUESTION *(from page ____)*	**ANSWER:**	
YOUR QUESTION *(from page ____)*	**ANSWER:**	
YOUR QUESTION *(from page ____)*	**ANSWER:**	
YOUR QUESTION *(from page ____)*	**ANSWER:**	

Finally, after answering these questions, recite this chapter's major points in your mind. Consider the following general questions to help you master this material.

▶ What was it about?
▶ What does it mean?
▶ What was the most important thing I learned? Why?
▶ What were the key points to remember?

CHAPTER 5
THINK

EXPANDING
YOUR APTITUDE
FOR CRITICAL
THINKING,
EMOTIONAL
INTELLIGENCE,
AND
INFORMATION
LITERACY SKILLS

"Many people think they are thinking when they are merely rearranging their prejudices."

—William James

WHY READ THIS CHAPTER?

What's in it for me?

WHY do I need to understand my emotions and know about emotional intelligence? WHY will a chapter on problem solving help me with my studies? WHY is information literacy important? WHY do I need to read a chapter on critical thinking when I'm thinking all the time?

Why? Because critical thinking affects your life positively or negatively every day. You use it when you go to the grocery store, you use it when you purchase gasoline, you use it when you choose what TV program to watch, you use it when you select classes for your degree, and you use it when you discuss important issues with your friends. Critical thinking is a major aspect of your daily life, affecting the very nature of the way you live and function in society. It helps you make decisions that will enhance your quality of life. Learning how to think more critically means that you are going to be able to look at situations differently, evaluate research sources more effectively, manage your emotions more closely, and solve problems more productively than ever before. Your ability to think critically, solve problems, and become information literate is going to help you greatly in all of your classes and well into your career.

By carefully reading this chapter and taking the information provided seriously, you will be able to:

▶ Define the eight steps in critical thinking, recognize their uses, and understand their importance.

▶ Use emotional restraint, emotional intelligence, and emotional guidelines to aid in logical, rational thinking.

▶ Manage information and become more information literate.

▶ Learn to identify, narrow, and solve problems.

▶ Learn to use creative thinking to become more resourceful.

CHAPTER 5 | THINK

"A person who does not think for himself does not think at all."

—Oscar Wilde

How my COMMUNITY COLLEGE changed my life

JENNIFER ADAMS
Graduate!
Florida State College at Jacksonville, Jacksonville, Florida

An interview conducted and written by
STEVE PISCITELLI
Professor of History and Student Success, Florida State College at Jacksonville

Jenna's initial college attempt had ended after three less-than-successful semesters. So when she decided to return, to say she had mixed emotions is an understatement. She was not only concerned about whether she would be able to handle the work, she was not sure she would fit in with the student population. After all, she was a 27-year-old divorcee—and she was nervous.

Although Jenna was not aware of it at the time, her choice to attend Florida Community College at Jacksonville proved to be the first of many wise decisions she was to make on her educational journey. She said, *"The community college professors and counselors helped me see that there is not a right or wrong way to succeed, it depends on the person and her goals. The smaller-sized classes, individual attention, and campus resources were invaluable to my success. I feel like I would have been lost in a larger institution. The freedoms and distractions of a university can be a lot to handle!"*

Jenna's age actually proved to be positive. Once again, in Jenna's words, *"There were times when my maturity was able to help a classmate understand a topic as I could relate to both the professor and the student. I feel like I was able to help some of my peers understand different points of view. Many students lack confidence to enter a dialogue with a professor, as they are used to being told what they need to know and do. College offers the opportunity to question material and discover knowledge."* Jenna found the college environment exhilarating. The smaller classes meant a greater opportunity to ask questions, have dialogue, and even try to debate with the professor!

After successfully completing her community college program, Jenna moved to California to attend Humboldt State University. And while she has happily adjusted to her new home and college campus, she still looks back with affection on her community college days. *"Attending community college,"* Jenna remembers, *"offered me the opportunity to avoid many of the struggles that I see students facing at my current university. Community college gave me the fundamental learning skills that I needed to be able to be successful without being distracted. Now that those skills are secure, I am far better at balancing tougher classes and the challenges of life in general."*

THINK ABOUT IT

1. What steps do you need to take to be able to establish better dialogue with your professors? What can you do this week to get started?

2. What kinds of skills and knowledge do you think you can learn from other students of all ages and backgrounds? How can you begin this week taking advantage of learning from your colleagues?

In the preface of this book (page xiv), you read about the **SQ3R study method.** Right now, take a few moments, **scan this chapter,** and on the SQ3R Mastery Study Sheet on page 141, write **five of your own questions** that you think will be important to your mastery of this material. In addition to the two questions below, you will find five questions from your authors on that study sheet. Use one of your **"Study for Quiz"** stickers to flag this page for easy reference.

EXAMPLES:

► Why is emotional intelligence important to critical thinking? (from page 117)

► What is information literacy? (from page 124)

THINKING ABOUT THINKING

Do You Know *Why* You Think *What* You Think?

Same-sex couples should be able to marry and adopt children. Think about that statement for a moment. You may be saying to yourself, *"I don't have to think about it—I know what my opinions on same-sex marriage and adoption are."* However, do you know WHY you have these opinions? Can you trace your decisions back to certain events or moments in your life? Do you think that your emotions cloud your thoughts on this issue? Is there a right or wrong side to this debate? Does your religion or culture come into play when thinking about this issue? Did someone else influence your thoughts or are they your very own, developed through research and conversations regarding this issue?

What are you thinking right now? More importantly, why are you thinking the way you are right now? What is causing you to believe, feel, or think one way or the other regarding this issue? What are the facts and/or opinions that have led you to your conclusion? At this moment, what are the origins on which you are basing your thoughts about this issue—emotions or facts, fallacies or truths, data or opinions, interviews or hearsay, reason or misjudgment, fear or empathy?

We purposefully chose a "hot topic" issue to open this chapter because understanding why and how we formulate thoughts and ideas is the main objective of this chapter and critical thinking in general. This chapter is about believing and disbelieving, seeking, uncovering, debunking myths, uncovering biases, identifying and solving problems, using information correctly, and proving the impossible possible. It is about proof, logic, evidence, and developing ideas and opinions based on hard-core facts and credible research. This chapter is about seeking truth and expanding your mind to unimaginable limits. This chapter is about the fundamental hallmarks of becoming an educated citizen; it is about human thought and reasoning.

THE IMPORTANCE OF CRITICAL THINKING

When Will I Ever Use it?

Have you ever made a decision that turned out to be a mistake? Have you ever said to yourself, *"If only I could go back and . . ."*? Have you ever regretted actions you took toward a person or situation? Have you ever planned a paper or speech that was flawless? Have you ever had to make a hard, painful decision that turned out to be "the best decision of your life"? If the answer to any of these questions is yes, you might be able to trace the consequences back to your *thought process* at the time of the decision. Let's face it, sometimes good and bad things just happen out of luck or circumstance. More often than not, however, many events in our lives are driven by the thought processes involved when we made the initial decision and chose to act on that decision.

Critical thinking can serve us in many areas as students and citizens in a free society. As a student, *critical thinking can help you*:

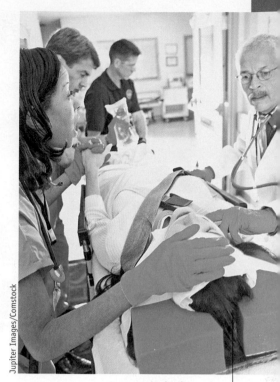

▶ Focus on relevant issues and problems and avoid wasting time on trivia.

▶ Gather relevant, accurate information regarding finances, goals, decision making, relationships, civic responsibility, and environmental issues, to name a few.

▶ Understand and remember facts and organize thoughts logically.

▶ Look more deeply at problems, analyze their causes, and solve them more accurately.

▶ Develop appropriate and meaningful study plans and manage your priorities.

▶ Improve your problem-solving skills.

▶ Control your emotions so that you can make rational judgments and become more open-minded.

▶ Produce new knowledge through research and analysis.

▶ Determine the accuracy of printed and spoken words.

▶ Detect bias and determine the relevance of arguments and persuasion.

Jupiter Images/Comstock

Can you think of a professional career in which critical thinking will not be required?

AN EIGHT-POINT PLAN FOR CRITICAL THINKING

Can You Really Make Critical Thinking Work for You in Everyday Life?

Does critical thinking really matter? Seriously? Can it do anything to improve the quality of your life? The answer is yes. Critical thinking has daily, practical uses, from making sound financial decisions to improving personal relationships to helping you become a better student. You can improve your critical thinking skills by watching your emotional reactions, using solid research and facts to build your examples and thoughts, and practicing open-mindedness.

Conversely, can the lack of critical thinking skills cause real problems? The answer, once again, is yes. Poor critical thinking skills can impair your judgment, lead you to make rash decisions, and even cause you to let your emotions rule (and sometimes ruin) your life. Critical thinking can be hampered by a number of factors including closed-mindedness, unflappable opinions based on rumor instead of facts, cultural and/or religious bias, lack of accurate information, faulty arguments, and negativity.

As you begin to build and expand your critical thinking skills, consider the eight steps in Figure 5.1.

Step 1: Understanding and Using Emotional Intelligence

Emotions play a vital role in our lives. They help us feel compassion, help others, reach out in times of need, and relate to others. On the other hand, emotions can also cause some problems in your critical thinking process. You do not—and should not have to—eliminate emotions from your thoughts, but it is crucial that you know when your emotions are clouding an issue and causing you to act and speak before thinking.

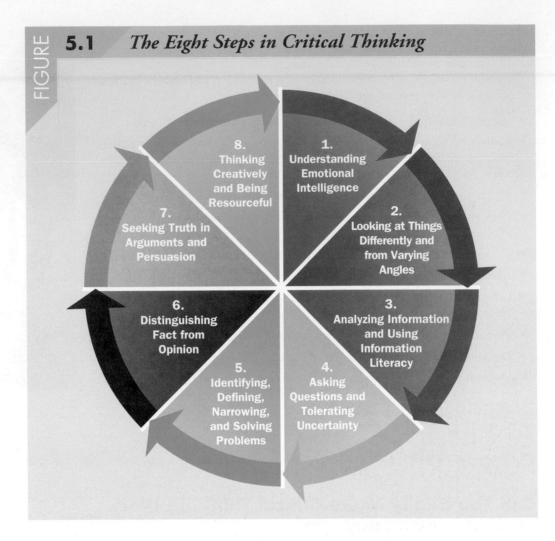

FIGURE 5.1 *The Eight Steps in Critical Thinking*

1. Understanding Emotional Intelligence
2. Looking at Things Differently and from Varying Angles
3. Analyzing Information and Using Information Literacy
4. Asking Questions and Tolerating Uncertainty
5. Identifying, Defining, Narrowing, and Solving Problems
6. Distinguishing Fact from Opinion
7. Seeking Truth in Arguments and Persuasion
8. Thinking Creatively and Being Resourceful

Consider the following topics:

▶ Should drugs and prostitution be totally legalized in the United States?
▶ Can the theories of evolution and creationism coexist?
▶ Can affirmative action reverse discrimination?
▶ Should illegal aliens be given amnesty and made U.S. citizens?
▶ Should the legal drinking age be lowered to 18?
▶ Should terminally ill patients have the right to assisted suicide?
▶ Should prayer be allowed in public schools?

As you read these topics, did you immediately form an opinion? Did old arguments surface? Did you feel your emotions coming into play as you thought about the questions? If you had an immediate answer, it is likely that you allowed some past judgments, opinions, and emotions to enter the decision-making process, unless you have just done a comprehensive, unbiased study of one of these issues. If you had to discuss these issues in class or with your friends and had to defend your position, how would you react? Do you think you would get angry? Would you find yourself groping for words? Would you find it hard to explain why you hold the opinion that you voiced? If so, these are warning signs that you are allowing your emotions to drive your decisions. If you allow your emotions to run rampant (not restrain them) and fail to use research, logic, and evidence, you may not be able to examine the issues critically or have a logical discussion regarding the statements.

"Simply stated, people who are emotionally intelligent harness emotions and work with them to improve problem solving and boost creativity."
—Snyder and Lopez

HOW DOES EI AFFECT CRITICAL THINKING AND PROBLEM SOLVING? If you have ever heard the old saying, "THINK before you act," you were actually being told to use *emotional intelligence (EI)*. Everyone knows that intelligence quotient (IQ) is important to success in college, work, and life, but many experts believe that *EI* is just as important to being successful. EI helps people cope with the social and emotional demands in daily life. "Emotional intelligence is the single most influencing variable in personal achievement, career success, leadership, and life satisfaction" (Nelson and Low, 2010). "The data that exist suggest it can be *as powerful,* and at times *more powerful,* than IQ" (Goleman, 2006).

Exactly what is EI? EI includes all the skills and knowledge necessary for building strong, effective relationships through managing and understanding emotions. *It is knowing how you and others feel and managing those feelings in a rational manner that is good for both parties.* Consider Figure 5.2.

We all have emotions and feelings that influence our thoughts and actions significantly. Emotions can manifest themselves in a wide range, from happiness to sadness, serenity to anger, and apathy to passion. You need to be able to recognize each of these emotions and employ appropriate skills for dealing with them. For example, let's say that you are discussing a political or religious issue with a friend of yours. You begin to sense that your friend is getting emotional and combative. You notice this in his or her voice and nonverbal behavior. An emotionally intelligent person would be able to sense what is going on, understand this situation and the consequences, and redirect the conversation to something more appropriate.

Our emotions originate in the brain. If you have EI skills, your *thinking mind* and *emotional mind* should function together, making it more likely that you will craft sound, rational decisions. In other words, you will **think** before you **act**. When these two minds do not operate in harmony, you might make highly emotional decisions that can be viewed as irrational (see Figure 5.3).

To become a successful, happy person, interpersonal relationships are important and learning to manage the entire spectrum of your personal emotions from the extreme **negative side** to the extreme **positive side** will be vitally important. This spectrum ranges from the darker side of your

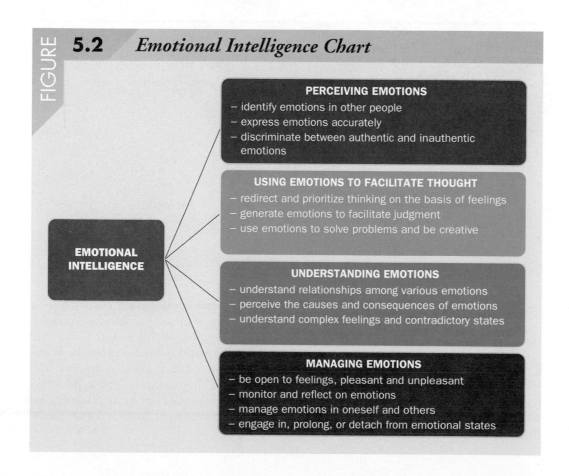

FIGURE 5.2 *Emotional Intelligence Chart*

EMOTIONAL INTELLIGENCE

PERCEIVING EMOTIONS
– identify emotions in other people
– express emotions accurately
– discriminate between authentic and inauthentic emotions

USING EMOTIONS TO FACILITATE THOUGHT
– redirect and prioritize thinking on the basis of feelings
– generate emotions to facilitate judgment
– use emotions to solve problems and be creative

UNDERSTANDING EMOTIONS
– understand relationships among various emotions
– perceive the causes and consequences of emotions
– understand complex feelings and contradictory states

MANAGING EMOTIONS
– be open to feelings, pleasant and unpleasant
– monitor and reflect on emotions
– manage emotions in oneself and others
– engage in, prolong, or detach from emotional states

5.3   *The Amygdala*

Don't let this word or concept frighten you. If you have never heard the word *"amygdala"* (pronounced ah-MIG-da-la), you're not alone. Most people have not. But this term and concept are important for you to be able to understand the overall aspects of EI. The amygdala, simply a part of the brain's emotional system, can cause us to go into default behavior based on what we remember from a similar experience. Do I use *fight* or *flight*? Basically, the amygdala is there to protect us when we become afraid or emotionally upset. When influenced by the amygdala, everything becomes *about us*. We become more judgmental. We don't stop to think about differences or the other person's feelings or the relationship. The amygdala can trigger an emotional response **before** the rest of the brain has had time to understand what is happening, and this situation causes us to have problems with others.

The amygdala remembers frustrations, fears, hurt feelings, and anger from our past. The tension from these past experiences causes the amygdala to go into default behavior—we *feel* before we *think*—and this can create a potentially explosive situation. If you had a bad experience several years ago and are placed in a similar situation today, the amygdala will remember and trigger emotions that cause the body to respond. These feelings often cause people to bypass critical thinking (the logical brain) and to respond with angry words or actions (the emotional brain). For example:

▶ They get angry—you get angry.

▶ They curse you—you curse them.

▶ They use physical violence—you use physical violence.

However, if you remain calm and level-headed, you will begin to see that the other person usually begins to calm down, too. He or she will follow your emotional lead, positive or negative, and if you're calm and rational, anger and violence become out of place for most people.

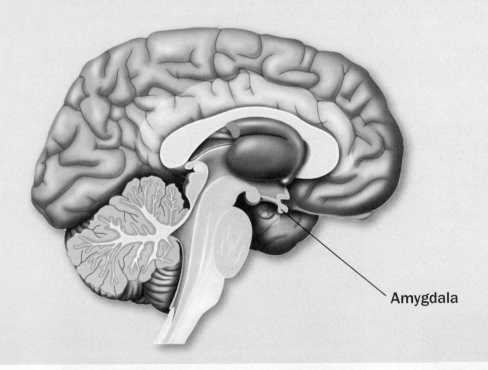

Amygdala

emotions (extreme negative pole) to the optimistic side (extreme positive pole). Study the spectrum of emotions illustrated in Figure 5.4. Think about which of these emotions you experience frequently and where you are located most of the time on this emotional continuum.

As you can see, the restraint and management of your personal emotional spectrum can impact you and your thinking skills greatly at home, at school, and at work. Today, this relatively new concept is being given a great deal of attention on college campuses and in the workplace. Not only will you find it helpful and necessary to manage your emotions at school, you will also need to be able to apply emotional management techniques at home and with family, friends, and work associates.

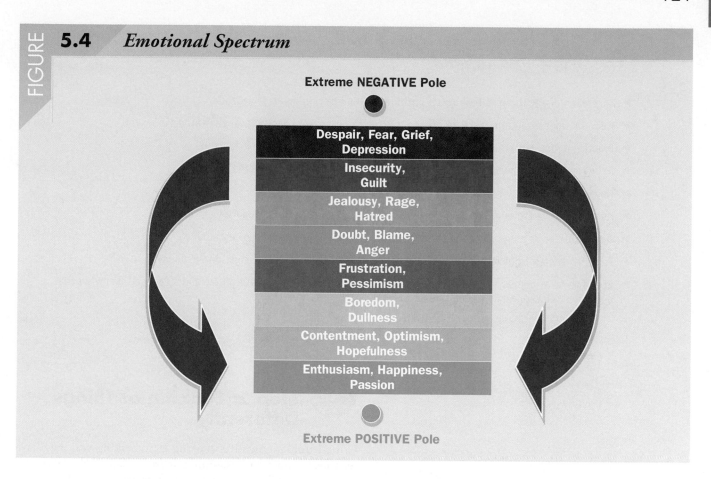

FIGURE 5.4   Emotional Spectrum

Think about one experience you've had in the past where your negative emotions "took over." Perhaps it was anger, fear, sorrow, hatred, or rage.

What was the situation and where were you when it happened? Be specific. _____

_____

_____

What triggered these emotions? _____

_____

_____

What were the negative consequences to you (or someone else) because of your emotions?

_____

_____

How did these emotions affect your ability to think clearly and critically? _____

_____

_____

_____

Because EI skills and knowledge are so important to your success in all areas of your life, you are encouraged to read extensively about this subject and to design your own personal plan for dealing with emotional concerns. Consider the tips in Figure 5.5 for managing your emotions on a daily basis.

FIGURE

5.5 *Guidelines for Emotional Management at School, Work, and Beyond*

- ▶ Face each day with an "I feel great, nothing is going to ruin my day" attitude.

- ▶ Hear all sides of an argument before you say anything, make a decision, or take an action.

- ▶ Practice a win-win philosophy at all times and work tirelessly to make it happen.

- ▶ Avoid letting your personal feelings about a person dictate your decisions.

- ▶ Never, never, never lose control!

- ▶ Avoid negative stereotyping and typecasting people into negative categories.

- ▶ Never look at or judge someone through someone else's eyes or experiences.

- ▶ Learn to keep a tight rein on any emotional "hotspots" such as anger, rage, and jealousy.

- ▶ Strive to treat people so well that you can always put your head on your pillow and sleep well, knowing that you have not been underhanded, rude, or unfair.

TIPS FOR PERSONAL SUCCESS

Use the following tips when you are faced with a situation that causes you to want to fight or flee.

- ▶ Stop and think before you act. Do not let past experiences influence this decision. This is a different person and a different situation.

- ▶ Think about the other person's feelings. How might past experiences be influencing him or her and causing this person to use poor judgment?

- ▶ Breathe deeply and focus on staying calm. Consider ways you can resolve this problem without fighting or running away.

Now it's your turn. Create a list of at least three more tips that you could share with a classmate to help him or her make better decisions when faced with a "fight or flight" situation.

1. _____

2. _____

3. _____

Step 2: Looking at Things Differently

Critical thinking involves looking at something you may have seen many times and examining it from many different angles and perspectives. It involves going beyond the obvious or beyond "easy" to seek new understanding and rare solutions. It encourages you to dig deeper than you have before, to get below the surface, to struggle, experiment, and expand. It asks you to look at something from an entirely different viewpoint so that you might develop new insights and understand more about the problem, situation, question, or solution. Critical thinking involves looking at **common issues** with uncommon eyes, **known problems** with new skepticism, **everyday conflicts** with probing curiosity, and **daily challenges** with greater attention to detail.

Review the "brain teasers" in Figures 5.6 to 5.8 and take the time to solve them even though you may not "get" them quickly. You may need to break down a few barriers in your thought processes and look at the puzzles from a new angle. Remember, these exercises do not measure intelligence. They are included to prod your thought processes along and help you look at things differently. Complete the puzzles before continuing.

How did you do? Was it hard to look at the situation backward or have to look for clues within a series of letters and numbers? Most of us are not used to that. But part of critical thinking is trying to find **clues** or **patterns.** Perhaps the easiest teaser in Figure 5.6 was number two. Most people know MLK as Martin Luther King, Jr. When you figure that part out, the name of his most popular speech, *I Have a Dream*, becomes easy to figure out. Often, when trying to solve problems or dealing with unknowns, things become easier when you can find a clue or a pattern and build from what you already know.

FIGURE 5.6 *Brain Teaser 1: Looking at Common Terms Abbreviated*

Consider the following clues. Two examples are given to help you get started. Answer the following ten teasers based on the clues.

Examples	4 W on a C	Four Wheels on a Car
	13 O C	Thirteen Original Colonies

1. SW and the 7D _____
2. I H a D by MLK _____
3. 2 Ps in a P _____
4. HDD (TMRUTC) _____
5. 3 S to a T _____
6. 100 P in a D _____
7. T no PLH _____
8. 4 Q in a G _____
9. I a SWAA _____
10. 50 S in t U _____

Examine the brain teaser in Figure 5.7. This teaser is included to help you look at an issue beyond what is actually given to you and to consider what is not given.

Once again, you are given a basic clue, but you must go beyond what is given. You must look at the nine dots, but you must NOT let them confine you. You can't let the nine dots control your thoughts—you must move beyond what is given, beyond what you actually see. When you do this, the answer will come to you.

As you continue to look at common things differently and think beyond the obvious, examine the penny in Figure 5.8.

Drawing inferences often requires the ability to look at things differently and take something very common and examine it like you have never examined it before. Just as you looked at the penny, you learned new things about it by studying it with different eyes. Think about

FIGURE 5.7 *Brain Teaser 2: Seeing What Is Not Given*

Look at the design below. You will find nine dots. Your mission is to connect all nine dots with four straight lines without removing your pencil or pen from the paper. Do not retrace your lines.

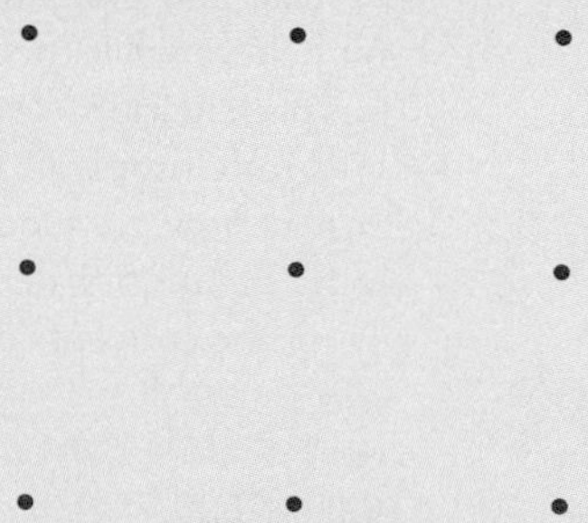

FIGURE

5.8 *Brain Teaser 3:*
The Penny

Pretend that all life on earth has ended and all traces of civilization are gone—there are no buildings, no people, no animals, no plants—nothing is left but dirt and one penny. Someone from another planet, who knows our language, comes to earth and finds the penny. List all of the things that could be inferred about our civilization based on this one small penny. You should find at least 10.

1. _____
2. _____
3. _____
4. _____
5. _____
6. _____
7. _____
8. _____
9. _____
10. _____

how you might solve a common problem that you face every day simply by looking at that problem with different eyes, too.

While these activities may seem somewhat trivial, they are provided to help you begin to think about and consider information from different angles. This is a major step in becoming a critical thinker: looking beyond the obvious, thinking outside the box, examining details, and exploring possibilities—basically, looking BEYOND what is given to you.

Step 3: Managing Information and Becoming Information Literate

Critical thinking involves knowing how to deal with all types of information, while ***information literacy*** refers to the skills a person needs to "recognize when information is needed and the ability to locate, evaluate, and effectively use the needed information" (American Library Association, 1989). *Information literacy* impacts all aspects of your college career and will later play a major role in your success in the workplace. You will use information literacy when you write a paper, read and evaluate an article, listen to presenters and determine if you believe what the speakers are saying, and prepare and make your own presentation.

Quite simply, if you are an information literate person, you have learned how to acquire and use information accurately and effectively. Figure 5.9 demonstrates a system for understanding and applying the concepts of information literacy.

"The sheer abundance of information will not in itself create a more informed citizenry without a complementary cluster of abilities necessary to use information correctly."

—ACRL

HOW CAN I EVALUATE MY RESEARCH SOURCES FOR VALIDITY, TIMELINESS, AND ACCURACY? A person who practices informa-

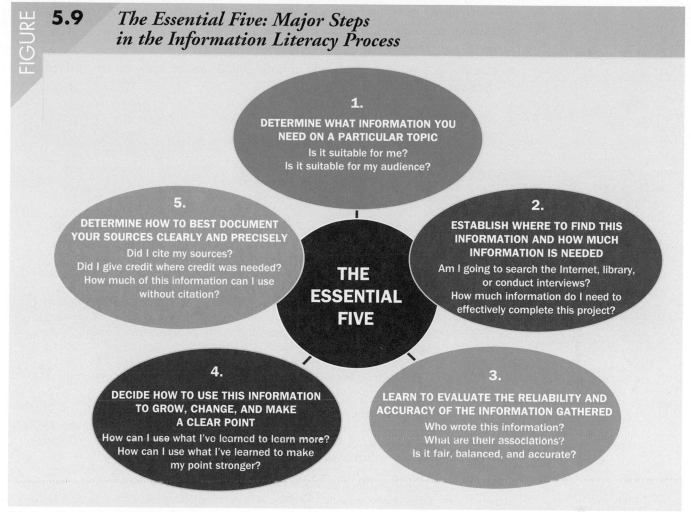

FIGURE 5.9 *The Essential Five: Major Steps in the Information Literacy Process*

1.
DETERMINE WHAT INFORMATION YOU NEED ON A PARTICULAR TOPIC
Is it suitable for me?
Is it suitable for my audience?

5.
DETERMINE HOW TO BEST DOCUMENT YOUR SOURCES CLEARLY AND PRECISELY
Did I cite my sources?
Did I give credit where credit was needed?
How much of this information can I use without citation?

2.
ESTABLISH WHERE TO FIND THIS INFORMATION AND HOW MUCH INFORMATION IS NEEDED
Am I going to search the Internet, library, or conduct interviews?
How much information do I need to effectively complete this project?

THE ESSENTIAL FIVE

4.
DECIDE HOW TO USE THIS INFORMATION TO GROW, CHANGE, AND MAKE A CLEAR POINT
How can I use what I've learned to learn more?
How can I use what I've learned to make my point stronger?

3.
LEARN TO EVALUATE THE RELIABILITY AND ACCURACY OF THE INFORMATION GATHERED
Who wrote this information?
What are their associations?
Is it fair, balanced, and accurate?

© Robert Sherfield and Patricia Moody

tion literacy not only knows **where** to find information, but **how to evaluate** the information found. Consider the steps to evaluating research sources in Figure 5.10.

IS THE LIBRARY STILL IMPORTANT IN THE DIGITAL AGE? Yes! The answer is yes! Many people think of libraries as places that are quiet as a tomb with a crabby old woman presiding over it who is prepared to pounce on you if you ask a question or touch one of her precious books. Fortunately, that stereotype went the way of the horse and buggy and today, libraries are literally the hub of a college campus. Your library is the key to unlock the secrets to your education and help you become more information literate. Your authors think it is safe to say, "You can't get an education if you try to bypass the library." Certainly, you can't write a solid research paper without using the library and its resources. Although the Internet is an amazing tool, serious research requires you to use the library and its tools such as print books, maps, charts, government data, periodicals, and your librarian. It may be fun and easy to use Google, Dogpile, or Wikipedia, but you will also need to hone your library research skills and critical thinking abilities.

Some of the ways your librarian can assist you include the following:

▶ Discovering, understanding, searching, and using the online catalog

▶ Narrowing your digital search to get to the information you need

▶ Searching other libraries for information and sources not available on your campus

▶ Discovering, using, and evaluating databases for almost every subject area

▶ Making use of interlibrary loan tools

▶ Introducing you to reference works in many critical areas of study that have proven validity, accuracy, and reliability

---

FIGURE

5.10 *Evaluating Research Sources*

Are the information and author credible, valid, accurate, and reliable?	▶ Who is the author and what are his or her credentials, educational background, past writings, or experience? Your task is to distinguish between the reliable and questionable, the knowledgeable and the amateur.
	▶ What edition is the source? Second and third editions suggest that the source has been updated to reflect changes and new knowledge.
	▶ Who is the publisher? If the source is published by a university press, it is likely to be a scholarly publication. There is a vast difference between information found in magazines such as *People* and *Us* versus information found in *The New England Journal of Medicine* and *The Journal of Social Archeology*.
	▶ Does the information appear to be valid and well researched or does it just gloss over the material? Does it have depth? Is it supported by evidence?
Is the article fact or opinion; popular or scholarly?	▶ What is the title of the source? This will help you determine if the source is popular, sensational, or scholarly and indicates the level of complexity. Popular journals are resources such as *Time, Newsweek, Vogue, Ebony,* and *Reader's Digest.* They seldom cite their sources. Sensational resources are often inflammatory and written on an elementary level. They usually have flashy headlines, and they cater to popular superstitions. Examples are *The Globe, The National Enquirer,* and *The Star.*
	▶ Is the source factually objective, is it opinionated, or is it propaganda? A factually objective article and credible opinion piece look at all angles, report on each one honestly, and cite their sources.
	▶ Are sources documented with footnotes or links? In scholarly works, the credibility of most assertions is proven through the footnote or endnote documentation.
Is it up to date and timely?	▶ When was the source published? If it is a webpage, the date is usually found on the last page or the home page. Is the source current or out of date for your topic?
	▶ When was the article last updated?
	▶ Is the page dated? Is it current enough for your research or is it "stale" and outdated?
Does it have depth?	▶ Who is the intended audience of your source? Is the information too simple, too advanced, or too technical for your audience?
Are the sources cited?	▶ Does the writer of the book, article, or website cite sources? If not, what does this mean to the credibility and reliability of the material?
Is it logical?	▶ Could the article be parody, humorous, or satire, yet cloaked as legitimate?
	▶ Does the information follow a logical flow of thoughts and arguments or make illogical leaps and assumptions?
Is it fair?	▶ Does the article present both sides of the argument? Is it balanced?
	▶ Was the article written by a neutral source on the topic or by someone with a vested interest in the topic or publication? Is this information an advertisement cloaked as a research article?

Source: Adapted from Ormondroyd, Engle, and Cosgrave (2001) and from Cornell University Libraries and UC Berkeley (2005).

Step 4: Asking Questions and Learning to Tolerate Uncertainty

You've asked questions all your life. As a child, you asked your parents, "What's that?" a million times. You probably asked them, "Why do I have to do this?" In later years, you've asked questions of your friends, teachers, strangers, store clerks, and significant others.

> *"It is not possible to become a good thinker and be a poor questioner. Thinking is not driven by answers, but, rather, by questions."*
> *—Paul and Elder*

Questioning is not new to you, but it may be a new technique to you for exploring, developing, and honing your critical thinking skills. Curiosity may have killed the cat, but it was a smart cat when it died! Your curiosity is one of the most important traits you possess. It helps you grow and learn, and sometimes it may cause you to be uncomfortable. That's OK. This section is provided to assist you in learning how to ask questions to promote knowledge, solve problems, foster strong relationships, and critically analyze difficult situations. It is also included to help you understand the value of knowing how to tolerate uncertainty and avoid jumping to faulty conclusions because uncertainty "got the better of you." It is important to know that sometimes, *the question is more important than the answer*—especially a faulty answer.

TYPES OF QUESTIONS. Basically, there are three types of questions, according to Paul and Elder (2006):

- ▶ **Questions of Fact**
  Require answers based in fact and evidence and have correct and incorrect reponses
  Example: What is the freezing point of water?

- ▶ **Questions of Preference**
  Require answers that state a subjective preference and do not necessarily have correct or incorrect responses
  Example: What is your favorite color?

- ▶ **Questions of Judgment**
  Require answers derived from your judgment based in logic and evidence and can have more than one defensible answer
  Example: Should *Roe vs. Wade* be overturned?

Asking questions helps us gain insight where we may have limited knowledge. Answering properly posed questions can also help us expand our knowledge base. For example, if you were assigned to write a paper or give a speech on the topic of *creationism versus evolution*, what five questions would you definitely want that paper or speech to answer when you are finished writing and delivering it? Take some time to think about this issue. Write down at least five questions that you consider essential to the topic of creationism versus evolution.

My five questions are:

1. _____

2. _____

3. _____

4. _____

5. _____

Learning to ask probing questions can help you in everyday situations by challenging you to look beyond the obvious and critically examine everyday situations. Examine the car advertisement in Figure 5.11. The car dealership has provided some information, but it is not enough to make a smart, rational decision. What other questions would you ask the dealer to make sure that you are getting a good deal?

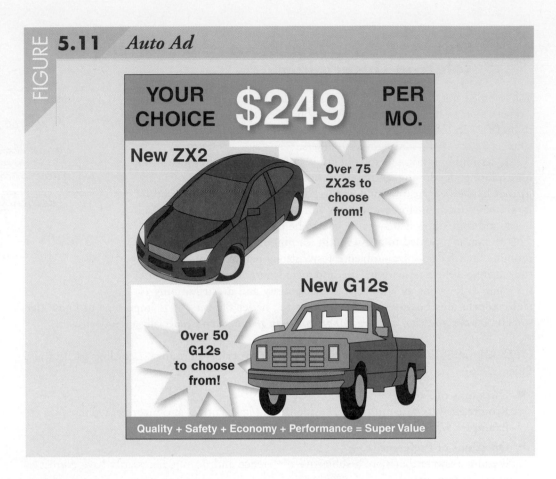

FIGURE 5.11 *Auto Ad*

What additional questions would you need to ask the dealer to ensure that you are getting a "good" deal?

1. _____

2. _____

3. _____

4. _____

5. _____

CAN YOU TOLERATE UNCERTAINTY? Asking questions that can be answered is vitally important to critical thinking, but so is learning to tolerate uncertainty and learning to ask questions that may not have an immediate answer. Uncertainty causes you to keep going—to not get lazy or give up. If we thought we knew the answers to everything, we would still be beating rocks together to make fire and we would still be walking everywhere instead of driving or flying. Uncertainty causes humanity to move forward and create new knowledge, to try new things, to consider the impossible. Uncertainty also breeds creative thinking.

Think about all of the uncertainty that can arise in your daily life:

"Can I be certain that my spouse/partner will not leave me?" No.
"Can I be certain that I will remain healthy?" No.
"Can I be certain that my children will turn out to be good, caring, loving adults?" No.
"Can I be certain what happens to me after I die?" No.
"Can I be certain that the plane won't crash or that someone won't crash into my car?" No.
"Can I be certain that this will not embarrass me or someone else?" No.
"Can I be certain that my investments will grow and I can retire comfortably?" No.

The inability to tolerate uncertainty can cause stress and anxiety. Sometimes, we just have to "let go" and accept that we do not know the answers. We can work hard to try to find the answers and/or direct our actions so that the answers will be favorable to us, but ultimately, many things in this universe require our tolerance of uncertainty. Sometimes, the best we can hope for is to keep asking questions and seeking the truth.

Think of the good things that initially unanswered questions and uncertainty brought to humanity in many fields of study.

"Can we send someone to the moon and have them return safely?"
"Can we transplant a human heart and have that person live and prosper afterward?"
"Can we establish a new country with a new constitution and have it work?"
"Can we design and build a skyscraper that is over 140 stories high and have it remain safe?"
"Can we create an automobile that will get over 50 miles per gallon of fuel?"
"Can we help reduce global warming and its effects on the polar ice caps?"

All of these uncertainties have contributed to the development of new knowledge, new skills, new jobs, new outlooks, and new ways of living. Therefore, it is important to remember that in your quest for answers, sometimes uncertainty can be the most important thing you discover.

Step 5: Identifying, Defining, Narrowing, and Solving Problems

What would your life be like if you had no problems? Most people do not like to face or deal with problems, but the critical thinker knows that problems exist every day and that they must be faced and hopefully solved. Some of our problems are larger and more difficult than others, but we all face problems from time to time. You may have transportation problems. You may have financial problems. You may have child care problems. You may have academic problems or interpersonal problems. Many people don't know how to solve problems at school, home, or work. They simply let the problem go unaddressed until it is too late to reach a reasonable solution. But there are many ways to address and solve problems. In this section, we will discuss how to **identify and narrow** the problem, **research and develop** alternatives, **evaluate** the alternatives, and **solve** the problem.

Every problem may not have a solution. That can be a hard pill for many people to swallow, but it is a raw truth and a part of the uncertainty we just discussed. Many problems have solutions, but the solution may not be the one you wanted. It is imperative to remember the words of Mary Hatwood Futrell, President of the National Education Agency. She states that *"finding the right answer is important, of course. But more important is developing the ability to see that many problems have multiple solutions, that getting from X to Y demands basic skills and mental agility, imagination, persistence, patience."* Consider the problem-solving model in Figure 5.12.

IDENTIFY THE SYMPTOMS. *Symptoms* and *problems* are not the same thing. Symptoms are PART of the problem, but may not be the problem itself. Think of a problem like you think of your health. For example, you may have aches in your joints, cold chills, and a severe headache. Those seem like problems, but in actuality they are really symptoms of something larger—perhaps the flu or an infection. You can treat the headache with medicine and soothe your joint pain with ointment, but until you get at the ROOT of the problem, these symptoms will come back. Problems are much the same way. If you don't move beyond the symptoms, the problem may seem to be solved, but shortly it will reappear, usually worse than before. Therefore, it is imperative that you identify the symptoms of the **greater problem** before you begin solving anything.

NARROW THE SYMPTOMS TO FIND THE ROOT PROBLEM. Often, problems keep coming up because we did not deal with the *real problem*— the root problem—but, rather, we dealt with a symptom. Getting to the

"When I'm getting ready to reason with a man, I spend one-third of my time thinking about myself and what I am going to say—and two-thirds thinking about him and what he is going to say."
—Abraham Lincoln

FIGURE **5.12** *Steps in the Problem-Solving Process*

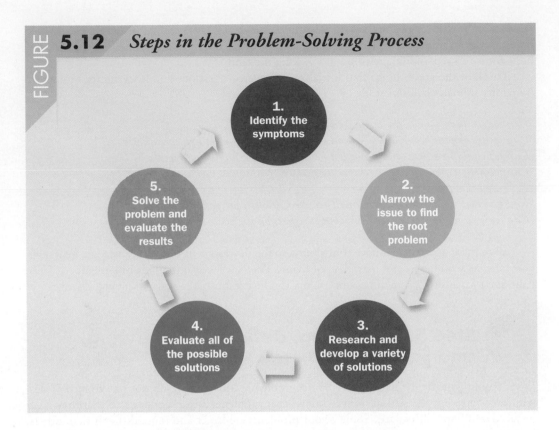

heart of a problem is hard work that requires a great deal of thought, research, and patience. Begin by putting your symptoms in writing, perhaps on note cards, so that you can lay them out and see them all at once. When doing this, be sure to jot down all of the major and minor symptoms as in the following list:

▶ What are the daily challenges that keep coming up?

▶ Who is involved?

▶ How are the symptoms hindering your overall goals?

▶ Who or what is responsible for creating these symptoms?

▶ Are the symptoms internal (self-inflicted) or external (other-inflicted)?

▶ What obstacles are these symptoms creating?

▶ Are the symptoms part of ONE major problem or several problems?

RESEARCH AND DEVELOP A VARIETY OF SOLUTIONS. It is a mistake to try to solve a problem when you don't have enough information to do so. It may be that you need to conduct interviews, research what others have done who face similar issues, read current data and reports, or even explore historical documents. Paul and Elder (2006) suggest that the type of information you need is determined by the type of problem you have and the question(s) you are trying to answer: "If you have a historical question, you need *historical information.* If you have a biological question, you need *biological information.* If you have an ethical question, you must identify at least one relevant *ethical principle.*" Therefore, part of the problem-solving process is to gather your facts—the correct facts—before you try to reach a resolution.

EVALUATE AND ANALYZE ALL OF THE POSSIBLE SOLUTIONS. After you have gathered your research (through formal methods and/or brainstorming), you must now evaluate your solutions to determine which would work best and why. After careful study and deliberation, without emotional interference, analyze the solutions you came up with and determine if they are appropriate or inappropriate. To analyze them, create Columns A and B. Write the possible *solutions in Column A* and an evaluative *comment in Column B.*

SUCCESSFUL DECISIONS: An Activity for Critical Reflection

Carson's class was assigned an activity asking them to determine whom they would like to meet if they could meet anyone and which questions they would like to ask them. Some of the class members thought it was a stupid assignment—and Carson was not so sure that she wanted to spend any time on this "weird" activity either. That evening, she began to think about the question seriously. "Who has been important to the world?" she thought. "Who has done something powerful and extraordinary?" "Who has been awful and caused needless pain?"

She decided that if she could ask anyone anything, she would choose Hitler. She decided that she would ask him these questions: (1) If you had to do it all over again, would you? (2) From where did your hatred come? (3) Why did you have everyone killed who could have revealed your own past? (4) You did not look like the master race you chose to promote. Why did you choose to promote it? (5) Why did you become such a coward in the end and kill yourself?

This interesting project led Carson to use WWII, Hitler, and the German occupation as the basis for her presentation in speech class. She did not just brush off what had seemed to be a "weird" assignment.

In your own words, what three suggestions would you give to a classmate who thinks an assignment is weird or useless? Be specific.

1. _____

2. _____

3. _____

Example (Using the problem "I don't have enough time to study due to my job"):
With your comments in Column B, you can now begin to eliminate some of the alternatives that are inappropriate at this time.

A (POSSIBLE SOLUTIONS)	B (COMMENTS)
Quit the job.	Very hard to do. I need the money for tuition and car.
Cut my hours at work.	Will ask my boss.
Find a new job.	Hard to do because of the job market—but will look into it.
Get a student loan.	Visit financial aid office tomorrow.
Quit school.	No—it is my only chance for a promotion.

SOLVE THE PROBLEM AND EVALUATE THE RESULTS. Now that you have a few strong possible solutions, you have some work to do. You will need to talk to your boss, go to the financial aid office, and possibly begin to search for a new job with flexible hours. Basically, you are creating a PLAN to bring this solution to life. After you have researched each possible solution further, you will be able to make a decision based on solid information and facts. You will be able to figure out which solution is the best option for you.

Using the diagram in Figure 5.13, work through the following situation and determine the steps that could be taken to solve this problem.

YOUR TURN: Pretend that your best friend, Nathan, has just come to you with a problem. He tells you that his parents are really coming down hard on him for going to college. It is a strange problem. They believe that Nathan should be working full time and that he is just wasting his time and money, because he did not do well in high school. They have threatened to take away his car and kick him out of the house if he does not find a full-time job. Nathan is doing well and does not want to leave college. He has a goal of

"Everyone is entitled to their own opinion, but not their own facts."
—Senator Daniel Patrick Moynihan

FIGURE

5.13 *Effective Problem Solving*

Summarize the situation in your own words.

_____
_____
_____
_____
_____
_____
_____

Symptom 1 that the problem is real

_____
_____

Symptom 2 that the problem is real

_____
_____

Symptom 3 that the problem is real

_____
_____

Identify the ROOT problem.

_____
_____
_____
_____
_____
_____
_____

Possible solution 1

_____
_____

Possible solution 2

_____
_____

Research possible solutions.
What did you find?

Possible solution 3

_____
_____

Evaluate the solutions.

Solution 1
Comments

_____
_____
_____

Solution 2
Comments

_____
_____
_____

Create a PLAN to solve the problem.
I plan to. . .

_____
_____
_____
_____
_____

Solution 3
Comments

_____
_____
_____

becoming an architect and knows that he has talent in this area. He is making A's and B's in all of his classes. This does not matter to his parents. They do not value education and see it as a luxury.

Step 6: Distinguishing Fact from Opinion

An important aspect of critical thinking is the ability to distinguish fact from opinion. *In most media—TV, radio, newspapers, magazines, and the Internet—opinions surface more often than facts. Reread the previous sentence.* This is an example of an opinion cloaked as a fact. There is no research supporting this opinion. It sounds as if it could be true, but without evidence and proof, it is just an opinion.

A fact is something that can be ***proven***, something that can be ***objectively veri-fied***. An opinion is a statement that is held to be true, but has no objective proof. *Statements that cannot be proven should always be treated as opinion.* Statements that offer valid proof and verification from credible, reliable sources can be treated as factual.

Learning to distinguish fact from opinion can be a paramount step in building your critical thinking skills at work, with family, and especially when analyzing media.

Step 7: Seeking Truth in Arguments and Persuasion

Whether or not you realize it, arguments and persuasive efforts are around you daily—hourly, for that matter. They are in newspaper and TV ads, editorials, news commentaries, talk shows, TV magazine shows, political statements, and religious services. It seems at times that almost everyone is trying to persuade us through arguments or advice. This section is included to assist you in recognizing faulty arguments and implausible or deceptive persuasion.

First, let's start with a list of terms used to describe faulty arguments and deceptive persuasion. As you read through the list in the terminology box on the next page, try to identify situations in which you have heard arguments that fit these descriptions.

IDENTIFYING FALLACIOUS ARGUMENTS. Below, you will find statements intended to persuade you or argue for a cause. Beside each statement, identify which type of faulty persuasion is used.

AB	Ad baculum	**SA**	Straw argument	**AH**	Ad hominem
AT	Appeal to tradition	**AP**	Ad populum	**PF**	Plain folks
AV	Ad verecundiam	**PM**	Patriotism	**BW**	Bandwagon
ST	Scare tactic	**GG**	Glittering generalities		

_____ 1. *This country has never faltered in the face of adversity. Our strong, united military has seen us through many troubled times, and it will see us through our current situation. This is your country; support your military.*

_____ 2. *If I am elected to office, I will personally lobby for lower taxes, a new comprehensive crime bill, a $2,500 tax cut on every new home, and better education, and I will personally work to lower the unemployment rate.*

_____ 3. *This is the best college in the region. All of your friends will be attending this fall. You don't want to be left out; you should join us, too.*

_____ 4. *If you really listen to Governor Wise's proposal on health care, you will see that there is no way that we can have a national system. You will not be able to select your doctor, you will not be able to go to the hospital of your choice, and you will not be able to get immediate attention. His proposal is not as comprehensive as our proposal.*

Terminology for Fallacious Arguments

Ad baculum	Ad baculum is an argument that tries to persuade based on force. Threats of alienation, disapproval, or even violence may accompany this type of argument.
Ad hominem	Ad hominem is when someone initiates a personal attack on someone else rather than listening to and rationally debating the person's ideas. This is also referred to as "slander."
Ad populum	An ad populum argument is based on the opinions of the majority of people. It assumes that because the majority says X is right, then Y is not. It uses little logic.
Ad verecundiam	This argument uses quotes and phrases from people in authority or popular people to support one's own views.
Appeal to tradition	This argument looks only at the past and suggests that because we have always done it "this way," we should continue to do it "this way."
Bandwagon	The bandwagon approach tries to convince you to do something just because everyone else is doing it. It is also referred to as "peer pressure."
Glittering Generalities	This type of persuasion or argumentation is an appeal to generalities (Bosak, 1976). It suggests that a person, candidate, or professional is for all the "right" things: justice, low taxes, no inflation, rebates, full employment, low crime, free tuition, progress, privacy, and truth.
Patriotism	This form of persuasion asks you to ignore reason and logic and support what is right for state A or city B or nation C.
Plain folks	This type of persuasion is used to make you feel that the people making the argument are just like you. Usually, they are not; they are only using this appeal to connect with your sense of space and time.
Scare tactic	A scare tactic is used as a desperate measure to put fear in your life. If you don't do X, then Y is going to happen to you.
Straw argument	The straw argument attacks the opponent's argument to make one's own argument stronger. It does not necessarily make argument A stronger; it simply discounts argument B.

_____ 5. *My father went to Honors College, I went to Honors College, and you will go to Honors College. It is the way things have been for the people in this family. There is no need to break with tradition now.*

_____ 6. *The witness's testimony is useless. He is an alcoholic; he is dishonest and corrupt. To make matters worse, he was a member of the Leftist Party.*

_____ 7. *The gentleman on the witness stand is your neighbor, he is your friend, he is just like you. Sure, he may have more money and drive a Mercedes, but his heart never left the Elm Community.*

_____ 8. *John F. Kennedy once said, "Ask not what your country can do for you; ask what you can do for your country." This is the time to act, my fellow citizens. You can give $200 to our cause and you will be fulfilling the wish of President Kennedy.*

_____ 9. *Out of the 7,000 people polled, 72 percent believe that there is life beyond our planet. Therefore, there must be life beyond earth.*

_____ 10. *Without this new medication, you will die.*

_____ 11. *I don't care what anyone says. If you don't come around to our way of thinking, you'd better start watching your back.*

> *"There is nothing so powerful as truth, and often, nothing so strange."*
> —Daniel Webster

As you develop your critical thinking skills, you will begin to recognize the illogical nature of many thoughts, the falsehoods of many statements, the deception in some advertisements, and the irrational fears used to persuade. You will also begin to understand the depths to which you should delve to achieve objectivity, the thought and care that you should give to your own decisions and statements, and the methods by which you can build logical, truthful arguments.

Step 8: Thinking Creatively and Being Resourceful

Creative thinking is a major and important aspect of critical thinking, in that you are producing something that is uniquely yours—introducing something to the world that is new, innovative, and useful. Creative thinking does not mean that you have to be an artist, a musician, or a writer. Creative thinking instead means that you have examined a situation and developed a new way of explaining information, delivering a product, or using an item. It can be as simple as discovering that you can use a small rolling suitcase to carry your books around campus instead of the traditional backpack. Creative thinking means that you have opened your mind to possibilities!

Creative thinking is really about being resourceful—and in today's times, resourcefulness is a powerful tool. Resourcefulness is an **internal** quality, not an **external** gift. If you have ever seen the TV series *Survivorman* or *Man vs. Wild*, you know that it takes a strong person to eat a slug just carved out of a tree trunk. It takes internal will to drink water with so many bacteria that flies die when they drink it. Yes, both shows are somewhat staged, but they show the basics of creativity, intelligence, imagination, and **resourcefulness**.

To truly understand resourcefulness, you need look no further than a child playing in the backyard. *"What does a worthless old stick become?"* Because of a child's inability to see limitations, the stick becomes a medieval sword, Luke Skywalker's light saber, an old man's cane, a crutch, a magic wand, a baseball bat, a witch's stirring stick, or a marshmallow roaster. An old stick now has limitless possibilities because the child refused to see it only as a stick. His refusal to be boxed into the confines of our adult reality created possibilities. Sometimes, we have to become that child and use every stick we have just to survive.

Think of internal resourcefulness as **renewable energy**. When you have to draw on your wits, creativity, and determination, these qualities multiply. The more you are required by circumstances to use these qualities, the stronger and more plentiful they become. Conversely, if you've always been able to buy anything you want or if all that you need is provided to you by an external force, your internal resourcefulness begins to wither and die like uneaten fruit on the winter vine. You are not forced to use the whole of yourself. Your energy fades. Your harvest dies.

Your inner resourcefulness and creativity also make you more secure and offer more protection from outside forces. When you know how to make ends meet, you can always do it. When you know how to pay the rent on limited income, you can always do it. When you know how to cut firewood to heat your home, you can always do it. When you know how to navigate the public transportation system in your town, you can always do it; even when the time comes that you don't have to "do it" anymore, you could if you had to. The more you know and the more inner strength and resourcefulness you have, the safer you are against the unknown. The more confidence you possess, the greater the likelihood that you can survive anything at any time. The more resourceful you are, the more you understand that this one quality will help you rebuild all that may have been lost. When the world *HAS* been handed to you on a silver platter, you cannot be ready for what the world *CAN* hand you.

To begin the creative process, consider the items in Figure 5.14. These are some of the characteristics creative thinkers have in common. Using your imaginative and innovative juices, think about how you would *creatively* solve the following problem. Write down at least five possibilities. Come on, make it count!

Jennifer is a first-year student who does not have enough money to pay her tuition, buy her books, and purchase a few new outfits and shoes to wear to class and her work-study job on campus.

Stockdisc

Why is it important to read and research possible solutions before you make decisions?

If you had to use your creativity to survive in the wild, could you do it?

Getty Images RF

From Ordinary to *Extraordinary*

DR. WAYNE A. JONES
Assistant Professor and Thurgood Marshall Pathways Fellow
Department of Political Science and Public Administration
Virginia State University, Petersburg, Virginia

I come from a fine family. My mother is a retired social worker, college professor and community activist and my father, a retired Presbyterian minister and college professor. They provided a safe, structured environment and always have encouraged me to do well. Clearly, I had the foundation to do well in school. However I have not always followed my parents' advice. This was especially true for my senior year in high school. The outcome was that I did not graduate. So at 18, I was working, had my own apartment and things were OK. At least, so I thought.

I had always been interested in anything that had wheels on it. If it has wheels, I could drive it —or wanted to! I drove a bus for a few years and then I drove an ambulance. One day, however, I saw our local bookmobile and I wanted to drive it. I applied to do so, but found out that I had to have a high school diploma to be able to drive the bookmobile. At 19, this was my reason for going back to get my GED. Now, I could master driving yet another "thing" with wheels. It was not, however, as exciting as I thought it would be.

My parents begged me to begin my college studies. Reluctantly, at age 21, I enrolled at Virginia Commonwealth University. After only one year, I knew that college was not for me. I dropped out. In 1975, I began working for the police department in Chesterfield, VA. I was only the second African American police officer on the force. I held this position for five years.

My desire for wheels was still with me. I left the police department and began working for the Virginia Overland Transportation Company as a safety supervisor. I worked my way up to become supervisor of transportation. With this experience under my belt, I went to work for a transit company in Richmond, Virginia, driving a city transit bus. I left the second bus company after a year to drive for a local construction company. This work, however, turned out to be very "seasonal" and I found myself frequently without income. I asked to be allowed to drive one of their trash trucks so that I could have a steady income and overtime, too. So, there I was in my late twenties, without a college degree,

driving a trash truck. There was not a lot to look forward to.

My late grandmother called me one day and asked me why I didn't go back to college. "You are far from dumb," I remember her telling me. I tried to explain to her that I was making decent money and I could not quit my job. I told her that it would take me at least eight years to get my degree. "I'll be too old by then," I told her. She then said the words that woke me up and changed my life. "Son," she said, "unless you die, you're going to be eight years older in eight years anyway, why not be eight years older with a college degree?"

That was my wake-up call. I found another job with more flexible hours and enrolled at John Tyler Community College with no idea of what I wanted to become. Shortly after I re-enrolled in college, my grandmother died. Her final gift to me was her wonderful words of wisdom.

So, there I was, working full time, going to college full time, and barely having enough time to even visit my family who lived nearby. One night, I received another phone call that changed my life again. My parents called me and told me that they wanted to talk with me about money. I visited them and to my surprise, they asked me to quit work and concentrate on my studies. "Grandmother had a vision," my mother told me. "She knew that you were going to do great things." They told me that if I quit, they would pay my bills until I finished college. I agreed to take their help.

I transferred from John Tyler Community College and enrolled again at Virginia Commonwealth University. My GPA was not great upon graduation. I took the Graduate Record Exam (GRE) and scored very badly. I was turned down for the graduate program in Public Administration. I was now 35. I met with the director of admissions and said to him, "Just give me a chance, I know I can do this."

In just a few short years, I managed to go from driving a trash truck to being a university professor.

After some conversation, he agreed to give me a chance. I completed my Masters of Public Administration in only 18 months. I applied to the doctoral program in public administration at VCU. The chairman of the doctoral program reviewed my GRE scores and basically told me that based on them, I should not have been able to obtain a master's degree. Then, I applied to George Washington University for their Ph.D. program.

Once again, the admissions office looked at my scores and basically told me that my master's degree was "just a fluke." I was accepted provisionally and only five years later, I graduated with a 3.85. My dissertation won the Outstanding Dissertation of the Year Award in 2000 from the George Washington University chapter of Phi Delta Kappa. I was not a fluke anymore.

I began working as Director of Adult Day Care for a United Way Agency and loved it. It was then that the thought of becoming a college professor came to mind. I saw an ad in the paper for a part-time teaching position working with advanced-placement students. I found the love of my life — teaching. I later applied to become a full-time faculty member at Virginia State University and today, I teach freshman studies and public administration.

EXTRAORDINARY REFLECTION

Read the following statement and respond in your online journal or class notebook.

Dr. Jones was brave enough to take an enormous risk, quit his full-time job, accept help, and reach his goals. Whom do you have in your life that you can depend on for support (maybe not monetary support, but crucial support of your goals, dreams, and educational plans)? Why?

What should she do? Should she pay her tuition and purchase her books, or pay her tuition and buy new clothes and shoes to wear to class and work? What creative, resourceful ideas (solutions) can you give Jennifer?

My Creative Solutions

1. _____

2. _____

3. _____

4. _____

5. _____

FIGURE

5.14   *Characteristics of Creative Thinking*

COMPASSION	Creative thinkers have a zest for life and genuinely care for the spirit of others.	**Example:** More than 40 years ago, community members who wanted to feed the elderly created Meals on Wheels, now a national organization feeding the elderly.
COURAGE	Creative thinkers are unafraid to try new things, to implement new thoughts and actions.	**Example:** An NBC executive moves the *Today Show* out of a closed studio onto the streets of New York, creating the number one morning news show in the United States.
TRUTH	Creative thinkers search for the true meaning of things.	**Example:** The astronomer and scientist Copernicus sought to prove that earth was *not* the center of the universe— an unpopular view at the time.
DREAMS	Creative thinkers allow themselves time to dream and ponder the unknown. They can see what is possible, not just what is actual.	**Example:** John F. Kennedy dreamed that space exploration was possible. His dream became reality.
RISK TAKING	Creative thinkers take positive risks every day. They are not afraid to go against popular opinion.	**Example:** Barack Obama took a risk and ran for president of the United States. He became one of only a few African Americans to ever run for the office and the only African American to be nominated by his party. In November of 2008, he became the first African American president of the United States.
INNOVATION	Creative thinkers find new ways to do old things.	**Example:** Instead of continuing to fill the earth with waste such as aluminum, plastic, metal, and old cars, means were developed to recycle these materials for future productive use.
COMPETITION	Creative thinkers strive to be better, to think bolder thoughts, to do what is good, and to be the best at any task.	**Example:** A textbook writer updates the publication every three years to include new and revised information so the product remains competitive.
INDIVIDUALITY	Creative thinkers are not carbon copies of other people. They strive to be true to themselves.	**Example:** A young man decides to take tap dancing instead of playing baseball. He excels and wins a fine arts dancing scholarship to college.
CURIOSITY	Creative thinkers are interested in all things; they want to know much about many things.	**Example:** A 65-year-old retired college professor goes back to college to learn more about music appreciation and computer programming to expand her possibilities.
PERSEVERANCE	Creative thinkers do not give up. They stick to a project to its logical and reasonable end.	**Example:** Dr. Martin Luther King, Jr., did not give up on his dream in the face of adversity, danger, and death threats.

CREATING your NEW REALITY

REFLECTIONS ON CRITICAL AND CREATIVE THINKING

Critical thinking, emotional intelligence, and information literacy require a great deal of commitment on your part. They may not be easy for everyone at first, but with practice, dedication, and an understanding of the immense need for all three, everyone can think more critically and logically, evaluate information sources, and use emotional intelligence to best advantage.

Critical thinking and emotional intelligence can affect the way you live your life, from strengthening relationships to purchasing a new car, from solving family problems to investing money, from taking the appropriate classes for graduation to getting a promotion at work. Both are vitally important to your growth and education.

As you continue on in the semester and work toward personal and professional motivation and change, consider the following ideas:

▶ Use only *credible* and *reliable* sources.
▶ Learn to distinguish *fact* from *opinion*.
▶ Be *flexible* in your thinking and *avoid* generalizations.
▶ Use emotional intelligence and *restraint* to your best advantage.
▶ Avoid *stereotyping* and prejudging and strive for *objectivity* in your thinking.
▶ *Reserve* judgment until you have looked at every side.
▶ Do *not* assume—do the research and *ask* questions.
▶ Work hard to distinguish *symptoms from problems*.

Critical thinking is truly the hallmark of an educated person. It is a hallmark of character and integrity, and a hallmark of successful students. Let it be yours.

> *"The significant problems we face cannot be solved at the same level of thinking we were at when we created them."*
>
> —*Albert Einstein*

ANSWERS TO TEASERS pp. 123–124

Brain Teaser #1, Looking at Common Terms Abbreviated

1. Snow White and the Seven Dwarfs
2. I Have a Dream by Martin Luther King, Jr.
3. Two peas in a pod
4. Hickory dickory dock, the mouse ran up the clock
5. Three sides to a triangle
6. One hundred pennies in a dollar
7. There's no place like home
8. Four quarts in a gallon
9. "It's A Small World After All"
10. Fifty states in the Union

Brain Teaser #2, Seeing What Is Not Given

(Hint: You have to think "outside the box." Look beyond what is given to you.)

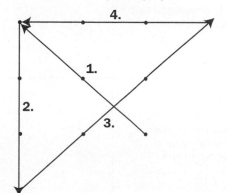

Brain Teaser #3, The Penny

Your answers might include ideas such as the following:

▶ We had more than one language.
▶ We knew geometry.
▶ We had a calendar system.
▶ We honored people.
▶ We knew metallurgy.
▶ We knew math.
▶ We knew architecture.
▶ We were united.
▶ We valued liberty.

CREATE SUCCESS
Your Journey to University, Career, and Life Beyond College

## Connecting Think about the people on your college campus. With whom can you make a connection to learn more about *emotional intelligence skills?* (Example: counselor, advisor, retention specialist, etc.) Why and how will this connection be important?	
## Reading Find one brief, relevant article (in print or online) relating to *information literacy.* After you have read the article, write a brief summary of the additional facts you have learned.	
## E-Learning Consider a real problem with which you are dealing that you would not mind sharing with someone else. Using your social networking site or even your cell phone, text or tell someone about your problem. Ask for advice. Seek several opinions. Now, using what you've learned about problem solving and the advice you have been given, work to solve your problem using the model in Figure 5.13.	
## Analyzing Choose one main idea or topic from this chapter. After exploring and researching this idea further, determine how this information can help you succeed in other classes.	
## Transitioning How will you use the content found in this chapter to help you create a successful transition plan to your next semester and beyond?	
## Empowering Thinking about the entire spectrum of your life (college, family, friends, finances, career, etc.), how can you empower yourself to be more successful through the information found in this chapter?	

SQ3R *Mastery* Study Sheet

EXAMPLE QUESTION *(from page 117)* Why is emotional intelligence important to critical thinking?		**ANSWER:**
EXAMPLE QUESTION *(from page 124)* What is information literacy?		**ANSWER:**
AUTHOR QUESTION *(from page 119)* Why is emotional intelligence important?		**ANSWER:**
AUTHOR QUESTION *(from page 125)* Discuss the steps in information literacy.		**ANSWER:**
AUTHOR QUESTION *(from page 127)* Why is asking questions so important in critical thinking?		**ANSWER:**
AUTHOR QUESTION *(from page 133)* Define *fact* and *opinion* and give an example of each.		**ANSWER:**
AUTHOR QUESTION *(from page 134)* Define *ad hominem* and find an example of this in a recent newspaper or magazine article.		**ANSWER:**
YOUR QUESTION *(from page ____)*		**ANSWER:**
YOUR QUESTION *(from page ____)*		**ANSWER:**
YOUR QUESTION *(from page ____)*		**ANSWER:**
YOUR QUESTION *(from page ____)*		**ANSWER:**
YOUR QUESTION *(from page ____)*		**ANSWER:**

Finally, after answering these questions, recite this chapter's major points in your mind. Consider the following general questions to help you master this material.

► What was it about?
► What does it mean?
► What was the most important thing I learned? Why?
► What were the key points to remember?

CHAPTER 6
PRIORITIZE

PLANNING
YOUR
TIME AND
REDUCING
STRESS

"If you want to make good use of your time, you've got to know what's most important and then give it all you've got."

—Lee Iacocca

WHY READ THIS CHAPTER?

What's in it for me?

WHY does time management play a role in my value system and self-discipline? WHY is time management so important to the quality of my life? WHY do I need to know about stress and what causes it? WHY is learning to reduce anxiety and manage stress important to my overall success?

Why? Because poor time management and stress are partners in crime. Poor time management leads to more stress and more stress leads to poor time management skills. It is a vicious cycle. Time, of course, is not the only thing in your life that can cause stress. Stress can be brought on by relationships, work, family issues, and money problems, to name a few. However, by learning to effectively manage your time, you can reduce a major factor that contributes to the stress levels in your life. Have you ever looked at your peers who have children, a full-time job (or two jobs), and outside activities, and yet they still get it all done? *"How do they do that?"* The answer is they have figured out what they value and how to apply their values to their time management plans.

By carefully reading this chapter and taking the information provided seriously, you will be able to:

▶ Discuss the relationship between time management, your value system, and self-discipline.

▶ Beat procrastination and get more done.

▶ Evaluate how you spend your time and develop a "to do" list based on your findings.

▶ Understand the relationship between poor time management and stress.

▶ Identify the major stressors in your life.

CHAPTER 6 | PRIORITIZE

"Nothing is a waste of time if you use the experience wisely."

—Rodin

PATTY MONTELLA
Graduate!

*Erie Community College,
Williamsville, New York*

How my COMMUNITY COLLEGE changed my life

An interview conducted and written by

SHERYL DUQUETTE
Asst. Project Director and Instructor, Erie Community College

Patty grew up in one of Buffalo's west-side neighborhoods. She shared the characteristic thinking of her friends and family that everything this world had to offer could be found within that three-block radius. Patty remembers never challenging nor wanting more than what her neighborhood offered. *"That was the way it was for all us living there,"* she recalls. *"Everything—school, shopping, and church were all within a short walk."*

Asked about high school, Patty recalls being an average student with average enthusiasm. *"I didn't really like English, yet somehow made it through."* Any interest to pursue higher education was quickly curtailed with the birth of her first child. Marriage and additional children helped replicate the insulated lifestyle she knew growing up. Like many moms in the neighborhood, Patty needed to work to help support the family income. She became a certified nurse's aide at the local nursing home. Patty said, *"I really loved caring for my patients . . . and I had a favorite. When she passed away, something triggered in me the idea that I needed to be able to do more with my patients . . . and that is what motivated me to go back to school."*

Patty enrolled at Erie Community College for the fall semester determined to become a nurse. She was registered in the pre-nursing track of courses including a health career exploration course. *"I loved that course! I was introduced to so many different health careers by the guest speakers . . . it was the first time I realized I had options outside of what I had been doing."* Patty recalls a required paper for the course. *"There was a cultural diversity paper we had to write. I remember interviewing my coworker from Cuba. I had known this guy for some time yet never really talked with him about his past. His story was so interesting and I was amazed by his struggles. I did a really good job on that paper. It built my confidence, not just with my education but with my appreciation for people from different backgrounds. It was the beginning of my learning not to pre judge and to listen to others. I still have the paper."*

Patty matriculated into the college's Ophthalmic Dispensing Program a few semesters later. With guidance and support from the department, her peers, and family, Patty continued to excel in her academics. *"I fell in love with learning and everyone who knew me could see it!"* What was so evident was her self-confidence and her personal development. Patty noted that she was exercising regularly, reading, and watching the evening news, activities that had never interested her prior to school. Patty graduated from the Ophthalmic Dispensing Program in spring 2009.

She is happily employed at the University of Buffalo's Ross Eye Institute assisting physicians. *"I love what I do today. Being situated at a university, I work with a variety of doctors, residents, and patients from diverse backgrounds. My community college experience has broadened my perspective of people, and of myself. It's wonderful!"*

THINK ABOUT IT

1. Patty's past work experiences helped her decide on a college major. What past experiences have you had that are impacting your career choices in college? Why?

2. Patty is now employed at the University of Buffalo's Ross Eye Institute working in her "dream job." What is your "dream job"? What are you doing to reach the goal of working in YOUR "dream job"?

SCAN & QUESTION

In the preface of this book (page xiv), you read about the **SQ3R study method**. Right now, take a few moments, **scan this chapter,** and on the SQ3R Mastery Study Sheet on page 173, write **five of your own questions** that you think will be important to your mastery of this material. In addition to the two questions below, you will find five questions from your authors on that study sheet. Use one of your *"Study for Quiz"* stickers to flag this page for easy reference.

EXAMPLES:

▶ What are the components of self-discipline? (from page 148)

▶ How can I simplify my life and get more done? (from page 151)

TIME—YOU HAVE ALL THERE IS

Can You Take Control of Your Life and Make the Most of Your Time?

You can definitely say four things about time: *It is fair. It does not discriminate. It treats everyone the same. Everyone has all there is.* No person has any more or fewer hours in a day than the next person. It may seem that Gary or Tamisha has more time than you do, but they do not. In a 24-hour span we all have 1,440 minutes. No more. No less. There is one more thing you can definitely say about time, too: *It can be cruel and unrelenting.* It is one of the few things in our lives that we cannot stop. There are no time-out periods, no breaks, and try as we might, we can't turn it back, shut it down, or stop it. The good news, however, is that by learning how to manage our time more effectively, we don't need to slow it down or stop it. We can learn how to get things done and have more time for joy and fun.

So how do you spend your time? Some people are very productive, whereas others scramble to find a few moments to enjoy life and have quality relationships. According to time management and personal productivity expert Donald Wetmore (2008), "The average working person spends less than two minutes per day in *meaningful* communication with their spouse or significant other and less than 30 seconds per day in *meaningful* communication with their children." Think about that for a moment. THIRTY seconds. If you think that is amazing, consider the following list. As strange as they may seem, these figures are taken from the Bureau of Labor Statistics of the U.S. Department of the Census (2006). During your *working years* (age 20 to 65, a 45-year span), you spend an average of:

▶ 16 years sleeping.

▶ 2.3 years eating.

▶ 3.1 years doing housework.

▶ 6 years watching TV.

▶ 1.3 years on the telephone.

This totals **28.7 years of your working life** doing things that you may not even consider in your time management plan. What happens to the remaining 16.3 years? Well, you will spend **14 of those years working**, which leaves you with 2.3 years, or only

Shutterstock

iStockPhoto

Shutterstock

Do the figures regarding how we spend our time surprise you? Where do you think most of your "free" time goes?

20,000 hours, during your working life to embrace joy, spend time with your family, educate yourself, travel, and experience a host of other life-fulfilling activities. Dismal? Scary? It does not have to be. By learning how to manage your time, harness your energy and passion, and take control of your day-to-day activities, 2.3 years can be a long, exciting, productive time.

Why is it that some people seem to get so much more done than other people? They appear to always be calm and collected and have it together. Many people from this group work long hours in addition to going to school. They never appear to be stressed out, and they seem to be able to do it all with grace and charm.

You are probably aware of others who are always late with assignments, never finish their projects on time, rarely seem to have time to study, and appear to have no concrete goals for their lives. Sometimes, we get the idea that the first group accomplishes more because they have more time or because they don't have to work or they don't have children or they are smarter or have more help. Actually, some of these reasons may be true, but in reality, many of the people in the first group have learned how to overcome and beat procrastination, tie their value systems to their time management plans, and use their personal energy and passion to accomplish more.

"I can't do any more than I am doing right now," you may say to yourself. But is that really true? One of the keys to managing your time is to consider your values. We discussed your value system in Chapter 2. What you value, enjoy, and love, you tend to put more passion, energy, and time toward. Do you value your family? If so, you make time for them. Do you value your friends? If so, you make time for them. Now you have to ask yourself, **how much do I value my education**? How important is it that I succeed in college and get my degree? If you make succeeding in college a high value for your life and your future, you will find that you make more time for your studies, your classes, and your projects. **We spend time on what we value!**

TIME MANAGEMENT AND SELF-DISCIPLINE

Do You Have What It Takes to Get It Done?

Time management is actually about managing you! It is about taking control and assuming responsibility for the time you are given on this earth. The sooner you understand this and take control of how you use your time, the quicker you will be on your way to becoming successful in college and many other activities. Learning to manage your time is a lesson that you will use throughout your studies and beyond. No, **you can't control time**, but you can control yourself. Time management is basically self-discipline—and self-discipline involves self-motivation. Time management is paying attention to how you are spending your most valuable resource—time—and then devising a plan to use it more effectively. This is one of the goals of this chapter.

The word *discipline* comes from a Latin word meaning "to teach." Therefore, **self-discipline** is really about "teaching ourselves" (Waitley, 1997). Self-discipline implies that you have the ability to teach yourself how to get more done when things are going well and when they are not going so well. If you have self-discipline, you have learned how to hold it all together when things get tough, when you feel beaten, and when defeat seems just around the corner. It also means that when you have important tasks to complete, you can temporarily pull yourself away from enjoyable situations and fun times until those tasks are completed. Consider the chart in Figure 6.1 regarding self-discipline. **Self-discipline is really about four things.**

"Self-discipline is teaching ourselves to do the things necessary to reach our goals without becoming sidetracked by bad habits."
—Denis Waitley

Once you have made the **choice** to engage in your education, stop procrastinating, and manage your time more effectively, you have to make the **changes** in your thoughts and behaviors to bring those choices to fruition. Then, you have to **accept responsibility** for your actions and take control of your life. You have to call upon your **inner strength** or **willpower**—

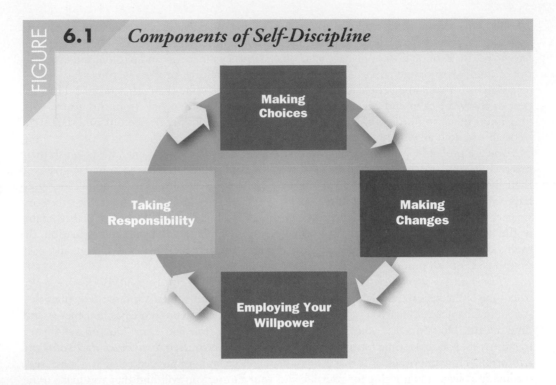

FIGURE **6.1** *Components of Self-Discipline*

Making Choices

Making Changes

Employing Your Willpower

Taking Responsibility

Shutterstock

How can becoming a more organized person help you manage your time more effectively?

and you DO have willpower; it may just be hidden or forgotten, but you do have it. You have the ability to empower yourself to get things done. No one can do this for you. You are responsible for your life, your actions, and your willpower. Self-discipline and willpower help you move in the direction of your dreams. Even in the face of fear, anxiety, stress, defeat, and darkness, self-discipline will help you find your way.

Willpower and self-discipline are all about *retraining your mind* to do what YOU want it to do and not what IT wants to do. It is about eliminating the negative self-talk that so often derails us and causes us to procrastinate and get stressed out. By retraining your mind and resisting the urge to simply "obey" your subconscious, you are basically retraining your life. Consider the following situations:

▶ You come home after three classes and are tired and weary. Your subconscious mind tells you to sit down, put your feet up, and watch TV for a while. But you have to tell your mind, *"NO! I am going to take a short walk around the block to get my adrenaline flowing and then I'm going to read my chapter for homework."*

▶ You look at your desk or study space, and you see all of the books and papers you have gathered for your research paper and your subconscious mind tells you to just ignore it for a while; there's still time to get it done! You have to tell your mind, *"ABSOLUTELY NOT! I'm going to get those articles organized and make an outline of my paper before I do anything else today. Period."*

▶ You come home tired and hungry, and your mind tells you to eat that candy bar or donut. You have to tell your mind, *"NO WAY! I am going to have an apple instead. It is better for me and my memory to avoid sugar right now."*

By retraining your mind and ignoring your subconscious, you can retrain yourself to develop the self-discipline and willpower you need to get things done and avoid the stress caused by procrastination. Willpower gives you strength to stay on track and avoid the guilt associated with putting things off or not doing them at all. Guilt turns into frustration and frustration turns into anger, and before you know it, your negative self-talk and subconscious mind have "won" and nothing gets done. You DO have the power to change this.

I'LL DO IT WHEN I HAVE A LITTLE FREE TIME

Is Time Really "Free"?

What is *"free time"* and when does it occur? We've all used that expression at one time or another: *"I'll do that when I get a little more free time,"* or *"I'm going to wait until I find a little more time."* Can time be found? Is time free? Do we ever have a moment to call our own? The answer is "maybe," but you have to create free time, and you can create it only by getting the things done that must be completed for your success.

Free time is NOT time that you simply create by putting off work that needs to be done. Free time is NOT time that is spent procrastinating. Free time is NOT time that you take away from your duties, chores, studies, family, and obligations. That is **borrowed time** and if you know the rules of good behavior, you know that anything you borrow, you must repay. When are you going to find the time to "repay" these blocks of time to yourself? Usually you don't, and that is when and where you get into trouble and your stress levels start to rise.

Free time IS time that you reward yourself when you have completed your studies, tasks, chores, and obligations. Free time IS time that you have created by planning ahead and avoiding procrastination. Free time IS time that you enjoy when your work is done and you can sit and enjoy your life, family, and friends because the pressures and guilt of poor time management are not haunting you. One of your goals in managing your time more effectively should be to create more free time in your life for joy. Joy will not come to you, however, if you have projects looming over your head.

> *"Begin doing what you want to do now. We are not living in eternity. We have only this moment, sparkling like a star in our hand and melting like a snowflake."*
> —Marie B. Ray

PLANNING, DOODLING, OR BEGGING

What Type of Person Are You, Anyway?

We all have different personality types, but did you know that we also have different time management personalities? Consider the list in Figure 6.2 explaining the different negative time management personalities. Respond YES or NO to the types you think most resemble you and your management style. Then, in the next column explain why you think this type represents you and your daily thoughts on time. Finally, in the last column, list at least one strategy that you can begin to implement to overcome this type of negative time management style.

ABSOLUTELY NO . . . WELL, MAYBE

Do You Know How to Say No?

"NO, I'm sorry, I can't do that" is perhaps one of the most difficult phrases you must learn to say when it comes to effective time management. *"Jeez, I should have never agreed to do this*

6.2 *Time Management Types*

Type	Explanation	Do You Have Any of These Tendencies?	What Actions Make You Like This Type of Person?	What Can You Do to Begin Eliminating This Type of Behavior?
THE CIRCLER	Doing the same things over and over again and again and hoping for a different result; basically, going around in circles.	YES / NO		
THE DOODLER	Not paying attention to details, doing things that do not really matter to the completion of your project.	YES / NO		
THE SQUANDERER	Wasting too much time trying to "get ready" to study or work and never really getting anything done until it is too late to do a good job.	YES / NO		
THE BEGGAR	Expecting time to "stop" for you after you've wasted time doing nothing or going in circles, then becoming frustrated when you don't have enough time.	YES / NO		
THE PLANNER	Planning out your project so carefully and meticulously that by the time you have everything you think you need, there is no time to really do the project.	YES / NO		
THE HUN	Waiting too late to plan or get things done and then stomping on anyone or anything to get the project done with no regard for others' feelings, time, or relationships.	YES / NO		
THE PASSIVIST	Convincing yourself that you'll never get it all done and that there is no use to try anyway.	YES / NO		

in the first place" is perhaps one of the most common phrases used when you don't know how to say no. If you continually say yes to everyone and every project, then you'll quickly have no time left for yourself, your family, your friends, and your other projects. Many of us are taught from an early age that *no* is a bad word and that we should always try to avoid saying it to others. However, we are not taught that never saying no can cause us undue stress and feelings of guilt and frustration and throw our time management plans into disarray. Now that you have so much going on from so many different projects, saying no needs to become a part of your everyday vocabulary. By learning to say "NO" to a few things, you can begin to say "YES" to many other things—things that you want to do, need to do, and that will actually help others in the long run. "No" is not rude; it is simply a way of managing your time so that you have more time to say yes to what is important and useful.

"Time is the most valuable and most perishable of our possessions."
—*John Randolph*

Steps to Learning to Say No—It's as Simple as NOT Saying Yes

▶ Think before you answer out loud with an insincere or untrue "Yes."

▶ Make sure you understand exactly what is being asked of you and what the project involves before you give a yes or no answer.

▶ Review your schedule to see if you really have the time to do a quality job. ("If you have to have an answer immediately, it is 'No.' If you can wait a few days for me to finish project X and review my schedule, the answer may be 'Yes.'")

▶ Learn the difference between assertiveness (politely declining) and rudeness (responding with "Have you lost your mind?").

▶ Say no at the right times (i.e., to the wrong things) so that you can say yes at the appropriate times (i.e., to the right things).

▶ Learn how to put yourself and your future first (for a change). By doing this, you can say yes more often later on.

▶ Inform others of your time management schedule so that they will have a better understanding of why you say no.

▶ If you must say yes to an unwanted project (something at work, for example), try to negotiate a deadline that works for everyone—you first!

▶ Keep your no short. If you have to offer an explanation, be brief so that you don't talk yourself into doing something you can't do and so that you avoid giving false hope to the other person. If the answer is no right now and it will be no in the future, say no now.

▶ Offer suggestions to the other person as to who may be able to help or when you might be available (if it is in your best interest to accept this request at any time).

▶ If you feel you simply have to say yes, try to trade off with the other person and ask him or her to do something on your list.

▶ Put a time limit on your "Yes." For example, you might agree to help someone, but you could say, "I can give you 30 minutes and then I have to leave."

Do you think saying no is rude or necessary?

YOUR TURN. You are taking four classes and the reading and homework are mounting day by day. Your family needs you, your friends think you've abandoned them, and you want to continue to do a good job at work. Your schedule is tight and you have things planned down to the hour in order to be able to get it all done and done well. Suddenly, you are asked to help with a project for disadvantaged children that seems very worthy and timely. You know that your schedule is full but your conscience begins to gnaw at you and you really do want to help.

Applying the tips from the list above, predict how you might be able to address this situation.

_____

_____

_____

BEGINNING YOUR DAY WITH PEACE

Can You Start Your Day as a Blank Page and Simplify Your Life?

Imagine a day with nothing to do! That may be difficult, if not impossible, for you to conceive right now. But as an exercise in building your own day from scratch and simplifying your life,

iStockPhoto

think about having a day where YOU build your schedule and where you do not have to be constrained by activities and projects that others have thrust upon you. Think about a day where you are in charge. Crazy? Impossible? Outrageous? Maybe not as much as you think.

Yes, you will need to plot activities such as work, class, and family duties into your daily calendar, but you also need to learn how to schedule time for fun activities, time for silence and peace, and time to be alone with your thoughts. By learning how to build your schedule each evening from scratch, you will have the opportunity to plan a day where you simplify your life. There is an old quote that states, "If you want to know what you value in your life, look at your checkbook and your calendar." Basically, this suggests that we spend our money and time on things we value.

Do you find it difficult or easy to simplify and de-clutter your life? Why?

12 Ways to Simplify Your Life

▶ Know what you value, and work hard to eliminate activities that are not in conjunction with your core value system. This can be whittled down to one statement: ***"Identify what is important to you. Eliminate everything else."***

▶ Get away from technology for a few hours a day. Turn off your computer, cell phone, iPod, and other devices that can take time away from doing what you value.

▶ Learn to delegate to others. You may say to yourself, "My family does not know how to use the washing machine." Guess what? When all of their underwear is dirty, they'll learn how to use it. Don't enable others to avoid activities that complicate your life.

▶ Make a list of everything you are doing. Prioritize this list into what you enjoy doing and what fits into your value system. If you can feasibly do only three or four of these activities per day, draw a line after number four and eliminate the rest of the list.

▶ Do what is essential for the well-being of you and your family and eliminate everything else.

SUCCESSFUL DECISIONS: An Activity for Critical Reflection

Darius is a single father of two young daughters. He and his wife divorced several years ago and he was granted custody of Alice and Marianne. Shortly after the divorce, Darius was laid off from his job as a construction foreman. He had been making a very good living, but now it was hard to make ends meet. He could not find another job that paid well enough to support the three of them.

Therefore, he decided to go back to school to pursue his dream of becoming a draftsman. His classes, along with his new part-time job, demand much of his time. He has found that he is spending much less time with his daughters than he had in the past—and he does not like this at all.

His daughters were cast in the school play and the performance is scheduled for Friday night—the same night as one of his drafting classes. He knows that he has a conflict on his hands. He knows that class is very important, but so is supporting his daughters. In your own words, what would you suggest that Darius do at this point? List at least three things that he could do handle this situation, manage his time to meet all of his obligations, and maintain his sanity.

1. _____

2. _____

3. _____

► Don't waste time saving money. Spend money to save time. In other words, don't drive across town to save 3 cents per gallon on fuel or 10 cents for a gallon of milk. Pay the extra money and have more time to do what you like.

► Clean your home of clutter and mess. Work from cleanliness. Declutter and organize. Make sure everything has a place.

► Donate everything you don't need or use to charity. Simplifying your life may also mean simplifying your closets, drawers, cabinets, and garage.

► Go through your home or apartment and eliminate everything that does not bring you joy or have sentimental value. If you don't love it, ditch it.

► Clean up the files on your computer. Erase everything that you don't need or want so that you can find material more easily. If you have not used the file in a month, put it on a flash drive for later use.

► Live in the moment. Yes, it is important to plan for the future, but if you ignore "the moment," your future will not be as bright.

► Spend a few moments each morning and afternoon reflecting on all of the abundance in your life. Learn to give thanks and learn to do nothing.

► Don't miss today worrying about yesterday and tomorrow. ("Zen Habits," 2008; *Get More Done,* 2008)

In the space in Figure 6.3, compile a list that can help you simplify your life in each category. Add ONLY those things to the list that you can actually DO on a daily basis.

FIGURE **6.3** *Ways to Simplify Your Life*

Two things I can do to simplify my life at home	
Two things I can do to simplify my life at work	
Two things I can do to simplify my life at school	
Two things I can do to simplify my life with my children	
Two things I can do to simplify my life with my spouse/partner/loved one	
Two things I can do to simplify my economics (financial matters)	

PROCRASTINATION: THE DREADED "P" WORD

How Can You Beat It Once and for All?

It's not just you! Almost everyone procrastinates, and then we worry and tell ourselves, "I'll never do it again if I can just get through this one project." We say things to ourselves like, "If I can just live through this paper, I will never wait until the last minute again." But then someone comes along with a great idea for fun, and off we go. Or there is a great movie on TV, the kids want to play a game of catch, you go to the refrigerator for a snack, and before you know it, you are rewarding yourself *with FREE time* before you have done your work.

The truth is simple: We tend to avoid the hard jobs in favor of the easy ones. Even many of the list makers fool themselves. They mark off a long list of easy tasks while the big ones still loom in front of them. Many of us put off unpleasant tasks until our backs are against the wall. So why do we procrastinate when we all know how unpleasant the results can be? Why aren't

> *"If you have to eat two frogs,*
> *eat the ugliest one first."*
> —Brian Tracy

we disciplined and organized and controlled so that we can reap the rewards that come from being prepared? Why do we put ourselves through so much stress by putting things off?

The biggest problem with procrastination, even beyond not getting the job, task, or paper completed on time, *is doing it poorly* and then suffering the stress caused by having put it off or turning in a subpar project. By putting the project off, you have cheated yourself out of the time needed to bring your best to the table and, most likely, you are going to hand over a project, with your name on it, that is not even close to your potential. And to top it off, more stress is created by this vicious cycle of "I'll do it tomorrow—or this weekend."

What has procrastination cost you? This is perhaps one of the most important questions that you can ask and answer with regard to managing your time more effectively. Did it cost you a good grade? Did it cost you money? Did it cost you your reputation? Did it cost you your dignity? Did it cost you your ability to do your best? *Procrastination is not free.* Every time you do it, it costs you something. You need to determine what it is worth.

In order to beat procrastination, you will also need to consider *what type* of procrastinator you are (Figure 6.4). Each type requires a different strategy and different energy to overcome, but make no doubt about it, success requires overcoming all degrees and types of procrastination. Before you complete the Time Management Assessment, examine Figure 6.4 to determine if any of these procrastination types fit you.

Take a moment to complete the **Time Management Assessment** in Figure 6.5. Be honest and truthful in your responses. The results of your score are located after the assessment.

Procrastination is quite simply a bad habit formed after many years of practice. There are reasons, however, that cause us to keep doing this to ourselves. Often, we let our negative self-

FIGURE

6.4 *Procrastinator Types*

CHRONIC Procrastinator 	You procrastinate all of the time on most everything in most aspects of your life including social situations, financial affairs, career decisions, personal responsibility, and academic projects. Usually, you do not meet any deadlines if you complete the project at all. It is going to take a great deal of thought, planning, and energy to overcome this type of procrastination.
MODERATE Procrastinator 	You procrastinate much of the time. You usually get things done, but it is not your best work and you create a great deal of stress in your own life. It is going to take a fair amount of planning and energy to overcome this type of procrastination. With some planning, your projects could be much more effective and you could eliminate much stress and guilt.
OCCASIONAL Procrastinator	You occasionally put things off. You do not do this often, but when you do, you feel guilty and rush to get the project completed. Sometimes, you turn in work that is not your best. You are good at planning most things, but you do need to concentrate on sticking to your plan and not letting unscheduled events obstruct your success.

FIGURE 6.5 *Time Management Assessment*

Answer the questions below with the following scale:

1 = Not at all   2 = Rarely   3 = Sometimes   4 = Often   5 = Very often

1. I prioritize my tasks every day and work from my priority list.	1 2 3 4 5
2. I work hard to complete tasks on time and not put them off until the last minute.	1 2 3 4 5
3. I take time to plan and schedule the next day's activities the night before.	1 2 3 4 5
4. I have made time during my daily schedule to study and get my projects completed so that I can have more quality time at home.	1 2 3 4 5
5. I study and get my work done before I take fun breaks.	1 2 3 4 5
6. I analyze my assignments to determine which ones are going to take the most time and then work on them first and most often.	1 2 3 4 5
7. I have analyzed my daily activities and determined where I actually spend my time.	1 2 3 4 5
8. I know how to say no and do so frequently.	1 2 3 4 5
9. I know how to avoid distractions and how to work through unexpected interruptions.	1 2 3 4 5
10. I do not let "fear of the unknown" keep me from working on a project.	1 2 3 4 5
11. I know how to overcome apathy toward a project.	1 2 3 4 5
12. I know how to fight and overcome my own laziness.	1 2 3 4 5
13. I know how to reframe a project that may not interest me so that I can see the benefits from it and learn from it.	1 2 3 4 5
14. I know how to break down a major, complex, or overwhelming task to get it done in pieces and then put it all together.	1 2 3 4 5
15. I build time into my schedule on a daily or weekly basis to deal with "unexpected" interruptions or distractions.	1 2 3 4 5

YOUR TOTAL SCORE: _____

RESULTS:		
60–75	You manage your time well and you know how to build a schedule to get things done. Your productivity is high. You don't let procrastination rule your life.
45–59	You are good at doing some things on time, but you tend to procrastinate too much. Learning how to build and work from a priority list may help you manage your time more effectively.
30–44	You need to work hard to change your time management skills and learn how to set realistic goals. Procrastination is probably a major issue for you, causing you much stress and worry. Working from a priority list can help you greatly.
29 or below	Your time management skills are very weak and without change and improvement, your success plan could be in jeopardy. You could benefit from learning to set realistic goals, working from a priority list, and reframing your thought process toward tasks.

talk cause us to procrastinate. We allow our negative attitude to override what we know is best for us. An attitude adjustment may be just the thing you need to overcome and beat the trap of procrastination.

Consider the following negative statements. On the right-hand side, rewrite each statement to make it a positive, procrastination-beating statement.

NEGATIVE STATEMENT	**POSITIVE STATEMENT**
I'll do it at 9:30 when this TV show is off.	_____
	_____
I'm tired.	_____
	_____

I can't concentrate.

_____

_____

This is too hard.

_____

This is boring.

_____

_____

I don't know why anyone would ask me to
do this crazy stuff.

_____

_____

Learning to apply this type of positive thinking can help you beat the procrastination trap and
manage your time and life more effectively.

GETTING THE MOST OUT OF THIS MOMENT

Do You Know the Causes of and Cures for Procrastination?

Below, you will find a list of the 10 most COMMON CAUSES of procrastination and some
simple, doable, everyday strategies that you can employ to overcome each cause. We have provided three strategies for each cause. Add at least two of your own strategies to overcome this
type of procrastination.

Superhuman Expectations and Trying to Be a Perfectionist

▶ Allow yourself **more time than you think you need** to complete a project.

▶ Realize that no one, including you, is (or ever will be) perfect. **Perfection does not exist.**

▶ **Allow enough time to do your very best** and let that be that. If you plan and allow time
for excellence, you can't do more.

_____

_____

Fear of Not Knowing How to Do the Task

▶ **Ask for clarification** from whomever asked you to do the project.

▶ **Read** as much as you can about the task at hand and **ask for help.**

▶ Break up big tasks into **small ones.**

_____

_____

Lack of Motivation and the Inability to Find Internal Motivation

▶ **Reframe your attitude** to find the good and beneficial in any task.

▶ Consider how this task will help you **reach your overall goals and dreams.**

▶ Take time to do the **things you love,** which will create a healthy balance in your life.

_____

_____

Fear of Failing or Fear of the Task Being Too Hard

▶ Start the project with **positive, optimistic thoughts.**

▶ **Face your fears;** look them right in the face and make a decision to defeat them.

▶ **Visualize your successful completion** of the project.

_____

_____

No Real Plan or Goal for Getting the Task Done

▶ Set reasonable, concrete goals that you can reach in about **20 to 25 minutes.**

▶ **Draw up an action plan** the night before you begin the project.

▶ Look at completing the project in terms of your **long-range goals** and your overall life plan.

_____

_____

Considering the Task Too Unpleasant or Uninteresting

▶ **Realize** that most tasks are not as unpleasant as we've made them out to be.

▶ **Do the hardest tasks first** and save the easiest for last.

▶ Schedule tasks that you consider unpleasant to be done **during your peak hours.**

_____

_____

Utter Laziness and/or Apathy

▶ **Concentrate on the rewards** of managing yourself and your time more effectively.

▶ Give yourself a **time limit** to accomplish a task.

▶ Set a regular, realistic time for study, and **stick to it.**

_____

_____

Photolibrary

Is there a difference between laziness, procrastination, and resting?

Distractions and/or Lack of Focus

▶ **Ask for help** from your professors, advisor, counselor, or other professionals.

▶ Start on the difficult, **most boring tasks first.**

▶ Weed out your personal belongings and living space. Organization helps you manage your time and **get to work.**

_____

_____

Choosing "Fun" Before Responsibility

▶ Actually **reward yourself** when you have accomplished an important body of work.

▶ **Don't get involved** in too many organizations, accept too many commitments, or overextend yourself so that you can concentrate on what needs to be done.

▶ **Consider the consequences** of not doing what you're responsible for doing.

_____

_____

Waiting for the "Right" Mood

▶ **Avoid whining and complaining** and realize that you can create the right mood at any time.

▶ **Just do it!** Force yourself to jump into the task.

▶ Work during your **peak hours of the day.**

_____

_____

From Ordinary to *Extraordinary*

MAUREEN RIOPELLE
President & Founder
Mary's Circle of Hope—The Mary Maguire Foundation
Milford, Ohio

Things could not have been going better! I was a star basketball player recruited by hundreds of colleges and was a top pick by the University of Iowa. My dream of going to college, becoming an Olympic athlete, and later a sportscaster was so close I could see it all happening. But life has a funny way of turning on a dime.

I had suffered knee problems for many years and most doctors attributed it to "growing pains." I continued to play sports in high school de-spite the pain. By the time I got to the University of Iowa, at the urging of my coaches I finally saw a few specialists but the diagnosis was inconclusive. They knew my knee was in serious disrepair and that I had lost over 35 percent of the range of motion. They just couldn't figure out why.

After surgery, my knees actually began to worsen. The doctors feared a massive infection and after more tests, another surgery was scheduled. It was then determined that the plica in my knees had hardened and formed so much scar tissue that it seemed to almost form another "bone" in my leg. I was told that I would probably have to have surgery every two years to repair the damage and that I only had a 50/50 chance of ever walking again.

In a relatively brief period of time, I went from a college basketball standout and Olympic hopeful to losing my scholarship, dropping out of college, and potentially facing the rest of my life on crutches or in a wheelchair. I had five surgeries in seven months and I spent that summer in a wheelchair and on crutches, but within a year, I was walking on my own again. Within a year and half I walked my first 5K.

I attribute my recovery to my drive and determination. When necessary, I am the most stubborn person you'll

> *In a relatively brief period of time, I went from a college basketball standout and Olympic hopeful to losing my scholarship, dropping out of college, and potentially facing the rest of my life on crutches or in a wheelchair.*

ever meet. When I was told that I would not walk, run, or play basketball again, I took it as a *personal challenge* to prove everyone wrong—*"I'll show you."* I eventually went back to college, graduating with a 4.0 GPA. After graduation, I began working, and life was moving along. Little did I know that within a few short years, I would have to call upon that teenager who years earlier had told herself, *"I'll show you."*

One morning I found a lump in my breast and immediately met with my doctor, who scheduled a mammogram. After the test, I was told that everything was fine. But there was a little voice in my head that said, "You need to ask someone else. Get a second opinion." This little voice saved my life. I did, indeed, have breast cancer and it had even spread to my

lymph nodes. My determination and strong will to live and beat the odds became my salvation once again. After surgery and treatment, there are no signs of cancer.

Both of these experiences, while trying and frightening, led me to my real calling in life—founding Mary's Circle of Hope—The Mary Maguire Foundation, a nonprofit organization dedicated to the support of women cancer survivors. We help provide financial assistance; health, fitness, and nutritional assistance; empowerment retreats and workshops; and additional services that help the women go from surviving to thriving. Being able to help others thrive in the face of adversity has become my passion and focus in life. Visit us at www.marymaguire foundation.org.

EXTRAORDINARY REFLECTION

Read the following statement and respond in your online journal or class notebook.

Ms. Riopelle suffered a major setback with her health, causing her to lose her scholarship and drop out of college for a time. What advice regarding persistence, internal motivation, positive thinking, and determination would you give to someone who is facing a life-threatening health problem?

EVALUATING HOW YOU SPEND YOUR TIME

Do You Know Where Your Time Goes?

So how do you find out where your time goes? The same way that you find out where your money goes—you track it. Every 15 minutes for one week, record exactly how you spent that time. This exercise may seem a little tedious at first, but if you complete the process over a period of a week, you will have a much better concept of where your time is being used. Yes, that's right—for a week you need to keep a written record of how much time you spend sleeping, studying, eating, working, getting to class and back, cooking, caring for children, watching television, doing yard work, going to movies, attending athletic events, hanging out, doing laundry, whatever.

Take your plan with you and keep track of your activities during the day. To make things simple, round off tasks to 15-minute intervals. For example, if you start walking to campus at 7:08, you might want to mark off the time block that begins with 7:00. If you finish eating and return home at 7:49, you can mark off the next two blocks. You will also want to note the activity so that you can later evaluate how you spent your time. Study the example that is provided for you in Figure 6.6.

In Figure 6.7 you will find a daily time log that you can use for this exercise. Remember to take these pages with you and record how you are spending your time during the day. As you progress through the week, try to improve the use of your time. When you finish this exercise, review how you spent your time.

FIGURE 6.6 *How You Really Spend Your Time*

7:00	get up	7:00			12:15
	+ shower	7:15			12:30
	X	7:30		Walked to Union	12:45
	Breakfast	7:45	1:00	Ate lunch	1:00
8:00		8:00			1:15
		8:15			1:30
	Read paper	8:30		Talked w/ Joe	1:45
	Walked to class	8:45	2:00		2:00
9:00	English 101	9:00		Went to book	2:15
		9:15		store	2:30
		9:30		Walked to	2:45
		9:45	3:00	my room	3:00
10:00		10:00		Called Ron	3:15
		10:15			3:30
		10:30			3:45
	Walked to class	10:45	4:00	Watched	4:00
11:00	History 210	11:00		TV	4:15
		11:15			4:30
		11:30		Walked to	4:45
		11:45	5:00	library	5:00
12:00		12:00			5:15

FIGURE **6.7** *Daily Time Sheet*

Monday		Tuesday		Wednesday	
6:00	6:00	6:00	6:00	6:00	6:00
	6:15		6:15		6:15
	6:30		6:30		6:30
	6:45		6:45		6:45
7:00	7:00	7:00	7:00	7:00	7:00
	7:15		7:15		7:15
	7:30		7:30		7:30
	7:45		7:45		7:45
8:00	8:00	8:00	8:00	8:00	8:00
	8:15		8:15		8:15
	8:30		8:30		8:30
	8:45		8:45		8:45
9:00	9:00	9:00	9:00	9:00	9:00
	9:15		9:15		9:15
	9:30		9:30		9:30
	9:45		9:45		9:45
10:00	10:00	10:00	10:00	10:00	10:00
	10:15		10:15		10:15
	10:30		10:30		10:30
	10:45		10:45		10:45
11:00	11:00	11:00	11:00	11:00	11:00
	11:15		11:15		11:15
	11:30		11:30		11:30
	11:45		11:45		11:45
12:00	12:00	12:00	12:00	12:00	12:00
	12:15		12:15		12:15
	12:30		12:30		12:30
	12:45		12:45		12:45
1:00	1:00	1:00	1:00	1:00	1:00
	1:15		1:15		1:15
	1:30		1:30		1:30
	1:45		1:45		1:45
2:00	2:00	2:00	2:00	2:00	2:00
	2:15		2:15		2:15
	2:30		2:30		2:30
	2:45		2:45		2:45
3:00	3:00	3:00	3:00	3:00	3:00
	3:15		3:15		3:15
	3:30		3:30		3:30
	3:45		3:45		3:45
4:00	4:00	4:00	4:00	4:00	4:00
	4:15		4:15		4:15
	4:30		4:30		4:30
	4:45		4:45		4:45
5:00	5:00	5:00	5:00	5:00	5:00
	5:15		5:15		5:15
	5:30		5:30		5:30
	5:45		5:45		5:45
6:00	6:00	6:00	6:00	6:00	6:00
	6:15		6:15		6:15
	6:30		6:30		6:30
	6:45		6:45		6:45
7:00	7:00	7:00	7:00	7:00	7:00
	7:15		7:15		7:15
	7:30		7:30		7:30
	7:45		7:45		7:45
8:00	8:00	8:00	8:00	8:00	8:00
	8:15		8:15		8:15
	8:30		8:30		8:30
	8:45		8:45		8:45
9:00	9:00	9:00	9:00	9:00	9:00
	9:15		9:15		9:15
	9:30		9:30		9:30
	9:45		9:45		9:45
10:00	10:00	10:00	10:00	10:00	10:00
	10:15		10:15		10:15
	10:30		10:30		10:30
	10:45		10:45		10:45
11:00	11:00	11:00	11:00	11:00	11:00
	11:15		11:15		11:15
	11:30		11:30		11:30
	11:45		11:45		11:45
12:00	12:00	12:00	12:00	12:00	12:00

(continued)

FIGURE

6.7 *Daily Time Sheet (continued)*

Thursday		Friday		Saturday		Sunday	
6:00	6:00	6:00	6:00	6:00	6:00	6:00	6:00
	6:15		6:15		6:15		6:15
	6:30		6:30		6:30		6:30
	6:45		6:45		6:45		6:45
7:00	7:00	7:00	7:00	7:00	7:00	7:00	7:00
	7:15		7:15		7:15		7:15
	7:30		7:30		7:30		7:30
	7:45		7:45		7:45		7:45
8:00	8:00	8:00	8:00	8:00	8:00	8:00	8:00
	8:15		8:15		8:15		8:15
	8:30		8:30		8:30		8:30
	8:45		8:45		8:45		8:45
9:00	9:00	9:00	9:00	9:00	9:00	9:00	9:00
	9:15		9:15		9:15		9:15
	9:30		9:30		9:30		9:30
	9:45		9:45		9:45		9:45
10:00	10:00	10:00	10:00	10:00	10:00	10:00	10:00
	10:15		10:15		10:15		10:15
	10:30		10:30		10:30		10:30
	10:45		10:45		10:45		10:45
11:00	11:00	11:00	11:00	11:00	11:00	11:00	11:00
	11:15		11:15		11:15		11:15
	11:30		11:30		11:30		11:30
	11:45		11:45		11:45		11:45
12:00	12:00	12:00	12:00	12:00	12:00	12:00	12:00
	12:15		12:15		12:15		12:15
	12:30		12:30		12:30		12:30
	12:45		12:45		12:45		12:45
1:00	1:00	1:00	1:00	1:00	1:00	1:00	1:00
	1:15		1:15		1:15		1:15
	1:30		1:30		1:30		1:30
	1:45		1:45		1:45		1:45
2:00	2:00	2:00	2:00	2:00	2:00	2:00	2:00
	2:15		2:15		2:15		2:15
	2:30		2:30		2:30		2:30
	2:45		2:45		2:45		2:45
3:00	3:00	3:00	3:00	3:00	3:00	3:00	3:00
	3:15		3:15		3:15		3:15
	3:30		3:30		3:30		3:30
	3:45		3:45		3:45		3:45
4:00	4:00	4:00	4:00	4:00	4:00	4:00	4:00
	4:15		4:15		4:15		4:15
	4:30		4:30		4:30		4:30
	4:45		4:45		4:45		4:45
5:00	5:00	5:00	5:00	5:00	5:00	5:00	5:00
	5:15		5:15		5:15		5:15
	5:30		5:30		5:30		5:30
	5:45		5:45		5:45		5:45
6:00	6:00	6:00	6:00	6:00	6:00	6:00	6:00
	6:15		6:15		6:15		6:15
	6:30		6:30		6:30		6:30
	6:45		6:45		6:45		6:45
7:00	7:00	7:00	7:00	7:00	7:00	7:00	7:00
	7:15		7:15		7:15		7:15
	7:30		7:30		7:30		7:30
	7:45		7:45		7:45		7:45
8:00	8:00	8:00	8:00	8:00	8:00	8:00	8:00
	8:15		8:15		8:15		8:15
	8:30		8:30		8:30		8:30
	8:45		8:45		8:45		8:45
9:00	9:00	9:00	9:00	9:00	9:00	9:00	9:00
	9:15		9:15		9:15		9:15
	9:30		9:30		9:30		9:30
	9:45		9:45		9:45		9:45
10:00	10:00	10:00	10:00	10:00	10:00	10:00	10:00
	10:15		10:15		10:15		10:15
	10:30		10:30		10:30		10:30
	10:45		10:45		10:45		10:45
11:00	11:00	11:00	11:00	11:00	11:00	11:00	11:00
	11:15		11:15		11:15		11:15
	11:30		11:30		11:30		11:30
	11:45		11:45		11:45		11:45
12:00	12:00	12:00	12:00	12:00	12:00	12:00	12:00

ELIMINATING DISTRACTIONS AND INTERRUPTIONS

When Is Enough Really Enough?

If you were diligent and kept an accurate account of all of your time, your evaluation probably reveals that much of your time is spent dealing with distractions, getting side-tracked, and handling interruptions. These three things account for much of the time wasted within a 24-hour period. In Figure 6.8 you will find a list of some of the most common distractions faced by college students. Consider how you might deal with these distractions in an effective, assertive manner.

PLANNING AND PREPARING

Is There a Secret to Time Management?

In the past, you may have said to yourself, *"I don't have time to plan." "I don't like to be fenced in and tied to a rigid schedule." "I have so many duties that planning never works."* Scheduling does not have to be a tedious chore or something you dread. Scheduling can be your lifeline to more free time. After all, if YOU build your own schedule, it is yours! As much as you are able, build your schedule the way you want and need it.

FIGURE 6.8 *Common Distractions*

Common Distractions	My Plan to Overcome These Distractions
Friends/family dropping by unexpectedly	
Technology (playing on YouTube, Facebook, iTunes, Google, etc.)	
Constant phone calls or texts that do not pertain to anything in particular or of importance	
Not setting aside any time during the day to deal with "the unexpected"	
Friends/family demanding things of you because they do not understand your schedule or commitments	
Not blocking private time in your daily schedule	
Being unorganized and spending hours upon hours dawdling and calling it "work"	
Playing with your children or pets before your tasks are complete (and not scheduling time to be with them in the first place)	
Saying "Yes" when you need to say "NO"	
Other distractions you face . . .	

To manage your time successfully, you need to spend some time planning. To plan successfully, you need a calendar that has at least a week-at-a-glance or a month-at-a-glance section as well as sections for daily notes and appointments. If you have not bought a calendar, you can download one from the Internet or create one using Word or another computer program.

Planning and Organizing for School

Each evening, you should take a few minutes (and literally, that is all it will take) and sit in a quiet place and make a list of all that needs to be done tomorrow. Successful time management comes from **planning the NIGHT BEFORE!** Let's say your list includes

Research speech project	Exercise
Study for finance test on Friday	Buy birthday card for Mom
Read Chapter 13 for chemistry	Wash the car
Meet with chemistry study group	Take shirts to dry cleaner
Attend English class at 8:00 a.m.	Buy groceries
Attend mgt. class at 10:00 a.m.	Call Janice about weekend
Work from 2:00 to 6:00 p.m.	

Now you have created a list of tasks that you will face tomorrow. Next, separate this list into three categories:

MUST DO	NEED TO DO	WOULD LIKE TO DO
Read Ch. 13 for chem.	Research speech project	Wash the car
Exercise	Buy birthday card for Mom	Call Janice
English class @ 8:00	Shirts to cleaner	
Mgt. class @ 10:00	Buy groceries	
Meet w/chem study gp.		
Work 2:00–6:00 p.m.		

Don't get too excited yet! Your time management plan is ***NOT finished***. The most important part is still ahead of you. Now you will need to rank the items in order of their importance. You will put a 1 by the most important tasks, a 2 by the next most important tasks, etc., in each category.

MUST DO	NEED TO DO	WOULD LIKE TO DO
1 Read Ch. 13 for chem.	1 Research speech project	2 Wash the car
2 Study for finance test on Fri.	2 Buy birthday card for Mom	1 Call Janice
3 Exercise	3 Shirts to cleaner	
1 English class @ 8:00	2 Buy groceries	
1 Mgt. class @ 10:00		
2 Meet w/chem study gp.		
1 Work 2:00–6:00 p.m.		

Now you have created a PLAN to actually get these tasks done! Not only have you created your list, but you have also divided them into important categories, ranked them, and made a written commitment to these tasks.

Now take these tasks and write them into your daily calendar (see Figure 6.9). You would schedule category 1 (MUST DO) first, category 2 (NEED TO DO) next, and category 3 (WOULD LIKE TO DO) next. Remember, NEVER keep more than one calendar. Always carry it with you and always schedule your tasks immediately so that you won't forget them.

FIGURE **6.9** *Daily Calendar*

DAY Monday		Priority	Complete?
Time	**Task**		
6:00			__ Yes __ No
6:30			__ Yes __ No
7:00	Study for finance		__ Yes __ No
7:30	↓		__ Yes __ No
8:00	English 101		__ Yes __ No
8:30			__ Yes __ No
9:00	↓		__ Yes __ No
9:30	Read Pg. 1-10 of Chem. Chapter		__ Yes __ No
10:00	Management 210		__ Yes __ No
10:30			__ Yes __ No
11:00	↓		__ Yes __ No
11:30	Finish Reading Chem. Chapter		__ Yes __ No
12:00			__ Yes __ No
12:30	↓		__ Yes __ No
1:00	Meet w/Chemistry group (take lunch)		__ Yes __ No
1:30	↓		__ Yes __ No
2:00	Work		__ Yes __ No
2:30			__ Yes __ No
3:00			__ Yes __ No
3:30			__ Yes __ No
4:00			__ Yes __ No
4:30			__ Yes __ No
5:00			__ Yes __ No
5:30			__ Yes __ No
6:00			__ Yes __ No
6:30	Dinner/run by grocery store		__ Yes __ No
7:00	↓		__ Yes __ No
7:30	Internet Research for speech		__ Yes __ No
8:00			__ Yes __ No
8:30	↓		__ Yes __ No
9:00	call Janice @ w/end		__ Yes __ No
9:30			__ Yes __ No

STRESS? I DON'T HAVE ENOUGH TIME FOR STRESS!

Do You Feel Like You're Going to Explode?

The word *stress* is derived from the Latin word *strictus,* meaning "to draw tight." Stress is your body's response to people and events in your life; it is the mental and physical wear and tear on your body as a result of everyday life and all that you have to accomplish. Stress is inevitable, but it is not in itself bad. It is your response to stress that determines whether it is good stress (**eustress**) or bad stress (**distress**). The same event can provoke eustress or distress, depending on the person experiencing the event; just as "one person's trash is another's treasure," so one person's eustress may be another person's distress.

The primary difference between eustress and distress is your body's response. It is impossible to exist in a totally stress-free environment; in fact, some stress is important to your health and well-being. Good stress can help you become more motivated and even more productive. It helps your energy level, too. It is only when stress gets out of hand that your body becomes distressed. Test your stress level in Figure 6.10.

Some Physical Signs of Distress

Headaches	Muscular tension and pain	Fatigue
Coughs	Abdominal pain and diarrhea	Mental disorders
Dry mouth	Hypertension and chest pain	Insomnia
Impotence	Heartburn and indigestion	Suicidal tendencies
Twitching/Trembling	Abdominal pain	Apprehension
Jitters	Diminished performance	Decreased coping ability

If you begin to experience any of these reactions for an extended period of time, you know that your body and mind are probably suffering from undue stress, anxiety, and pressure. This can lead to a very unhealthy situation. You may even require medical attention for hypertension.

FIGURE 6.10 *Test Your Stress*

Take the following **Stress Assessment** to determine the level of distress you are currently experiencing in your life. Check the items that reflect your behavior at home, work, or school, or in a social setting.

☐ 1. Your stomach tightens when you think about your schoolwork and all that you have to do.
☐ 2. You are not able to sleep at night.
☐ 3. You race from place to place trying to get everything done that is required of you.
☐ 4. Small things make you angry.
☐ 5. At the end of the day, you are frustrated that you did not accomplish all that you needed to do.
☐ 6. You get tired throughout the day.
☐ 7. You need some type of drug, alcohol, or tobacco to get through the day.
☐ 8. You often find it hard to be around people.
☐ 9. You don't take care of yourself physically or mentally.
☐ 10. You tend to keep everything inside.
☐ 11. You overreact.
☐ 12. You fail to find the humor in many situations others see as funny.
☐ 13. You do not eat properly.
☐ 14. Everything upsets you.
☐ 15. You are impatient and get angry when you have to wait for things.
☐ 16. You don't trust others.
☐ 17. You feel that most people move too slowly for you.
☐ 18. You feel guilty when you take time for yourself or your friends.
☐ 19. You interrupt people so that you can tell them your side of the story.
☐ 20. You experience memory loss.

Total Number of Check Marks

0–5 = Low, manageable stress

6–10 = Moderate stress

11+ = High stress, could cause medical or emotional problems

I DON'T THINK I FEEL SO WELL

What Is the Relationship Between Poor Time Management, Monumental Stress, and Your Health?

There are probably as many stressors in this world as there are people alive. For some people, loud music causes stress. For others, a hectic day at the office, with people demanding things and equipment breaking down, causes stress. For others, that loud music and busy day at the office are just what the doctor ordered—they love it and thrive off of the energy and demands. For some people, being idle and sitting around reading a book cause stress, while others long for a moment of peace walking on the beach or just sitting out in the backyard with a good book. One thing is for sure: Poor planning and "running out of time" are on most people's lists of major stressors.

Most stress does not "just happen" to us. We allow it to happen by not planning our day or week. We allow our "to do" list to get out of hand (or we do not create a to-do list), and before we know it, our lives are out of control because of all the activities we are required to accomplish or because of all the things we agreed to by saying "Yes." Because of poor planning and procrastination, we become anxious and nervous about not getting it all done. By planning, prioritizing, and developing an action strategy, we can actually lower our stress level and improve our general overall health and our memory.

Medical research has shown that exposure to stress over a long period of time can be damaging to one's body. Besides the physical and mental symptoms of stress previously mentioned, consider this as well: Stress can also have an effect on *memory.* When you are stressed, your brain releases ***cortisol,*** which has effects on the neurons in your brain. Over time, cortisol can be toxic and damage parts of the hippocampus—the part of the brain that deals with memory and learning. Therefore, learning to control stress through managing your time more effectively can be a key to better memory. In Chapter 5, "Think," we discussed the amygdala (the part of the brain that causes "fight or flight"). The amygdala is also affected negatively by prolonged stress, causing you to say and do things you regret later.

Other physical symptoms include ***exhaustion,*** in which one part of the body weakens and shifts its responsibility to another part and causes complete failure of key organ functions. ***Chronic muscle pain*** and malfunction are also caused by unchecked stress. "Chronically tense muscles also result in numerous stress-related disorders including headaches, backaches, spasms of the esophagus and colon (causing diarrhea and constipation), posture problems, asthma, tightness in the throat and chest cavity, some eye problems, lockjaw, muscle tears and pulls, and perhaps rheumatoid arthritis" (Girdano et al., 2009).

As you can see from this medical research, stress is not something that you can just ignore and hope it will go away. It is not something that is overblown and insignificant. It is a real, bona fide condition that can cause many physical and mental problems from simple exhaustion to death. By learning how to recognize the signs of stress, what causes you to be "stressed out," and effectively dealing with your stress, you can actually control many of the negative physical and emotional side effects caused by prolonged stress (see Figure 6.11).

IndexOpen

Have you ever allowed procrastination to stress you out? What was the result?

TIPS FOR PERSONAL SUCCESS

Consider the following tips for dealing with and reducing stress in your life:

▶ Use relaxation techniques such as visualization, listening to music, and practicing yoga.

▶ Let minor hassles and annoyances go. Ask yourself, *"Is this situation worth a heart attack, stroke, or high blood pressure?"*

▶ Don't be afraid to take a break. Managing your time can help you take more relaxation breaks.

Now it is your turn. Create a list of at least three more tips that you would offer a fellow classmate to assist him or her with reducing unhealthy stress in his or her life.

1. _____

2. _____

3. _____

6.11 *Three Types of Major Stressors in Life*

Type	Cause	What You Can Do to Reduce Stress
Situational		
	Change in physical environment	▶ If at all possible, change your residence or physical environment to better suit your needs. If you can't change it, talk to the people involved and explain your feelings.
	Change in social environment	▶ Work hard to meet new friends who support support you and on whom you can rely in times of need. ▶ Get involved in some type of school activity. ▶ Enroll in classes with friends and find a campus support group.
	Daily hassles	▶ Try to keep things in perspective and work to reduce the situations that you allow to stress you out. ▶ Allow time in your schedule for unexpected events. ▶ Find a quiet place to relax and study.
	Poor time management	▶ Work out a time management plan that allows time to complete your projects while allowing time for rest and joy too. ▶ Create "to-do" lists.
	Conflicts at work, home, and school	▶ Read about conflict management (Chapter 4 in this text) and realize that conflict can be managed. ▶ Avoid "hot" topics such as religion or politics if you feel these discussions cause you to engage in uncomfortable conflicts. ▶ Be assertive, not aggressive or rude.
	People	▶ Try to avoid people who stress you out. ▶ Put people into perspective and realize that we're all different with different needs, wants, and desires. ▶ Realize that not everyone is going to be like you.
	Relationships	▶ Work hard to develop healthy, positive relationships. ▶ Move away from toxic, unhealthy relationships and people who bring you down. ▶ Understand that you can NEVER change the way another person feels, acts, or thinks.

FIGURE 6.11 *Three Types of Major Stressors in Life (continued)*

Type	Cause	What You Can Do to Reduce Stress
Situational *(continued)*		
	Death of a loved one	▶ Try to focus on the good times you shared and what they meant to your life. ▶ Remember that death is as much a part of life as living. ▶ Talk about the person with your friends and family—share your memories. ▶ Consider what the deceased person would have wanted you to do.
	Financial problems	▶ Cut back on your spending. ▶ Seek the help of a financial planner. ▶ Determine why your financial planning or spending patterns are causing you problems. ▶ Apply for financial assistance.
Psychological		
	Unrealistic expectations	▶ Surround yourself with positive people and work hard to set realistic goals with doable timelines and results. ▶ Expect and anticipate less.
	Homesickness	▶ Surround yourself with people who support you. ▶ Call or visit home as often as you can until you get more comfortable. ▶ Meet new friends on campus through organizations and clubs.
	Fear	▶ Talk to professors, counselors, family, and friends about your fears. Put them into perspective. ▶ Visualize success and not failure. ▶ Do one thing every day that scares you to expand your comfort zone.
	Anxiety over your future and what is going to happen	▶ Put things into perspective and work hard to plan and prepare, but accept that life is about constant change. ▶ Talk to a counselor or advisor about your future plans and develop a strategy to meet your goals. ▶ Don't try to control the uncontrollable.

(continued)

FIGURE

6.11   *Three Types of Major Stressors in Life (continued)*

Type	Cause	What You Can Do to Reduce Stress
Psychological *(continued)*		
	Anxiety over your past	▶ Try to see the big picture and how "the puzzle" is going to come together. ▶ Work hard to overcome past challenges and remember that your past does not have to dictate your future. ▶ Learn to forgive. ▶ Focus on your future and what you really want to accomplish.
Biological		
	Insomnia	▶ Watch your caffeine intake. ▶ Avoid naps. ▶ Do not exercise two hours prior to your normal bedtime. ▶ Complete all of your activities before going to bed (studying, watching TV, e-mailing, texting, etc.). Your bed is for sleeping.
	Anxiety	▶ Laugh more. Share a joke. ▶ Enjoy your friends and family. ▶ Practice breathing exercises. ▶ Talk it out with friends. ▶ Learn to say "No" and then say it as often as necessary. ▶ Turn off the TV if the news makes you anxious or nervous.
	Weight loss/gain	▶ Develop an exercise and healthy eating plan. ▶ Meet with a nutrition specialist on campus or in the community. ▶ Join a health-related club or group.
	Reduced physical activities	▶ Increase your daily activity. ▶ If possible, walk to class instead of driving. ▶ Take the stairs instead of using the elevator.
	Sexual difficulties/ dysfunction	▶ Seek medical help in case something is physically wrong. ▶ Determine if your actions are in contradiction with your value system.

REFLECTIONS ON TIME AND STRESS MANAGEMENT

Managing your time and reducing your levels of stress are two skills that you will need for the rest of your life. By learning to avoid procrastinating and taking the time to enhance the quality of your life, you are actually increasing your staying power as a college student. Further, as you enter the world of work, both of these skills will be necessary for your success. Technological advances, fewer people doing more work, and pressure to perform at unprecedented levels can put your life in a tailspin, but with the ability to plan your time and reduce your own stress level, you are making a contribution to your own success.

As you continue this term in college and work toward managing your time and stress levels, consider the following ideas:

► Make a to-do list every evening to plan for the next day.
► Always include time for friends, joy, and adventure in your schedule.
► Avoid procrastination by practicing the "Just Do It" mentality.
► Work hard to lose the "Superhuman" and perfectionist attitudes.
► Delegate everything that you can.
► Plan your day and week to avoid becoming too stressed.
► To reduce stress, take a few moments to relax in private.
► When stress is overwhelming, take time to decompress.

Good luck to you as you develop your plan for managing your time and stress.

> "I wanted a perfect ending. Now I've learned, the hard way, that some poems don't rhyme, and some stories don't have a clear beginning, middle and end. Life is about knowing, having to change, taking the moment and making the best of it without knowing what is going to happen next."
> —Gilda Radner

CREATE SUCCESS
Your Journey to University, Career, and Life Beyond College

Connecting

Think about the people on your college campus. With whom can you make a connection to learn more about *self-discipline as related to time management?* (Example: counselor, advisor, retention specialist, etc.) Why and how will this connection be important?

Reading

Find one brief, relevant article (in print or online) relating to *simplifying your life.* After you have read the article, write a brief summary of the additional facts you have learned.

E-Learning

Using your social networking site or a text message, ask your friends and associates **WHY they procrastinate.** After you have compiled your list of reasons they procrastinate (use at least five reasons), develop two action steps for each that could be used to reduce procrastination (you should have 10 in total).

Analyzing

Choose one main idea or topic from this chapter. After exploring and researching this idea further, determine how this information can help you succeed in other classes.

Transitioning

How will you use the content found in this chapter to help you create a successful transition plan to your next semester and beyond?

Empowering

Thinking about the entire spectrum of your life (college, family, friends, finances, career, etc.), how can you empower yourself to be more successful through the information found in this chapter?

SQ3R *Mastery* Study Sheet

EXAMPLE QUESTION *(from page 148)* What are the components of self-discipline?		**ANSWER:**
EXAMPLE QUESTION *(from page 151)* How can I simplify my life and get more done?		**ANSWER:**
AUTHOR QUESTION *(from page 147)* What is self-discipline and how is it related to time management?		**ANSWER:**
AUTHOR QUESTION *(from page 149)* What are the benefits of learning how to say no?		**ANSWER:**
AUTHOR QUESTION *(from page 163)* What are three strategies to effective time management and planning?		**ANSWER:**
AUTHOR QUESTION *(from page 165)* How does good stress differ from bad stress?		**ANSWER:**
AUTHOR QUESTION *(from page 167)* What are some of the physical and mental symptoms of stress?		**ANSWER:**
YOUR QUESTION *(from page ____)*		**ANSWER:**
YOUR QUESTION *(from page ____)*		**ANSWER:**
YOUR QUESTION *(from page ____)*		**ANSWER:**
YOUR QUESTION *(from page ____)*		**ANSWER:**
YOUR QUESTION *(from page ____)*		**ANSWER:**

Finally, after answering these questions, recite this chapter's major points in your mind. Consider the following general questions to help you master this material.

► What was it about?
► What does it mean?
► What was the most important thing I learned? Why?
► What were the key points to remember?

CHAPTER 7
LEARN

USING YOUR DOMINANT INTELLIGENCE, PREFERRED LEARNING STYLE, AND UNIQUE PERSONALITY TYPE TO BECOME AN ACTIVE LEARNER

"We are led to truth by our weaknesses as well as our strengths."

—Parker Palmer

WHY READ THIS CHAPTER?

What's in it for me?

WHY is it important to understand what some old guys say about learning theory? *WHY* do I need to know my personality type? *WHY* will a chapter on discovering my learning style and dominant intelligence help me study better? *WHY* is it important to know the difference between my learning style and a learning strategy?

Why? Because discovering how "*TO* LEARN" and discovering how "*YOU* LEARN" are two of the most important things you will ever do for yourself as a college student. Learning **how TO learn** means that you know where to find information, how to store information in your brain so that it is easily retrievable, and how to make connections between one thing and another. Learning **how you learn** means that you know your own learning style, your primary intelligence, and your personality type and understand how to apply these characteristics to various learning situations. Knowing how you learn also affects the way you approach the task of mastering content. It is a dynamic discovery that will help you change your academic performance.

By carefully reading this chapter and taking the information provided seriously, you will be able to:

▶ Define learning and discuss several historical learning theories.

▶ Identify and discuss the steps in the learning process.

▶ Identify and use your learning style to increase active and authentic learning.

▶ Identify and use your primary intelligence to increase active and authentic learning.

▶ Identify and use your personality type to increase active and authentic learning.

CHAPTER 7 | LEARN

"Learn everything you can, anytime you can, from anyone you can—there will always come a time when you will be grateful you did."

—*Sarah Caldwell*

How my
COMMUNITY
COLLEGE
changed my life

ALENCIA ANDERSON
Graduate!
Delgado Community College, New Orleans, Louisiana

An interview conducted and written by
MELANIE DEFFENDALL
Director, Women's Center and Coordinator of College Success, Delgado Community College

She was 27 years old with a baby and a seven-year-old, working a job in retail when she decided to go back to school. She knew she was supposed to go to college, but had let life get in the way of her dreams. She said, *"I was working, paying bills, but ends were not meeting, so I said that Delgado Community College is where my life began. Change just happened; overnight my entire life just changed."*

Alencia caught my attention because she seemed to hang onto every word that was being said. She was a young, professionally dressed woman who seemed older than the fresh-out-of-high-school student. During the semester I related my story of returning to school at the age of 35 after a divorce. We had a lot in common and had many discussions regarding her future. *"I didn't know for certain if I wanted to go to a four-year college, even at that time. I thought I wanted to major in English. After talking with Ms. Deffendall, I did transfer to a four-year college after completing my basics and majored in sociology. I now have a master's degree in criminal justice and will begin law school in the fall at Southern University."*

"It all began at Delgado. I was a first-generation college student, the first to enter college, the first in my family on both sides, now the first to hold a degree, two degrees. I asked myself if I was smart enough to go to college. Your words spoke to me, to my life; you cared and I felt that. When I think about community college, I think that is where my self-esteem developed. It gave me the confidence to believe that the goals I had thought about and wrote down could be achieved. It opened doors for me even before I graduated. I am so grateful for community college, for this community college."

Alencia's confidence grew and so did her abilities. Students need to believe they can succeed. Her success is my success, because that is why I teach at a community college, to change lives. She still has her textbook and remarks that: *"Knowledge is power. I just believe that before you can do something, you have to have knowledge. This is where the knowledge began. I thought I knew a great deal, but there was so much more I needed to know. This is where the knowledge started, where the doors opened. Not just walking through one door, but so many more doors; so many more opportunities that I didn't even know existed. Until you go to college and learn what is available, you have no idea what you can become. This was a great start."*

THINK ABOUT IT

1. Alencia had several home and family issues that could have prevented her from attending college. However, she determined that her best bet for the future was to secure her education. What obstacles will you need to overcome to make your dream of a college degree a reality?

2. How has community college helped you develop your self-esteem and personal passion? What have you learned about careers since you began your community college experience?

In the preface of this book (page xiv), you read about the **SQ3R study method.** Right now, take a few moments, **scan this chapter,** and on the SQ3R Mastery Study Sheet on page 199 write **five of your own questions** that you think will be important to your mastery of this material. In addition to the two questions below, you will find five questions from your authors on that study sheet. Use one of your *"Study for Quiz"* stickers to flag this page for easy reference.

EXAMPLES:

▶ What is the difference between a learning style and a learning strategy? (from page 186)

▶ What is the definition of tactile learning and how do you use it? (from page 188)

Bananastock

Have you encountered people with a learning style different from yours? How?

WE HOPE YOU LEARNED YOUR LESSON!

What Is This Thing Called Learning, Anyway?

In its purest and simplest form, learning is a *cognitive mental action* in which new information is acquired or in which you learn to use old information in a new way. Learning can be *conscious* and/or *unconscious.* Do you remember the very day you learned how to walk or talk? Probably not. This learning was more of an unconscious nature. However, you probably do remember learning about the 50 states or subtraction or reading an Edgar Allan Poe poem for the first time. This learning was more conscious in nature. Learning can also be *formal* (schooling) or *informal* ("street knowledge"). Learning can happen in many ways such as through play, trial and error, mistakes, successes, repetition, environmental conditioning, parental discipline, social interactions, media, observation, and, yes, through formal study methods.

Learning is what you do *FOR* yourself; it is not done *TO* you. Parents may discipline you time and time and time again, but try as they might, until YOU learn the lesson trying to be taught, it will NOT be learned. Teachers can preach and talk until they are blue in the face about the 13 original colonies, but until you learn them and commit them to memory, they will NOT be learned. That is what this chapter is all about—helping you discover how you learn, why you learn, and assisting you in finding the best way to learn so that you can DO the learning for yourself on a more effective level.

What Do the Experts Say?

The question still begs: *HOW do we really learn?* By studying a textbook? By reading a newspaper? By looking at pictures? By interviewing someone about a topic? By watching a movie? By trying something to see if it works? Yes, but the process is much more complex than this. Around 300 BC, the great Greek philosopher **Socrates** introduced his theory of learning. He believed that we learn by asking questions. This is called the Socratic Method. His student, **Plato,** expanded on this theory, believing that we learn best by dialogue, called the Dialectic Method, which involves "the searcher" beginning a conversation on a topic and having a dialogue with "an expert" on the other side. He believed that through this back-and-forth conversation, knowledge could be acquired.

In the 5th century BC, the Chinese philosopher **Lao-Tse** wrote, "*If you tell me, I will listen. If you show me, I will see. But if you let me experience, I will learn.*" He was one of the first to proclaim that active, involved learning was a viable form of acquiring information. **Kung Fu-tse (Confucius)** first introduced the case study, which includes telling stories or parables and then having people discuss the issues or the case to learn and acquire knowledge. In 1690, the English philosopher **John Locke** introduced the theory of "the blank slate." He believed that all humans were born with empty minds and that we learn information about the world through what our senses bring to us (sensory learning). He felt that learning was like a pyramid—we learn the basics and then build on those simple principles until we can master complex ideas.

In the 1760s, the French philosopher **Jean-Jacques Rousseau** expanded on a theory that suggested that people learn best by experiencing rather than by authority. In other words, we learn best by doing something rather than being told how someone else did it. He was the first to thoroughly introduce the concept of individual learning styles, believing that learning should be natural to us and follow our basic instincts and feelings. In the early 1900s, the American psychologist **J. B. Watson** developed the theory of behaviorism, believing that we learn best by conditioning. His theory was based on that of Pavlov (and his dog) and held the tenet that we act and learn in certain ways because we have been conditioned to do so. If a dog (or a person) is fed when it rings a bell, the dog (or the person) quickly learns to ring the bell when it *wants* to be fed.

In the mid 1900s, Swiss psychologist **Jean Piaget** introduced the groundbreaking theory of holistic learning. This theory is widely held today as one of the most important breakthroughs in educational psychology. Piaget believed that we learn best by experiencing a wide variety of stimuli such as reading, listening, experimenting, exploring, and questioning. In 1956, **Benjamin Bloom** introduced his taxonomy of learning. Bloom believed in a mastery approach to learning. This theory suggests that we learn simple information and then transform that information into more complex ideas, solutions, and creations. His was an idea of learning how to process and actually use information in a meaningful way.

As you can see from these historical experts in the fields of learning, educational psychology, and philosophy, there are many theories on just HOW we learn best. Perhaps the most important thing to take from these examples is tied into Jean Piaget's theory of holistic learning—that as individuals with diverse and varied needs, backgrounds, and experiences, we require a variety of stimuli to help us learn and that we all learn differently at different stages in our lives.

GIVE YOUR BRAIN A WORKOUT

Can I Really Learn All This Stuff?

Yes! Yes! Yes! You can learn! Think about all that you have already learned in your lifetime. You learned how to eat, walk, talk, play, make decisions, dress yourself, have a conversation, tie your shoes, make your bed, ride a bicycle, play a sport, drive a car, protect yourself, make associations based on observations, use a cell phone, play a video game, ask questions, and countless other simple and highly complex skills. The *proof* that you **CAN learn** is that you **HAVE learned** in the past. The old excuse of "*I can't learn this stuff*" is simply hogwash! You have the capacity to know more, do more, experience more, and acquire more knowledge. Your

> "The mind is not a vessel to be filled, but rather a fire to be kindled."
> —Plutarch

> "Many things in life cannot be transmitted well by words, concepts, or books. Colors that we see cannot be described to a person born blind. Only a swimmer knows how swimming feels; the non-swimmer can get only the faintest idea of it with all the words and books in the world. And so it goes. Perhaps it is better to say that all of life must first be known experientially. There is no substitute for experience, none at all."
> —Abraham H. Maslow

brain is a natural learning machine just as your heart is a natural pumping machine. It is in our nature to learn every single day. You just have to understand how this process works in order to make the most of your brain's natural learning power. And you have to **devote the time necessary to learn** the basics of something new and then build on that knowledge base. Time and effort are very important aspects of the learning process.

You also have to give your brain a "workout" to make sure it stays in shape. Just as your body needs exercise and activities to stay in shape, your brain does too. When you "work out" your brain and use it to learn new material, your brain releases a chemical called **cypin** (SIGH-pin). Cypin is found throughout the body, but in the brain, it helps build new branches, like a tree sprouting new growth. In a nutshell, when you exercise your brain, your brain rewards you with new learning patterns and new learning receptors. This is sometimes referred to as **neuroplasticity** (new-ro-plas-TIS-i-ty), or the brain's ability to change with new knowledge.

THE LEARNING PROCESS
What Are the Steps to Active, Authentic Learning?

"Human beings have an innate learning process, which includes a motivation to learn" (Smilkstein, 2003). You may be saying to yourself, *"If I have a natural, innate ability to learn, then why is chemistry so difficult for me to master?"* or *"Why is English such a crazy language with so many rules?"* The answer to both could rest in the notion that you are going AGAINST your natural, neurological learning pattern—that you are being taught, or are trying to learn by yourself, in a way that is unnatural to you, and your brain simply is having trouble adapting to this unnatural process.

If you learn best by doing and touching, **you need to do and touch.** If you learn best by listening and questioning, you need to **listen and question.** If you learn best by reading and studying in a quiet place, you need to **find a quiet place to read and study.** Basically, you must figure out your natural inclination for learning and build on it. You will also need to understand that learning takes time and that people need different amounts of time to master material. Janet may learn Concept X in a few hours, but it may take William three days of constant practice to learn the same concept. One thing is true for everyone: The more INVOLVED you are with the information you are trying to learn, the more you will retain.

In Figure 7.1 we have tried to simplify thousands of years of educational study on the topic of learning. Basically, learning something new can happen in the six steps outlined in Figure 7.1.

If you are trying to learn new facts, concepts, procedures, principles, systems, solutions, or processes, you could achieve this goal by using these six steps. Take a moment and carefully review them now.

As a practice activity, research one of the following topics (all of which we purposefully chose because of their uniqueness . . . OK, weirdness) using the six steps in the Learning Process chart (Figure 7.1). You can do this in your notebook or online journal. Remember, however, that you will need to devote some time to this activity. Learning new information does not happen instantaneously. You will also need to use a variety of sources. Do not depend solely on Wikipedia! Yes, there are other sources out there!

Possible topics:

▶ What was The Night of Long Knives?
▶ What is the mystery of the pyramid at Cheops?
▶ Why and how long can a cockroach live without a head?
▶ Who invented the electric chair and why?
▶ What is Sanskrit?
▶ How is paper made?
▶ Who invented the zero and what is its duel function?
▶ Who was Vlad the Impaler? What famous character did his life inspire?

FIGURE 7.1 *The Learning Process*

1. Motivation to learn the material is the first step in the learning process. You have to possess the internal motivation and passion to WANT to learn what is being presented or what you are studying. You must also be motivated enough to devote the time to learning something new. Deep, purposeful learning does not happen in an instant; it takes work, patience, and yes, motivation.

2. Understand the material through ambitious curiosity, keen observations, purposeful questioning, intense studying, eager determination, robust effort, and time devoted to task. You must answer questions such as: Who is involved? What happened? When did it happen? Where did it happen? How did it happen? How could it have happened? What does it all mean? Why is it important? What is the relationship between x and y? You should be able to describe it, discuss it, give examples, put the information into your own words, and tell others about it clearly.

3. Internalize the material by asking: How can this information affect my life, my career, my studies, and my future? Why does this information matter? How can I control my emotions regarding the value of this information? If I think this information is useless, how can I change this perception?

4. Apply the material by asking: How can I use this information to improve? How can I use this information to work with others, to develop new ideas, or to build meaningful conclusions? Can I demonstrate it? Can I share this information with, or teach this information to, others intelligently? Is it possible to practice what I have learned?

5. Evaluate the material by determining the value of what you just learned. Ask: Do I trust my research and sources? Have I consulted others about their findings and knowledge? What did they learn? What can I learn from them? Have I asked for feedback? Can I debate this information with others?

6. Use the material to grow and change. How could I take this information (or the process of learning this information) and change my life, attitudes, or emotions? How could this information help me grow? What can I create out of this new information? How can I expand on this knowledge to learn more?

UNDERSTANDING YOUR STRENGTHS

What Are the Advantages of Discovering and Polishing Your Talents?

On the next few pages, you will have the opportunity to complete three inventories: one to identify your **learning style** (Figure 7.5), one to identify your **personality type** (Figure 7.7), and one to identify your **dominant intelligence** (Figure 7.2). At the end of the chapter, you will have the opportunity to pull all of this information together to help you understand your learning patterns and to formulate a learning plan for the future.

7.2 *Take the MIS*

The Multiple Intelligences Survey

Directions: Read each statement carefully and thoroughly. After reading the statement, rate your response using the scale below. There are no right or wrong answers. This is not a timed survey. The MIS is based, in part, on *Frames of Mind* by Howard Gardner, 1983.

3 = Often Applies

2 = Sometimes Applies

1 = Never or Almost Never Applies

_____ 1. When someone gives me directions, I have to visualize them in my mind in order to understand them.

_____ 2. I enjoy crossword puzzles and word games like Scrabble.

_____ 3. I enjoy dancing and can keep up with the beat of music.

_____ 4. I have little or no trouble conceptualizing information or facts.

_____ 5. I like to repair things that are broken such as toasters, small engines, bicycles, and cars.

_____ 6. I enjoy leadership activities on campus and in the community.

_____ 7. I have the ability to get others to listen to me.

_____ 8. I enjoy working with nature, animals, and plants.

_____ 9. I know where everything is in my home such as supplies, gloves, flashlights, camera, and compact discs.

_____10. I am a good speller.

_____11. I often sing or hum to myself in the shower or car or while walking or just sitting.

_____12. I am a very logical, orderly thinker.

_____13. I use a lot of gestures when I talk to people.

_____14. I can recognize and empathize with people's attitudes and emotions.

_____15. I prefer to study alone.

_____16. I can name many different things in the environment such as clouds, rocks, and plant types.

_____17. I like to draw pictures, graphs, or charts to better understand information.

_____18. I have a good memory for names and dates.

_____19. When I hear music, I "get into it" by moving, humming, tapping, or even singing.

_____20. I learn better by asking a lot of questions.

_____21. I enjoy playing competitive sports.

_____22. I communicate very well with other people.

_____23. I know what I want and I set goals to accomplish it.

_____24. I have some interest in herbal remedies and natural medicine.

_____25. I enjoy working puzzles or mazes.

_____26. I am a good storyteller.

_____27. I can easily remember the words and melodies of songs.

_____28. I enjoy solving problems in math and chemistry and working with computer programming problems.

_____29. I usually touch people or pat them on the back when I talk to them.

_____30. I understand my family and friends better than most other people do.

_____31. I don't always talk about my accomplishments with others.

_____32. I would rather work outside around nature than inside around people and equipment.

_____33. I enjoy and learn more when seeing movies, slides, or videos in class.

_____34. I am a very good listener and I enjoy listening to others' stories.

_____35. I need to study with music.

_____36. I enjoy games like Clue, Battleship, chess, and Rubik's Cube.

_____37. I enjoy physical activities such as bicycling, jogging, dancing, snowboarding, skateboarding, or swimming.

_____38. I am good at solving people's problems and conflicts.

_____39. I have to have time alone to think about new information in order to remember it.

_____40. I enjoy sorting and organizing information, objects, and collectibles.

FIGURE

7.2   *Take the MIS (continued)*

Refer to your score on each individual question. Place that score beside the appropriate question number below. Then, tally each line at the side.

Score					Total Across	Code
1 ___	9 ___	17 ___	25 ___	33 ___	_____	Visual/Spatial
2 ___	10 ___	18 ___	26 ___	34 ___	_____	Verbal/Linguistic
3 ___	11 ___	19 ___	27 ___	35 ___	_____	Musical/Rhythmic
4 ___	12 ___	20 ___	28 ___	36 ___	_____	Logical/Mathematical
5 ___	13 ___	21 ___	29 ___	37 ___	_____	Bodily/Kinesthetic
6 ___	14 ___	22 ___	30 ___	38 ___	_____	Interpersonal
7 ___	15 ___	23 ___	31 ___	39 ___	_____	Intrapersonal
8 ___	16 ___	24 ___	32 ___	40 ___	_____	Naturalistic

MIS Tally

Multiple Intelligences

Look at the scores on the MIS. What are your top three scores? Write them in the spaces below.

Top Score	_____	Code	_____
Second Score	_____	Code	_____
Third Score	_____	Code	_____

This tally can help you understand where some of your strengths may be. Again, this is not a measure of your worth or capacities, nor is it an indicator of your future successes. Read the following section to better understand multiple intelligences.

© Robert M. Sherfield, Ph.D.

These assessments are in no way intended to "label you." They are not a measure of how smart you are. They do not measure your worth or your capacities as a student or a citizen. The three assessments are included so that you might gain a better understanding of your dominant intelligence, identify your learning style, and discover your strongest personality type.

There are no right or wrong answers and there is no one best way to learn. We hope that by the end of this chapter, you will have experienced a "Wow" or "Ah-ha!" moment as you explore and discover new and exciting components of your education. We also hope that by the end of this chapter, you will have the skills you need to more effectively use your dominant traits and improve your less dominant characteristics.

UNDERSTANDING MULTIPLE INTELLIGENCES

Why Is It Important to Discover New Ways of Looking at Yourself?

In 1983, Howard Gardner, a Harvard University professor, developed a theory called Multiple Intelligences. In his book *Frames of Mind,* he outlines seven intelligences that he feels are possessed by everyone: visual/spatial, verbal/linguistic, musical/rhythmic, logical/mathematical, bodily/kinesthetic, interpersonal, and intrapersonal. In 1996, he added an eighth intelligence: naturalistic (Figure 7.3). In short, if you have ever done things that came easily for you, you were probably drawing on one of your well-developed intelligences. On the other hand, if you have tried to do things that are very difficult to master or understand, you may be dealing with

DID YOU KNOW

George Stroud/Hulton Archives/Getty Images

PABLO PICASSO, the world-renowned, trend-setting artist, was born in Spain. He had a hard time in school and is said to have had a very difficult time with reading. He was diagnosed with a learning disability and his formal education never really benefited him. He left his college-level courses at the Academy of Arts in Madrid after less than a year of study. However, because of his immense artistic talent and his cubist interpretation of the universe, he changed the way the world looks at art. He is listed in the *Guinness Book of World Records* as THE most prolific painter in history, having completed nearly 14,000 paintings.

FIGURE

7.3   *The Eight Intelligences*

VISUAL/SPATIAL
- Picture Smart
- Thinks in pictures; knows where things are in the house; loves to create images and work with graphs, charts, pictures, and maps.

VERBAL/LINGUISTIC
- Word Smart
- Communicates well through language, likes to write, is good at spelling, great at telling stories, loves to read books.

MUSICAL/RHYTHMIC
- Music Smart
- Loves to sing, hum, and whistle; comprehends music; responds to music immediately; performs music.

LOGICAL/MATHEMATICAL
- Number Smart
- Can easily conceptualize and reason, uses logic, has good problem-solving skills, enjoys math and science.

BODILY/KINESTHETIC
- Body Smart
- Learns through body sensation, moves around a lot, enjoys work involving the hands, is graced with some athletic ability.

INTERPERSONAL
- People Smart
- Loves to communicate with other people, possesses great leadership skills, has lots of friends, is involved in extracurricular activities.

INTRAPERSONAL
- Self Smart
- Has a deep awareness of own feelings, is very reflective, requires time to be alone, does not get involved with group activities.

NATURALISTIC
- Environment Smart
- Has interest in the environment and in nature; can easily recognize plants, animals, rocks, and cloud formations; may like hiking, camping, and fishing.

material that calls on one of your less developed intelligences. If playing the piano by ear comes easily to you, your musical/rhythmic intelligence may be very strong. If you have trouble writing or understanding poetry, your verbal/linguistic intelligence may not be as well developed.

This does not mean that you will never be able to write poetry; it simply means that this is not your dominant intelligence and you may need to spend more time on this activity.

USING MULTIPLE INTELLIGENCES TO ENHANCE STUDYING AND LEARNING

Can You Make Them Work for You?

In Figure 7.4, you will find some helpful tips to assist you in creating a study environment and study habits using your multiple intelligences. Read each category because you may need to improve your less dominant intelligence in some of the classes you take. This list can help you build on your strengths and develop your less dominant areas.

FIGURE 7.4 *Using the Multiple Intelligences*

VISUAL/SPATIAL 	• Use visuals in your notes such as timelines, charts, graphs, and geometric shapes. • Work to create a mental or visual picture of the information at hand. • Use colored markers to make associations or to group items together. • Use mapping or webbing so that your main points are easily recognized. • When taking notes, draw pictures in the margins to illustrate the main points. • Visualize the information in your mind.
VERBAL/LINGUISTIC 	• Establish study groups so that you will have the opportunity to talk about the information. • Using the information you studied, create a story or a skit. • Read as much information about related areas as possible. • As you read chapters, outline them in your own words. • Summarize and recite your notes aloud.
MUSICAL/RHYTHMIC 	• Listen to music while studying (if it does not distract you). • Write a song, jingle, or rap about the chapter or information. • Take short breaks from studying to listen to music. • Associate the information being studied to the music from your favorite song.
LOGICAL/ MATHEMATICAL	• Strive to make logical connections between subjects. • Don't just memorize the facts; apply them to real-life situations. • As you study the information, think of problems in society and how this information could solve those problems. • Create analyzing charts. Draw a line down the center of the page, put the information at hand in the left column and analyze, discuss, relate, and synthesize it in the right column. • Allow yourself some time to reflect after studying.

(continued)

FIGURE

7.4 *Using the Multiple Intelligences (continued)*

BODILY/KINESTHETIC

- Don't confine your study area to a desk or chair; move around, explore, go outside.
- Act out the information.
- Study in a group of people and change groups often.
- Use charts, posters, flash cards, and chalkboards to study.
- When appropriate or possible, build models using the information studied.
- Verbalize the information to others.
- Use games such as chess, Monopoly, Twister, or Clue when studying.
- Trace words as you study them.
- Use repetition to learn facts; write them many times.
- Make study sheets.

INTERPERSONAL

- Study in groups.
- Share the information with other people.
- Teach the information to others.
- Interview outside sources to learn more about the material at hand.
- Have a debate with others about the information.

INTRAPERSONAL

- Study in a quiet area.
- Study by youself.
- Allow time for reflection and meditation about the subject matter.
- Study in short time blocks and then spend some time absorbing the information.
- Work at your own pace.

NATURALISTIC

- Study outside whenever possible.
- Relate the information to the effect on the environment whenever possible.
- When given the opportunity to choose your own topics or research projects, choose something related to nature.
- Collect your own study data and resources.
- Organize and label your information.
- Keep separate notebooks on individual topics so that you can add new information to each topic as it becomes available to you.

UNDERSTANDING LEARNING STYLES THEORY

Why Is It Important to Know HOW I Learn?

A learning style is "the way in which each learner begins to concentrate on, process, and retain new and difficult information" (Dunn and Griggs, 2000). There is a difference between a *learning style* and a *learning strategy.* A learning *style* is innate and involves your five senses. It is how you best process information that comes to you. A learning *strategy* is how you might choose to learn or study, such as by using note cards, flip charts, color slides, or cooperative learning groups. Your learning strategy also involves where you study (such as at a desk, in bed, at the library, in a quiet place, with music, etc.), how long you study, and what techniques you use to help you study (such as mnemonics, cooperative learning teams, or SQ3R).

If you learn best by *seeing* information, you have a more dominant *visual learning style.* If you learn best by *hearing* information, you have a more dominant *auditory learning style.* If you learn best by *touching or doing,* you have a more dominant *tactile learning style.* You may also hear the tactile learning style referred to as *kinesthetic* or *hands-on.*

Some of the most successful students master information and techniques by using all three styles. If you were learning how to skateboard, you might learn best by *hearing someone* talk about the different styles or techniques. Others might learn best by *watching a video* in which someone demonstrates the techniques. Still others would learn best by actually getting on the board and *trying it out.* Those who engage all of their senses gain the most.

After taking the LEAD (Figure 7.5) and reading more about learning styles (Figure 7.6), list at least three concrete strategies that you can employ to enhance your learning strategies for each of the three areas.

FIGURE 7.5 *Take the LEAD*

The Learning Evaluation and Assessment Directory

Directions: Read each statement carefully and thoroughly. After reading the statement, rate your response using the scale below. There are no right or wrong answers. This is not a timed survey. The LEAD is based, in part, on research conducted by Rita Dunn.

3 = Often Applies
2 = Sometimes Applies
1 = Never or Almost Never Applies

_____ 1. I remember information better if I write it down or draw a picture of it.
_____ 2. I remember things better when I hear them instead of just reading or seeing them.
_____ 3. When I get something that has to be assembled, I just start doing it. I don't read the directions.
_____ 4. If I am taking a test, I can "see" the page of the text or lecture notes where the answer is located.
_____ 5. I would rather the professor explain a graph, chart, or diagram than just show it to me.
_____ 6. When learning new things, I want to "do it" rather than hear about it.
_____ 7. I would rather the instructor write the information on the board or overhead instead of just lecturing.
_____ 8. I would rather listen to a book on tape than read it.
_____ 9. I enjoy making things, putting things together, and working with my hands.
_____ 10. I am able to quickly conceptualize and visualize information.
_____ 11. I learn best by hearing words.
_____ 12. I have been called hyperactive by my parents, spouse, partner, or professor.
_____ 13. I have no trouble reading maps, charts, or diagrams.
_____ 14. I can usually pick up on small sounds like bells, crickets, or frogs, or distant sounds like train whistles.
_____ 15. I use my hands and gesture a lot when I speak to others.

Refer to your score on each individual question. Place that score beside the appropriate question number below. Then, tally each line at the side.

Score					Total Across	Code
1 _____	4 _____	7 _____	10 _____	13 _____	_____	Visual
2 _____	5 _____	8 _____	11 _____	14 _____	_____	Auditory
3 _____	6 _____	9 _____	12 _____	15 _____	_____	Tactile

LEAD (Learning Styles) SCORE
Look at the scores on the LEAD. What is your top score?

Top Score _____

Code _____

© Robert M. Sherfield, Ph.D.

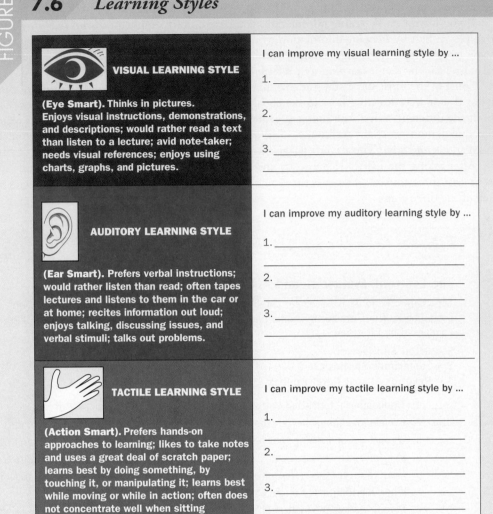

FIGURE 7.6 *Learning Styles*

VISUAL LEARNING STYLE

(Eye Smart). Thinks in pictures. Enjoys visual instructions, demonstrations, and descriptions; would rather read a text than listen to a lecture; avid note-taker; needs visual references; enjoys using charts, graphs, and pictures.

I can improve my visual learning style by ...

1. _____
_____
2. _____
_____
3. _____
_____

AUDITORY LEARNING STYLE

(Ear Smart). Prefers verbal instructions; would rather listen than read; often tapes lectures and listens to them in the car or at home; recites information out loud; enjoys talking, discussing issues, and verbal stimuli; talks out problems.

I can improve my auditory learning style by ...

1. _____
_____
2. _____
_____
3. _____
_____

TACTILE LEARNING STYLE

(Action Smart). Prefers hands-on approaches to learning; likes to take notes and uses a great deal of scratch paper; learns best by doing something, by touching it, or manipulating it; learns best while moving or while in action; often does not concentrate well when sitting and reading.

I can improve my tactile learning style by ...

1. _____
_____
2. _____
_____
3. _____
_____

WANTED: A VISUAL LEARNER WITH TACTILE SKILLS

Do You Know the Differences Between Your Primary Learning Style and Your Dominant Intelligence?

As discussed previously, a *learning style* and a *learning strategy* are different. A learning style and a *dominant intelligence* are also quite different. When you read over the descriptions of multiple intelligences theory and learning styles theory, you probably noticed several common elements. Both theories deal with the visual, auditory, and tactile (or kinesthetic). There are also similarities between the two theories, but the differences are great and important.

SUCCESSFUL DECISIONS: An Activity for Critical Reflection

Kristin knew that her most powerful learning style was visual. She knew that she had always learned best when she could "see" the information in pictures, charts, graphs, PowerPoint slides, videos, or other powerful visuals. Kristin also knew that when she was able to get involved with the information, she seemed to retain it better. She did not at first know what this was called, but later learned that she was also a tactile or "hands-on" learner.

When she discovered that different people have different ways of learning and instructors have different ways of teaching, things began to make more sense to her. She had wondered why she had always done poorly in classes that were all lecture—like her history class. This semester, she was becoming increasingly worried about her performance in her literature class. It, too, was all lecture—information about poems, plays, and sonnets. She decided to go to the Tutoring Center to find out what she could do to retain the information more effectively. Her tutor showed her how to make the terms and ideas more "visual" by drawing pictures beside each one, using colors in her notes, creating small story boards, and creating a visual image of what was being discussed.

In your own words, what would you suggest that a classmate do if he or she is having trouble understanding, interpreting, or remembering information from a class where there is very little discussion or lecture and he or she is a very strong auditory learner? List at least three things that your classmate could do to strengthen his or her less dominant intelligence or learning style. Think about what services are offered on your campus and what people might be of assistance to him or her.

1. _____

2. _____

3. _____

Simply stated, you can have a visual learning style and yet **not have** visual/spatial as your dominant intelligence. *"How can this be possible?"* you may be asking. It may be that you **learn best** how to paint a picture by watching someone paint a picture—watching his or her brushstrokes, his or her method of mixing paints, and his or her spatial layout (this is your dominant visual *learning style*). However, you may not be as engaged or as talented at actually painting as the person you watched. Your painting may lack feeling, depth, and expression. You may find it hard to paint anything that is not copied from something else. You can't visualize a landscape in your mind because your visual/spatial intelligence is not very strong. In other words, you are not an innate artist at heart. This is an example of how your *visual learning style* can be a strong way for you to learn, but your visual/spatial intelligence may not be your dominant intelligence.

In your own words, compare and contrast YOUR primary learning style with your dominant intelligences. Give one example.

_____

_____

_____

_____

From Ordinary to *Extraordinary*

REAL PEOPLE | REAL LIVES | REAL CHANGE

CHEF ODETTE SMITH-RANSOME

Hospitality Instructor

The Art Institute of Pittsburgh, Pittsburgh, Pennsylvania

At the age of 15, I found myself constantly in conflict with my mother, until one day I stood before her as she held a gun to my head. It was at that moment I knew I had to leave my parents' home, not just for my emotional well-being, but for my actual life and survival. My father was a good man, but he did not understand the entire situation with my mother's alcohol and diet pill addiction and he could do little to smooth out the situation between my mother and me. To complicate matters even more, my brother had just returned home from fighting in Vietnam and everyone was trying to adjust. It was a horrible time in the house where my ancestors had lived for over 100 years. So, I packed my clothes, dropped out of the 10th grade, and ran away over 1,000 miles to Charleston, South Carolina.

My first job was as a waitress. I worked in that job for over three years, realizing more every day that I was not using my talents and that without an education, I was doomed to work for minimum wage for the rest of my life. During this time, I met a friend in Charleston who was in the Navy. When he was released, he offered to take me back to Pittsburgh. I agreed and upon my return, I went to work in the kitchen of a family-owned restaurant. They began to take an interest in me and made me feel proud of my work. I then decided to get my GED and determine what road to take that would allow me to use my culinary talents and help others at the same time.

I began my associate's degree, which required that students complete an apprenticeship. We worked 40 hours per week, Monday through Thursday, under the direction of a master chef and we were in class eight hours a day on Friday. My apprenticeship was at the Hyatt Regency in Pittsburgh. In order to obtain my degree, I had to pass the apprenticeship, all of the classes, and a bank of tests that proved

> *So, I packed my clothes, dropped out of the 10th grade, and ran away over 1,000 miles to Charleston, South Carolina.*

my proficiency in a variety of areas. If I failed one part of the tests, I could not get my degree. Proudly, I passed every test, every class, and my apprenticeship.

My first professional job came to me upon the recommendation of a friend. I interviewed for and was hired to become the private chef for the Chancellor of the University of Pittsburgh. I loved the job and it afforded me the opportunity to get my bachelor's degree. So, I juggled a full-time job, a two-year-old child, and a full load of classes. As I neared the end of my degree, I was offered a fellowship at the University of Pittsburgh that trained people to teach students with special needs. I graduated Cum Laude and began teaching and working with people who had cerebral palsy at Con-

nelley Academy. I loved the work, and the position solidified my desire to work with adults.

From there I taught at the Good Will Training Center and later at the Pittsburgh Job Corps, where my culinary team won a major national competition. Today, I am an Instructor at The Art Institute of Pittsburgh, helping others reach their dreams of working in the hospitality industry. In 2005, I was named *Culinary Educator of the Year* by the American Culinary Federation. I try to let my life and my struggles serve as a light for students who have faced adversity and may have felt that their past was going to determine their future. My advice to my students—and to you—is this: NEVER let anyone tell you that you can't do it, that you're not able to do it,

that you don't have the means to do it, or that you'll never succeed. YOU set your own course in life and you determine the direction of your future.

EXTRAORDINARY REFLECTION

Read the following statement and respond in your online journal or class notebook.

Chef Smith-Ransome had to literally leave her family to protect her life. Think about your family situation at the moment. Are your family members supportive of your efforts? Do they offer you support? Are they working with you to help you achieve your goals? If so, how does this make you stronger? Do they offer you guidance?

UNDERSTANDING PERSONALITY TYPE

Are You ENFJ, ISTP, or ENTJ, and Why Does It Matter?

In 1921, Swiss psychologist **Carl Jung** (1875–1961) published his work *Psychological Types*. In this book, Jung suggested that human behavior is not random. He felt that behavior follows patterns and that these patterns are caused by differences in the way people use their minds. In 1942, Isabel Briggs-Myers and her mother, Katharine Briggs, began to put Jung's theory into practice. They developed the Myers-Briggs Type Indicator, which after more than 50 years of research and refinement, has become the most widely used instrument for identifying and studying personality.

Personality typing can "help us discover what best motivates and energizes each of us as individuals" (Tieger and Barron-Tieger, 2007). The questions on the PAP (Figure 7.7) will help you discover whether you are an **E** or an **I** (**E**xtroverted or **I**ntroverted), an **S** or an **N** (**S**ensing or i**N**tuitive), a **T** or an **F** (**T**hinking or **F**eeling), and a **J** or a **P** (**J**udging or **P**erceiving). When all of the combinations of E/I, S/N, T/F, and J/P are combined, there are 16 personality types. Everyone will fit into *ONE* of the following categories:

ISTJ	ISFJ	INFJ	INTJ
ISTP	ISFP	INFP	INTP
ESTP	ESFP	ENFP	ENTP
ESTJ	ESFJ	ENFJ	ENTJ

Let's take a look at the four major categories of typing (Figure 7.8). Notice that the higher your score in one area, the stronger your personality type is for that area. For instance, if you scored 15 on the E (extroversion) questions, this means that you are a strong extrovert. If you scored 15 on the I (introversion) questions, this means that you are a strong introvert. However, if you scored 7 on the E questions and 8 on the I questions, your score indicates that you possess almost the same amount of extroverted and introverted qualities. The same is true for every other category of the PAP.

E VERSUS I (EXTROVERSION/INTROVERSION). This category deals with the way we *interact with others and the world around us, how we draw our energy.*

Extroverts prefer to live in the outside world, drawing their strength from other people. They are outgoing and love interaction. They usually make decisions with others in mind. They enjoy being the center of attention. There are usually few secrets about extroverts.

Introverts draw their strength from the inner world. They need to spend time alone to think and ponder. They are usually quiet and reflective. They usually make decisions by themselves. They do not like being the center of attention. They are private.

S VERSUS N (SENSING/INTUITION). This category deals with the way we *learn and deal with information.*

Sensing types gather information through their five senses. They have a hard time believing something if it cannot be seen, touched, smelled, tasted, or heard. They like concrete facts and details. They do not rely on intuition or gut feelings. They usually have a great deal of common sense.

TIPS FOR PERSONAL SUCCESS

Consider the following tips for making the most of your learning style, personality type, and dominant intelligence.

▶ Improve your weaker learning styles by incorporating at least one aspect of those learning styles into your daily study plans.

▶ If your personality type clashes with your professor's personality type, try to make adjustments that enable you to get through the class successfully.

▶ Adjust your learning style to match your professor's teaching style if possible.

▶ Use your primary intelligence to help you decide on your life's vocation.

Now it is your turn. Create a list of at least three more tips that you would offer to assist a fellow classmate in making the most of his or her learning style, intelligence, and personality type. Develop one strategy for each category.

1. Learning Style Tip _____

2. Multiple Intelligence Tip _____

3. Personality Type Tip _____

FIGURE

7.7 *Take the PAP*

The Personality Assessment Profile

Directions: Read each statement carefully and thoroughly. After reading the statement, rate your response using the scale below. There are no right or wrong answers. This is not a timed survey. The PAP is based, in part, on the Myers-Briggs Type Indicator (MBTI) by Katharine Briggs and Isabel Briggs-Myers.

3 = Often Applies
2 = Sometimes Applies
1 = Never or Almost Never Applies

_____ 1a. I am a very talkative person.
_____ 1b. I am a more reflective person than a verbal person.
_____ 2a. I am a very factual and literal person.
_____ 2b. I look to the future and I can see possibilities.
_____ 3a. I value truth and justice over tact and emotion.
_____ 3b. I find it easy to empathize with other people.
_____ 4a. I am very ordered and efficient.
_____ 4b. I enjoy having freedom from control.
_____ 5a. I am a very friendly and social person.
_____ 5b. I enjoy listening to others more than talking.
_____ 6a. I enjoy being around and working with people who have a great deal of common sense.
_____ 6b. I enjoy being around and working with people who are dreamers and have a great deal of imagination.
_____ 7a. One of my motivating forces is to do a job very well.
_____ 7b. I like to be recognized. I am motivated by my accomplishments and awards.
_____ 8a. I like to plan out my day before I go to bed.
_____ 8b. When I get up on a non-school day or non-work day, I just like to let the day "plan itself."
_____ 9a. I like to express my feelings and thoughts.
_____ 9b. I enjoy a great deal of tranquility and quiet time to myself.
_____ 10a. I am a very pragmatic and realistic person.
_____ 10b. I like to create new ideas, methods, or ways of doing things.
_____ 11a. I make decisions with my brain.
_____ 11b. I make decisions with my heart.
_____ 12a. I am a very disciplined and orderly person.
_____ 12b. I don't make a lot of plans.
_____ 13a. I like to work with a group of people.
_____ 13b. I would rather work independently.
_____ 14a. I learn best if I can see it, touch it, smell it, taste it, or hear it.
_____ 14b. I learn best by relying on my gut feelings or intuition.
_____ 15a. I am quick to criticize others.
_____ 15b. I compliment others very easily and quickly.
_____ 16a. My life is systematic and organized.
_____ 16b. I don't really pay attention to deadlines.
_____ 17a. I can be myself when I am around others.
_____ 17b. I can be myself when I am alone.
_____ 18a. I live in the here and now, in the present.
_____ 18b. I live in the future, planning and dreaming.
_____ 19a. I think that if someone breaks the rules, the person should be punished.

(continued)

FIGURE

7.7 *Take the PAP (continued)*

_____ 19b. I think that if someone breaks the rules, we should look at the person who broke the rules, examine the rules, and look at the situation at hand before a decision is made.

_____ 20a. I do my work, then I play.

_____ 20b. I play, then do my work.

Refer to your score on each individual question. Place that score beside the appropriate question number below. Then, tally each line at the side.

Score					Total Across	Code
1a _____	5a _____	9a _____	13a _____	17a _____	_____	E Extrovert
1b _____	5b _____	9b _____	13b _____	17b _____	_____	I Introvert
2a _____	6a _____	10a _____	14a _____	18a _____	_____	S Sensing
2b _____	6b _____	10b _____	14b _____	18b _____	_____	N Intuition
3a _____	7a _____	11a _____	15a _____	19a _____	_____	T Thinking
3b _____	7b _____	11b _____	15b _____	19b _____	_____	F Feeling
4a _____	8a _____	12a _____	16a _____	20a _____	_____	J Judging
4b _____	8b _____	12b _____	16b _____	20b _____	_____	P Perceiving

PAP Scores

Personality Indicator

Look at the scores on your PAP. Is your score higher in the *E or the I* line? Is your score higher in the *S or the N* line? Is your score higher in the *T or the F* line? Is your score higher in the *J or the P* line? Write the code to the side of each section below.

Is your higher score **E or I** Code _____

Is your higher score **S or N** Code _____

Is your higher score **T or F** Code _____

Is your higher score **J or P** Code _____

© Robert M. Sherfield, Ph.D.

FIGURE

7.8 *Personality Typology*

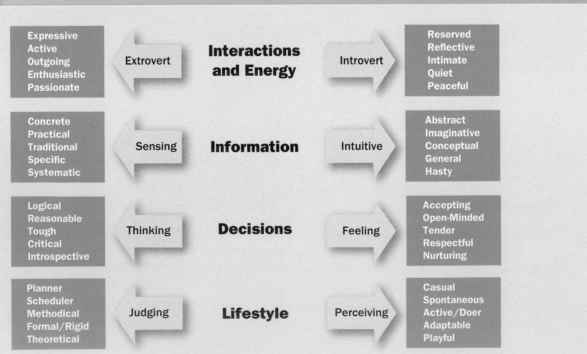

Intuitive types are not very detail-oriented. They can see possibilities, and they rely on their gut feelings. Usually, they are very innovative people. They tend to live in the future and often get bored once they have mastered a task.

T VERSUS F (THINKING/FEELING). This category deals with the way we *make decisions.*

Thinkers are very logical people. They do not make decisions based on feelings or emotions. They are analytical and sometimes do not take others' values into consideration when making decisions. They can easily identify the flaws of others. They can sometimes be seen as insensitive and lacking compassion.

Feelers make decisions based on what they feel is right and just. They like to have harmony, and they value others' opinions and feelings. They are usually very tactful people who like to please others. They are very warm people.

J VERSUS P (JUDGING/PERCEIVING). This category deals with the way we *live and our overall lifestyle.*

Judgers are very orderly people. They must have a great deal of structure in their lives. They are good at setting goals and sticking to them. They are the type of people who would seldom, if ever, play before their work was completed.

Perceivers are just the opposite. They are less structured and more spontaneous. They do not like timelines. Unlike the judgers, they will play before their work is done. They will take every chance to delay a decision or judgment. Sometimes, they can become involved in too many things at one time.

After you have studied the the personality type chart (Figure 7.9) and other information in the chapter regarding your personality type, you can make some decisions about your study

FIGURE 7.9 A Closer Look at Your Personality Type

Personality Type	Characteristics	Possible Careers
ISTJ—The Dutiful (7–10% of Americans)	Have great power of concentration; very serious; dependable; logical and realistic; take responsibility for their own actions; they are not easily distracted.	Accountant, purchasing agent, real estate, IRS agent, corrections officer, investment counselor, law researcher, technical writer, judge, mechanic
ISTP—The Mechanic (4–7% of Americans)	Very reserved; good at making things clear to others; interested in how and why things work; like to work with their hands; can sometimes be misunderstood as idle.	Police officer, intelligence officer, firefighter, athletic coach, engineer, technical trainer, logistic manager, EMT, surgical technician, banker, office manager, carpenter, landscape architect
ISFJ—The Nurturer (7–10% of Americans)	Hard workers; detail-oriented; considerate of others' feelings; friendly and warm to others; very conscientious; they are down-to-earth and like to be around the same.	Dentist, physician, biologist, surgical technician, teacher, speech pathologist, historian, clerical, bookkeeper, electrician, retail owner, counselor
ISFP—The Artist (5–7% of Americans)	Very sensitive and modest; adapt easily to change; they are respectful of others' feelings and values; take criticism personally; don't enjoy leadership roles.	Artist, chef, musician, nurse, medical assistant, surgeon, botanist, zoologist, science teacher, travel agent, game warden, coach, bookkeeper, clerical, insurance examiner
INFJ—The Protector (2–3% of Americans)	Enjoy an atmosphere where all get along; they do what is needed of them; they have strong beliefs and principles; enjoy helping others achieve their goals.	Career counselor, psychologist, teacher, social worker, clergy, artist, novelist, filmmaker, health care provider, human resource manager, agent, coach, crisis manager, mediator

(continued)

FIGURE **7.9** *Continued*

Personality Type	Characteristics	Possible Careers
INFP—The Idealist (3–4% of Americans)	They work well alone; must know others well to interact; faithful to others and their jobs; excellent at communication; open-minded; dreamers; tend to do too much.	Entertainer, artist, editor, musician, professor, researcher, counselor, consultant, clergy, dietitian, massage therapist, human resources manager, events manager, corporate leader
INTJ—The Scientist (2–3% of Americans)	They are very independent; enjoy challenges; inventors; can be skeptical; they are perfectionists; they believe in their own work, sometimes to a fault.	Economist, financial planner, banker, budget analyst, scientist, astronomer, network specialist, computer programmer, engineer, curriculum designer, coroner, pathologist, attorney, manager
INTP—The Thinker (3–4% of Americans)	Extremely logical; very analytical; good at planning; love to learn; excellent problem solvers; they don't enjoy needless conversation; hard to understand at times.	Software designer, programmer, systems analyst, network administrator, surgeon, veterinarian, lawyer, economist, architect, physicist, mathematician, college professor, writer, agent, producer
ESTP—The Doer (6–8% of Americans)	They are usually very happy; they don't let trivial things upset them; they have very good memories; very good at working with things and taking them apart.	Police officer, firefighter, detective, military, investigator, paramedic, banker, investor, promoter, carpenter, chef, real estate broker, retail sales, insurance claims
ESTJ—The Guardian (12–15% of Americans)	They are "take charge" people; they like to get things done; focus on results; very good at organizing; good at seeing what will not work; responsible; realists.	Insurance agent, military, security, coach, credit analyst, project manager, auditor, general contractor, paralegal, stockbroker, executive, information officer, lawyer, controller, accounts manager
ESFP—The Performer (8–10% of Americans)	Very good at sports and active exercises; good common sense; easygoing; good at communication; can be impulsive; do not enjoy working alone; have fun and enjoy living and life.	Nurse, social worker, physician assistant, nutritionist, therapist, photographer, musician, film producer, social events coordinator, news anchor, fund raiser, host, retail sales
ESFJ—The Caregiver (11–14% of Americans)	Enjoy many friendly relationships; popular; love to help others; do not take criticism very well; need praise; need to work with people; organized; talkative; active.	Medical assistant, physician, nurse, teacher, coach, principal, social worker, counselor, clergy, court reporter, office manager, loan officer, public relations, customer service, caterer, office manager
ENFP—The Inspirer (6–7% of Americans)	Creative and industrious; can easily find success in activities and projects that interest them; good at motivating others; organized; do not like routine.	Journalist, writer, actor, newscaster, artist, director, public relations, teacher, clergy, psychologist, guidance counselor, trainer, project manager, human resources manager
ENFJ—The Giver (3–5% of Americans)	Very concerned about others' feelings; respect others; good leaders; usually popular; good at public speaking; can make decisions too quickly; trust easily.	Journalist, entertainer, TV producer, politician, counselor, clergy, psychologist, teacher, social worker, health care provider, customer service manager
ENTP—The Visionary (4–6% of Americans)	Great problem solvers; love to argue either side; can do almost anything; good at speaking/motivating; love challenges; very creative; do not like routine; overconfident.	Entrepreneur, manager, agent, journalist, attorney, urban planner, analyst, creative director, public relations, marketing, broadcaster, network solutions, politician, detective
ENTJ—The Executive (3–5% of Americans)	Excellent leaders; speak very well; hard-working; may be workaholics; may not give enough praise; like to learn; great planners; enjoy helping others reach their goals.	Executive, senior manager, administrator, consultant, editor, producer, financial planner, stockbroker, program designer, attorney, psychologist, engineer, network administrator

Source: Adapted from Tieger and Baron Tieger, *Do What You Are* (2001), and the Personality Type Portraits at www.personalitypage.com

habits and even your career choices. For instance, if you scored very high in the extroversion section, it may not serve you well to pursue a career where you would be forced to work alone. It would probably also be unwise to try to spend all of your time studying alone. If you are a strong extrovert, you would want to work and study around people.

REFLECTIONS ON LEARNING HOW TO LEARN

Unlike an IQ test, learning style, multiple intelligence, and personality type assessments do not pretend to determine if you are "smart" or not. These assessments simply allow you to look more closely at how you learn, what innate strengths you possess, and what your dominant intelligence may be.

Discovering your learning style can greatly enhance your classroom performance. For example, finally understanding that your learning style is visual and that your professor's teaching style is totally verbal (oral) can answer many questions about why you may have performed poorly in the past in a "strictly lecture" class. Now that you have discovered that you are a feeling extrovert, you can better understand why you love associating with others and learn a great deal by working in groups. And now that you have discovered that your primary intelligence is logical/mathematical, you know why math and science are easier for you than history or literature.

Possessing this knowledge and developing the tools to make your learning style, dominant intelligence, and personality type work for you, not against you, will be paramount to your success. As you continue to use your learning style, dominant intelligence, and personality type to enhance your learning, consider the following:

▶ Get involved in a *variety* of learning and social situations.
▶ Use your less dominant areas more often to *strengthen* them.
▶ *Read more* about personality typing and learning styles.
▶ *Surround yourself* with people who learn differently from the way you do.
▶ Try *different ways* of learning and studying.
▶ Remember that inventories *do not* measure your worth.

By understanding how you process information, learning can become an entirely new and exciting venture for you. Good luck to you on this new journey.

"Education is learning what you did not know you did not know."
—Daniel Boorstin

CREATE SUCCESS
Your Journey to University, Career, and Life Beyond College

CONNECTING Think about the people on your college campus. With whom can you make a connection to learn more about *integrating your learning style into your study plan?* (Example: counselor, advisor, retention specialist, etc.) Why and how will this connection be important?	
READING Find one brief, relevant article (in print or online) relating to *the theory of Multiple Intelligences and its use in education and learning.* After you have read the article, write a brief summary of the additional facts you have learned.	
E-LEARNING Go to any search engine and research **learning styles inventories.** Find one that you can take for free. Take the inventory. Do the results match the results from the inventory you took in the text? How are they similar? How do they differ? Which do you think is more accurate? Why?	
ANALYZING Choose one main idea or topic from this chapter. After exploring and researching this idea further, determine how this information can help you succeed in other classes.	
TRANSITIONING How will you use the content found in this chapter to help you create a successful transition plan to your next semester and beyond?	
EMPOWERING Thinking about the entire spectrum of your life (college, family, friends, finances, career, etc.), how can you empower yourself to be more successful through the information found in this chapter?	

SQ3R *Mastery* Study Sheet

EXAMPLE QUESTION *(from page 186)* What is the difference between a learning style and a learning strategy?		**ANSWER:**
EXAMPLE QUESTION *(from page 188)* What is the definition of tactile learning and how do you use it?		**ANSWER:**
AUTHOR QUESTION *(from page 178)* Describe at least three theories of learning from the historical figures discussed.		**ANSWER:**
AUTHOR QUESTION *(from page 183)* Who is Howard Gardner and why is his work important?		**ANSWER:**
AUTHOR QUESTION *(from page 188)* Explain the difference between your learning style and your dominant intelligence.		**ANSWER:**
AUTHOR QUESTION *(from page 189)* What is the difference between a visual learning style and visual intelligence?		**ANSWER:**
AUTHOR QUESTION *(from page 192)* How can your personality type affect your study time?		**ANSWER:**
YOUR QUESTION *(from page ____)*		**ANSWER:**
YOUR QUESTION *(from page ____)*		**ANSWER:**
YOUR QUESTION *(from page ____)*		**ANSWER:**
YOUR QUESTION *(from page ____)*		**ANSWER:**
YOUR QUESTION *(from page ____)*		**ANSWER:**

Finally, after answering these questions, recite this chapter's major points in your mind. Consider the following general questions to help you master this material.

► What was it about?
► What does it mean?
► What was the most important thing I learned? Why?
► What were the key points to remember?

CHAPTER 8
READ

BUILDING YOUR READING AND COMPREHENSION SKILLS

"The difference between the right word and the almost right word is the difference between lightning and the lightning bug."

—Mark Twain

PART TWO CHANGING YOUR PERFORMANCE

WHY READ THIS CHAPTER?

What's in it for me?

WHY is it important to know my reading speed? *WHY* will a chapter on reading and comprehension help me study better? *WHY* do I need to know how to identify a main point? *WHY*, since I'm already in college, is learning how to read more effectively such a big deal?

Why? Because there is a monumental difference between recognizing and pronouncing the words on a page and being able to comprehend, interpret, analyze, evaluate, and remember those written words. Your having hands does not make you a mechanic. Having a voice does not make you a singer, and being able to read words does not mean that you comprehend what the author intended. Reading makes you smarter and more knowledgeable about many subjects. You can sit in your easy chair and read all about the Renaissance, the painting of Mona Lisa, the statue of David, the Gold Coast of Australia, the battles of Alexander the Great, or the priceless antiquities of China. You might one day learn to do your job better by reading professional journals. Reading covers many terrains, from history to human-interest stories to cutting-edge ideas to scholars' research results. If you really want to learn, reading is the key. No other single skill comes close to offering you the benefits of knowing how to effectively read and comprehend information.

By carefully reading this chapter and taking the information provided seriously, you will be able to:

▶ Understand the value of reading and identify whether you are an active or a passive reader.

▶ Calculate and understand your reading speed and how it affects your study time.

▶ Apply strategies to increase your reading comprehension.

▶ Understand the skills associated with effective reading, including dictionary usage, fixation, and locating main ideas.

▶ Understand and use the SQ3R method of reading.

CHAPTER 8 | READ

"I read myself out of poverty long before I worked myself out of poverty."

—*Walter Anderson*

How my
COMMUNITY
COLLEGE
changed my life

PATRICIA WALLS
Graduate!

The College of Southern Nevada and The University of Nevada, Las Vegas, Las Vegas, Nevada

An interview conducted and written by

T. D. ELIOPULOS
Professor, The College of Southern Nevada

Nearly 25 years ago, during my first year at Eastern Washington University, one of my professors told a group of us first-time graduate teaching assistants that one day we would meet a student who would possess greater writing and critical thinking skills than we did. We should not fear this student, but rather use the experience to learn *from* the student. *"This student will offer you new truths yet to discover."* I am certain that I encountered students who were better writers than I very early on in my career, but never had I been so struck by a student's natural ability to write, think, and communicate as I was when I met Patricia (Pat) Walls at the College of Southern Nevada (CSN). Perhaps even more surprising than Pat's innate writer's ability was her genuine modesty about it.

CSN is an institution proud to educate those students returning to education after years spent in the work- and/or parent-force. Pat, born in Atlanta, Georgia, in 1950, was one of those students. She had already navigated her roles of wife and mother of five when she decided to pursue higher education in the summer of 2000. Pat decided to follow a new dream and study education at CSN.

Pat and I met when she enrolled in my Composition One course. After reading her first essay, I knew I had found the student whom my professor had predicted all those years earlier. Assignment after assignment, Pat wrote with insightful intellect and rhetorical command. Her eye for description, her humor, and her precise language were those of the already published writer, not those of an uncertain community college student. But much to my amazement, uncertain she was. During one of our first conversations, Pat shared with me her apprehension: *"I'm worried someone's going to tap me on the shoulder and tell me to go home."* At that time, Pat actually believed she did not belong in college. For years she had possessed such an inflated idea of what the college experience was that she had convinced herself she was

not "worthy" of it. Luckily, after a semester or two, she realized that she did belong in college. Pat recalled, *"After a few semesters at CSN, I realized that I was wrong in placing education on a pedestal, that it was something that was achievable."*

After spending two years at CSN, where she earned her AA in education, she transferred to University of Nevada, Las Vegas, where in 2006 she received her degree in secondary education along with a TESOL certificate. Removed from her college and university experiences, she can now distinguish the differences between the college and university environments. According to Pat, CSN is *"a very positive learning community"* whereas UNLV *"is a place of greater ambition, a place to jump-start a career."* She added that the community college experience gives a student the opportunity to engage in the "learning process" whereas the university environment toughens its members through experience. Her experience in both places has allowed her to pass along her knowledge to her own students. Pat insists it is not the smartest student who succeeds, but those who stay the course, those who do not allow the many forms of discouragement to impede their learning process and shake them loose.

Four years into her own professional career, Pat teaches three courses for English language learners and two courses of sophomore English at Rancho High School in Las Vegas, Nevada, benefiting the lives of nearly 125 students each year. Clearly, Pat Walls continues to instill the learning and life processes, and fortunately for the Clark County School District, she is gifting her students with a desire to engage in the same activity that she once thought above her. I am certain that learning *from* her has been among the most satisfying moments of my professional career.

THINK ABOUT IT

1. Pat states that she was afraid that someone was going to tap her on the shoulder and tell her to go home. What has been your greatest fear since beginning your studies? How have you dealt with this fear?
2. What differences do you perceive between the community college and university experiences? Who can you talk with to clarify some of your ideas about the differences in a community college and a university?

BEFORE YOU READ

SCAN & QUESTION

In the preface of this book (page xiv), you read about the **SQ3R study method.** Right now, take a few moments, **scan this chapter,** and on the SQ3R Mastery Study Sheet on page 225, write **five of your own questions** that you think will be important to your mastery of this material. In addition to the two questions below, you will find five questions from your authors on that study sheet. Use one of your *"Study for Quiz"* stickers to flag this page for easy reference.

EXAMPLES:

▶ What is a logodaedalian? (from page 206)

▶ Describe the process of fixation. (from page 209)

IS READING *FUNDAMENTAL* OR JUST PURE TORTURE?

The Answer Can Change Your Life

Quick question: "What are the top two academic problems among college students today?" According to faculty members, assessments, national tests, and yes, even your peers around the nation, the two greatest problems students face today are college math classes and reading comprehension—and some of the math problems can even be attributed to poor reading skills.

How many times have you read to the bottom of a page or completed a section in a textbook and said to yourself, *"I don't remember a thing I just read"*? In actuality, all of us have experienced this at one time or another. The strategies outlined in this chapter will help you eliminate this common occurrence from your study time. By applying the strategies discussed herein, you will be able to read a page, a section, or an entire chapter so that when you reach the end, you will *comprehend and remember* what you just read.

DISCOVERING YOUR READING STYLE

Are You Active or Passive?

Take a few moments and circle TRUE or FALSE for each of the statements in Figure 8.1 to determine whether you are more of an active or a passive reader.

FIGURE

8.1   *Discovering Your Reading Style*

1. I enjoy reading for pleasure.	TRUE	FALSE
2. College textbooks have little connection to my real life.	TRUE	FALSE
3. I look for the deeper meaning in words and phrases.	TRUE	FALSE
4. I seldom visualize what I am reading.	TRUE	FALSE
5. I look up words that I do not understand.	TRUE	FALSE
6. I read only what I have to read, and that is a stretch for me.	TRUE	FALSE
7. I stop reading to ponder what something means.	TRUE	FALSE
8. I never take notes when reading.	TRUE	FALSE
9. Reading brings me great joy.	TRUE	FALSE
10. My mind wanders constantly when I read.	TRUE	FALSE
11. I make time for reading even when I am not required to read.	TRUE	FALSE
12. Words are just words—they add no real meaning to my life or work.	TRUE	FALSE
13. I get excited about reading something new because I know I will learn something new and useful.	TRUE	FALSE
14. When reading, I just want to get it over with.	TRUE	FALSE
15. I usually have no trouble concentrating when reading.	TRUE	FALSE
16. I never look up words; I just read on.	TRUE	FALSE

Total of even-numbered TRUE responses _____

Total of odd-numbered TRUE responses _____

If you answered TRUE to more even numbers, you tend to be a more passive reader.
If you answered TRUE to more odd numbers, you tend to be a more active reader.

Active reading is really nothing more than a mindset. It is the attitude you have as you begin the reading process. For the next few days, try approaching your reading assignments with a positive, open-minded approach and notice the difference in your own satisfaction, understanding, and overall comprehension. Instead of saying things like "I hate reading" or "This stuff is worthless," reframe your self-talk into statements such as "I'm going to learn from this" and "I think I can apply this to my life now."

I FEEL THE NEED . . . THE NEED FOR SPEED!

Do You Know Your Personal Reading Rate?

You've heard the advertisements: "Breeze through a novel on your lunch hour," "Read an entire computer instruction book over dinner," or "Read the *New York Times* in 10 minutes." Sure, there are people who have an incredible gift for speed reading and a photographic memory, but those people are not the norm.

This section is included in your text to give you some idea about how long it will take to read a chapter so that you can *plan your reading time* more effectively. There is an average of 450 words on a college textbook page. If you read at 150 words per minute, each page may take you an average of three minutes to read.

This is a **raw number** for basic reading. It DOES NOT allow for marking, highlighting, taking notes, looking up words, reflecting, or comprehending. When these necessary skills are coupled with basic reading, they can sometimes triple the amount of reading time required. So that page that you estimated would take you 3 minutes to read may actually take you 9 to 10 minutes to read.

In the reading activity (Figure 8.2), you will find a passage about binge drinking. Read the section at your normal pace. Use a stopwatch or a watch with a second hand to accurately

iStockPhoto

Have you ever timed yourself to determine how long it takes you to read a complete chapter?

record your reading time, and then calculate your rate and comprehension level using the directions provided.

Speed and Comprehension: How Does It Impact My Education?

According to Brenda D. Smith (2007), professor and reading expert, "rate calculators vary according to the difficulty of the material. Research indicates, however, that on relatively easy material, the average adult reading speed is approximately 250 words per minute at 70 percent comprehension. For college students, the rate is sometimes estimated at closer to 300 words per minute." The passage that you just read in Figure 8.2 would be classified as relatively easy.

If you are reading below the average 250-words-per-minute rate, several factors could be contributing to this situation.

▶ Not concentrating on the passage
▶ Vocabulary words with which you are not familiar
▶ Stopping too long on any given single word (called fixations, discussed later)
▶ Not reading often enough to build your speed

The remainder of this chapter is intended to assist you with improving your reading speed AND comprehension.

VOCABULARY AND COMPREHENSION

Do You Have to Be a Logodaedalian to Enjoy Words?

Thankfully, it is not every day that you run across words like *logodaedalian*. (A logodaedalian is a person who has a great passion for unique, sly, and clever words and phrases.) Perhaps the best way to develop a dynamic vocabulary is by reading. While reading, you may come across words with which you are not familiar. You may be exposed to aspects of language that you have not experienced from your family, friends, or geographic location. These unfamiliar words will not become a part of your *vernacular* unless you STOP and look them up. This is the way to begin building a masterful vocabulary.

Let's start by looking up the word *vernacular*. Take a moment and jot down the definition of this term.

Vernacular means: _____

_____

_____

_____

See how simple that was? Now you have a new word in your vocabulary—actually, you have two new words from just a few paragraphs: *vernacular* and *logodaedalian*. You have taken a step toward becoming a logophile!

How Can a Dictionary Aid in Reading Comprehension?

Your dictionary will become a good friend to you in college. There may be many words and phrases that you do not understand when reading your college textbooks. This is somewhat

FIGURE

8.2   *Calculating Your Reading Rate*

Start Time _____ : _____ : _____
          Hour   Min.   Sec.

BINGE DRINKING

Binge drinking is classified as having more than five drinks at one time. Many people say, "I only drink once a week." However, if that one drinking spell includes drink after drink after drink, it can be extremely detrimental to your liver, your memory, your digestive system, and your overall health.

Most college students report that they do not mean to binge drink, but it is caused by the situation, such as a ballgame, a party, a campus event, or special occasions. Researchers at Michigan State University found that only 5 percent of students surveyed say they party to "get drunk" (Warner, 2002).

In their breakthrough work, *Dying to Drink*, Harvard researcher Henry Wechsler and science writer Bernice Wuethrich explore the problem of binge drinking. They suggest, "two out of every five college students regularly binge drink, resulting in approximately 1,400 student deaths, a distressing number of assaults and rapes, a shameful amount of vandalism, and countless cases of academic suicide" (Wechsler and Wuethrich, 2002).

It is a situation reminiscent of the old saying, "Letting the fox guard the henhouse." After a few drinks, it is hard to "self-police," meaning that you may not be able to control your actions once the drinking starts.

Perhaps the greatest tragedy of drug and alcohol abuse is the residual damage of pregnancy, sexually transmitted diseases, traffic fatalities, verbal/physical abuse, and accidental death. You know that drugs and alcohol lower your resistance and can cause you to do things that you would not normally do, such as drive drunk or have unprotected sex. Surveys and research results suggest that students who participate in heavy episodic (HE) or binge drinking are more likely to participate in unprotected sex with multiple sex partners. One survey found that 61 percent of men who do binge drink participated in unprotected sex as compared to 23 percent of men who do not binge drink. The survey also found that 48 percent of women who do binge drink participated in unprotected sex as compared to only 8 percent of women who do not binge drink (Cooper, 2002).

These staggering statistics suggest one thing: alcohol consumption can cause people to act in ways in which they may never have acted without alcohol—and those actions can result in personal damage from which recovery may be impossible.
(387 words)

Finishing Time _____ : _____ : _____
          Hour   Min.   Sec.

Reading time in SECONDS = _____

Words per MINUTE (use the following chart) = _____

Example: If you read this passage in 2 minutes and 38 seconds, your reading time in seconds would be 158. Using the Rate Calculator Chart, your reading rate would be about 146 words per minute.

RATE CALCULATOR FOR "BINGE DRINKING" PASSAGE

Time in Seconds	Words Per Minute
40	581
50	464
60 (1 minute)	387
120 (2 minutes)	194
130	179
140	165
150	155
160	145
170	137
180 (3 minutes)	129
190	122
200	116
210	110
220	106
230	101

(continued)

FIGURE 8.2 *Calculating Your Reading Rate (continued)*

Test Your Comprehension Skills

Answer the following questions with T (true) or F (false) without looking back over the material.

_____ 1. Binge drinking has resulted in the deaths of students.

_____ 2. Men who binge drink have unprotected sex more often than men who do not binge drink.

_____ 3. Women who binge drink have unprotected sex no more often than women who do not binge drink.

_____ 4. "Self-policing" means that you are able to look out for yourself.

_____ 5. Binge drinking is classified as having more than three drinks at one time.

Each question is worth 20%.   Comprehension = _____%

Example: If you answered two correctly, your comprehension rate would be 40% (2 × 20%). If you answered four correctly, your comprehension rate would be 80% (4 × 20%).

Test Your Comprehension Skills Answers: 1 = T, 2 = T, 3 = F, 4 = T, 5 = F.

common, as many college texts are written on the 13th- and 14th-grade levels. You will need to stop and look up the words you don't understand. When you look up a word in the dictionary, you are given more than just a definition (see Figure 8.3). You are also given the phonetic pronunciation, the spelling, the meaning, the part of speech in which the word can be used, the origin of the word, and usually several definitions. You may have to choose the definition that best suits the context of the sentence. It can be beneficial to you to jot down definitions in the margins of your text.

Using the definition for *magnitude,* determine which definition would be best suited to this sentence: ***The magnitude of the power she had over him was truly amazing.***

FIGURE 8.3 *Annotated Dictionary Entry*

The word · Pronunciation · Part of speech

mag-ni-tude (mag'ni-tood) *n.* **1. a.** High rank or status: "The General's character rose to the magnitude of his rank." **b.** Great amount, size or statue: "The magnitude of his personal loss" **c.** Greatness of one's ability to influence or sway: "The magnitude of her personality overwhelmed the group." **2. Astron.** How bright a star or other celestial body measures on a numerical scale with the brightest degree registering as the "first magnitude." Those less bright would measure second, third, or fourth degree. **3. Math.** A number is assigned to a certain quantity in order for comparisons to be made with other quantities in the same class. **Geol.** Having to do with energy released: "The energy of the earthquake was of a tremendous magnitude."

Syllable breakdown · Usage · Meanings

LEARNING TO READ FASTER AND SMARTER

Can Speed and Comprehension Be Improved?

As you begin to practice your reading comprehension, review the following tips for helping you read the material more quickly and understand it more clearly. Whenever you are faced with having to choose between comprehension and speed, choose comprehension every time.

CONCENTRATION. Speed and comprehension both require deep, mindful concentration. Neither can be achieved without it. Your body needs to be ready to concentrate. It will be nearly impossible to concentrate if you are tired and hungry. To increase your concentration for active reading, consider doing the following:

▶ Reduce outside distractions such as people talking, rooms that are too hot or cold, cell phones ringing, and so on.

▶ Reduce internal distractions such as fatigue, self-talk, daydreaming, hunger, and emotions that cause you to think of other things.

▶ Set a goal of reading a certain amount of material in an allotted time. This goal can help you focus.

▶ Take a short break every 20 minutes. Don't get distracted and go off and do something else; come back to your reading in three to five minutes.

▶ Take notes as you read. This helps reading become an active process.

VOCABULARY. Building a strong vocabulary may not be the easiest thing to do, and you will not build it overnight. However, it is important that you work on this aspect of reading as often as possible. If you do not know a word, you must stop and look it up. Having to stop and look up a word that you do not know may slow you down and cause you to lose concentration; however, the more words you have in your vocabulary, the fewer times you will need to stop and look up a word. It is difficult and nearly impossible to read, comprehend, and remember a passage when you do not know or understand one or more words.

FIXATION. *Fixation* occurs when your eyes stop on a single word to read it. Your eyes stop for only a fraction of a second, but those fractions add up over the course of a section or chapter. Your mind sees the words something like this:

> **Nutrition   is   important   to   good   health.**

As you read this, you probably had six fixations because the words are spaced out. However, even if they were not spaced out, many people would still have six fixations. To increase your speed, try to see two or three words with one fixation; this will cut your reading time nearly in half. Try to see the sentence like this:

> **Nutrition is important   to good health.**

Smith (2007) states: "Research has shown that the average reader can see approximately 2.5 words per fixation."

SUCCESSFUL DECISIONS: An Activity for Critical Reflection

Whitney is 19 years old and has just completed high school. She enrolled at Seymore Technical Institute with dreams of becoming a phlebotomist. She had done well in high school, but reading had never been her strongest talent.

She became increasingly worried when she began to review her texts for the first semester. The readings were much more difficult than she expected. Furthermore, she was stunned at the amount of reading required by each instructor.

Realizing that reading AND comprehending were going to play a major role in her academic success, Whitney began to set aside two hours per day devoted strictly to reading, taking notes, vocabulary building,

and comprehension. She was doing better but still struggling with her difficult texts and handouts.

Pretend that Whitney is a student at YOUR campus. What services are available that you could recommend to help her improve reading and comprehension skills?

1. _____

2. _____

What would you recommend that she do on a daily basis to improve her reading and comprehension?

1. _____

2. _____

To reduce your fixation time for active reading, consider the following:

▶ Practice seeing two or more words with one fixation.

▶ As you practice, try to read in phrases like the example below:

*Nutrition is important   to good health. Therefore,   you should
work hard   to eat   proper meals   every day.   By doing this
you can maintain   good health.*

Read the following passage using the fixation procedure:

Motivation is an important asset to all students, and it must come from within. No one—not your professors, your parents, or your friends—can motivate you unless you want to be motivated. You will be motivated by one of two things—fear or desire. Fear will cause you to be afraid and not take risks, whereas desire will make you take a chance on yourself and move out of your comfort zone.

How did you do? Was this easy or difficult? Why?

_____

_____

FINDING THE TOPIC AND MAIN IDEAS IN PARAGRAPHS AND SECTIONS

Can You Get to the Main Point?

Typically, each paragraph has a main idea. You're no doubt familiar with this from your English classes. It is usually called a topic sentence. The topic statement is what the paragraph is about.

Identifying the main idea of a paragraph can greatly aid your comprehension of that paragraph and eventually the entire section or chapter.

Read the following paragraph and determine the main idea—the point.

Without exception, the conclusion should be one of the most carefully crafted components of your paper or speech. Long after your reader has finished reading or your listener has finished listening, the last part of your work is more than likely going to be the part they remember the most. Some writers and speakers suggest that you write your conclusion first, so that your paper or speech is directed toward a specific end result. That decision, of course, is up to you. However, a great piece of advice from writing experts tells us that captivating writers always know how their stories will end long before they begin writing them. (Cornerstone: Building on Your Best, 5th edition)

Can you determine what the above paragraph is about? We know that the opening statement talks about writing the conclusion of a paper or speech. But it also talks about the importance of your conclusion and that some writers actually write their conclusions first. The main topic of this paragraph happens to be the first sentence. The remaining sentences simply add information and credibility to the topic sentence.

Read and study the following paragraph.

Do you remember where you were and what you were doing when you heard that Barack Obama had been elected the first African American president of the United States? Chances are good that you remember some of the details surrounding what you were doing when you heard this historic news. Experts report that most people remember exactly where they were and what they were doing when a major event occurred. Depending on your age, you or your parents probably remember where you were when you heard about the World Trade Center attacks. Many people who were alive when John Kennedy was assassinated still remember vividly where they were when they heard the news, even though this event happened many years ago. Events of this magnitude seem to be seared into our memories.

Circle the one option below that best describes the topic sentence of this paragraph.

1. The election of Barack Obama

2. John Kennedy's assassination

3. The fact that we tend to remember what we were doing when events of great magnitude happened

Which did you choose? Statements one and two have very little to do with the paragraph's intended message. They are simply prompts or examples. Statement three is the correct topic for this paragraph.

According to Dorothy Seyler (2003), professor and reading expert, you can identify the topic of a paragraph in four easy steps:

▶ The topic is the subject of the paragraph.

▶ You can identify the topic by answering the question, "What or who is the paragraph about?"

▶ The topic statement should be general enough to cover all of the specifics of the paragraph.

▶ The topic statement should be specific enough to exclude other paragraphs on related topics.

Shutterstock

When reading, do you stop after each paragraph and think about the meaning?

Finding the topic sentence or main idea of a paragraph, section, or chapter is not hard, but it does take concentration and a degree of analytical skills. If you approach each paragraph as a detective searching for clues, you will soon find out how easy and effortless it is to determine main points.

From Ordinary to *Extraordinary*

REAL PEOPLE | REAL LIVES | REAL CHANGE

SYLVIA EBERHARDT
Fashion Model, Abercrombie and Fitch, *Hollister Magazine,*
and Other Top Agencies
Honors Graduate, Fairfax High School, Fairfax, Virginia
Honors Student—Howard University, Washington, D.C.

If you read my resumé and looked at my professional credits, you might think I had it made—that the world had been handed to me on a silver platter and that I never wanted for anything. Nothing could be further from the truth. Although I am an honors student at Howard University and a fashion model who has worked with some of the top stores and magazines in the nation, my beginnings were anything but easy and beautiful.

I was born into a crack-infested, gang-ridden, one-bedroom house in inner-city Washington, D.C. I was raised a few doors down from a major crack house, where I saw junkies, prostitutes, and pimps on a daily basis. It was simply a way of life. Poverty surrounded me and my two siblings at every turn. Unemployment was rampant and the streets were filled with trash and used needles. I slept in a bunk bed where nightly I could hear drug deals being made outside my window. The iron bars on the windows were the only things that separated me from the ugliness of the world outside my home.

My mother died just before I entered high school and I was raised from that point on by my father. I was constantly teased and tormented growing up because I was so thin. My peers nicknamed me Anna (for "Anorexic"). What they did not know was that I suffered (and continue to suffer) from Crohn's disease, a life-threatening disability. Crohn's is an autoimmune disease that affects the gastrointestinal system and causes rashes, severe abdominal pain, arthritis, vomiting, and weight loss.

How did I survive? How did I become an honors student at one of the top high schools in the nation? How did I become a fashion model at the age of 15? I am blessed to have an amazing, supportive father who taught me that you never have to let your past or present dictate your future. He believed and taught me that no matter how humble one's beginnings, no matter where you were born

> *My father taught me that "you may live in the ghetto, but the ghetto does not have to live in you."*

or the circumstances of your life, the test of a person's character is knowing that he or she holds his or her destiny in his or her own hands.

He taught me that I had to take responsibility for my own life. I had to be my own savior. Further, he taught my siblings and me that "you may live in the ghetto, but the ghetto does not have to live in you." He always told us that you do not have to think and act poor simply because you live in a lower-class neighborhood. He also taught us that in order to enjoy the finer things in life, you first have to experience hard times. He would say to us, "You have to ride in an old, ragged car before you can appreciate a Mercedes." His attitude helped guide and change my life.

After we moved to Virginia, I began working hard and taking college-level classes at Northern Virginia Community College while still in high school. My dream is to become a heart surgeon. I knew from the very beginning that I would have to study hard and give up many things I enjoyed doing. It paid off, however. By the end of my senior year in high school, I had over 30 college credits in math, science, anatomy, microbiology, calculus, and physiology, with a 4.0 grade point average. I won a full scholarship to Howard University and finished my first semester with a 3.92 GPA.

I write all of this to you to say, "Your life is what you make of it. You can let your past and present dictate and ruin your future, or you can get over it, work hard, believe in yourself, push yourself, and work toward your dreams." I wish you so much good luck and good fortune in your future.

EXTRAORDINARY REFLECTION

Read the following statement and respond in your online journal or class notebook.

Sylvia mentions that her father would say to her, "in order to enjoy the finer things in life, you first have to experience hard times. You have to ride in an old, ragged car before you can appreciate a Mercedes." How do you plan to use your past experiences, positive or negative, to bring about positive change in your future?

Read the following paragraph about emotion and identify the topic in your own words. Justify your answer. Then, identify the main idea of the paragraph. See if you can determine what the author really wants you to know.

You *will not* have to do this for every paragraph you read in college. As you become a stronger reader, you will do this type of analysis after each heading or chapter section. But for now, as you work on building your skills as a reader, take the time to learn how to fully analyze a small portion of a chapter.

> *The origin of emotion is the brain. You might say that there are two minds—one that thinks (the thinking mind) and one that feels (the emotional mind). Think of thoughts and emotions as two different mechanisms for knowing and making sense of the world. The two minds are not adversarial or physically separate; rather, they operate interactively to construct your mental life. Passion (the heart) dominates reason (the mind) when feelings are intense. (Nelson & Low, 2010)*

Define the following terms found in the passage and answer the questions that follow.

mechanism _____

adversarial _____

dominate _____

The TOPIC of this paragraph is _____

_____

_____

Who or what is the paragraph about (the MAIN IDEA*)?* _____

_____

_____

_____

What do the authors of the paragraph really want you TO KNOW? _____

_____

_____

_____

_____

SQ3R TO THE RESCUE
How Can You Do It Right the First Time?

There are as many ways to approach a chapter in a textbook as there are students who read textbooks. One of the most effective and often-used reading and studying systems is the **SQ3R Method**, developed by Francis P. Robinson in 1941. This simple yet highly valuable system has proved to be a successful study tool for millions of students. SQ3R involves five steps: **S**can, **Q**uestion, **R**ead, **R**ecite, and **R**eview. The most important thing to remember about SQ3R is that it should be used on a daily basis, not as a method for cramming. See Figure 8.4.

SCAN. The first step of SQ3R is to *scan,* or preread, an assigned chapter. You've been doing this since you began reading Chapter 1 of this text. You begin by reading the title of the chapter, the headings, and each subheading. Look carefully at the vocabulary, timelines, graphs, charts, pictures, and drawings included in each chapter. If there is a chapter summary, read it.

FIGURE **8.4** *SQ3R Design*

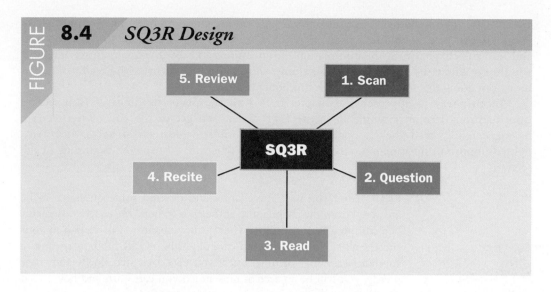

Scanning also includes reading the first and last sentences in each paragraph. Scanning is not a substitute for reading a chapter. Reading is discussed later. Before going any further, scan Chapter 9 of this text using the following seven questions.

*What is the title of the chapter?*_____

*What is the subtitle of the chapter?*_____

*List the chapter's major headings.*_____

_____

_____

_____

Who is introduced in the "How My Community College Changed My Life?" feature? List one thing you learned about him or her.

_____

_____

_____

If the chapter contains quotations, which one means the most to you? Why?

_____

_____

_____

What is the most important graph or chart in the chapter? Why?

_____

_____

_____

Without looking back, list six topics that this chapter will cover.

1. _____   4. _____

2. _____   5. _____

3. _____   6. _____

QUESTION. The second step is to *question.* There are five common questions you should ask yourself when you are reading a chapter: Who? When? What? Where? and Why? As you scan and read the chapter, turn the information into questions and see if you can answer them. If you do not know the answers to the questions, you should find them as you read along. You have been doing this for each chapter in this book thus far.

Another way to approach the chapter is to turn the major headings of each section into questions (see an example in Figure 8.5). When you get to the end of the section, having carefully read the material, looked up unfamiliar words, taken notes, and highlighted important information, answer the questions that you wrote at the beginning of the section.

READ. After you scan the chapter and develop some questions to be answered from the chapter, the next step is to *read the chapter.* Remember, scanning is not reading. There is no substitute for reading in your success plan. Read slowly and carefully. The SQ3R method requires a substantial amount of time, but if you take each step slowly and completely, you will be amazed at how much you can learn and how much your grades will improve.

Read through each section. It is best not to jump around or move ahead if you did not understand the previous section. Paragraphs are usually built on each other, and so you need to understand the first be-

> "There are worse crimes than burning books. One of them is not reading them."
> —Joseph Brodsky

FIGURE 8.5 *Forming Questions from Headings*

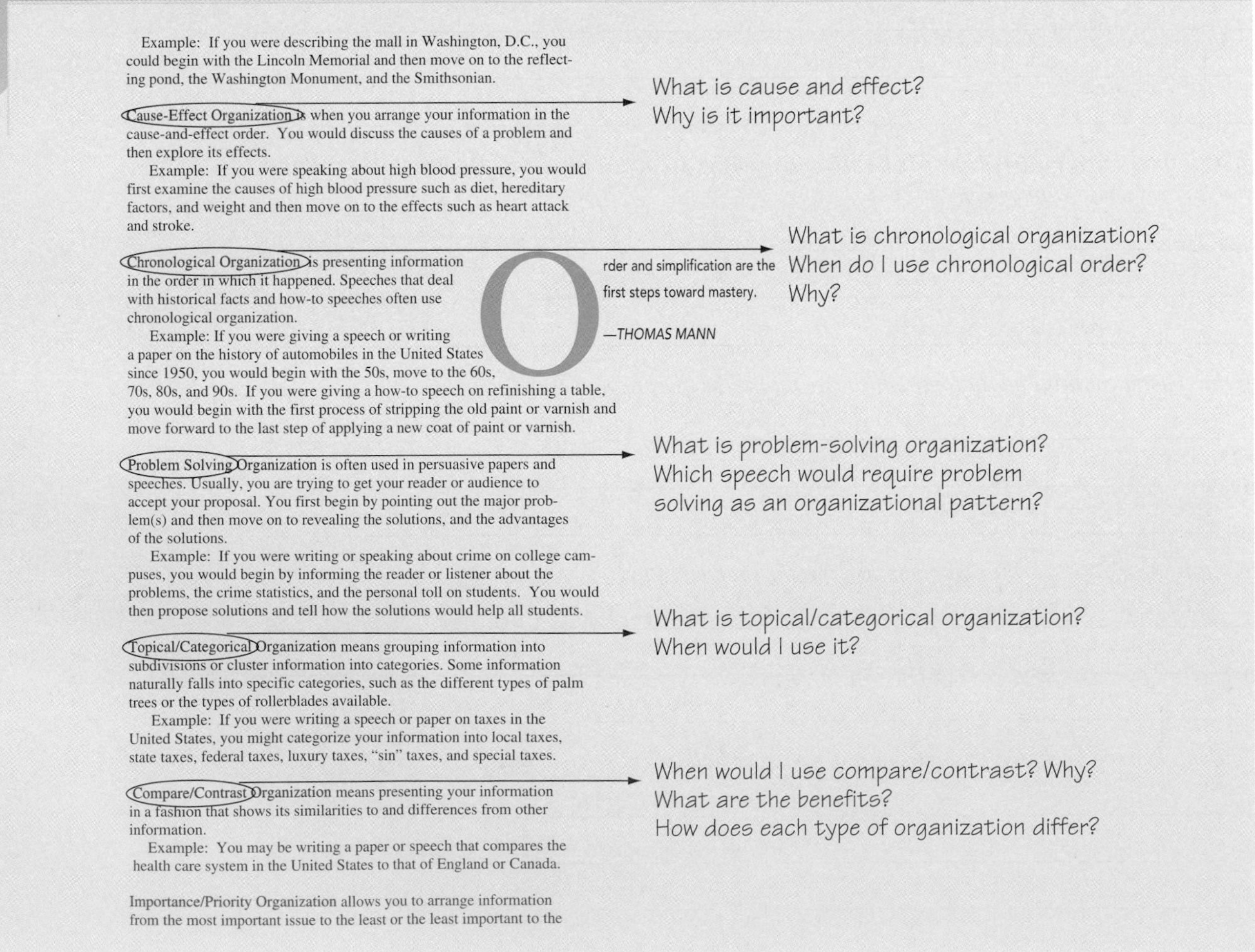

fore you can move on to the next. You may have to read a chapter or section more than once, especially if the information is new, technical, or difficult.

Take notes, highlight, and make marginal notes in your textbook as you read along. You own your textbook and should personalize it as you would your lecture notes. Highlight areas that you feel are important, underline words and phrases that you do not understand or that you feel are important, and jot down notes in the margins. Refer to page xv in the preface to see how a text page should look after using SQ3R.

As you begin to read your chapter, mark the text, and take notes, keep the following in mind:

- ▶ Read the entire paragraph before you mark anything.
- ▶ Identify the topic or thesis statement of each paragraph and highlight it.
- ▶ Highlight key phrases.
- ▶ Don't highlight too much; the text will lose its significance.
- ▶ Stop and look up words that you do not know or understand.

"The man who does not read good books has no advantage over the man who can't read."
—*Mark Twain*

While reading, you will want to take notes that are more elaborate than your highlighting or marginal notes. Taking notes while reading the text will assist you in studying the material and committing it to memory. **This is a major part of LEARNING ACTIVELY.** There are several effective methods of taking notes while reading (see Figure 8.6), including the following:

Charts	Outlines	Flash cards
Mind maps	Timelines	Summaries
Key words		

As you read through a chapter in your textbook, you may find that you have to use a variety of these techniques to capture information. Try them for one week. Although taking notes while reading a chapter thoroughly is time consuming, you will be amazed at how much you remember and how much you are able to contribute in class after using these techniques. They work!

READING PIECE BY PIECE

If you are reading material that is completely **new to you—difficult to understand** yet important to remember—you may have to disregard entire paragraphs or read only pieces of certain paragraphs. When you get to a point where you have "read enough," or your mind begins to wander, put a tick mark at that point (see Figure 8.7). The placement of the tick marks will be different for every person reading based on individual skills and experience. After your first tick mark, continue reading until you get to another stopping point, putting tick marks in the places where you feel you have read a complete thought. You will not want to read an entire chapter at one time this way— only sections.

When you get to the end of a major section, reread the material in your first "ticked section." Out to the side, paraphrase that section (indicated in matching colors in Figure 8.7). Then go on to the next section. Figure 8.7 gives you a visual of this technique. The paragraph on criminal justice is shown with its original paragraph breaks. However, you will also see **"tick marks"** indicated with a "/" showing where the reader felt this was enough to try to comprehend at one time. The "ticked section" and paraphrased remarks are shown in corresponding colors.

TIPS FOR PERSONAL SUCCESS

Consider the following strategies for making the most of your reading time:

- ▶ Reduce the distractions around you. Try to find an atmosphere that is comfortable and effective for you.

- ▶ Discover what time of day is best for you to read and concentrate on your material.

- ▶ Read in sections. Don't try to read an entire chapter in one sitting. Divide it up and take breaks.

- ▶ Never just skip over words or phrases that you don't understand. Look them up in a dictionary.

Now it is your turn. Make a list of three tips that you would share with a classmate to assist him or her in becoming a better reader.

1. _____
2. _____
3. _____

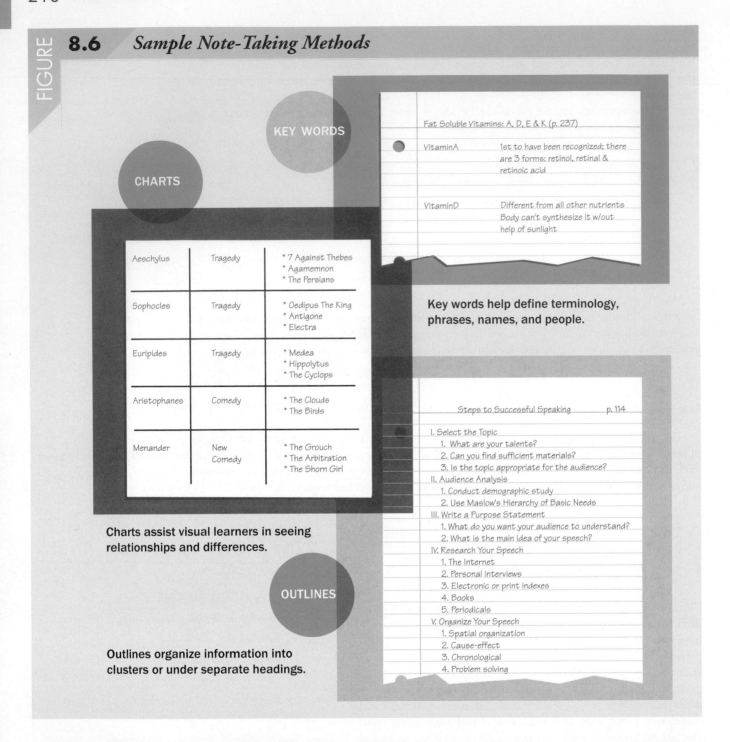

FIGURE 8.6 *Sample Note-Taking Methods*

KEY WORDS

Fat Soluble Vitamins: A, D, E & K (p. 237)

VitaminA   1st to have been recognized; there
                  are 3 forms: retinol, retinal &
                  retinoic acid

VitaminD   Different from all other nutrients
                  Body can't synthesize it w/out
                  help of sunlight

Key words help define terminology, phrases, names, and people.

CHARTS

Aeschylus	Tragedy	* 7 Against Thebes * Agamemnon * The Persians
Sophocles	Tragedy	* Oedipus The King * Antigone * Electra
Euripides	Tragedy	* Medea * Hippolytus * The Cyclops
Aristophanes	Comedy	* The Clouds * The Birds
Menander	New Comedy	* The Grouch * The Arbitration * The Shorn Girl

Charts assist visual learners in seeing relationships and differences.

OUTLINES

                Steps to Successful Speaking   p. 114

I. Select the Topic
   1. What are your talents?
   2. Can you find sufficient materials?
   3. Is the topic appropriate for the audience?
II. Audience Analysis
   1. Conduct demographic study
   2. Use Maslow's Hierarchy of Basic Needs
III. Write a Purpose Statement
   1. What do you want your audience to understand?
   2. What is the main idea of your speech?
IV. Research Your Speech
   1. The Internet
   2. Personal interviews
   3. Electronic or print indexes
   4. Books
   5. Periodicals
V. Organize Your Speech
   1. Spatial organization
   2. Cause-effect
   3. Chronological
   4. Problem solving

Outlines organize information into clusters or under separate headings.

Few techniques will assist your comprehension and retention more than this one because it requires you to be actively involved in the reading process.

Recite

Recitation is simple, but crucial. Skipping this step may result in less-than-full mastery of the chapter. Once you have read a section using one or more of the techniques already discussed, ask yourself this simple question: *"What was that all about?"* Find a classmate, sit down together, and ask questions of each other. Discuss with each other the main points of the chapter. Try to explain the information to each other without looking at your notes. If you are at home, sit back in your chair, recite the information, and determine what it means. If you have trouble

FIGURE **8.7** *Original Paragraph Breaks and New "Tick Mark Breaks" Indicated with a "/" and a Number*

A Brief History of Crime in America
(from F. Schmalleger, *Criminal Justice: A Brief Introduction,* 6th Edition. Prentice Hall, 2006.)

1 What we call criminal activity has undoubtedly been with us since the dawn of history, and crime control has long been a primary concern of politicians and government leaders world-wide./ 2 Still, the American experience with crime during the last half century has been especially influential in shaping the criminal justice system of today./

3 In this country, crime waves have come and gone, including an 1850-1880 crime epidemic, which was apparently related to social upheaval caused by large-scale immigration, and the spurt of widespread organized criminal activity associated with the prohibition years of the early twentieth century./ 4 Following World War II, however, American crime rates remained relatively stable until the 1960s./

5 The 1960s and 1970s saw a burgeoning concern for the rights of ethnic and racial minorities, women, the physically and mentally challenged, and many other groups. The civil rights movement of the period emphasized the equality of opportunity and respect for individuals, regardless of race, color, creed, or personal attributes./ 6 As new laws were passed and suits filed, court involvement in the movement grew. Soon, a plethora of hard-won individual rights and prerogatives, based on the U.S. Constitution, the Bill of Rights, and the new federal and state legislation, were recognized and guaranteed. By the 1980s, the civil rights movement had profoundly affected all areas of social life—from education throughout employment to the activities of the criminal justice system./

1) *Criminal activity has been around since the beginning of time and has been a concern to politicians and leaders.*

2) *Crime in Am. has greatly shaped our criminal justice system in the past 50 years.*

3) *Crime in Am. has come in waves including the 1850-1880 epidemic due to immigration and a later one due to prohibition.*

4) *After WWII, crime in Am. remained stable until the 60s.*

5) *During the 60s and 70s, Am. saw the rise of individual rights regardless of race, creed, or attributes.*

6) *Due to laws based on the US Constitution the C.R. Movement profoundly impacted all aspects of life in Am. including the C.J. system.*

explaining the information to your friend or reciting it to yourself, you probably did not understand the section and you should go back and reread it. If you can tell your classmate and yourself exactly what you just read and what it means, you are ready to move on to the next section of the chapter.

Review

After you have read the chapter, immediately go back and read it again. **"What?!! I just read it!"** Yes, you did. And the best way to determine whether you have mastered the information is once again to survey the chapter; review marginal notes, highlighted areas, and vocabulary words; and determine whether you can answer the questions you posed during the *"Question Step"* of SQ3R. This step will help you store and retain this information in long-term memory.

PRACTICE READING

It has often been stated that there is a huge difference between *learning to read* and *reading to learn.* Now that you have a deeper understanding of the reading and comprehension process, it is time to put your reading skills to practice and learn something new. On the following pages you will find an essay about Harvey Milk. As you read the essay, stop and look up words that you do not understand. In the right-hand column, paraphrase what you have read making certain to check for accuracy and detail. At the end of the essay, you will be asked to summarize the entire article. Happy reading.

The Life and Death of Harvey Milk

DIRECTIONS: READ THIS SECTION, IDENTIFY UNFAMILIAR WORDS <u>WITH</u> <u>UNDERLINING</u>, HIGHLIGHT IMPORTANT WORDS AND PHRASES	LOOK UP WORDS THAT NEED TO BE DEFINED	PARAPHRASE THE MAIN IDEA IN YOUR OWN WORDS
More <u>perplexing</u> things have happened, but a Twinkie caused the death of Harvey Milk. That's right. In 1978, defense lawyers using the "Twinkie Defense" explained an <u>inexplicable</u> murder away. This was the first mainstream trial to use the, "I am not responsible for my actions" defense.	*Unfamiliar words and definitions* *Perplexing = confusing or puzzling* *Inexplicable = not easily explained, unreasonable*	*The main idea of this paragraph is: In 1978, defense lawyers used a new strategy called "the Twinkie Defense" (I'm not responsible for my actions) to explain why someone murdered Harvey Milk.*
Harvey Milk was the first openly gay man elected to a significant office in America. In 1977, Milk was elected as a member of the San Francisco Board of Supervisors. This was quite arduous at this point in American history, when most people, including many psychologists and religious leaders, still classified homosexuality as deviant and a mental illness.	*Unfamiliar words and definitions*	*The main idea of this paragraph is:*
Harvey Milk is to the Gay Rights Movement what Martin Luther King, Jr. is to the Civil Rights Movement. Before King, little was happening with the CRM, and before Milk, little was happening with the GRM. He changed the face of California politics and paved the way for countless other gays and lesbians to enter the world of politics.	*Unfamiliar words and definitions*	*The main idea of this paragraph is:*
Dan White, a staunch antigay advocate, served on the board with Milk. They were constantly at odds with each other and often engaged in verbal confrontations.	*Unfamiliar words and definitions*	*The main idea of this paragraph is:*
White had been a policeman and a fireman in San Francisco before running for office. While running for office, he vowed to restore "family values" to the city government. He vowed to "rid San Francisco of radicals, social deviants, and incorrigibles."	*Unfamiliar words and definitions*	*The main idea of this paragraph is:*
Dan White was one of the most conservative members of the board, and many proposals brought to the board by Milk and the mayor of San Francisco, George Moscone, were defeated because of the heavily conservative vote led by White.	*Unfamiliar words and definitions*	*The main idea of this paragraph is:*

DIRECTIONS: READ THIS SECTION, IDENTIFY UNFAMILIAR WORDS <u>WITH UNDERLINING</u>, HIGHLIGHT IMPORTANT WORDS AND PHRASES	LOOK UP WORDS THAT NEED TO BE DEFINED	PARAPHRASE THE MAIN IDEA IN YOUR OWN WORDS
At that time, the Board of Supervisors was made up of 11 members; six of them, including Dan White, were conservative and had the power to defeat most, if not all, of the liberal measures brought before the board. This did not fare well with Harvey Milk and the other liberal members of the board.	*Unfamiliar words and definitions*	*The main idea of this paragraph is:* _____ _____ _____ _____ _____ _____
Because the job offered diminutive wages, Dan White soon realized that he could not support his family on $9,800 per year, and he submitted his resignation to Mayor Moscone. This did not sit well with the people who'd elected him. They urged him to reconsider and when he tried to rescind his resignation, Mayor Moscone refused. This decision was made, in part, because Harvey Milk had convinced Moscone to deny White's reinstatement.	*Unfamiliar words and definitions*	*The main idea of this paragraph is:* _____ _____ _____ _____ _____ _____ _____ _____ _____ _____
In a fit of wrath over the decision, Dan White entered the San Francisco City Hall on the morning of November 27, 1978, through a basement window. He went to Mayor Moscone's office and shot him in the chest, and as he lay dying, shot him again in the head.	*Unfamiliar words and definitions*	*The main idea of this paragraph is:* _____ _____ _____ _____ _____ _____ _____
He then walked calmly down the hall and asked to see Harvey Milk. Once inside the office, he slew Milk with two bullets to the brain. He then left City Hall, called his wife, spoke with her in person at St. Mary's Cathedral, and then turned himself in.	*Unfamiliar words and definitions*	*The main idea of this paragraph is:* _____ _____ _____ _____ _____ _____ _____ _____
It is reported that policemen representing the city of San Francisco shouted, cheered, and applauded when news of the murders reached the police department.	*Unfamiliar words and definitions*	*The main idea of this paragraph is:* _____ _____ _____ _____

DIRECTIONS: READ THIS SECTION, IDENTIFY UNFAMILIAR WORDS <u>WITH UNDERLINING</u>, HIGHLIGHT IMPORTANT WORDS AND PHRASES	LOOK UP WORDS THAT NEED TO BE DEFINED	PARAPHRASE THE MAIN IDEA IN YOUR OWN WORDS
Dan White's defense lawyers used a "diminished capacity" defense, suggesting that he was led to his actions by too much sugar from junk food. The lawyers convinced a jury that he was not himself and his senses were off-kilter. This became known as the "Twinkie Defense."	*Unfamiliar words and definitions*	*The main idea of this paragraph is:* _____ _____ _____ _____
Dan White was convicted of second-degree manslaughter and was sentenced to only seven years for two premeditated murders. After serving only five years, he was released. The "Twinkie Defense" had worked.	*Unfamiliar words and definitions*	*The main idea of this paragraph is:* _____ _____ _____ _____
In 1985, after being released from Soledad Prison, Dan White walked into his garage, took a rubber hose, connected it to his car's exhaust, and killed himself with carbon monoxide poisoning. He was 39 years old. His tombstone reads, *"Daniel J. White (1946–October 21, 1985), Sgt. U. S. Army, Vietnam. Cause of death: Suicide."*	*Unfamiliar words and definitions*	*The main idea of this paragraph is:* _____ _____ _____ _____

Sources: "He Got Away with Murder," retrieved from www.findagrave.com; "The Pioneer Harvey Milk," retrieved from www.time.com; "Remembering Harvey Milk," retrieved from www.lambda.net.

In 100 words or less, thoroughly summarize this entire article. Be certain to include dates, names, places, and circumstances. Pretend that you have to explain this entire story to someone else. This exercise will help you become more adept at paraphrasing and summarizing.

_____
_____
_____
_____
_____
_____
_____
_____
_____
_____
_____
_____
_____
_____
_____

FIGURE **8.8** *A Six Pack That Can Help You with Effective Reading*

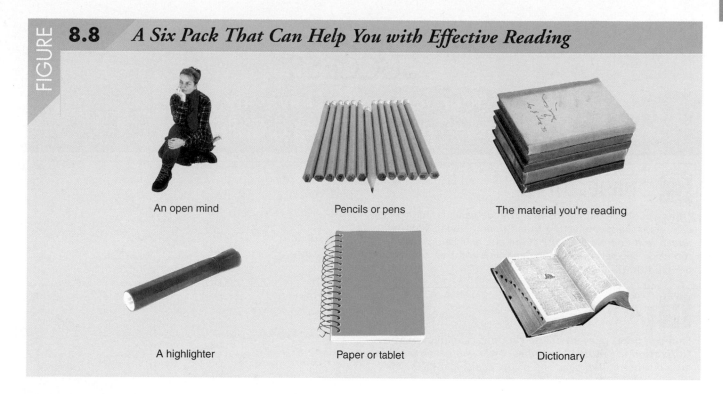

An open mind   Pencils or pens   The material you're reading

A highlighter   Paper or tablet   Dictionary

REFLECTIONS ON READING AND COMPREHENSION

SQ3R can be a lifesaver when it comes to understanding material that is overwhelming. It is an efficient, comprehensive, and DOABLE practice that can dramatically assist you in your reading efforts. It may take more time than your old method, but you will begin to see the results almost immediately. Seriously considering and practicing the strategies outlined in this chapter will help increase your comprehension level and also help your ability to recall the information when you need it later on.

As you continue to work to become an active, engaged learner, consider the following tips for reading comprehension and retention:

▶ Approach the text, chapter, or article with an *open mind.*

▶ *Free your mind* to focus on your reading.

▶ Always read with your *"six pack"* at your side (Figure 8.8).

▶ Underline and look up words you do not *understand.*

▶ Write down your *vocabulary words,* and review them often.

▶ Use *SQ3R* to increase and test your comprehension.

▶ If you're having trouble, *get a tutor* to help you.

▶ Understand that *the more you read,* the better you'll become at it.

"The knowledge of words is the gateway to learning."
—Woodrow Wilson

CREATE SUCCESS
Your Journey to University, Career, and Life Beyond College

CONNECTING

Think about the people on your college campus. With whom can you make a connection to learn more about *Reading Speed and Comprehension?* (Example: counselor, advisor, retention specialist, etc.) Why and how will this connection be important?

READING

Find one brief, relevant article (in print or online) relating to *fixation in reading strategies.* After you have read the article, write a brief summary of the additional facts you have learned.

E-LEARNING

Go to any search engine and research *"increasing reading comprehension."* Develop a list of at least 10 strategies to help you build your reading comprehension (NOT speed) skills. How do you plan to use these strategies?

ANALYZING

Choose one main idea or topic from this chapter. After exploring and researching this idea further, determine how this information can help you succeed in other classes.

TRANSITIONING

How will you use the content found in this chapter to help you create a successful transition plan to your next semester and beyond?

EMPOWERING

Thinking about the entire spectrum of your life (college, family, friends, finances, career, etc.), how can you empower yourself to be more successful through the information found in this chapter?

SQ3R *Mastery* Study Sheet

EXAMPLE QUESTION *(from page 206)* What is a logodaedalian?		**ANSWER:**
EXAMPLE QUESTION *(from page 209)* Describe the process of fixation.		**ANSWER:**
AUTHOR QUESTION *(from page 204)* Differentiate between passive and active reading.		**ANSWER:**
AUTHOR QUESTION *(from page 206)* Why is having a dictionary on hand important to developing good reading comprehension?		**ANSWER:**
AUTHOR QUESTION *(from pages 217–218)* What are some effective methods to take notes while reading?		**ANSWER:**
AUTHOR QUESTION *(from pages 217–219)* How can you use tick marks to help you improve your reading ability?		**ANSWER:**
AUTHOR QUESTION *(from page 218)* Why is recitation an important part of reading comprehension?		**ANSWER:**
YOUR QUESTION *(from page _____)*		**ANSWER:**
YOUR QUESTION *(from page _____)*		**ANSWER:**
YOUR QUESTION *(from page _____)*		**ANSWER:**
YOUR QUESTION *(from page _____)*		**ANSWER:**
YOUR QUESTION *(from page _____)*		**ANSWER:**

Finally, after answering these questions, recite this chapter's major points in your mind. Consider the following general questions to help you master this material.

- ▶ What was it about?
- ▶ What does it mean?
- ▶ What was the most important thing I learned? Why?
- ▶ What were the key points to remember?

CHAPTER 9
RECORD

CULTIVATING
YOUR
LISTENING
SKILLS AND
DEVELOPING
A NOTE-TAKING
SYSTEM
THAT WORKS
FOR YOU

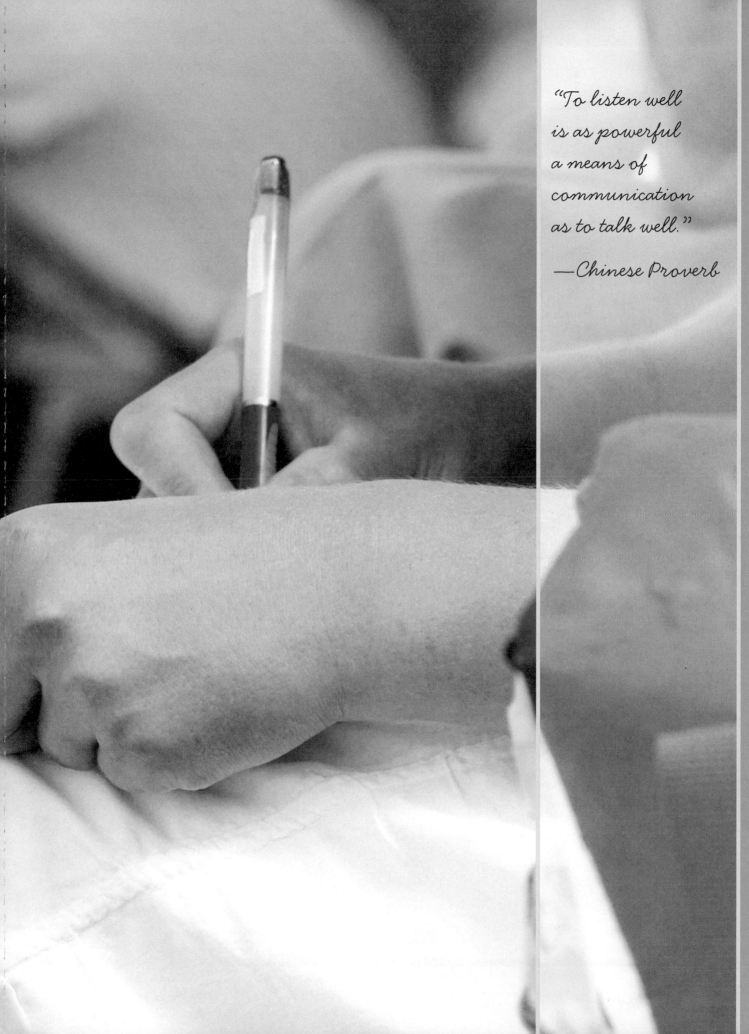

"To listen well is as powerful a means of communication as to talk well."

—Chinese Proverb

WHY READ THIS CHAPTER?

What's in it for me?

WHY do I need to become a better listener? WHY will a chapter on listening and note taking help me become a better student? WHY do instructors make such a big deal about note taking anyway? WHY is listening so important to my overall quality of life?

Why? Because listening is considered by many communication experts to be one of the, if not THE, most essential skills for building healthy relationships, solving problems, becoming open-minded, learning new information, and getting along in life. Listening will help you in terms of note taking, retaining information, and becoming actively involved in the learning process. The ability to listen in a variety of situations will also help you become a more efficient note-taker. Listening and note taking are important because well-designed notes create a history of your time in class, what you have read in your text and various articles, and what you might have studied with a group. You will find that there are different listening styles and note-taking styles and you will have to experiment to find which work best for you.

By carefully reading this chapter and taking the information provided seriously, you will be able to:

▶ Understand the difference between listening and hearing.

▶ Define the four listening styles.

▶ Overcome the obstacles to listening and how to listen in different situations.

▶ Discuss the importance of note taking and list specific tips to increase effectiveness.

▶ Identify, discuss, and use the three types of note-taking systems: Cornell, outline, and mapping.

CHAPTER 9 | RECORD

"You cannot truly listen to anyone and do anything else at the same time."

—M. Scott Peck

AMY GEDDINGS
Graduate!
Central Carolina Technical College, Sumter, South Carolina

How my
COMMUNITY
COLLEGE
changed my life

An interview conducted and written by
ANN A. COOPER
Vice President for Academic Affairs, Central Carolina Technical College

Amy Geddings began her experience with Central Carolina Technical College while still in high school. Long before dual enrollment became so popular in education, Amy decided to take a basic computer course with Central Carolina while a senior in high school, and she liked the hands-on instruction and engagement with the faculty members. Amy states, *"I received personal attention with the admissions counselor, who even walked me to my first class."* Amy was continually aware of personal attention from faculty and staff members throughout the college, and she decided to attend full time following her graduation from high school. She states that even today—over ten years later—the faculty members still remember her and stay in contact with her.

Amy relays that the technical college experience changed her life in many ways. She feels the confidence she gained while taking courses has benefited her tremendously in her present job as the marketing representative for Farmers Telephone Cooperative, where she makes presentations to employees. While attending college, she was reluctant to take the public speaking course and was not sure she would succeed in this particular course. Quite the contrary—this is the course where she gained communication skills that she uses frequently in her present position. The small classes and supportive faculty helped build her confidence and prepare her for the world of work. She talks about how learning to work with people while attending Central Carolina Technical College has prepared her for the working environment.

Amy feels her experience at CCTC provided exceptional technical training and experience in her field of telecommunications; and because of this knowledge, she has been very successful in her career. The educational preparation also provided her with the skills that she needed when she chose to continue her education in the pursuit of a bachelor's degree

from a senior institution. She states, *"Because of my time at Central Carolina, I already knew how to study and be successful in classes."*

Amy Geddings has been very successful in her career because of a positive combination of technical skills, confidence, and personal self-awareness in the pursuit of her career goals. However, she attributes much of her success to beginning her studies at a two-year college, learning from the rich experiences there, and then transferring those skills into her four-year degree and the world of work.

THINK ABOUT IT

1. Amy states that she received personal attention from the faculty and staff at her community college? In what areas do you feel you need more personal attention? Who can help?

2. What "real world" skills are you gaining at your two-year college that will help you become more successful in your chosen field?

In the preface of this book (page xiv), you read about the **SQ3R study method**. Right now, take a few moments, **scan this chapter**, and on the SQ3R Mastery Study Sheet on page 249, write **five of your own questions** that you think will be important to your mastery of this material. In addition to the two questions below, you will find five questions from your authors on that study sheet. Use one of your "***Study for Quiz***" stickers to flag this page for easy reference.

EXAMPLES:

▶ What are the four components of the Chinese verb "to listen"? (from page 231)

▶ Why is it important to identify key words during a lecture? (from page 235)

THE IMPORTANCE OF LISTENING

Why Does Listening Really Matter in Classes and Relationships?

Listening is a survival skill. Period! It is that simple! *"I know listening is important,"* you might say, but few ever think of the paramount significance listening has in our everyday lives. It is necessary for all of the following:

How can becoming a critical listener help you in and out of the classroom?

▶ Establishing and improving relationships
▶ Personal growth
▶ Showing respect to others
▶ Professional rapport
▶ Showing empathy and compassion
▶ Learning new information
▶ Understanding others' opinions and views
▶ Basic survival
▶ Entertainment
▶ Health

How much time do you think you spend listening every day? Research suggests that we spend almost 70 percent of our waking time communicating, and **53 percent of that time is spent in listening situations** (Adler et al., 2006). Effective listening skills can mean the difference between A's and F's; relationships and loneliness; and, in some cases, careers, success and failure.

LISTENING DEFINED

Is There Really a Difference Between Listening and Hearing?

No doubt you've been in a communication situation in which a misunderstanding has taken place. Either you hear something incorrectly or someone hears you incorrectly OR it could be that someone hears your message but misinterprets it. These communication blunders arise because we tend to view listening (and communicating in general) as an automatic response, when in fact it is not.

Listening is a learned, voluntary activity. You must choose to do it. It is a skill just like driving a car, painting a picture, or playing the piano. Becoming an active listener requires practice, time, mistakes, guidance, and active participation. **Hearing, however, is not learned; it is automatic and involuntary.** If you are within range of a sound, you will probably hear it even though you may not be listening to it. Hearing a sound does not guarantee attention. Listening actively, though, means making a conscious effort to focus on the sound and to determine what it is.

According to Ronald Adler (Adler et al., 2006), the Chinese character "to listen" provides a comprehensive and practical definition of listening (see Figure 9.1).

In this figure, listening involves the ears, the eyes, undivided attention, and the heart. Do you make it a habit to listen with more than your ears? The Chinese view listening as a whole-body experience. At its core, listening is "the ability to hear, understand, analyze, respect, and appropriately respond to the meaning of another person's spoken and nonverbal messages" (Daly and Engleberg, 2006). Although this definition involves the word "hear," listening goes far beyond just the physical ability to catch sound waves.

FIGURE **9.1** *Chinese Verb "To Listen"*

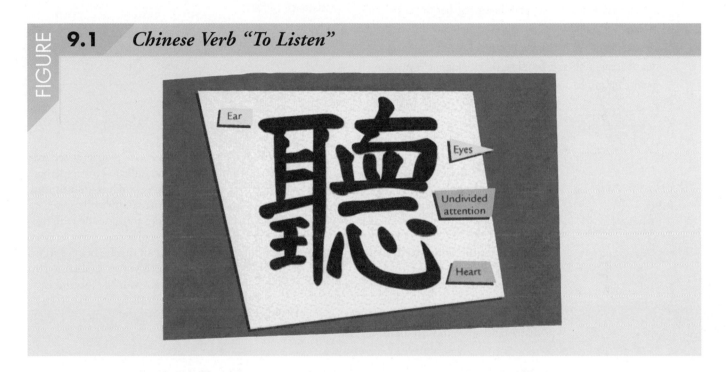

Categories of Listening

The first step of listening *is* hearing, but true listening involves one's full attention and the ability to filter out distractions, emotional barriers, cultural differences, and religious biases. Listening means that you are making a conscious decision to understand and show respect for the other person's communication efforts. Listening involves being open-minded as well. To understand listening as a whole-body experience, we can divide it into three different categories:

1. Listening with a **purpose**
2. Listening **objectively**
3. Listening **constructively**

Listening with a purpose suggests a need to recognize different types of listening situations—for example, class, worship, entertainment, and relationships. People do not listen the same way in every situation.

SUCCESSFUL
DECISIONS: An Activity for Critical Reflection

Jennifer greatly disliked her biology instructor. She could not put her finger on exactly WHY she disliked her; she just knew that Dr. Lipmon rubbed her the wrong way. This had been the case since the first day of class. Other students seemed to like her and were able to carry on conversations with her—but Jennifer could not. "Why?" she thought. "Why do I dislike her so much? She's not a bad teacher," she reasoned, "but I just can't stand to listen to her."

Jennifer decided to sit in class for the next week and really try to figure out what the main problem was. As she sat in class and listened, she finally put her finger on the problem: She and Dr. Lipmon had completely different views on many things including evolution and women's reproductive rights. Every time Dr. Lipmon made a statement contrary to Jennifer's core beliefs, Jennifer cringed.

She "shut down" and refused to listen any further. She then transferred her dislike of Dr. Lipmon's lectures and opinions onto her as a person. She knew this was affecting her grade and her knowledge base in class, but did not know how to manage or change the situation.

In your own words, what would you suggest that Jennifer do at this point? Pretend that she is enrolled at your institution. List at least three things she could do to ensure her success in her biology class. Think about what services are offered and what people might be of assistance to her.

1. _____

2. _____

3. _____

Listening objectively means listening with an open mind. You can give yourself few greater gifts than the gift of knowing how to listen without bias or prejudice. This is perhaps the most difficult aspect of listening. If you have ever been cut off in mid-conversation or mid-sentence by someone who disagreed with you, or if someone has left the room while you were giving your opinion of a situation, you have had the experience of talking to someone who does not know how to listen objectively.

Listening constructively means listening with the attitude "How can this be helpful to my life, my education, my career, or my finances?" This type of listening involves evaluating the information you are hearing and determining whether it has meaning to your life. Sound easy? It is more difficult than it sounds because, again, we all tend to shut out information that we do not view as immediately helpful or useful. To listen constructively, you need to know how to listen and store information for later.

THE FOUR LISTENING STYLES

What Is Your Orientation?

According to Steven McCornack (2007), interpersonal communication expert, author, and educator, there are **four different listening styles**: action-oriented, time-oriented, people-oriented, and content-oriented. Study Figure 9.2 to determine which style best describes you as a listener.

Which style best describes you? _____

What are the pros of this type of listening? _____

_____

_____

_____

FIGURE

9.2   *Four Listening Styles*

ACTION-ORIENTED LISTENERS

✓ want to get their messages quickly and to-the-point.

✓ do not like fluff and grow impatient when they perceive people to be "wasting their time."

✓ become frustrated when information is not orderly.

✓ are quick to dismiss people who "ramble" and falter when they speak.

TIME-ORIENTED LISTENERS

✓ want their information in brief, concise meetings

✓ are consumed with how much time is taken to convey a message

✓ set time limits for listening (and communicating in general

✓ will ask people to "move the message along" if they feel it takes too long

PEOPLE-ORIENTED LISTENERS

✓ focus less on content than other listeners

✓ view listening as a chance to connect with other people

✓ enjoy listening to people so that relationships can be built

✓ become emotionally involved with the person communicating

CONTENT-ORIENTED LISTENERS

✓ seek intellectual challenges

✓ like to listen to technical information, facts, and evidence

✓ enjoy complex information that must be deciphered and filtered

✓ carefully evaluate information and facts before forming an opinion

✓ ask many questions

What are the cons of this type of listening?   _____

_____

_____

_____

LISTENING CAN BE SO HARD

Can You Really Overcome the Obstacles to Listening?

Several major obstacles stand in the way of becoming an effective listener. To begin building active listening skills, you first have to remove some barriers.

Obstacle 1: Prejudging

Prejudging, the act of automatically shutting out what is being said, is one of the biggest obstacles to active listening. You may prejudge because you don't like or agree with the information or the person communicating it. You may also have prejudging problems because of your environment, culture, religion, social status, or attitude.

DO YOU PREJUDGE INFORMATION OR ITS SOURCE? Answer yes or no to the following questions:

1. I tune out when something is boring.	YES	NO
2. I tune out when I do not agree with the information.	YES	NO
3. I argue mentally with the speaker about information.	YES	NO
4. I do not listen to people I do not like.	YES	NO
5. I make decisions about information before I understand all of its implications or consequences.	YES	NO

If you answered yes to two or more of these questions, you tend to prejudge in a listening situation.

TIPS FOR OVERCOMING PREJUDGING

▶ Listen for information that may be valuable to you as a student. Some material may not be pleasant to hear but could be useful to you later on.

▶ Listen to the message, not the messenger. If you do not like the speaker, try to go beyond personality and listen to what is being said, without regard to the person saying it. Conversely, you may like the speaker so much that you automatically accept the material or answers without listening objectively to what is being said.

▶ Try to remove cultural, racial, gender, social, and environmental barriers. Just because a person is different from you or holds a different point of view does not make that person wrong; and just because a person is like you or holds a similar point of view does not make that person right. You sometimes have to cross cultural and environmental barriers to learn new material and see with brighter eyes.

Obstacle 2: Talking

Not even the best listener in the world can listen while he or she is talking. The next time you are in a conversation with a friend, try speaking while your friend is speaking—then see if you know what your friend said. To become an effective listener, you need to learn the power of silence. Silence gives you the opportunity to think about what is being said before you respond. The first rule of listening is: Stop talking. The second rule of listening is: Stop talking. And, you guessed it, the third rule of listening is: Stop talking.

ARE YOU A TALKER RATHER THAN A LISTENER? Answer yes or no to the following questions:

1. I often interrupt the speaker so that I can say what I want.	YES	NO
2. I am thinking of my next statement while others are talking.	YES	NO
3. My mind wanders when others talk.	YES	NO
4. I answer my own questions.	YES	NO
5. I answer questions that are asked of other people.	YES	NO

If you answered yes to two or more questions, you tend to talk too much in a listening situation.

TIPS FOR OVERCOMING THE URGE TO TALK TOO MUCH

▶ Avoid interrupting the speaker. Force yourself to be silent at parties, family gatherings, and friendly get-togethers. You should not be unsociable, but force yourself to be silent for 10 minutes. You'll be surprised at what you hear. You may also be surprised how hard it is to do this. Test yourself.

▶ Ask someone a question and then allow that person to answer the question.

▶ Too often we ask questions and answer them ourselves. Force yourself to wait until the person has formulated a response. If you ask questions and wait for answers, you will force yourself to listen.

▶ Concentrate on what is being said at the moment, not on what you want to say next.

Obstacle 3: Becoming Too Emotional

Emotions can form a strong barrier to active listening. Worries, problems, fears, and anger can keep you from listening to the greatest advantage. Have you ever sat in a lecture and before you knew what was happening, your mind was a million miles away because you were angry or worried about something? If you have, you know what it's like to bring your emotions to the table.

DO YOU BRING YOUR EMOTIONS TO THE LISTENING SITUATION? Answer yes or no to the following questions:

1. I get angry before I hear the whole story. YES NO
2. I look for underlying or hidden messages in information. YES NO
3. Sometimes, I begin listening on a negative note. YES NO
4. I base my opinions of information on what others are saying or doing. YES NO
5. I readily accept information as correct from people whom I like or respect. YES NO

If you answered yes to two or more of these questions, you tend to bring your emotions to a listening situation.

TIPS FOR OVERCOMING EMOTIONS

▶ Know how you feel before you begin the listening experience. Take stock of your emotions and feelings ahead of time.

▶ Focus on the message; determine how to use the information.

▶ Create a positive image about the message you are hearing.

▶ Avoid overreacting and jumping to conclusions.

LISTENING FOR KEY WORDS, PHRASES, AND HINTS

iStockPhoto

> Do you find it easy or hard to pick up on a professor's clues in class that may indicate important test information?

Do Professors Really Offer Test Clues in Their Lectures?

Learning how to listen for key words, phrases, and hints can help you become an active listener and an effective note-taker. For example, if your English instructor begins a lecture by saying, "There are 10 basic elements to writing poetry," jot down the number 10 under the heading "Poetry" or write the numbers 1 through 10 on your notebook page, leaving space for notes. If at the end of class you find that you listed only six elements to writing poetry, you know that you missed part of the lecture. At this point, you need to ask the instructor some questions.

Here are some key phrases and words to listen for:

in addition to	another way	above all
most important	such as	specifically
you'll see this again	therefore	finally
for example	to illustrate	as stated previously
in contrast	in comparison	nevertheless
the characteristics of	the main issue is	moreover
on the other hand	as a result of	because

From Ordinary to *Extraordinary*

Kerri Edwards, Red Light Management

LUKE BRYAN

Country Music Singer/Songwriter

2010 Top New Solo Vocalist, Academy of Country Music Awards

Basically, I'm a country boy who grew up in the very small town of Leesburg, Georgia. During high school, I worked on my Dad's farm and in his peanut and fertilizer businesses. I played sports and loved everything about outdoors. Because I loved country music, my mother often urged me to belt out George Strait songs over and over while she drove me into town to shop. When I was 14, my parents bought me an Alvarez guitar. By age 15, my father would take me down to a nearby club, Skinner's, where I shared guitar licks and lead vocals with other local country singers.

At age 16, two local songwriters who'd enjoyed some success providing tunes for Nashville artists invited me to join their twice-a-week writing sessions at a local church. By that time, I was leading my own band, playing at Skinner's and various community events.

> *One of the biggest days of my life was signing a contract with Capitol Records. All my dreams and wishes came together right there in that room.*

Encouraged by everyone who heard me play, I planned to move to Nashville after high school graduation. Supported by my family, I was loading my car for the move when tragedy struck. My older brother Chris, one of my biggest supporters and one of my best friends, was killed in an auto accident the day I was to leave town. This was a devastating blow to me that still impacts me today. All I wanted to do was be close to my family so my plans for Nashville were put on hold.

I continued to devote myself to my music, finding escape and emotional release in my songs. I poured my feelings into my songwriting and, after enrolling at Georgia Southern University, my band and I performed nearly every weekend on campus or at nearby clubs or parties. I eventually recorded an album of 10 songs, nine of which I wrote. I played throughout my college career and was able to pay my way through Georgia Southern University playing and singing country music.

After I graduated from college, I went back home to work for my dad. I did this for a year and a half, but my heart just wasn't in it. By then, I had begun to realize that I was way too passionate about country music to turn it loose without going for it. One day my father took me for a drive. "Look, your heart is in your music," my father told me. "It's what you were meant to do. You either quit this job and move to Nashville, or I'm going to fire you." With the encouragement of my family, I headed for Nashville. My dad agreed to help support me for a year to see if I could make it in the country music business. He said, "You will always wonder if you could have made it, so you need to go try." Within two months I had signed a recording contract. I will always be grateful to my parents for their support and encouragement.

Like most new artists, I struggled in the beginning, but I tried to keep a level head and to plug myself into a positive community of singers and performers. I can tell you for sure that who you hang out with has a great impact on who you become. I advise you to surround yourself with people in your field who seem to be moving and shaking. I watched lots of my friends succeed, and this made me feel that I could make it, too. It's easy to get in with the wrong crowd in college or after you graduate, so I highly recommend that you associate with a good group of people who are trying to make something of themselves. My fellow writers and performers had a major impact on my life.

One of the biggest days in my life was signing a contract with Capitol Records. When they offered me a contract, all I could think about is "I've got to call Mama and Daddy." All my dreams and wishes came together right there in that room.

I spent many long hours preparing to tour and sing in front of big crowds. Becoming a recording artist encompasses many hours of hard work, but it has paid off. Capitol Records released my debut album in 2006. Now, I am living my dream! I have a tour bus and I have been fortunate enough to open for some of the greats in the business like Kenny Chesney. I am very happy when my wife and our little son, Bo, travel with me.

I can't say that it's been easy breaking into a competitive field; I've worked very hard for many years, but it's all been worth it because I am beginning to see success. I've written several songs that have been well received, including "Good Directions" that climbed to number one and was recorded by Billy Currington. My "Country Man" song, which I recorded, made top ten. Another big hit for me was "All My Friends Say." I recently released "We Rode in Trucks" and "Do I." I wrote "Do I" with Lady Antebellum, a trio of popular, well-known country music stars. We were all thrilled when "Do I" went to the top of the charts and stayed there several weeks. Our record company, Capitol Records, gave us a Number One party in Nashville.

The best advice I can give you is to follow your dreams; do what you love; trust your instincts. Don't get trapped into doing something you don't love and look forward to every day.

EXTRAORDINARY REFLECTION

Read the following statement and respond in your online journal or class notebook.

Luke mentions that he was encouraged to go after his dream by his family and friends. He also states how important it is to surround yourself with people who are on the move and believe in their dreams. Who supports you and your dreams? How have your family and friends helped you reach your goals thus far?

Picking up on *transition words* such as these will help you filter out less impor-
tant information and thus listen more carefully to what is most important.

LISTENING IN DIFFICULT SITUATIONS

What Do You Do When English Is Your Second Language?

For students whose first language is not English, the college classroom can
present some uniquely challenging situations. One of the most pressing and important challenges is the ability to listen, translate, understand, and capture the
message on paper in a quick and continuous manner. According to Lynn Forkos,
professor and coordinator of the Conversation Center for International Students
at the College of Southern Nevada, the following tips can be beneficial:

▶ Don't be afraid to stop the instructor to ask for clarification. Asking questions
allows you to take an active part in the listening process. If the instructor doesn't
answer your questions sufficiently, make an appointment to speak with him or
her during office hours.

▶ If you have questions in a situation when the instructor can't stop or you're
watching a movie or video in class, listen for words that you do understand
and try to figure out unfamiliar words in the context of the sentence. Jot
down questions to ask later.

▶ Enhance your vocabulary by watching and listening to TV programs such as *Dateline,
20/20, Primetime Live, 60 Minutes,* and the evening news. You might also try listening to
radio stations such as National Public Radio as you walk or drive.

▶ Write down everything that the instructor puts on the board, overhead, or PowerPoint
slides. You may not need every piece of this information, but this technique gives you (and
hopefully your study group) the ability to sift through the information outside of class. It
also gives you a visual history of what the instructor said.

▶ Join a study group with people who speak English well and have the patience to assist you.

▶ Finally, if there is a conversation group or club that meets on campus, take the opportunity
to join. **By practicing language,** you become more attuned to common words and phrases.
If a conversation group is not available, consider starting one of your own.

TAKING EFFECTIVE NOTES

Is It Just a Big, Crazy Chore?

Go to class, take notes. Listen, take notes. Read a text, take notes. Watch a film, take notes.
Jeez! Is it really that important? Actually, knowing how to take useful, accurate notes can
dramatically improve your academic life. If you are an effective listener and note-taker, you
have two of the most valuable skills any student could ever use. There are several reasons why it
is important to take notes:

▶ You become an active part of the listening process.

▶ You create a history of your course's content when you take notes.

▶ You have written criteria to follow when studying.

▶ You create a visual aid for your material.

▶ Studying becomes much easier.

- ▶ You retain information at a greater rate than non-note-takers.
- ▶ Effective note-takers average higher grades than non-note-takers. (Kiewra and Fletcher, 1984)

TIPS FOR EFFECTIVE NOTE TAKING

How Can I Write It Right?

You have already learned several skills that you will need to take notes, such as cultivating your active listening skills, overcoming obstacles to effective listening, and familiarizing yourself with key phrases used by instructors. Next, prepare yourself mentally and physically to take notes that are going to be helpful to you. Consider the following ideas as you think about expanding your note-taking abilities.

Bananastock

- ▶ **Physically AND mentally attend class.** This may sound like stating the obvious, but it is surprising how many college students feel they do not need to go to class. Not only do you have to physically show up, you also have to be there mentally and emotionally—ready to listen, take notes, question, scrutinize, and interpret.
- ▶ **Come to class prepared.** Scan, read, and use your textbook to establish a basic understanding of the material before coming to class. It is always easier to take notes when you have a preliminary understanding of what is being said. Coming to class prepared also means bringing the proper materials for taking notes: lab manuals, pens, a notebook, and a highlighter.
- ▶ **Bring your textbook to class.** Although many students think they do not need to bring their textbooks to class if they have read the homework assignment, you will find that many instructors repeatedly refer to the text while lecturing. The instructor may ask you to highlight, underline, or refer to the text in class. Following along in the text as the instructor lectures may also help you organize your notes.
- ▶ **Ask questions and participate in class.** Two of the most critical actions you can perform in class are to ask questions and participate in the class discussion. If you do not understand a concept or theory, ask questions. Don't leave class without understanding what has happened and assume you'll pick it up on your own.

> Good note-taking skills help you do more than simply record what you learn In class or read in a book so that you can recall it. These skills can also help reinforce that information so that you actually know it.

THE L-STAR SYSTEM

Are You Seeing Stars?

One of the most effective ways to take notes begins with the **L-STAR system.** This five-step program will enable you to compile complete, accurate, and visual notes for future reference. Along with improving your note-taking skills, using this system will enhance your ability to participate in class, help other students, study more effectively, and perform well on exams and quizzes.

L: LISTENING. One of the best ways to become an effective note-taker is to become an active listener. A concrete step you can take toward becoming an active listener in class is to sit near the front of the room, where you can hear the instructor and see the board and overheads. Choose a spot that allows you to see the instructor's mouth and facial expressions. If you see that the instructor's face has become animated or expressive, you can bet that you are hearing

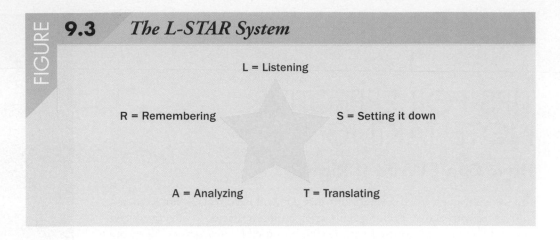

FIGURE **9.3**   *The L-STAR System*

L = Listening

R = Remembering   S = Setting it down

A = Analyzing   T = Translating

important information. Write it down! If you sit in the back of the room, you may miss out on these important clues.

S: SETTING IT DOWN. The actual writing of notes can be a difficult task. Some instructors are organized in their delivery of information; others are not. Some stick to an easy-to-follow outline and others ramble around, making it more difficult to follow them and take notes. Your listening skills, once again, are going to play an important role in determining what needs to be written down. In most cases, you will not have time to take notes verbatim. Some instructors talk very fast. You will thus have to be selective about the information you choose to set down. One of the best ways to keep up with the information being presented is to develop a shorthand system of your own. Some symbols, pictures, and markings in it will be uniquely your own. But many of the symbols you use will be universal:

w/	with	w/o	without
=	equals	≠	does not equal
<	less than	>	greater than
%	percentage	#	number
&	and	^	increase
+	plus or addition	–	minus
*	important	etc.	and so on
e.g.	for example	vs.	against
esp	especially	"	quote
?	question	…	and so on

These symbols can save you valuable time when taking notes. Because you will use them frequently, it might be a good idea to memorize them.

T: TRANSLATING. Translating can save you hours of work as you begin to study for exams. Many students feel that this step is not important, or is too time-consuming, and leave it out. Don't! Often, students take notes so quickly that they make mistakes or use abbreviations that they may not be able to decipher later.

After each class, go to the library or some other quiet place and review your notes. You don't have to do this immediately after class, but before the end of the day, you will need to rewrite and translate your classroom notes. This process gives you the opportunity to put the notes in your own words and to incorporate your text notes into your classroom notes. This practice also provides a first opportunity to commit this information to memory.

Translating your notes helps you make connections between previous material discussed, your own personal experiences, readings, and new material presented. Translating aids in recalling and applying new information. Few things are more difficult than trying to reconstruct your notes the night before a test, especially when they were made several weeks previously.

A: ANALYZING. This step takes place while you translate your notes from class. When you analyze your notes, you are asking two basic questions: (1) What does this mean? and (2) Why is it important? If you can answer these two questions about your material, you have almost mastered the information. Though some instructors will want you to spit back the exact same information you were given, others will ask you for a more detailed understanding and a synthesis of the material. When you are translating your notes, begin to answer these two questions using your notes, textbook, supplemental materials, and information gathered from outside research. Once again, this process is not simple or quick, but testing your understanding of the material is important. Remember that many lectures are built on past lectures. If you do not understand what happened in class on September 17, you may not be able to understand what happens on September 19. Analyzing your notes while translating them will give you a more complete understanding of the material.

R: REMEMBERING. Once you have listened to the lecture, set your notes on paper, and translated and analyzed the material, it is time to study, or remember, the information. Some effective ways to remember information include creating a visual picture, speaking the notes out loud, using mnemonic devices, and finding a study partner. Chapter 10 will help you with these techniques and other study aids.

TIPS FOR PERSONAL SUCCESS

Consider the following tips for improving your listening skills and taking notes more effectively:

▶ Sit near the front of the room and establish eye contact with the instructor.

▶ Read the text or handouts beforehand to familiarize yourself with the upcoming information.

▶ Come to class with an open mind and positive attitude about learning. Listen purposefully, objectively, and constructively.

Now it is your turn. Create a list of at least three more tips that you would offer a fellow classmate to assist him or her with bringing about positive change in his or her listening and note-taking skills.

1. _____

2. _____

3. _____

THREE COMMON NOTE-TAKING SYSTEMS

Why Doesn't Everyone Take Notes the Same Way?

There are three common note-taking systems: (1) the **outline** technique; (2) the **Cornell,** or split-page, technique (also called the T system); and (3) the **mapping** technique. You may find each technique useful or you may find that one is more effective for you than the others.

THE OUTLINE TECHNIQUE

Easy As A, B, C—1, 2, 3?

The outline system uses a series of major headings and multiple subheadings formatted in hierarchical order (Figure 9.4). The outline technique is one of the most commonly used note-taking systems, yet it is also one of the most misused systems. It can be difficult to outline notes in class, especially if your instructor does not follow an outline format while lecturing.

When using the outline system, it is best to get all the information from the lecture and, afterward, combine your lecture notes and text notes to create an outline. Most instructors would advise against trying the outline system of note taking during class, although you may be able to use a modified version. The most important thing to remember is not to get bogged down in a system during class; what is critical is getting the ideas down on paper. You can always go back after class and rearrange your notes as needed.

If you are going to use a modified or informal outline while taking notes in class, you may want to consider grouping information together under a heading as a means of outlining. It is easier to remember information that is logically grouped than information scattered across

9.4 *The Outline Technique*

October 20

Topic: Maslow's Hierarchy of Basic Needs

I. Abraham Maslow (1908–1970)
- American psychologist
- Born - Raised Brooklyn, N.Y.
- Parents = Uneducated Jewish immigrants
- Lonely - unhappy childhood
- 1st studied law @ city coll. of N.Y.
- Grad school - Univ of Wisconsin
- Studied human behavior & experience
- Leader of humanistic school of psy.

II. H of B. Needs (Theory)
- Written in <u>A Theory of Human Motivation</u> in 1943
- Needs of human arranged like a ladder
- Basic needs of food, air, water at bottom
- Higher needs "up" the ladder
- Lower needs must be met to experience the higher needs

III. H of B. Needs (Features)
- Physiological needs
 - Breathing
 - Food
 - Air & water
 - Sleep
- Safety needs
 - Security of body
 - Employment

several pages. If your study skills lecture is on listening, you might outline your notes using the headings "The Process of Listening" and "Definitions of Listening."

After you have rewritten your notes using class lecture information and material from your textbook, your notes may look like those in Figure 9.4.

THE CORNELL (MODIFIED CORNELL, SPLIT-PAGE, OR T) SYSTEM

A Split Decision?

The basic principle of the Cornell system, developed by Dr. Walter Pauk of Cornell University, is to split the page into two sections, each to be used for different information (see Figure 9.5).

FIGURE **9.5** *Cornell Note-Taking System Example*

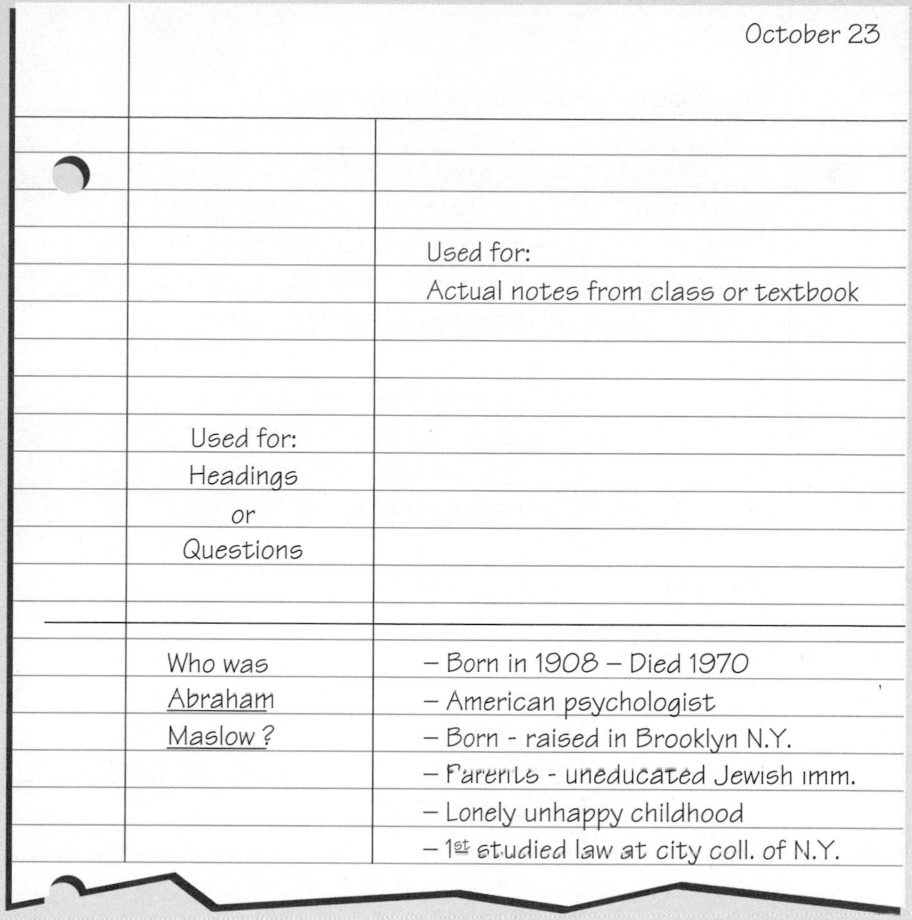

October 23

Used for: Headings or Questions	Used for: Actual notes from class or textbook
Who was Abraham Maslow ?	– Born in 1908 – Died 1970 – American psychologist – Born - raised in Brooklyn N.Y. – Parents - uneducated Jewish imm. – Lonely unhappy childhood – 1st studied law at city coll. of N.Y.

Section B (the larger section) is reserved for the actual notes from class or your text. Section A (the smaller section) should be used for headings OR questions. Review Figure 9.5 to see an example of Cornell note taking. An example of outline notes following the Cornell system appears in Figure 9.6.

THE MAPPING SYSTEM
Are You Going Around in Circles?

If you are a visual learner, the mapping system may be especially useful for you. Generating a picture of information (Figure 9.7) by creating a map, or web, of information allows you to see the relationships between facts or ideas. Figure 9.8 (page 246) shows how to use the mapping system in a Cornell frame.

A note-taking system ***must work for you.*** Do not continue with an ineffective system because your friends use it or because you feel it is the proper format. Experiment with each system or combination to determine which is best for you.

Always remember to keep your notes organized, dated, and neat. Notes that cannot be read are no good to you or to anyone else.

9.6 *Outline Using a Cornell Frame*

October 30

Topic: Maslow's Hierarchy of Basic Needs

What is the theory of basic needs ?	I. Published in 1943 in — "A Theory of human motivation" — Study of human motivation — Observation of innate curiosity — Studied exemplary people II. Needs arranged like ladder — Basic needs at the bottom — Basic needs = deficiency needs — Highest need = aesthetic need

What are the Steps in the Hierarchy ?	I. Physiological needs
	— Breathing
	— Food, water
	— Sex
	— Sleep
	
	II. Safety needs
	— Security of body
	— Security of employment
	— Resources of
	    — Family
	    — Health
	
	III. Love - Belonging needs
	— Friendships
	— Family
	— Sexual intimacy

TMI! TMI! (TOO MUCH INFORMATION)

What Do I Do If I Get Lost While Taking Notes During the Lecture?

Have you ever been in a classroom trying to take notes, but the instructor is speaking so rapidly that you cannot possibly get all of the information? And just when you think you're caught up, you realize that he or she has made an important statement and you missed it. What do you do? How can you handle, or avoid, this difficult note-taking situation? Here are several hints:

▶ Raise your hand and ask the instructor to repeat the information.

▶ Ask your instructor to slow down.

▶ If he or she will do neither, leave a blank space with a question mark in the side margin (Figure 9.9, p. 247). You can get this information after class from your instructor, a classmate, or your study buddy. This can be a difficult task to master. The key is to focus on the information at hand. Focus on what is being said at the exact moment. Don't give up!

▶ Meet with your instructor immediately after class or at the earliest time convenient for both of you. Ask for clarification of items missed.

▶ Form a note-taking group that meets after each class. This serves two purposes: (1) You can discuss and review the lecture, and (2) you will be able to get the notes from one of your note-taking buddies.

▶ Never lean over and ask questions of another student during the lecture. This will cause that person to miss information as well. It will probably also annoy your peers and the instructor.

▶ Rehearse your note-taking skills at home by taking notes from TV news magazines or documentaries such as on the History Channel.

▶ Ask the instructor's permission to use a tape recorder during the lecture. Do not record a lecture without permission. We suggest trying the other suggestions before taping your notes, however. It is a time-consuming task to listen to the lecture for a second time. However, if this system works for you, use it.

FIGURE 9.7 *The Mapping System*

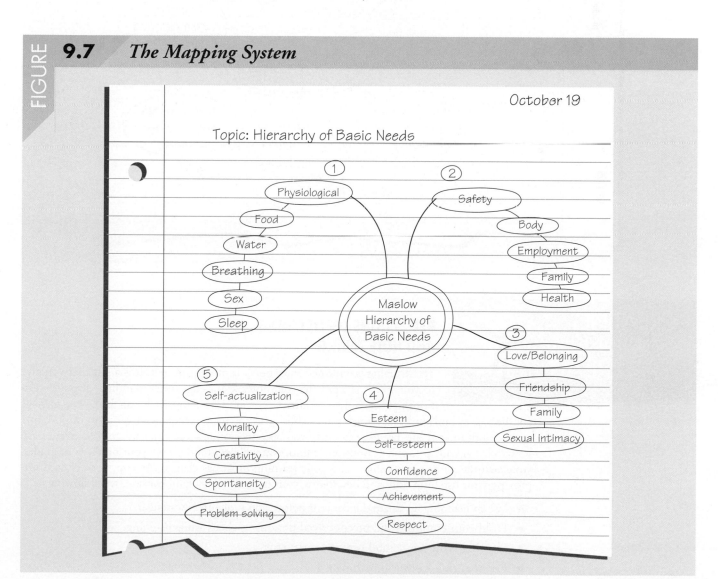

FIGURE

9.8 *The Mapping System in a Cornell Frame*

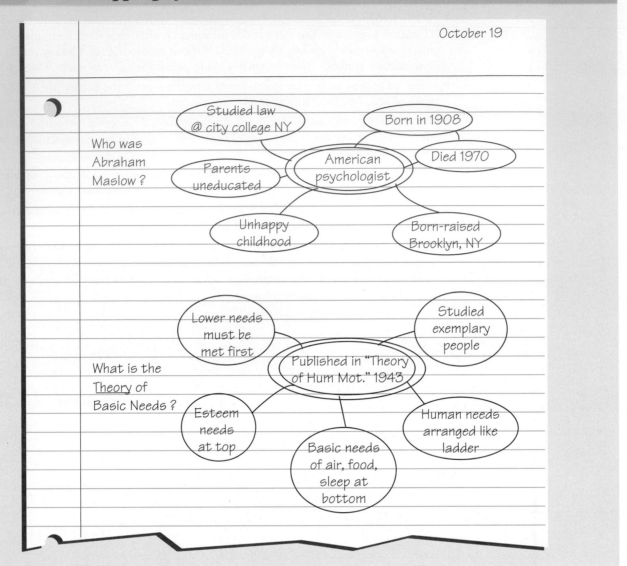

October 19

Who was Abraham Maslow?

- Studied law @ city college NY
- Born in 1908
- American psychologist
- Died 1970
- Parents uneducated
- Unhappy childhood
- Born-raised Brooklyn, NY

What is the Theory of Basic Needs?

- Lower needs must be met first
- Studied exemplary people
- Published in "Theory of Hum Mot." 1943
- Esteem needs at top
- Basic needs of air, food, sleep at bottom
- Human needs arranged like ladder

CREATING your NEW REALITY

REFLECTIONS ON LISTENING AND NOTE TAKING

Yes, listening is a learned skill, but it is more than that. It is a gift that you give to yourself. It is a gift that promotes knowledge, understanding, stronger relationships, and open-mindedness. Good listening skills can help you manage conflicts, avoid misunderstandings, and establish trusting relationships. Perhaps most importantly at this point in your life, listening can help you become a more successful student. Once you learn how to listen with your whole body and mind, you will begin to see how your notes, your grades, your attitude, your relationships, and your learning processes change. As you work toward improving your listening skills and developing your note-taking system, consider the following:

► When listening, evaluate the content before you judge the messenger.

► Hold your emotions and preconceived notions in check while listening.

► Sit where you can see and hear the instructor.

► Pay attention to *how* something is said.

FIGURE **9.9** *What to Do If You Get Lost*

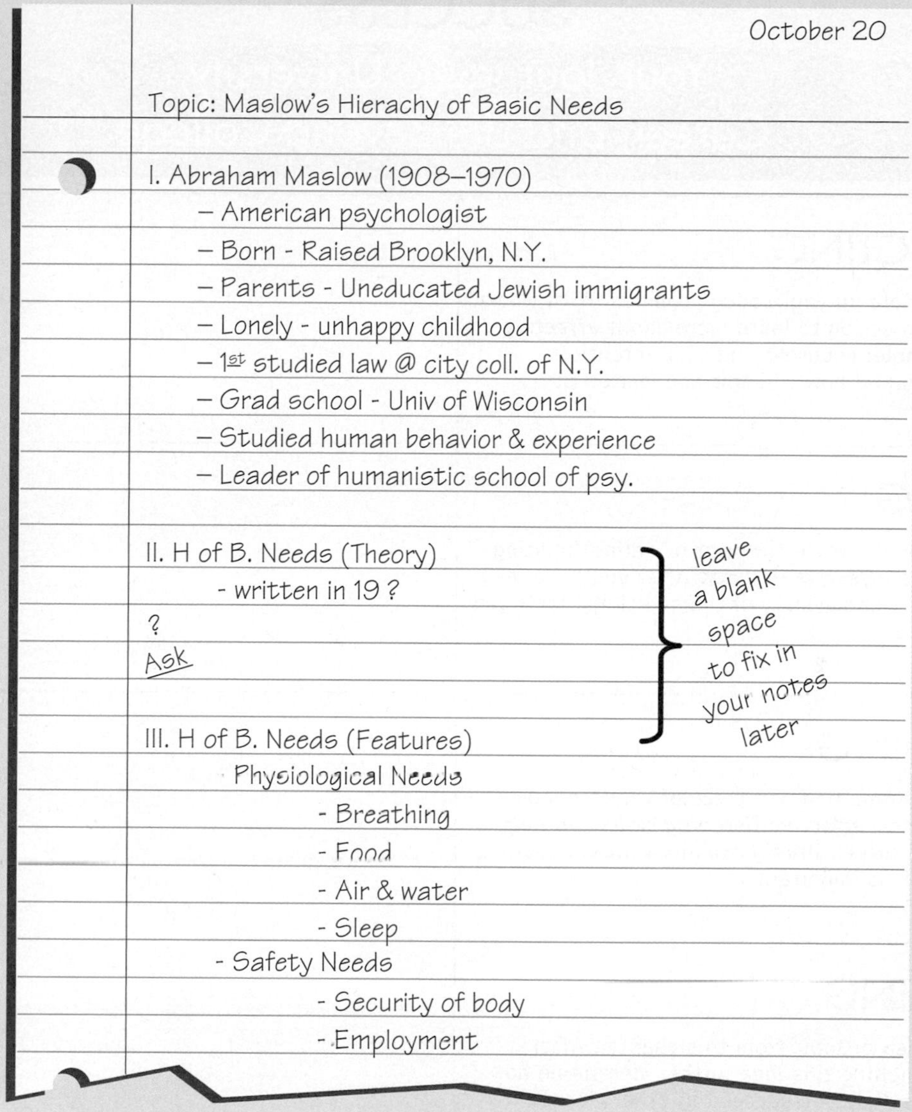

October 20

Topic: Maslow's Hierachy of Basic Needs

I. Abraham Maslow (1908–1970)
 — American psychologist
 — Born - Raised Brooklyn, N.Y.
 — Parents - Uneducated Jewish immigrants
 — Lonely - unhappy childhood
 — 1st studied law @ city coll. of N.Y.
 — Grad school - Univ of Wisconsin
 — Studied human behavior & experience
 — Leader of humanistic school of psy.

II. H of B. Needs (Theory)
  - written in 19 ?
?
<u>Ask</u>

III. H of B. Needs (Features)
  Physiological Needs
    - Breathing
    - Food
    - Air & water
    - Sleep
  - Safety Needs
    - Security of body
    - Employment

leave a blank space to fix in your notes later

▶ Hear the "entire story" before making a judgment call.
▶ Listen for major ideas and key words.
▶ Keep a separate notebook for every class.
▶ Use abbreviations whenever possible.
▶ Write down what the instructor puts on the board or PowerPoint slide.

Becoming adept at listening and developing your own note-taking system are two essential skills that can help you become a more active learner.

"Listening is an attitude of the heart, a genuine desire to be with another person."

—J. Isham

CREATE
SUCCESS
Your Journey to University, Career, and Life Beyond College

CONNECTING Think about the people on your college campus. With whom can you make a connection to learn more about *effective note taking?* (Example: counselor, advisor, retention specialist, etc.) Why and how will this connection be important?	
READING Find one brief, relevant article (in print or online) relating to *becoming a more effective listener.* After you have read the article, write a brief summary of the additional facts you have learned.	
E-LEARNING Using any search engine, find one piece of valid, reliable information about how *effective listening skills can help you in your chosen career.* Briefly explain what you learned and why you think it is important.	
ANALYZING Choose one main idea or topic from this chapter. After exploring and researching this idea further, determine how this information can help you succeed in other classes.	
TRANSITIONING How will you use the content found in this chapter to help you create a successful transition plan to your next semester and beyond?	
EMPOWERING Thinking about the entire spectrum of your life (college, family, friends, finances, career, etc.), how can you empower yourself to be more successful through the information found in this chapter?	

SQ3R *Mastery* Study Sheet

EXAMPLE QUESTION *(from page 231)* What are the four components of the Chinese verb "to listen"?		**ANSWER:**
EXAMPLE QUESTION *(from page 235)* Why is it important to identify key words during a lecture?		**ANSWER:**
AUTHOR QUESTION *(from page 231)* What is objective listening?		**ANSWER:**
AUTHOR QUESTION *(from page 232)* List and define the four listening styles.		**ANSWER:**
AUTHOR QUESTION *(from page 239)* Discuss the five steps in the L-STAR note-taking system.		**ANSWER:**
AUTHOR QUESTION *(from pages 241–242)* Discuss the benefits and drawbacks of the outline technique to take notes during class.		**ANSWER:**
AUTHOR QUESTION *(from pages 243–246)* When would be the best time to use the mapping system of note taking? Justify your answer.		**ANSWER:**
YOUR QUESTION *(from page ____)*		**ANSWER:**
YOUR QUESTION *(from page ____)*		**ANSWER:**
YOUR QUESTION *(from page ____)*		**ANSWER:**
YOUR QUESTION *(from page ____)*		**ANSWER:**
YOUR QUESTION *(from page ____)*		**ANSWER:**

Finally, after answering these questions, recite this chapter's major points in your mind. Consider the following general questions to help you master this material.

▶ What was it about?
▶ What does it mean?
▶ What was the most important thing I learned? Why?
▶ What were the key points to remember?

CHAPTER 10
UNDERSTAND

EMPOWERING
YOUR MEMORY,
STUDYING
EFFECTIVELY,
AND TAKING
TESTS WITH
CONFIDENCE

"Anyone who stops learning is old, whether at twenty or eighty. Anyone who keeps learning stays young. The greatest thing in life is to keep your mind young."

—Henry Ford

WHY READ THIS CHAPTER?

What's in it for me?

Why? Because when you read and study information, you learn amazing things. You may learn that Whoopi Goldberg has dyslexia, or that the Oedipus complex you read about in psychology class has its roots in a 2,500-year-old Greek tragedy, or that the first copying machine was invented in 1778. Although you may not be tested on this material, you will certainly have many tests in college and beyond. You will most likely be studying and taking tests for years to come. When you accept your first job, management may have you study their way of doing business and, in some cases, they will require you to pass an exam. If you go to graduate school, you will have to pass a test such as the G-MAT or the GRE or the MAT. Learning to study well and prepare for and take tests will be valuable lessons for you all your life. That is what this chapter is all about—learning how to study, how to increase your memory capacity, and how to take assessments more effectively.

By carefully reading this chapter and taking the information provided seriously, you will be able to:

▶ Understand the importance of studying, how your memory works, and how to help it work better.

▶ Identify the differences between short-term and long-term memory and how to commit information to long-term memory by using VCR3.

▶ Use mnemonics to help you remember information.

▶ Know at least three different study strategies and how to apply these strategies to all your classes, including math and science.

▶ Learn the causes of your test anxiety and how to reduce anxiety by predicting test questions and formulating appropriate responses.

WHY do I need to keep remembering information and cramming my brain full? *WHY* will a chapter on studying and remembering help me pass my classes? *WHY* is it so important, considering that I'm not going to be in school forever, to learn how to take tests? *WHY* will learning how to use mnemonic devices help me in all my courses?

CHAPTER 10 | UNDERSTAND

"We can learn something new at any time we believe we can."

—*Virginia Satir*

MARK D. WEBER
Graduate!

Moraine Valley Community College, Palos Hills, Illinois, and University of Illinois at Urbana-Champaign

How my
COMMUNITY
COLLEGE
changed my life

An interview conducted and written by
DONNA J. MCCAULEY
Professor, Moraine Valley Community College

The best kept secret about Moraine Valley? It's the total package, says a former student who now serves on the college's board of trustees.

"When folks think about a community college, it's not always looked at the same as going away to a university or college out of state," says Mark Weber, a 2003 Moraine Valley Community College graduate who was appointed to the board in 2008 and elected to a full term thereafter. *"But once they're enrolled, I think people realize and can see community college is the total package."*

"I was very involved while I was attending Moraine Valley," said Mark, who, in addition to his club affiliations on campus, served as a student trustee. *"I really enjoyed my time here and I found it very unique to find an organization like this college that truly values people—whether it's students or staff."*

Mark believes it was his community college experience that broadened his perspective on individuals from other cultures and socioeconomic backgrounds. *"I met individuals who walked into college with only the clothes on their back and graduated with the skills and opportunity to become self-sufficient and upwardly mobile,"* he said. *"I had a more valuable resource of knowledge and aptitude combined with access to my local community college. I had to prove myself in the university system and then the workforce, which all resulted from the foundational skills I learned at Moraine Valley."*

After earning a bachelor's degree in political science with a concentration in business from the University of Illinois at Urbana-Champaign, Mark began working for the State of Illinois in Springfield, but never lost sight of his first alma mater. *"I always wanted to maintain that connection to Moraine Valley, so when I heard about the referendum, I would drive back every weekend just to help out with phone calls,*

pass out literature, whatever was needed,*"* he said. Mark's volunteer efforts on behalf of the 2006 $89 million bond referendum helped the college earn voter approval for new instructional buildings, technology upgrades, and enhanced student services.

Mark, who is currently working for one of the largest professional service firms in the world, says he finds serving as a trustee for Moraine Valley very gratifying. *"I'm very involved with one of the highest priorities for this board,"* Mark said. *"It's seeing the capital construction come to fruition. That's very important. But also, at the end of the day, it's what the college can offer our students. Maybe it's an additional course, a new course, or an online course so a working mom can take a class. It's the personal things that resonate with me."*

THINK ABOUT IT

1. What skills do you think you are learning right now at your community college that will serve you well at a university or the world of work?
2. What could you do right now to help your community college?

In the preface of this book (page xiv), you read about the **SQ3R study method**. Right now, take a few moments, **scan this chapter**, and on the SQ3R Mastery Study Sheet on page 277, write **five of your own questions** that you think will be important to your mastery of this material. In addition to the two questions below, you will find five questions from your authors on that study sheet. Use one of your **"Study for Quiz"** stickers to flag this page for easy reference.

EXAMPLES:

▶ Why are mnemonics important? (from page 259)

▶ Discuss three strategies for studying math. (from page 273)

I FORGOT TO REMEMBER!

Do You Understand the FACTS and MYTHS about Memory Function?

"My brain is full." *MYTH*
"Certain foods can help with memory development." *FACT*
"Proper sleep and exercise can help you retain more information." *FACT*
"I can't remember another thing." *MYTH*
"Being closed-minded can hurt your memory development." *FACT*
"Drugs and alcohol can help me remember more." *MYTH*

Several studies suggest that it is impossible to fill our brains completely. One study in the 1970s concluded that if our brains were fed 10 new items of information every second for the rest of our lives, we would never fill even half of our memory's capacity (Texas A&M University, n.d.).

At times, you may feel that if you study or read or learn any more, you'll forget everything. Some researchers suggest that we never forget anything—that the material is simply "covered up" by other material, but it is still in our brain. The reason we can't recall that information is that it was not important enough, not stored properly, or not used sufficiently to keep it from being covered up. According to the German philosopher Friedrich Nietzsche (1844–1900), "The *existence of forgetting has never been proved;* we only know that some things don't come to mind when we want them."

So why is it so hard to remember the dates of the Civil War or who flew with Amelia Earhart or how to calculate the liquidation value of stocks or the six factors in the communication process? The primary problem is that we never properly filed or stored this information.

What would happen if you typed your English research paper into the computer and did not give it a file name? When you needed to retrieve that paper, you would not know how to find it. You would have to search through every file until you came across the paper you needed. Memory works in much the same way. We have to store it properly if we are to retrieve it easily at a later time.

> What study techniques have you used in the past to help you commit information to long-term memory?

Shutterstock

This section will detail how memory works and why it is important to your studying efforts.

Basic Facts about Memory

▶ Everyone remembers some information and forgets other information.

▶ Your senses help you take in information.

▶ With very little effort, you can remember some information.

▶ With rehearsal (study), you can remember a great deal of information.

▶ Without rehearsal or use, information is forgotten.

▶ Incoming information needs to be filed in the brain if you are to retain it.

▶ Information stored, or filed, in the brain must have a retrieval method.

▶ Mnemonic devices, repetition, association, and rehearsal can help you store and retrieve information.

Psychologists have determined that there are three types of memory: sensory, short-term (or working), and long-term memory.

Sensory memory stores information gathered from the five senses: taste, touch, smell, hearing, and sight. Sensory memory is usually temporary, lasting about one to three seconds, unless you decide that the information is of ultimate importance to you and make an effort to transfer it to long-term memory.

Short-term, or **working, memory** holds information for a short amount of time. Consider the following list of letters:

jmplngtoplntstsevng

Now, cover them with your hand and try to recite the letters.

It is almost impossible for the average person to do so. Why? Because your working memory bank can hold a limited amount of information, usually about five to nine separate new facts or pieces of information at once (Woolfolk, 2006). However, consider this exercise. If you break the letters down into smaller pieces and add MEANING, you are more likely to retain them. Example:

jmp lng to plnts ts evng

This may still not mean very much to you, but you can probably remember at least the first two sets of information, "jmp" and "lng."

Now, if you were to say to yourself that this sentence means "Jump Long To Planets This Evening," you would be much more likely to begin to remember this information. Just as your memory can "play tricks" on you, you can "play tricks" on your memory.

Although it is sometimes frustrating when we "misplace" information, it is also useful and necessary to our brain's survival that every piece of information that we hear and see is not in the forefront of our minds. If you tried to remember everything, you would not be able to function. As a student, you would never be able to remember all that your instructor had said during a 50-minute lecture. You have to take steps to help you to remember important information. Taking notes, making associations, drawing pictures, and visualizing information are all techniques that can help you move information from your short-term memory to your long-term memory bank.

Long-term memory stores a lot of information. It is almost like a computer disk. You have to make an effort to put something into your long-term memory, but with effort and memory techniques such as rehearsal, practice, and mnemonic devices, you can store anything you want to remember there. Long-term memory consists of information that you have heard often, information that you use often, information that you might see often, and information that you have determined necessary or important to you. Just as you name a file on a computer disk, you name the files in your long-term memory. Sometimes, you have to wait a moment for the information to come to you. While you are waiting, your "brain disk" is spinning; if the information you seek is in long-term memory, your brain will eventually find it if you stored it properly. You may have to assist your brain in locating the information by using mnemonics and other memory devices.

VCR3: THIS ISN'T YOUR DADDY'S VCR

How Can You Use VCR3 to Increase Memory Power?

Countless pieces of information are stored in your long-term memory. Some of them are triggered by necessity, some by the five senses, and some by experiences. The best way to commit information to long-term memory and retrieve it when needed can be expressed as a process:

V Visualizing
C Concentrating
R Relating
R Repeating
R Reviewing

Consider the following story:

As Katherine walked back to the dorm room after her evening class, she heard someone behind her. She turned to see two students holding hands walking about 20 feet behind her. She was relieved. This was the first night that she had walked back to the residence hall alone.

Katherine pulled her book bag closer to her as she increased her pace along the dimly lit sidewalk between the Salk Biology Building and the Horn Center for the Arts. "I can't believe that Shana didn't call me," she thought to herself. "She knows I hate to leave class alone."

As Katherine turned the corner onto Suddith Street, she heard someone else behind her. She turned but did not see anyone. As she continued to walk toward the residence hall, she heard the sound again. Turning to see if anyone was there, she saw a shadow disappear into the grove of hedges along the sidewalk.

Startled and frightened, Katherine crossed the street to walk beneath the streetlights and sped up to get closer to a group of students about 30 feet in front of her. She turned once more to see if anyone was behind her. Thankfully, she did not see anyone.

By this time, she was only one block from her residence hall. The lighting was better and other students were around. She felt better, but vowed never again to leave class alone at night.

Shutterstock

Do you find that studying in the library, at home, or somewhere else is most effective for you? Why?

"If a man is given a fish, he eats for a day. If a man learns to fish, he eats forever."
—Chinese Proverb

To visualize information, try to create word pictures in your mind as you hear the information. If you are being told about a Revolutionary War battle in Camden, South Carolina, try to see the soldiers and the battlefield, or try to paint a mind picture that will help you to remember the information. You may also want to create visual aids as you read or study information.

As you read Katherine's story, were you able to visualize her journey? Could you see her walking along the sidewalk? Did you see the two buildings? What did they look like? Could you see the darkness of her path? Could you see the shadow disappearing into the bushes? Could you see her increasing her pace to catch up to the other students? What was she wearing?

If you could see all of this, then you were using your visual skills—your mind's eye. This is one of the most effective ways to commit information to long-term memory. See it, live it, feel it, and touch it as you read and study it, and it will become yours.

Concentrating on the information given will also help you commit it to long-term memory. Don't let your mind wander. Stay focused. If you find yourself having trouble concentrating, take a small break (two to five minutes) and then go back to work.

Relating the information to something that you already know or understand will assist you in filing or storing the information for easy retrieval. Relating the appearance of the African zebra to the American horse can help you remember what the zebra looks like. You may not know what the buildings in Katherine's story looked like, but try to see her in front of a building on *your campus*. Creating these types of relationships increases memory retention.

Repeating the information out loud to yourself or to a study partner facilitates its transfer to long-term memory. Some people have to hear information many times before they can commit it to long-term memory. Memory experts agree that repetition is one of the STRONGEST ways to increase the retention of material.

Reviewing the information is another means of repetition. The more you see and use the information, the easier it will be to remember it when the time comes. As you review, try to remember the main points of the information.

Walter Pauk (2007), educator and inventor of the Cornell note-taking method, concluded from a research study that people reading a textbook chapter forget 81 percent of what they had read after 28 days. With this in mind, it may behoove you to review Katherine's story (and other material in your texts) on a regular basis. Reviewing is a method of keeping information fresh. Using the five points just discussed, work through the questions in Figure 10.1.

FIGURE 10.1 *Remembering Katherine*

Without looking back, answer the following questions about Katherine. Use the power of your visualization and concentration to recall the information.

1. What was the name of the biology building? _____

2. Did she see the shadow before or after she saw the two people behind her? _____

3. What were the two people behind her doing?_____

4. What was the name of the arts building? _____

5. Why did she cross the street? _____

6. How far ahead of her was the group of students? _____

7. When she saw the group of students in front of her, how far was she from her residence? _____

8. What was Katherine's friend's name? _____

THE CAPABILITY OF YOUR MEMORY

What Is the Difference Between Memorizing and Owning?

Why don't you forget your name? Why don't you forget your address? The answer is that you KNOW that information. **You OWN it.** It belongs to you. You've used it often enough and repeated it often enough that it is highly unlikely that you will ever forget it. Conversely, why might you have trouble remembering the details of Erickson's Stages of Development or Maslow's Hierarchy of Basic Needs? Most likely because you memorized it and never "owned" it.

Knowing something means that you have made a personal commitment to make this information a part of your life. For example, if you need to remember the name "Stephen" and his phone number of 925-6813, the likelihood of your remembering this information depends on *attitude*. Do you need to recall this information because he is in your study group and you might need to call him, or because he is the caregiver for your infant daughter while you are in class? How badly you need that name and number will determine the commitment level that you make to either *memorizing* it (and maybe forgetting it) or *knowing* it (and making it a part of your life).

Take a moment and refer to the Learning Process chart in Chapter 7 (Figure 7.1 on page 181). This will give you a good reminder of what it takes to learn new information and how to adjust your attitude about the value of that information. Next, study the **first picture** in Figure 10.2. Then, look at it again with the specific pointers. Finally, answer the questions on page 259.

FIGURE

10.2 *Seeing Clearly*

Consider the first picture only. Study it carefully.
Look at everything from left to right, top to bottom.

Now, notice the picture and pay close attention to the areas marked.

Notice the number of people on the trampoline   Notice the storage building

Notice the color
of the protective
padding

Notice the
green foliage

Notice the utility meter

FIGURE 10.2 *Seeing Clearly (continued)*

Now, cover this picture and answer the following questions:

1. How many people are on the trampoline? _____
2. What color is the protective padding on the edge? _____
3. What is the season of the year based on the foliage color? _____
4. What colors are used on the storage building? _____
5. Is there one utility meter or two? _____
6. How many children are in the air? _____
7. Are the children all male, female, or mixed? _____
8. How many people are wearing striped shirts? _____
9. What type of fence surrounds the house? _____
10. What colors are used on the house? _____
11. Is the house made of one material or more? _____
12. What color are the flowers on the bush? _____

Photo copyright Sonya Etchison/Fotolia

"NOT FAIR!" you may be saying right now. "We were not asked to look at the fence, the colors on the house, or what people are wearing." Regardless, could you answer all of the questions without looking? The purpose of this exercise is to help you understand the real difference between casually looking at something and REALLY looking at something. To truly know something, you have to go beyond what is on the surface—even going beyond reading and studying what was asked of you. You have to look and examine more than you are told or more than what is pointed out to you. In order to own information, you have to be totally committed to examining every detail, every inch, and every angle of it. You will need to practice and master the technique of "going beyond."

The Greek goddess of memory, Mnemosyne.

Leighton, Frederic (1830–96)/Bridgeman Art Library

USING MNEMONIC DEVICES

What Does a Greek Goddess Have to Do with *My Memory?*

The word *mnemonic* is derived from the name of the Greek Goddess of Memory, **Mnemosyne** (pronounced Ne-MO-ze-knee). She was considered one of the most important goddesses of all time because it was believed that memory separates us from lower animal life forms. It was believed that memory is the very foundation of civilization (The Goddess Path, 2009). Memory was so very important because most of the transmission of human history depended on oral stories and parables committed only to memory, not on paper.

In modern times, a mnemonic (pronounced ni-MON-ik) device is a memory trick or technique that assists you in putting information into your long-term memory and pulling it out when you need it. According to research into mnemonics and their effectiveness, it was found that mnemonics can help create a phenomenon known as the ***bizarreness effect.*** This effect causes us to remember information that is "bizarre" or unusual more rapidly than "normal," everyday facts. "The bizarreness effect occurs because unusual information and events trigger heightened levels of our attention and require us to work harder to make sense of them; thus we remember the information and its associated interaction better" (McCornack, 2007). The following types of mnemonics may help you process information in your long-term memory.

JINGLES/RHYMES. You can make up rhymes, songs, poems, or sayings to assist you in remembering information; for example, "Columbus sailed the ocean blue in fourteen hundred and ninety-two."

As a child, you learned many things through jingles and rhymes. You probably learned your ABC's, as well as your numbers, through a song pattern. If you think about it, you can probably still sing your ABC's, and maybe your numbers through the "Ten Little Indians" song. You can probably also sing every word to the opening of *The Brady Bunch, Scooby Doo,* or *Gilligan's Island* because of the continual reruns on TV. Some advertisements and commercials seem to stick with us even if we find them annoying. Jingles and rhymes have a strong and lasting impact on our memory—especially when repetition is involved.

SENTENCES. You can make up sentences such as "Some men can read backward fast" to help you remember related terms beginning with the same first letters For example, "**P**lease **e**xcuse **m**y **d**ear **A**unt **S**ally" corresponds to the order of mathematical operations (**p**arentheses, **e**xponents, **m**ultiplication, **d**ivision, **a**ddition, and **s**ubtraction).

Other mnemonic sentences in academic areas include the following:

1. **My Very Elderly Mother Just Saved Us Nicely.** This is a sentence mnemonic for the eight planets in order from the sun: Mercury, Venus, Earth, Mars, Jupiter, Saturn, Uranus, Neptune.

2. **Every Good Bird Does Fly** is a sentence mnemonic for the line notes in the treble clef in music.

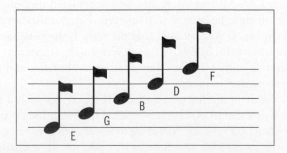

3. **Some Men Help Each Other** is a sentence mnemonic for the Great Lakes from west to east: Superior, Michigan, Huron, Erie, Ontario.

WORDS. You can also create words. For example, **Roy G. Biv** may help you to remember the colors of the rainbow: **r**ed, **o**range, **y**ellow, **g**reen, **b**lue, **i**ndigo, and **v**iolet. Other word mnemonics include the following:

1. **HOMES** is a word mnemonic for the Great Lakes in no particular order: **H**uron, **O**ntario, **M**ichigan, **E**rie, **S**uperior.

2. **FACE** is a word mnemonic for the space notes in the treble clef.

STORY LINES. If you find it easier to remember stories than raw information, you may want to translate the information into a story that you can easily tell. Weave the data and facts into a creative story that can be easily retrieved from your long-term memory. This technique can be especially beneficial if your instructor gives essay exams, because the "story" that you remember can be what was actually told in class.

ACRONYMS. An acronym is a word that is formed from the first letters of other words. You may see reruns for the famed TV show *M*A*S*H*. This is an acronym for "Mobile Army Surgical Hospital." If you scuba dive, you know that *SCUBA* is an acronym for "Self-Contained Underwater Breathing Apparatus."

Other Common Acronyms

NASA (**N**ational **A**eronautics and **S**pace **A**dministration)
NASCAR (**N**ational **A**ssociation for **S**tock **C**ar **A**uto **R**acing)
NASDAQ (**N**ational **A**ssociation of **S**ecurities **D**ealers **A**utomated **Q**uotations)
NATO (**N**orth **A**tlantic **T**reaty **O**rganization)
BART (**B**ay **A**rea **R**apid **T**ransit)

From Ordinary to *Extraordinary*

H. P. RAMA
CEO, JHM Hotels
Greenville, South Carolina

I have led a life filled with a great variety of experiences, trials, challenges, and triumphs. Born in Africa, I was sent to India to live with my grandparents and go to school when I was just five years old. I lived away from my parents, whom I missed greatly, in a little farming village in India, where I finished school and ultimately earned an undergraduate degree. I knew I wanted to go to America and pursue the American dream, so at age 21 I left India and arrived in this country with only $2 in my pocket.

I had to get a job quickly, so I took the first job offered to me, a dishwasher, which I quit after just four hours. My next job was as a waiter at a Howard Johnson's restaurant in Manhattan. While I worked as a waiter to support myself, I attended Xavier University to pursue my MBA. My life was primarily one of work and sacrifice as I worked hard to pay my expenses and to graduate with this degree I prized so much. While working at Howard Johnson's, I paid attention to everything that happened around me because I had no intention of remaining a waiter all my life. I was absorbing knowledge of the hotel and restaurant business, which I would put to use later. At the time, I had no intention of becoming a hotelier. My goal was to go into banking. I always say that I became an accidental hotelier, but this field has served me well and offered me many opportunities. I was pursuing the American dream, and that was all that mattered.

I considered myself fortunate to have this great opportunity to be in America, to be going to school, and to have a job that supported me.

After receiving my MBA from Xavier, I worked as a staff accountant for 14 months. In 1973 I had an opportunity to buy my first hotel in Pomona, California. My brother and I bought the hotel, and we had only two employees other than the two of us. We worked 24/7 and lived behind the office. There was no job that we did not do. But we were chasing the dream, and we were off and running with no idea of how many opportunities we would have.

> At age 21 I left India and arrived in this country with only $2 in my pocket.

Then I moved East, still focused on achieving the American dream, and bought a 36-room hotel in Buffalo, Tennessee. My wife and I did everything—front desk, night duty, all the maintenance. We both worked very hard, long hours. In 1977 we moved to Greenville, South Carolina, and bought a foreclosed property from a bank. In 1983 I bought four Howard Johnson's hotels—just 13 years after working for HJ as a waiter. Over the years my brothers and I have owned and developed 78 hotels and still own 38 today.

We developed a five-star hotel in India in 1990, and today we are expanding and adding other hotels. We are most proud of the fact that we are developing a mixed-use development in India that will include a Hospitality College campus, a retailing and entertainment campus, a hospital campus, and luxury accommodations. We are using our knowledge learned in this wonderful country to continue the dream in India.

In 1999, I was named chairman of the American Motel and Hotel Lodging Association, which was a significant honor for me. Because I wanted to give back to the field that has done so much for me, I donated $1 million for scholarships for hospitality students. In 1989 I was the founding member of the Asian American Hotel Owners Association. Today I serve on several boards of advisors for hospitality programs and was named an executive ambassador by Cornell University, a position in which I speak to graduate students about my experiences.

My advice to students today is this: Anything is possible if you have the vision, pay the price, work hard, and take risks. I have been very blessed, but I have also worked very hard. And I am living proof that the American dream is alive and well.

EXTRAORDINARY REFLECTION

Read the following statement and respond in your online journal or class notebook.

Mr. Rama worked his way up the ladder and became chairman of the American Motel and Hotel Lodging Association, a major organization. What top honors do you hope to achieve in your own career? Why? How would they change your life?

FIGURE

10.3 *The Pegging System*

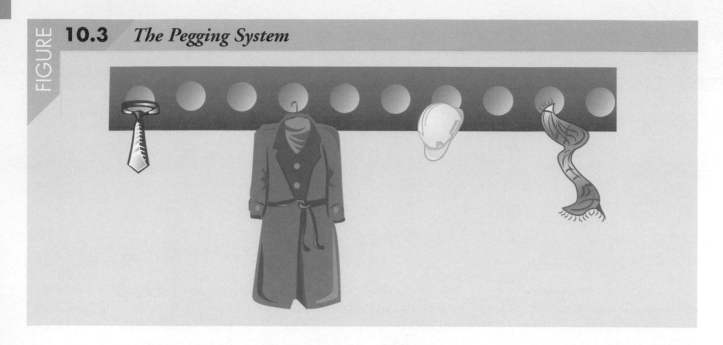

PEGGING. The pegging system uses association, visualization, and attachment to aid in memory. With this system, you literally "attach" what you want to remember to something that is already familiar to you—the pegs that you create. This is a visual means of remembering lists, sequences, and even categories of information.

Pretend that you are looking at a coat rack mounted on the wall, like Figure 10.3, with 10 pegs sticking out of it. Just as you would hang a hat or coat on the pegs of a rack, you can hang information there, too.

For the sake of explaining this technique more thoroughly, we have named the 10 pegs for you with corresponding rhyming words. You, however, can name your pegs anything that would be easy for you to remember. Once you memorize these peg names, you can attach anything to them with visualization and imagination. The key to using the pegging mnemonic system is to name your pegs ONCE and use those names each time you hook information to them. This way, they become second nature to you. For our example, our 10 pegs are named:

1	=	sun	6 =	sticks
2	=	shoe	7 =	heaven
3	=	bee	8 =	gate
4	=	shore	9 =	line
5	=	alive	10 =	pen

Repeat these until you have memorized them.

Let's use an example from your *Cornerstone* text. In Chapter 1 you were introduced to the ***Ten Essential Cornerstones for Success in a Changing World*** (passion, motivation, knowledge, resourcefulness, creativity, adaptability, openmindedness, communication, accountability, and vision). Using visualization, attach one of the cornerstones to each peg.

1 - sun	I look at the ***sun*** on a beautiful day with ***passion***.
2 - shoe	I walk in my ***shoes*** with ***motivation***.
3 - bee	I see a ***bee*** flying around that seems to be very ***knowledgeable***.
4 - shore	The ***shore*** washes many ***resources*** to the beach.
5 - alive	My brain is ***alive*** because I use ***creativity***.
6 - sticks	I see a ***stick*** bending into a half circle, making it very ***adaptable***.
7 - heaven	Believing in ***heaven*** takes ***openmindedness***.
8 - gate	Many ***gates*** open for people who know how to ***communicate***.
9 - line	If you walk a straight ***line***, you are ***accountable***.
10 - pen	Use a ***pen*** to write your ***vision***.

Read these over one more time, and then cover the list. You'll be amazed at how easy it is to repeat it. You will, of course, need to study each one to know what it means, but now, you have the list memorized, in order.

HAKUNA MATATA

How in the World Can I Study with Small Children in the House?

For many college students, finding a place or time to study is the hardest part of studying. Some students live at home with younger siblings; some students have children of their own. If you have young children in the home, you may find the following hints helpful when it comes time to study.

STUDY AT SCHOOL. Your schedule may have you running from work to school directly to home. Try to squeeze in even as little as half an hour at school for studying, perhaps immediately before or after class. A half hour of pure study time can prove more valuable than five hours at home with constant interruptions.

CREATE CRAFTS AND HOBBIES. Your children need to be occupied while you study. Choose projects your children can do by themselves, without your help. Explain to your children that you are studying and that they can use this time to be creative; when everyone is finished, you'll share with each other what you've done. Give them little rewards for their work and for helping you have quiet time to study.

STUDY WITH YOUR CHILDREN. One of the best ways to instill the value of education in your children is to let them see you participating in your own education. Set aside one or two hours per night when you and your children study. You may be able to study in one place, or you may have separate study areas.

RENT MOVIES OR LET YOUR CHILDREN WATCH TV. Research has shown that viewing a limited amount of educational television, such as *Sesame Street, Reading Rainbow,* or *Barney and Friends,* can be beneficial for children. If you do not like what is on television, you might consider renting or purchasing age-appropriate educational videos for your children.

INVITE YOUR CHILDREN'S FRIENDS OVER. What?! That's Right. A child who has a friend to play or study with may create less of a distraction for you. Chances are your children would rather be occupied with someone their own age, and you will gain valuable study time.

HIRE A SITTER OR EXCHANGE SITTING SERVICES WITH ANOTHER STUDENT. Arrange to have a sitter come to your house a couple of times a week if you can afford it. If you have a classmate who also has children at home, you might take turns watching the children for each other. You could each take the children for one day a week, or devise any other schedule that suits you both best.

FIND OUT IF YOUR COLLEGE HAS AN ON-SITE DAY-CARE CENTER SUCH AS THE BOYS AND GIRLS CLUB. Some colleges provide day-care facilities at a reduced cost, and some provide day care at no charge. It is certainly worth checking out.

TALK TO THE FINANCIAL AID OFFICE ON YOUR CAMPUS. In some instances, there may be grants or aid to assist you in finding affordable day care for your child.

IndekOpen

Do you think it is a good idea to involve your children (or younger siblings) in your education? Why or why not?

STUDYING IN A CRUNCH

TOMORROW? What Do You Mean the Test Is Tomorrow?

Let's be straight up front. No study skills textbook will ever advise you to cram. It is simply a dangerous and often futile exercise in desperation. You will *never read the words*, "Don't waste your time studying; just CRAM the night before so you can party harder and longer!" in a study skills textbook. Cramming is the complete opposite of what this whole chapter is about—knowing versus memorizing. Cramming will not help you own the material; it can only help you memorize a few things for storage in short-term memory. You may spend several hours cramming, and shortly after the test, the information is gone, evaporated, vanished! If you find yourself in this spot, consider the following tips and suggestions for cramming. These probably won't get you an A, but they may help you with a few questions.

DEPRESSURIZE. Just tell yourself up front what you are doing. Don't pretend that cramming is going to save you. Let yourself realize that you are memorizing material for short-term gain and that you won't be able to keep it all. With this admission, your stress will diminish.

KNOW THE SCORE. When cramming, it is important to know what you're cramming for. If you're cramming for a multiple-choice test, you'll need different types of information than for an essay test. Know the type of test for which you are studying.

READ IT QUICKLY. Think about **H2 FLIB.** This is a mnemonic for: read the **h**eadings, **h**ighlight the important words, read the **f**irst sentence of every paragraph, read the **l**ast sentence of every paragraph, read the **i**ndented and **b**oxed material. This can help you get through a chapter when pinched for time.

> *"Don't just learn something from every experience, learn something positive."*
> —Al Neuharth

MAKE CONNECTIONS. As you are reading, quickly determine if any of the information has a connection with something else you know. Is there a relationship of any kind? Is there a cause and effect in motion? Can you pinpoint an example to clarify the information? Is there a mnemonic that can help you with this information? These questions can help you with retention and long-term memory commitment.

USE YOUR SYLLABUS OR STUDY GUIDE. If your instructor lists questions in the syllabus to which you should know the answers (mastery questions) or has given you a study sheet (or you have developed your own study sheet, like the one you have created at the end of each *Cornerstone* chapter), this is the place to start. Answer those questions. If you don't have either, look to see if the text gives study questions at the end of the chapter.

SEE IT. Visualizing the information through mapping, diagrams, photos, drawings, and outlines can help you commit this information to short-term memory.

CHECK YOUR NOTES. Did the professor indicate that certain things are important to know for the test?

CHOOSE WISELY. If you're cramming, you can't do it all. Make wise choices about which material you plan to study. This can be driven by your study sheet, your lecture notes, or questions in your syllabus (if they are listed).

Information you've crammed is going to leave you after the test. Don't rely on it for the next test or the final. You will need to go back and relearn (truly understand) the information you "crammed" in order to commit it to long-term memory.

THINKING ABOUT TESTING

Can Changing My Attitude and Reducing Stress Really Help?

Yes, both are necessary to help you get through tests. A positive or negative attitude can truly mean the difference between success and failure. With an attitude adjustment from negative to positive and some basic preparation, you can overcome a good deal of your anxiety about tests and do well. You can reduce anxiety when you are in control of the situation, and you can gain control by convincing yourself that you *can be* and *will be* successful. If you think positively and can honestly say that you have done everything possible to prepare for a test, then the results will most likely be positive.

Silencing *your negative self-talk* is one of the most powerful things you can do for yourself. Consider the following tips for reducing test anxiety during your next test. You will not be able to employ them all, but if you learn and use a few new ones each time, before you know it, you'll be a testing pro!

- ▶ Prepare yourself emotionally for the test, control your self-talk, and be positive.
- ▶ Study and learn the material—NO! You can't study too much.
- ▶ Ask peers who have had a certain professor what type of tests he or she gives.
- ▶ Arrive early for the test (at least 15 minutes early).
- ▶ Go to the test with everything you need: pencils, calculator, and other supplies.
- ▶ Listen to the instructor before the test begins, know his or her rules about testing, and READ the instructions.
- ▶ Keep an eye on the clock during the test so that you can finish on time. However, don't let time cause you undue stress or anxiety.
- ▶ Answer what you know first, the questions that are easiest for you.
- ▶ Check your answers, but remember, your first response is usually correct.
- ▶ Find out ahead of time exactly what the test will cover.
- ▶ Ask the instructor for a study sheet; you may not get one, but it does not hurt to ask!
- ▶ When you get the test, jot down on the back or at the top of a page any mnemonics you might have developed.

PREPARING FOR THE TEST

What Should I Find Out Before Studying?

Several classes before the test is scheduled to be given, **quiz your instructor** about the logistics and specifics of the test. This information can help you study more effectively and eliminate the anxiety that comes with uncertainty. If you don't know whether the test is going to be true-false or essay or both, it is much more difficult to study. The questions you need to ask include the following:

1. What types of questions will be on the test?
2. How many questions will be on the test?

TIPS FOR PERSONAL SUCCESS

Consider the following tips for making time for studying and committing information to long-term memory:

- ▶ Study daily to avoid having to "cram" the night before your test.
- ▶ Form a study group with people who are motivated and keep you on track.
- ▶ Keep up with your daily readings and homework.

Now, it is your turn. Create a list of at least three more tips that would assist a fellow classmate in making time in his or her life to study.

1. _____
2. _____
3. _____

What techniques help you reduce your anxiety and negative self-talk during quizzes and exams?

Patrick White/Merrill

3. Is there a time limit on the test?

4. Will there be any special instructions, such as "use pen only" or "use a number 2 pencil"?

5. Is there a study sheet?

6. Will there be a review session?

7. What is the grade value of the test?

8. What chapters or sections will the test cover?

Asking these simple questions will help you know what type of test will be administered, how you should prepare for it, and what supplies you will need.

TEST-TAKING STRATEGIES AND HINTS FOR SUCCESS
What Do I Do When I Can't Remember the Answer?

Almost every test question will elicit one of three types of responses from you as the test-taker:

▶ Quick-time response
▶ Lag-time response
▶ No response

A *quick-time response* occurs when you read a question and know the answer immediately. You may need to read only one key word in the test question to know the correct response. Even if you have a quick-time response, however, always read the entire question before answering it. The question may be worded in such a way that the correct response is not the one you originally thought of.

You have a *lag-time response* when you read a question and the answer does not come to you immediately. You may have to read the question several times or even move on to another question before you think of the correct response. Information in another question will sometimes trigger the response you need. Once you've begun to answer other questions, you usually begin to remember more, and the response may come to you.

No response is the least desirable situation when you are taking a test. You may read a question two or three times and still have no response. At this point, you should move on to another question to try to find some related information. You should also consider your options:

1. Leave this question until the very end of the test.

2. Make an intelligent guess.

3. Try to eliminate all unreasonable answers by association.

4. Watch for modifiers within the question.

Remember these important tips about the three types of responses:

1. Don't be overly anxious if your *response is quick;* read the entire question and be careful not to make a mistake.

2. Don't get nervous if you have a *lag-time response;* the answer may come to you later, so just relax and move on.

3. Don't put down just anything if you have *no response;* take the remaining time and use intelligent guessing, if you can (less appropriate for essay or fill-in-the-blank questions).

SUCCESSFUL DECISIONS: An Activity for Critical Reflection

After the second week of classes, Jose was devastated by his first test score. The instructor put the range of grades on the board, and he was shocked to see that many people passed the test and that his score was in the bottom 10 percent.

He began asking classmates if they did well or not and found some who had made A's and others who had made D's. When he spoke with one classmate, Letty, she told him that he should just chill and take a "cheat sheet" to class. "The instructor never looks, man, and she left the classroom twice. She'll never know. That's how I got my A."

"Cheat," Jose thought, "I don't think I can do that." He knew that others had made better grades than he over the years, but he also knew that he had never once cheated on an exam. Never.

Jose went to the Tutoring Center and worked with a tutor on content and on how to take a test more effectively. On the next test, Jose scored a C. "It may not be the best grade in the class," he thought, "but it is all mine. I did it."

In your own words, what two suggestions would you give Jose to improve his grades without cheating?

1. _____

2. _____

What Are Some Tips for Taking Tests?

Before you read about the strategies for answering different types of questions, think about this: *There is no substitute for studying!* You can know all the tips, ways to reduce anxiety, mnemonics, and strategies on earth, but if you have not studied, they will be of little help to you.

STRATEGIES FOR MATCHING QUESTIONS. Matching questions frequently involve knowledge of people, dates, places, or vocabulary. Try the following strategies when answering matching questions:

▶ Study the directions carefully.

▶ Read each column before you answer.

▶ Determine whether there is an equal number of items in each column.

Sample Test 1 MATCHING

DIRECTIONS: Match the information in column A with the correct information in column B. Use uppercase letters.

GOALS, MOTIVATION, & SELF-ESTEEM

A

_____ They can be long or short, social, academic, religious, or financial

_____ They bring out the worst in you

_____ I CAN'T Syndrome

_____ Your "true self"

_____ Listening with an open mind

B

A. Child within

B. Objectivity

C. Contaminated people

D. Negative thoughts

E. Goals

- ▶ Match what you know first.
- ▶ Cross off information that has already been used.
- ▶ Apply a process of elimination for answers you might not know.
- ▶ Look for logical clues.
- ▶ Use the longer statement as a question; use the shorter statement as an answer.

STRATEGIES FOR TRUE-FALSE QUESTIONS. True-false questions ask whether a statement is true or not. True-false questions can be some of the trickiest questions ever developed. Some students like them; some hate them. There is a 50/50 chance of answering correctly, but you can use the following strategies to increase your odds with true-false questions:

- ▶ Read each statement carefully and watch for key words in each statement.
- ▶ Look closely for double negatives such as "not untruthful."
- ▶ Pay attention to words that may indicate that a statement is true, such as *some, few, many,* and *often.*
- ▶ Pay attention to words that may indicate that a statement is false, such as *never, all, every,* and *only.*
- ▶ Remember that if any part of a statement is false, the entire statement is false.
- ▶ Answer every question unless there is a penalty for guessing.

Sample Test 2 TRUE-FALSE

Place "T" for true or "F" for false beside each statement.

NOTE-TAKING SKILLS

1. _____ Note taking creates a history of your course content.
2. _____ "Most importantly" is not a key phrase.
3. _____ You should always write down everything the instructor says.
4. _____ You should never ask questions in class.
5. _____ The L-STAR system is a way of studying.

STRATEGIES FOR MULTIPLE-CHOICE QUESTIONS. Many college instructors give multiple-choice tests because they are easy to grade and provide quick, precise responses. A multiple-choice question asks you to choose from among, usually, two to five answers to complete a sentence. The following strategies can increase your success when answering multiple-choice questions.

- ▶ Read the question and try to answer it before you read the answers provided.
- ▶ Look for similar answers; one of them is usually the correct response.
- ▶ Recognize that answers containing extreme modifiers, such as *always, every,* and *never,* are usually wrong.
- ▶ Cross off answers that you know are incorrect.
- ▶ Read all the options before selecting your answer. Even if you believe that A is the correct response, read them all.
- ▶ When the answers are all numbers, the highest and lowest numbers are usually incorrect.
- ▶ Understand that the most inclusive and longest answers are often correct.
- ▶ If you cannot answer a question, move on to the next one and continue through the test; another question may trigger the answer you couldn't come up with previously.
- ▶ Answer every question unless there is a penalty for guessing.

Sample Test 3 MULTIPLE CHOICE

DIRECTIONS: Read each statement and select the best response from the answers given below.

STUDY SKILLS

1. Which statement is true according to the 2009 Labor Statistics, Bureau of Census?
   A. Men earn less than women.
   B. Women earn more than men.
   C. People with a master's degree earn the most money of any education level.
   D. Unemployment is greatest among those with a doctorate degree.

2. To calculate a GPA, you would:
   A. Divide quality points by the number of semester hours.
   B. Multiply total points by quality points.
   C. Divide total points by the number of semester hours.
   D. Multiply the quality points by the total points.

3. To be an effective priority manager, you have to:
   A. Be very structured, organized, and self-disciplined.
   B. Be very unstructured and disorganized.
   C. Be mildly structured and organized.
   D. Know what type of person you are and avoid working from that perspective.

STRATEGIES FOR SHORT-ANSWER QUESTIONS. Short-answer questions, also called fill-in-the-blanks, ask you to supply the answer yourself, not select it from a list. Although "short answer" sounds easy, these questions are often very difficult. Short-answer questions require you to draw from your long-term memory. The following hints can help you answer this type of question successfully:

▶ Read each question and be sure that you know what is being asked.

▶ Be brief in your response.

▶ Give the same number of answers as there are blanks; for example, _____ and _____ would require two answers.

▶ Never assume that the length of the blank has anything to do with the length of the answer.

Sample Test 4 SHORT ANSWER

DIRECTIONS: Fill in the blanks with the correct response. Write clearly.

LISTENING SKILLS

1. Listening is a _____ act. We choose to do it.
2. The three elements of listening involve listening objectively, _____, and _____.
3. _____ is the same as listening with an open mind.
4. Prejudging is an _____ to listening.
5. Leaning forward, making eye contact, being patient, and leaving your emotions at home are characteristics of _____ listeners.

▶ Remember that your initial response is usually correct.

▶ Pay close attention to the word immediately preceding the blank; if the word is "an," give a response that begins with a vowel (*a, e, i, o, u*).

▶ Look for key words in the sentence that may trigger a response.

STRATEGIES FOR ESSAY QUESTIONS. Most students look at essay questions with dismay because they take more time. Yet essay tests can be one of the easiest tests to take because they give you a chance to show what you really know. An essay question requires you to supply the information. If you have studied, you will find that once you begin to answer an essay question, your answer will flow more easily. The following tips can help in answering essay questions:

▶ More is not always better; sometimes more is just more. Try to be as concise and informative as possible. An instructor would rather see one page of excellent material than five pages of fluff.

▶ Pay close attention to the action word used in the question and respond with the appropriate type of answer. Key words used in essay questions include the following:

discuss	illustrate	enumerate	describe
compare	define	relate	list
contrast	summarize	analyze	explain
trace	evaluate	critique	interpret
diagram	argue	justify	prove

▶ Write a thesis statement for each answer.

▶ Outline your thoughts before you begin to write.

▶ Watch your spelling, grammar, and punctuation.

▶ Use details, such as times, dates, places, and proper names, where appropriate.

▶ Be sure to answer all parts of the question; some essay questions have more than one part.

▶ Summarize your main ideas toward the end of your answer.

▶ Write neatly.

▶ Proofread your answer.

Sample Test 5 ESSAY

DIRECTIONS: Answer each question completely. Use a separate paper if you wish.

STUDY SKILLS

1. Identify and discuss two examples of mnemonics.
2. Justify why it is important to use the SQ3R method when reading.
3. Compare an effective study environment with an ineffective study environment.

Learning how to take a test and learning how to reduce your anxiety are two of the most important gifts you can give yourself as a student. Although tips and hints may help you, don't forget that there is no substitute for studying and knowing the material.

FIGURE 10.4   *A Quick Reference Guide to Studying Math and Science*

Before Class

▶ **NEVER** take a math or science course (or any course for that matter) for which you are not prepared. If you think you need or test into a basic, remedial, or transitional class, *take it*!!! Look at it as a chance to start over with new hope and knowledge.

▶ **UNDERSTAND** that most math and science classes build on previous knowledge. If you begin the class with a weak background, you must work very hard to learn missed information.

▶ **AVOID** taking math or science classes during "short" terms if possible. The more time you spend with the material, the better, especially if math and science are not your strong suits.

▶ **KNOW** your own learning style. If you're visual, use colors, charts, and photos. If you're auditory, practice your listening skills. If you're tactile, work to create situations where you can "act out" or touch the material.

▶ **PREPARE** yourself *before class* by reading the chapter. EVEN if you don't understand all of it, read through the material and write down questions about material you did not understand.

▶ **SCAN** all of the introductory and summation materials provided in the text or study guides.

▶ **JOIN** a study group. If there is not one, start one. Cooperative learning teams can be lifesavers.

▶ **SEEK** tutorial assistance on campus from the first day. Go visit the center and get familiar with how it operates. Get to know the people who work there. Don't wait until you get behind to seek assistance.

During Class

▶ **COME to EVERY** class, study group, or lab.

▶ **CONTROL** your own anger and frustration. The past is the past and you can't change any part of it—but you can change YOUR future. Learn to make your negative self-talker "be quiet!"

▶ **ASK** questions. **ASK** questions. **ASK** questions. **ASK** questions. And be specific in your questioning. Don't just say, "I don't understand that." Ask detailed and specific questions such as "*I don't understand why f(x + h) doesn't equal f(x) + f(h)*. Or "*I don't understand the difference between 'algia' and 'dynia.' Why are two different words used for pain?*"

▶ **SLOW DOWN** and read the material carefully.

▶ **FIND** the formulas and write them down on note cards.

▶ **WRITE** down explanatory remarks made by the instructor, such as the following:

  ▶ How do you get from one step to the next?

  ▶ How does this problem differ from other problems?

  ▶ Why do you need to use formula "x" instead of formula "y"?

  ▶ Were any steps combined—why or why not?

▶ **TRY** to learn from a *general to specific* end. That is, try to get a feeling of the overall goal of the material before you hone in on smaller problems.

▶ **WRITE** down any theorem, formula, or technique that the instructor puts on the board, overhead, or PowerPoint.

▶ **LEAVE** a space in your notes for any material you missed or did not understand. This will help you keep your notes organized when you go back after class and add the explanation.

▶ **BRING** Post-it notes, strips of paper, or bookmarks to class with you so that you can "tag" pages with important information and concepts. Use the tabs included with your text to help you mark important information.

After Class

▶ **VISIT** your instructor's office (make an appointment to visit during office hours).

▶ **FILL** in the missing information in your notes by reviewing the text, going to your study group, or getting clarification from your instructor.

▶ **PRACTICE** the problems in your text or study guide and then practice them again, and again, and again until they become second nature. Much of math and science is learned by DOING . . . so DO . . . and then DO again.

(continued)

FIGURE

10.4   *A Quick Reference Guide to Studying Math and Science (continued)*

▶ **APPLY** what you learned in class or lab. Find a way to make it "speak" to your life in a practical way.

▶ **CONTINUALLY** review all of the theorems, formulas, concepts, and terms from each chapter so they become second nature to you.

▶ When doing practice tests, **PRETEND** that you are in an actual test and adhere to the timelines, rules, and policies of your instructor. This helps replicate the actual testing situation.

Before the Test

▶ **ASK** questions that will reduce your anxiety, such as the following:

  ▶ What is the point value of each question?

  ▶ How many questions will be on the test?

  ▶ Will the questions be multiple choice, true-false, or other types?

  ▶ What materials do I need to bring to class?

  ▶ Will I be allowed to use a calculator or any other technology?

  ▶ Is there a time limit on the test?

  ▶ What is the overall grade value of the test?

▶ **MAKE** every effort to attend any study or review sessions offered by the instructor or peers.

During Tests

▶ **READ** the directions carefully.

▶ **QUICKLY** glance over the test to determine the number of questions and the degree of difficulty as related to the time you have to complete the test.

▶ **WORK** by the clock. If you have 60 minutes to take a test that has 120 questions, this means you have about 30 seconds per question.

▶ **BEGIN** by solving the problems that are easiest or most familiar to you.

▶ **READ** the questions on the test carefully and MORE than once and don't jump to conclusions.

▶ **DETERMINE** which formulas you will need to use.

▶ **DECIDE** how you want to solve the problem.

▶ **CHECK** your work by using multiple solving techniques. (If the problem is division, can it be rechecked with multiplication? This is called Opposite Operations).

▶ **DRAW** pictures if you encounter word problems. Visualization is very important.

▶ **SHOW** all of your work, even if it is not required. This will help the instructor (and you) see what you did correctly or incorrectly.

▶ **RECHECK** every answer if you have time.

▶ **WORK** backward if at all possible. This may help answer the question and catch mistakes.

▶ After you've completed the answer, **REREAD** the question to determine if you did everything the question asked you do to.

▶ **NEVER** erase your margin work or mistakes. This wastes time and you may erase something that you need (or worse, something that was correct).

After Tests

▶ **IMMEDIATELY** after the test, try to determine whether the majority of test questions came from classroom notes, your textbook, the study guide, or from your homework. This will help you prepare for the next test.

▶ **THINK** about the way you studied for this test and how you could improve your techniques for the next time. Consider the amount of time spent studying for this test.

▶ Once the test is graded, **DETERMINE** what caused you to lose the most points: Simple errors? Applying incorrect formulas or theorems? Misunderstanding of the questions asked? Intensified test anxiety? Poor study habits in general?

REFLECTIONS ON NOTE TAKING AND TESTING

Just as reading is a learned skill, so are memory development, studying, and learning how to take assessments. You can improve your memory, but it will take practice, patience, and persistence. You can improve your study skills, but it will take time and work. And you can increase your ability to do well on tests, but it will take a commitment on your part to study smarter and put in the time and dedication required. By making the decision "I CAN DO THIS," you've won the battle, for when you make that decision, your studying and learning become easier.

Your challenge is to focus on developing excellent memory techniques, study patterns, and test-taking abilities while earning the best grades you can. When you have done this, you can look in the mirror and be proud of the person you see without having to be ashamed of your character or worry about being caught cheating or wondering if you really did your best. When studying for your next class or taking your next test, consider the following:

- ▶ Study the hardest material first.
- ▶ Review your classroom and textbook notes frequently.
- ▶ Use mnemonics to help you remember lists.
- ▶ Learn the material from many different angles.
- ▶ *Ask* questions of the instructor before the test.
- ▶ Glance at the entire test *before* beginning.
- ▶ *Ignore* the pace of your classmates.
- ▶ Watch *time* limits.
- ▶ Practice academic integrity.

As you study and learn to enter your chosen profession, remember this: You are building your character for the long haul—not just a few short years.

"Change occurs, progress is made, and difficulties are resolved if people merely do the right thing—and rarely do people NOT KNOW what the right thing is."
—*Father Hessburgh*

CREATE SUCCESS
Your Journey to University, Career, and Life Beyond College

CONNECTING Think about the people on your college campus. With whom can you make a connection to learn more about **developing your memory?** (Example: counselor, advisor, retention specialist, etc.) Why and how will this connection be important?	
READING Find one brief, relevant article (in print or online) relating to **studying for math classes.** After you have read the article, write a brief summary of the additional facts you have learned.	
E-LEARNING Access the website **Test Taking Strategies** at Bucks County Community College (www.bucks.edu/~specpop/tests.htm). Scroll down to Test Taking and read the article on general strategies for taking tests. After studying the article and tips, develop a list of 10 strategies that you can immediately employ in **your** studying. Why do you think these 10 strategies will help you?	
ANALYZING Choose one main idea or topic from this chapter. After exploring and researching this idea further, determine how this information can help you succeed in other classes.	
TRANSITIONING How will you use the content found in this chapter to help you create a successful transition plan to your next semester and beyond?	
EMPOWERING Thinking about the entire spectrum of your life (college, family, friends, finances, career, etc), how can you empower yourself to be more successful through the information found in this chapter?	

SQ3R *Mastery* Study Sheet

EXAMPLE QUESTION *(from page 259)* Why are mnemonics important?		**ANSWER:**
EXAMPLE QUESTION *(from page 273)* Discuss three strategies for studying math.		**ANSWER:**
AUTHOR QUESTION *(from page 255)* What is the difference between short-term and long-term memory?		**ANSWER:**
AUTHOR QUESTION *(from page 256)* Discuss the five steps in VCR3.		**ANSWER:**
AUTHOR QUESTION *(from page 266)* What is H2 FLIB and how can it help you?		**ANSWER:**
AUTHOR QUESTION *(from page 267)* Discuss five ways to reduce test anxiety.		**ANSWER:**
AUTHOR QUESTION *(from page 269)* Discuss one strategy for each type of testing situation.		**ANSWER:**
YOUR QUESTION *(from page ____)*		**ANSWER:**
YOUR QUESTION *(from page ____)*		**ANSWER:**
YOUR QUESTION *(from page ____)*		**ANSWER:**
YOUR QUESTION *(from page ____)*		**ANSWER:**
YOUR QUESTION *(from page ____)*		**ANSWER:**

Finally, after answering these questions, recite this chapter's major points in your mind. Consider the following general questions to help you master this material.

▶ What was it about?
▶ What does it mean?
▶ What was the most important thing I learned? Why?
▶ What were the key points to remember?

CHAPTER 11
PROSPER

MANAGING YOUR MONEY AND DEBTS WISELY

"I've been rich and I've been poor—and rich is better."

—Sophie Tucker

WHY READ THIS CHAPTER?

What's in it for me?

WHY is learning to manage money so important at this stage of my life? WHY does it matter if I have big student loans and credit card debt when I graduate? WHY is it such a big deal to know how much my next semester will cost? WHY is it important to know and protect my FICO score?

Why? Because changing and strengthening your money management skills can impact your life forever and make you fiscally fit! You have probably heard the old saying, "Money won't buy happiness." Well, neither will poverty. As in many areas of your life, wealth accumulation needs to be balanced with solid work experience, physical health, good relationships, hobbies, travel, and other things that you enjoy. Managing money—or the lack of managing money—will affect what kind of house you live in, what brand of car you drive, what type of education your children will have, how much you can give to charities, and what sort of retirement you will have. Few skills will have more of a direct impact on your quality of life than managing your personal finances.

By carefully reading this chapter and taking the information provided seriously, you will be able to:

▶ Understand the ramifications and the pitfalls of crushing, overwhelming debt.

▶ Identify the types of financial aid available to you and identify how each type differs from the others.

▶ Understand the importance of your credit history, how to keep it healthy, and how to protect your FICO score.

▶ Construct and use a budget.

▶ Protect your credit cards and other vital information from identity theft.

CHAPTER 11 | PROSPER

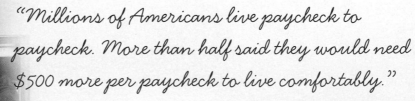

"Millions of Americans live paycheck to paycheck. More than half said they would need $500 more per paycheck to live comfortably."

—Careerbuilder.com, 2007

JEFFREY STEELE
Graduate!
Wor-Wic Community College, Salisbury, Maryland

How my COMMUNITY COLLEGE changed my life

An interview conducted and written by
RYAN MESSATZZIA
Academic and Disabilities Counselor, Wor-Wic Community College

At the age of 20, Jeff Steele found himself a college dropout and homeless. Growing up in rural Ohio, Jeff was a bright student who graduated from high school after his sophomore year and enrolled at a local university. However, he had a problem.

"No one had explained to me how financial aid worked, and my parents couldn't afford my schooling," he laments. To meet his steep tuition bills, Jeff started working full time as a busboy while also working part time in his residence hall on campus.

For two years, Jeff managed to work these jobs while also attending school full time. However, the stress and strain of this lifestyle started to take its toll. As Jeff puts it, *"With the heavy curriculum and my overworked body, I didn't last long."*

Before the start of his fifth semester in college, Jeff received a letter from the college that would change his life. *"I could no longer attend until I paid my tuition,"* he remembers. *"I was officially a college dropout."*

Kicked out of his dorm room, Jeff found himself "homeless," "helpless," and "severely depressed." He slept for two months at a local bus stop before saving up enough money to get his own apartment. However, after a year he still felt powerless. *"I knew I had to try and gain my college education again,"* he remarks.

Seeking to gain access to another chance at higher education, Jeff enlisted in the United States Air Force. This was the first step towards bettering his life. *"My military life gave me a chance to earn back my confidence and reestablish my strengths."*

After serving a four-year tour of duty in Germany, Jeff relocated to Maryland to be closer to family. This is where Jeff made a decision that would change his life forever—he enrolled at Wor-Wic Community College with a major in nursing.

"In finding Wor-Wic Community College, I found the help I needed to reach my goals. The faculty and staff were quick to respond to my needs," Jeff says. He learned from the college's

veterans coordinator that he could use his GI Bill benefits to pay for the costs of college. His nursing advisor helped to establish his career goals, and the director of student activities helped him gain leadership skills. Jeff became active on campus, participating in special events and even starting a new student organization.

"Wor-Wic gave me not only an education that I could afford, it has made a better person all-around. The people of my community college have helped me gain back the dignity I lost after my first attempt at a college education," he says gratefully.

Jeff graduated from Wor-Wic Community College with honors and gained employment at a local hospital while also continuing to pursue a bachelor's degree in nursing. *"My education has given me a purpose for my life,"* Jeff states, calling his current position *"the perfect job."*

Despite many trials and tribulations, Jeff persevered. And thanks to his community college, Jeff can now call himself a college graduate and a registered nurse.

THINK ABOUT IT

1. Finances derailed Jeff's first attempt at a college education. What financial hurdles will you have to overcome to continue your studies? What plans are you making now to overcome potential money-related obstacles you might face?

2. Jeff chose a major in nursing for his community college career and after graduation pursued a bachelor's degree. What advanced degrees can you pursue with your community college major if you decide to attend a university?

In the preface of this book (page xiv), you read about the **SQ3R study method.** Right now, take a few moments, **scan this chapter,** and on the **SQ3R Mastery Study Sheet** on page 303, write **five of your own questions** that you think will be important to your mastery of this material. In addition to the two questions below, you will find five questions from your authors on that study sheet. Use one of your *"Study for Quiz"* stickers to flag this page for easy reference.

EXAMPLES:

▶ What are four types of financial aid? (from page 284)

▶ How does a grant differ from a loan? (from page 284)

THE OVERWHELMING BURDEN OF CRUSHING DEBT

Can You Take Control Before It's Too Late?

Most of this chapter will be devoted to teaching you vital points about your current and future finances. We'll discuss the many ways that you can get into financial trouble and incur the feeling of being literally crushed by debt, as well as ways you can avoid these problems. Several very serious facts quoted by Erica Williams (2008), in her testimony before the House Financial Services Sub-Committee on Financial Institutions and Consumer Credit, should get your attention and make you determined not to become one of these statistics:

▶ A 2006 poll of three million twenty-somethings from *USA Today* and Experian, the credit-reporting agency, found that nearly half had stopped paying a bill, forcing lenders to "charge off" the debt and sell it to a collection agency, or had cars repossessed or sought bankruptcy protection.

▶ Thirty percent of twenty-somethings say they worry frequently about their debt.

▶ The Boomerang Effect, young adults returning to live with their parents, is quickly increasing. In 2006, Experience, Inc., which provides career services to link college grads with jobs, found that 58 percent of the twentysomethings it surveyed had moved home after college for a year or longer.

▶ Debt forces some young people to change their career plans. Of those surveyed in the 2006 *USA Today* NEFE poll, 22 percent said they'd taken a job they otherwise wouldn't have because they needed the money to pay off student loan debt.

iStockPhoto

Have you ever had a class or workshop on money management?

▶ Average credit card debt among indebted young adults increased by 55 percent between 1992 and 2001, to $4,088.

▶ The average credit card–indebted young adult household now spends nearly 24 percent of its income on debt payments.

▶ Among young adult households with incomes below $50,000 (two-thirds of young households), nearly one in five with credit card debt is in debt hardship—spending over 40 percent of their income servicing debt, including mortgages and student loans.

▶ Young Americans now have the second highest rate of bankruptcy, just after those aged 35 to 44.

PRACTICING DISCIPLINE AT THE RIGHT TIME

Can You Mind Your Own Business?

The time to learn to take care of your business and finances is right now so that you can hit the ground running when you graduate. You might already be working in a full-time position with an opportunity to participate in a 401(k) program. Many people neglect to enroll because they don't understand the program and don't want to appear ignorant by asking someone to explain it. You may feel that you simply can't afford to enroll and allocate that money to a retirement fund. The truth? You really can't afford not to enroll! Your future depends on it. Even if you are a typical college student who is struggling to make ends meet and can't invest right now, this is the time to prepare for what comes ahead. We highly encourage you to make up your mind that you are going to be financially secure and that you are going to master the keys to wise investing.

How many credit cards do you currently have? Do you use them wisely?

Some important ways to prepare for the future RIGHT NOW include the following tips:

▶ Practice *delayed gratification.* This is the first key to personal wealth accumulation. Even though it will probably require changing your habits, learn to develop this habit now.

▶ Take a *personal finance course* as soon as possible. You will be able to put the information into practice much sooner if you take the course early in your college career.

▶ Learn to understand *financial lingo.* A beginning list is shown later in Figure 11.3. Add to the list as you learn more in-depth information.

▶ If you plan to operate any kind of business, *take accounting and tax law courses.* Even if you plan to run a dance studio or a physical fitness center, this tip applies to you.

▶ *Save your change every day.* You will be surprised how quickly it adds up. You can put it in savings or invest it. You may even need it to pay the rent one month.

▶ *Write down everything you spend.* Where can you cut costs? In what ways are you wasting money? At the end of this chapter in Figure 11.9, you will find a worksheet titled **Tracking Your Expenditures and Spending Habits Chart.** Use this sheet to track all of your spending for three days, and then analyze your habits and develop a change plan. You'll be amazed at where your money goes.

▶ *Apply for every type of financial aid* available to assist with your education. You may not be awarded every type, but every cent helps. The following section will help you with this.

11.1 *Types of Aid*

TYPE	DESCRIPTION
Federal and state loans	Money that must be **repaid** with interest—usually beginning six months after your graduation date.
Federal and state grants	Monies you **do not have to repay**—often need-based awards given on a first-come, first-served basis.
Scholarships (local, regional, and national)	Money **acquired from public and private sources** that does not have to be repaid. Often, scholarships are merit based.
Work study programs	Money **earned** while working on campus for your institution. This money does not have to be repaid.

FINANCIAL AID

Is There Such a Thing as Pennies from Heaven?

Nearly two of every three undergraduate students are going into debt to go to college, owing an average of more than $19,000, most often to the government (Barrett, 2008). Chances are good that you have already borrowed money or might need to in the future. Therefore, understanding financial aid, scholarships, loans, and grants is very important as you make decisions that will impact you for a long time. If you have to borrow money to go to college, we think you should; on the other hand, we urge you to be very frugal—even stingy—when it comes to borrowing money. A day of reckoning will come, and for many people, that day is like getting hit by a freight train, when they realize what this debt means to them. Because they are relatively uninformed about personal finances, many young people make really bad financial decisions. Many college students don't have a clue as to the impact large student loans and other debts will have on their future well-being.

The most well-known sources of financial assistance are from federal and state governments. Federal and state financial aid programs have been in place for many years and are a staple of assistance for many college students. Figure 11.1 indicates the sources of aid.

Not every school participates in every federal or state assistance program. To determine which type of aid is available at your school, you need to contact the financial aid office.

One of the biggest mistakes students make when thinking about financial aid is forgetting about scholarships from private industry and social or civic organizations. Each year, millions of dollars are unclaimed because students do not know about these scholarships or where to find the necessary information about them. Speak with someone in your financial aid office regarding all types of scholarships.

How can learning about different loans, scholarships, and work study help you reach your goals?

Federal Financial Aid Types and Eligibility

PELL GRANT. This is a need-based grant awarded to qualified undergraduate students who have not been awarded a previous degree. Amounts vary based on need and costs.

FEDERAL SUPPLEMENTAL EDUCATIONAL OPPORTUNITY GRANT (FSEOG). This is a need-based grant awarded to institutions to allocate through their financial aid offices to students.

STAFFORD LOAN (FORMERLY KNOWN AS THE GUARANTEED STUDENT LOAN). The Stafford Direct Loan Program furnishes low-interest subsidized loans. You must show need to qualify. The government pays the interest

Thinkstock

FIGURE

11.2 *Student Eligibility for Federal Financial Aid*

To receive aid from the major federal student aid programs, you must meet the following conditions:

▶ Have financial need, except for some loan programs.

▶ Hold a high school diploma or GED, pass an independently administered test approved by the U.S. Department of Education, or meet the standards established by your state.

▶ Be enrolled as a regular student working toward a degree or certificate in an eligible program. You may not receive aid for correspondence or telecommunications courses unless they are a part of an associate, bachelor, or graduate degree program.

▶ Be a U.S. citizen.

▶ Have a valid Social Security number.

▶ Make satisfactory academic progress.

▶ Sign a statement of educational purpose.

▶ Sign a statement of updated information.

▶ Register with the Selective Service, if required.

▶ Some federal financial aid may be dependent on your not having a previous drug conviction.

Source: Adapted from U.S. Department of Education. (2008–2009). *The Student Guide: Financial Aid from the U.S. Department of Education.* Washington, DC: Author.

while you are in school, but you must be registered for at least half-time status. You begin re-payments six months after you leave school.

UNSUBSIDIZED STAFFORD LOAN. This type of Stafford loan is a low-interest nonsubsi-dized loan. You DO NOT have to show need to qualify. You are responsible for the interest on the loan while you are enrolled. Even though the government does not pay the interest, you can defer the interest and the payment until six months after you have left school.

PLUS LOAN. This is a federally funded, but state-administered, low-interest loan to qualified parents of students in college. The student must be enrolled at least half-time. Parents must pass a credit check and payments begin 60 days after the last loan amount has been received.

WORK STUDY. Work study is a federally funded, need-based program that pays students an hourly wage for working on (and sometimes off) campus. Students earn at least minimum wage.

HOPE SCHOLARSHIP TAX CREDIT. This tax credit is for students in their first two years of college who are enrolled at least half-time in a degree or certificate program. Each student taxpayer may receive a 100 percent tax credit for each year for the first $1,000 of qualified out-of-pocket expenses. They also may claim a 50 percent credit on the second $1,000 used for qualified expenses (U.S. Bank, 2002).

PERKINS LOAN. This is a need-based loan in which the amount of money you can borrow is determined by the government and the availability of funds. The interest rate is 5 percent, and repayment begins nine months after you leave school or drop below half-time status. You can take up to 10 years to repay the loan.

Bob Daemmrich/PhotoEdit

Have you allotted enough time in your schedule to fill out your financial aid application completely and accurately?

Applying for Financial Aid

You MUST complete a Free Application for Federal Student Aid (FAFSA) to be eligible to re-ceive ANY federal or state assistance. ***You AND your parents*** must apply for and obtain a PIN number to complete the FAFSA *if you are considered a dependent.* Because much federal and state money is awarded on a first-come, first-served basis, it is advisable to complete your application as soon after January 1 as possible—even if you have to use the previous year's tax returns and update your application later. Your college's financial aid office can assist you with this process. You can also log onto www.fafsa.ed.gov to learn more. The financial aid glossary in Figure 11.3 will be helpful to you as well.

▶ *Do not miss a deadline.* There are *no* exceptions that allow you to make up for missing deadlines for federal financial aid!

▶ *Read all instructions* before beginning the process, always fill out the application completely, and have someone proof your work.

▶ If documentation is required, submit it according to the instructions. Do not fail to do all that the application asks you to do.

▶ Never lie about your financial status.

▶ Begin the application process as soon as possible. Do not wait until the last moment. Some aid is given on a first-come, first-served basis. Income tax preparation time is usually also financial aid application time.

▶ Talk to the financial aid officer at the institution you will attend. Person-to-person contact is always best. Never assume anything until you get it in writing.

▶ Take copies of fliers and brochures that are available from the financial aid office. Private companies and civic groups will often notify the financial aid office if they have funds available.

▶ Always apply for financial aid when seeking admission. Many awards are given by the college to students who have already been accepted.

▶ If you are running late with an application, find out if there are electronic means of filing.

▶ Always keep a copy of your tax returns for each year!

FIGURE 11.3 *Financial Aid Glossary*

Borrower—The person who borrows the funds and agrees to repay them.
COA—Cost of attendance. This is the total amount it will cost you to go to college.
Cosigner—A person who signs a promissory note and agrees to repay the debt should the borrower default.
Default—The term used when you do not repay your student loan. This will prevent you from receiving any further funding. Your wages can be garnished until full restitution is made. Your tax refunds will also be applied to the balance. This default will also be reported to credit agencies and your credit will be scarred for seven to ten years.
Deferment—A period of time when you do not have to make loan payments. Deferment usually applies to education loans and customarily lasts only six to nine months.
EFC—Expected Family Contribution. The amount of money your family contributes to your educational costs.
FAFSA—Free Application for Federal Student Aid. The application that you (or your parents) fill out to determine your financial needs. This is the first step in any financial aid process.
FAT—Financial Aid Transcript. A record of your financial assistance from all institutions.
Gross income—Your income before taxes and deductions.
Interest—The fee (or amount of money) charged to you to borrow money.
Late fee—A fee charged if you do not make your payment on time.
Need analysis—A formula established by Congress to determine your financial need, based on the information in your FAFSA form.
Net income—Your income after taxes and deductions.
Payoff—The total amount owed on a loan if you were to pay it off in one lump sum.
Principal—The exact dollar amount that you borrowed and the amount on which interest is charged.
Promissory note—A legal document that obligates the borrower to repay funds.
Selective Service Registration—If you are required by law to register with Selective Service, you must do so before you can qualify for federal student aid.

▶ To receive almost any money, including some scholarships, you must fill out the FAFSA form.

▶ Apply for everything possible. You will get nothing if you do not apply.

STUDENT LOANS

A Day of Reckoning Will Come. Will You Be Ready?

The high cost of college makes tuition out of reach for many families. In recent years, "college tuition has risen at twice the rate of consumer prices. Tuition has soared much faster than pay has for the kinds of low-wage jobs that students tend to hold" (Block, 2006), making it much more difficult for students to work in the summer and pay for the coming year of college. Today a student would have to work an entire year to pay for one year of public college education, and that assumes that he or she saved every penny of his or her earnings. For many students, the only way they can attend college is with student loans. If this is the only way you can go to college, borrow the money—but borrow no more than you absolutely must. Try not to borrow anything but tuition and perhaps for books. Get a job, budget, cut out extras, work in the summers, attend college via a cooperative program, enroll in online courses, take fewer credits even though it delays graduation, live at home—do everything possible not to borrow more money than you must.

Many students are finding it necessary to extend their student loans over a period of 30 years just to keep their heads above water; of course, if one does that, the interest paid is also higher. For example, a student who takes 30 years to pay off a $20,000 loan at 6.8% will pay about $27,000 in interest plus the principal, compared to $7,619 interest on a loan paid off in 10 years (Block, 2006). You will have to repay the money that you have borrowed. Period! *Even bankruptcy will not relieve you of this debt* because student loans are not subject to bankruptcy laws; so again, don't borrow any money that you don't absolutely need. Consider the examples in Figure 11.4.

FIGURE 11.4 *Total Interest Paid*

AMOUNT OF MONEY BORROWED BY YOU	YOUR INTEREST RATE (AVERAGE)	TOTAL YEARS TO REPAY (20 YEARS IS THE AVERAGE)	YOUR MONTHLY PAYMENT	TOTAL INTEREST PAID BY YOU (YOUR COST TO BORROW THE MONEY)
$ 5,000	7%	10	$ 58.05	$ 1,966.00
		20	$ 38.76	$ 4,302.40
		30	$ 33.27	$ 6,977.20
$ 10,000	7%	10	$ 116.11	$ 3,933.20
		20	$ 77.53	$ 8,607.20
		30	$ 66.53	$ 13,950.80
$ 15,000	7%	10	$ 174.16	$ 5,899.20
		20	$ 116.29	$ 12,909.60
		30	$ 99.80	$ 20,928.00
$ 20,000	7%	10	$ 232.22	$ 7,866.40
		20	$ 155.06	$ 17,214.40
		30	$ 133.06	$ 27,901.60
$ 30,000	7%	10	$ 348.33	$ 11,799.60
		20	$ 232.59	$ 25,821.60
		30	$ 199.59	$ 41,852.40

YOUR CREDIT HISTORY

Do You Know the Score?

Many college students don't even know they have a credit score, yet this score is the single most important factor that will determine if you get approved for a mortgage, car loan, credit card, insurance, and so on. Furthermore, if you get approved, this credit score will determine what rate of interest you have to pay (Broderick, 2003). You can order one free credit score online by accessing the website www.annualcreditreport.com.

Range of Scores and What FICO Means for You

This information may seem trivial right now, and you might not want to be bothered with more information, but the truth is, you must pay attention to this because your credit score has long-lasting implications for almost everything you want to do. The sooner you understand the importance of this score and take steps to keep it healthy, the better off you will be.

> "Just about every financial move you make for the rest of your life will be somehow linked to your FICO score."
>
> —Suze Orman,
> Financial Planning Expert

Your credit score is referred to as the FICO score. FICO is the acronym for **Fair Isaac Corporation,** the company that created the widely used credit score model. This score is calculated using information from your credit history and files. The FICO score is the reason it matters if you accumulate large debts, if you go over your credit card limits, if you are late with payments—these offenses stick with you and are not easily changed. Based on this score, you can be denied credit, pay a lower or higher interest rate, be required to provide extensive asset information in order to even get credit, or sail right through when you seek a loan.

FICO scores range from 300 to 850. A good score is considered 720 or above. The lower your FICO score, the higher the interest rate you will have to pay because you will be considered a poor risk. So what's the big deal about a few points? Study the chart (Figure 11.5), and you will see how important your FICO score is when you want to finance a house or seek credit for other reasons.

FIGURE 11.5 *The Impact of FICO on Buying a Home*

FICO SCORE	INTEREST RATE	PAYMENT	30 YEARS OF INTEREST
500	9.3%	$1651	$394,362
560	8.5%	$1542	$355,200
620	7.3%	$1373	$294,247
675	6.1%	$1220	$239,250
700	5.6%	$1151	$214,518

B IS FOR BUDGETING

Where Does My Money Go?

Most people have no idea where their money goes. Many just spend and spend and then borrow on credit cards to pay for additional expenses for which they had not budgeted. Knowing how much money you have and exactly how you spend it is a very important step toward financial security. Many college students pay more attention to buying than they do to budgeting, watching their credit scores, or controlling their credit card debt. If you fit that mold, this is one area where change is needed.

One of the main reasons to budget is to determine the exact amount of money you need to borrow to finance your college education. Poor planning while in college can easily result in a lower standard of life after you graduate and begin paying back enormous loans. Deciding how much to borrow will impact your life long after you have completed your degree. You should also remember that you will be required to repay your student loans even if you do not graduate. As previously mentioned, even bankruptcy won't eliminate student loans.

When budgeting, you must first determine how much income you earn monthly. Complete the following chart:

SOURCE OF INCOME	ESTIMATED AMOUNT
Work	$ _____
Spouse/Partner/Parental Income	$ _____
Scholarships/Loans	$ _____
Savings/Investments	$ _____
Alimony/Child Support	$ _____
Other	$ _____
TOTAL INCOME	$ _____

Next, you must determine how much money you spend in a month. Complete the following chart:

SOURCE OF EXPENDITURE	ESTIMATED AMOUNT
Housing	$ _____
Utilies (water, gas, power, etc.)	$ _____
Phone (home and cell)	$ _____
Internet Access	$ _____
Car Payment	$ _____
Car Insurance	$ _____
Fuel	$ _____
Clothing	$ _____
Food	$ _____
Household Items	$ _____
Personal Hygiene Items	$ _____
Health Care and/or Health Insurance	$ _____
Entertainment/Fun	$ _____
Savings	$ _____
Other	$ _____
TOTAL EXPENDITURES	$ _____

Total Income _____ **minus Total Expenses** _____ = $_____

If the amount of your total expenditures is smaller than your monthly income, you are on your way to controlling your finances. If your total expenditures figure is larger than your monthly income, you are heading for a financial crisis. Furthermore, you are establishing bad habits for money management that may carry over into your life after college.

Now, consider your education and the costs associated with everything from books to supplies. Using the **Economic Readiness Assessment** (Figure 11.6), *do the research* to determine how much your education (tuition, books, room, board, etc.) will cost you next semester. You will have to go to the bookstore (or online) to research the cost of your texts, and you may need to refer to your college catalog for rules regarding some of the other questions. You can also use the Internet to answer a few of the questions, but it is important that you answer them all.

FIGURE

11.6   *Economic Readiness Assessment*

Please read each question carefully and respond with Yes or No. Then in the spaces provided, answer the question based on your financial research for **next semester.** Be specific. You may have to visit the financial aid office, bookstore, or other campus resource center to answer the questions.

QUESTION	ANSWER	RESPONSE
I know exactly how much my tuition will cost next semester.	YES NO	Answer: $_____
I know the totals for lab fees, technology fees, and other fees associated with my courses.	YES NO	Answer: $_____
I know how much I will pay for textbooks next semester.	YES NO	Answer: $_____
I know how much my transportation will cost next semester (car payment, gas, insurance, bus passes, etc.).	YES NO	Answer: $_____
I know how much I need to spend on supplies for next semester.	YES NO	Answer: $_____
I know how much child care will cost next semester.	YES NO	Answer: $_____
I know where my GPA must remain to keep my financial aid.	YES NO	Answer: _____
I know how much money I can borrow through the Guaranteed Student Loan Program in one academic year.	YES NO	Answer: $_____
I know how much money I need to manage my personal budget in a single semester.	YES NO	Answer: $_____
I have estimated miscellaneous and unexpected costs that might occur during the semester.	YES NO	Answer: $_____
I know what a FAFSA is and how and WHEN to apply.	YES NO	Answer: _____
I know how a drug arrest could affect my financial aid.	YES NO	Answer: _____
I know the scholarships available to me and how, when, and where to apply for them.	YES NO	Answer: _____
I know how and where to apply for work study.	YES NO	Answer: _____
I know how a felony charge affects my ability to get a job after graduation.	YES NO	Answer: _____
		TOTAL $_____

CREDIT CARDS: LIVING ON BORROWED MONEY

Are Credit Cards Really the WORST Kind of Debt?

"If you can eat it, wear it, or drink it, it is not an emergency."
—Kim Rebel, Credit Counselor

Credit card debt—one of the worst kinds of debt—is rising rapidly among college students as they struggle to pay tuition, buy books, and cover day-to-day living expenses. According to a Nellie Mae study (2005), 76 percent of all undergraduate college students have at least one credit card and carry an average balance of $2,169. One of the results of high credit card debt is lower GPAs and a higher dropout rate (Cooper-Arnold, 2006). As a result of over-the-top credit card marketing on campuses, terrible credit card terms and conditions, and an economy that no longer provides as many well-paying jobs with good benefits as it once did, graduates are facing overwhelming odds to achieve financial health, in large part as a result of the credit card debt from their undergraduate years (Williams, 2008).

Studies show that credit card shoppers, in general, are less price sensitive and more extravagant. When you pay with plastic, you lose track of how much you are spending. According to the article "Live Without Plastic" (Rosato, 2008), after McDonald's started accepting credit and debit cards in 2004, diners who paid with plastic spent $7 a visit on average compared to $4.50

when they paid in cash. The article also suggests that you are less aware of what you spend if you use plastic. For example, 68 percent of cash-paying students exiting a college bookstore knew how much they'd spent. Conversely, only 35 percent of students using plastic knew what they'd spent. Rosato also reports that you are willing to pay more for the same stuff if you are using plastic instead of real money.

"Imagine being 30 years old and still paying off a slice of pizza you bought when you were 18 and in college. Sounds crazy, but for plenty of people problems with credit card debt can lead to that very situation" (Collegeboard, 2008). If you borrow excessively and pay only the minimum each month, it will be very easy to find yourself over your head with credit card problems. Take the case of Joe. "Joe's average unpaid credit card bill over a year is $500, and his finance charge is 20 percent. He pays a $20 annual fee plus a $25 late fee (he was up late studying and forgot to mail in his check). Joe ends up owing $145 to his credit card company, and he still hasn't paid for any of his purchases" (Collegeboard, 2008).

iStockPhoto

Can you imagine paying for a piece of pizza for 12 years?

Most credit card companies charge a very high rate of interest—18 to 21 percent or higher. If you are late with a payment, the interest rate can go even higher. For every $1,000 you charge, you will pay from $180 to $210 in interest each year, states Konowalow (2003). Don't be fooled by the ploy of "1.5 percent interest." This means 1.5 percent each month, which equates to 18 percent per year. The best practice is to charge no more than you can pay off each month while avoiding high interest rates. Consider the tips in Figure 11.7.

SUCCESSFUL DECISIONS: An Activity for Critical Reflection

Jonathon is having a great time at college. He has joined a social club, is loving going to football games, and is managing to keep his grades up. But he's already got a major problem—keeping up with his expenses. He is spending much more money than he has coming in. His parents told him he could join a campus club, but that he would have to pay these expenses from the allowance they provide him every month. He and his parents made the decision for him not to work his first year, so he is in a bind.

To compound his problems, he has met a great girl, and he has tried hard to impress her by taking her to expensive clubs and restaurants. He took her to a dance that cost a bundle. He didn't have the funds so he charged everything on his new credit card. Jonathon is getting very stressed about his money situation. He's having trouble sleeping well. Club dues are coming up again soon. There is a big campus dance at the end of the semester that is high on his new girlfriend's list. Now

she is talking about going on a cruise for spring break. He is very worried because he has already maxed out one credit card and has heavy charges on the other one. Jonathon has calculated that if he charges $1,000 on his card and makes only the minimum payment, it will take 15½ years for him to pay for the cruise. He doesn't want to disappoint his girlfriend and fears losing her if he doesn't go on the cruise. But clearly, he has to make some changes.

What are two things you would advise Jonathon to do right away?

1. _____

2. _____

List two other suggestions that you would make to Jonathon to help him get control of his expenses.

1. _____

2. _____

FIGURE **11.7** *Important Facts You Need to Know about Credit Cards*

What you don't know can wreck your credit rating or ruin your life. Listed below are some of the most important things you can learn about managing credit card debt.

✔ Understand that credit cards are nothing more than high interest loans—in some cases, very high! The system is designed to keep you in debt.

✔ Be aware that companies often add on new fees and change policies after customers already have signed up.

✔ If you fall behind on payments to one creditor or if your credit score drops for any reason, your rates can be raised on all your credit cards.

✔ Banks can and will abruptly switch your due date, so pay attention. Always check your bill to see if any fees or charges have been added.

✔ Avoid cards that charge an annual fee just for the privilege of carrying their card. This fee can be as high as $100–$400 per year. If you charge this fee, it will be automatically added to your card and then you begin paying interest on the fee.

✔ Be sure your card allows for a grace period before interest is charged.

✔ Carry only one or two credit cards so you can manage your debt and not get in over your head. Do not accept or sign up for cards that you don't need.

✔ When you accept a card, sign it right away and keep records of your credit card numbers (in a secure location) and the phone number to contact in case they are lost or stolen. If you lose your card, report it immediately to avoid charges.

✔ Avoid the temptation to charge. You should use credit cards only when you absolutely must and only when you can pay the full amount before interest is added. "Buy now, pay later" is a dangerous game.

✔ When you pay off a card, celebrate and don't use that as a reason to charge again. Lock that card in a safe place and leave it there.

✔ Each month, always try to pay more than the "minimum payment due."

✔ Send the payment at least five days in advance. Late fees now represent the third-largest revenue stream for banks.

✔ Call the credit card company and negotiate a better rate. If they won't give you a better rate, tell them you are going to transfer the debt.

✔ If you have several credit card debts, consolidate all the amounts on the card on which you have the lowest balance. Don't cancel your cards, because it helps your credit score if you have cards on which you have no debt. Just don't use them again!

✔ Do not leave any personal information (credit cards, Social Security numbers, checking accounts) in places where roommates or other students have access to them. Purchase a metal file box with a lock and keep it in a secure place.

✔ Consider using a debit card. Money is deducted directly from your bank account and you cannot spend more than you actually have.

✔ If you have already gotten into credit card trouble, get *reputable* counseling. One of the best agencies is the National Foundation for Credit Counseling (NFCC).

✔ Be aware that using a credit card carelessly is similar to a drug addiction. Credit card use is habit forming and addictive!

✔ Ask yourself these questions: "If I can't pay this credit card in full this month, what is going to change next month? Will I have extra income or will I reduce my spending enough to pay for this purchase?" If the answers are no, you don't need to make the purchase.

Once you get a credit card, immediately write, "CHECK ID" across the back in RED, permanent ink.

✔ Realize that you are building your future credit rating even though you are a student.

THE PITFALLS OF PAYDAY LOANS, CAR TITLE LOANS, AND RENT-TO-OWN CONTRACTS

Did You Know There's Someone Lurking on Every Corner to Take Your Money?

Many unsuspecting consumers have been duped into signing car title loans, payday loans, or rent-to-own contracts that resulted in very high monthly payments and penalties. Some were told by their title loan broker before they signed the contract that they could make a partial payment if they needed to and this would be OK. Unfortunately, the unsuspecting victims find out too late that their car is going to be repossessed due to one late or partial payment. Others realize too late that on a loan of $400, they must pay back over $500 that month. According to recent reports from consumer affairs groups, some institutions have been charging as much as 250 percent interest on an annualized basis (Cojonet, 2003). In some instances, interest rates as high as 900 percent have been charged due to poor government regulatory policies. Some states have recently enacted laws to prevent this.

Payday loans are extremely expensive compared to other cash loans. For example, a $300 cash advance on the average credit card, repaid in one month, would cost $13.99 in finance charges and an annual interest rate of almost 57 percent, which is very high. By comparison, however, a payday loan costing $17.50 per $100 for the same $300 would cost $105 if renewed one time or 426 percent annual interest (Payday Loan Consumer Information, 2008). As bad as credit card debt is, it pales in comparison to the pitfalls of payday loans.

SMALL COSTS ADD UP!

How Much Money Will You Throw Down the Drain in 10 Years?

Many people pay more money for convenience. If you are on a tight budget, you might want to give up some of the conveniences so that you can hold onto more of your money. Although we want you to really live and enjoy life, we also want you to take a hard look at where your money goes. Those dimes, quarters, and dollars add up quickly. In fact, small-amount money drains for the typical person can add up to $175,000 over a 10-year period. What if you could hold onto some of that money and invest it? What would that money be worth to you when you are 65 and want to retire? Is having sausage biscuits and orange juice from a fast-food restaurant really worth $3.50 a day or $1,274 if you have that *every day for one year?* Did you ever stop to think that if you spend $3.50 every day on fast food or coffee or whatever for 10 *years,* you would be spending $12,740?

THE 10-YEAR PLAN. According to the website The Digerati Life (2008), some other prime causes of money drain include the following:

▶ **Gum**—A pack a day will cost you $5,488 in 10 years.

▶ **Bottled water**—One bottle a day will cost you almost $5,500 in 10 years. (Most bottled water comes from no special source and is no better than tap water.)

TIPS FOR PERSONAL SUCCESS

Consider the following suggestions for improving your financial status during the semester:

▶ Practice delayed gratification.

▶ Reduce your Latte Factor (Figure 11.8).

▶ Talk to an advisor about taking a personal finance course next semester as an elective.

Now it is your turn. What three changes could you implement to improve your financial management practices?

1. _____

2. _____

3. _____

▶ **Eating lunch out daily**—Even if you spend only $9, this will cost you over $35,000 in 10 years. If you can eat lunch at home or take your lunch, you will save so much money.

▶ **Junk food, vending machine snacks**—This will cost you at least $4,000 in 10 years if you are a light snacker, and they are empty calories.

▶ **Unused memberships**—Those gym memberships that look so enticing, and for many people go unused, will total over $7,500 in 10 years.

▶ **Expensive salon visits**—Fake nails along with the salon visit can cost over $30,000 in 10 years. Is that really how you want to spend your money?

▶ **Cigarettes**—Not only will this terrible habit kill you and make people want to avoid you, it will cost you over $25,000 in 10 years if you smoke a pack a day.

These are just a few of the drains that take our money and keep us from being wealthy when we are older. Maybe you want to splurge at times and go for convenience, but day in and day out, you can really save a lot of money if you budget your time and do some of these things for yourself.

Examine the following information about *The Latte Factor* (Figure 11.8), and apply it to your own spending habits.

Calculate Your Own Latte Factor. For example, if you buy one diet soda each morning for $1.81, then your Latte Factor is $685.84 per year ($1.81 × 7 days/week × 52 weeks/year).

My daily "have to have it" is _____

It costs $ _____ per day

My Latte Factor is $ _____

Small expenditures add up. What you do today may inhibit your ability to buy a car, purchase a house, and even get certain jobs!

PROTECT YOURSELF FROM IDENTITY THEFT

Why Are College Campuses Ground Zero?

"Amid all the back-to-school activities and tasks that college students face, one of the most important is to protect their identities. You have such busy schedules that you may unknowingly expose yourself to identity theft and fraud, particularly when you're making online purchases or engaging in social-networking websites. We're all living in an extremely open environment where free flow of information is the norm, as opposed to the exception," said Adam Levin, cofounder of Identity Theft 911 (Yip, 2008). Because college students tend to move often, their mail service may be interrupted if they don't follow through with change-of-address cards. By the time their information catches up to them, they may have already suffered from identity theft. "All these things make this group vulnerable," said Thomas Harkins, chief strategy officer of Secure Identity Systems (Yip, 2008).

People who may steal your identity include roommates, relatives, friends, estranged spouses, restaurant servers, and others who have ready access to your papers. They may steal your wallet, go through your trash, or take your mail. They can even legally photocopy your vital information at the courthouse if, for exam-

FIGURE **11.8** *The Latte Factor*

In his book *The Finish Rich Notebook* (2003), Bach states, "How much you earn has no bearing on whether or not you will build wealth." As a rule, the more we make, the more we spend. Many people spend far more than they make and subject themselves to stress, exorbitant debt, fear, and an ultimate future of poverty.

Bach uses the Latte Factor to call people's attention to how much money we carelessly throw away when we should be saving and investing for the future. He uses the story of a young woman who said she could not invest because she had no money. Yet, almost every day she bought a large latte for $3.50 and a muffin for $1.50. If you add a candy bar here, a drink there, a shake at the gym, you could easily be spending $10 a day that could be invested.

If you take that $10 per day and invest it faithfully until retirement, you would have enough money to pay cash for a home and a new car, and have money left over. This is the power of compound interest! If you are a relatively young person, you will probably work that many years and more, so you could retire with an extra $1 million in addition to any other savings you might have accumulated.

The point is that most of us have the ability to become rich, but we either lack the knowledge or the discipline to do so. Remember the Latte Factor as you begin your college career and practice it, along with other sound financial strategies, if you want to become a millionaire.

ple, you have been divorced. The Internet provides thieves many other opportunities to use official-looking e-mail messages designed to obtain your personal information. Do not provide personal information over the Internet no matter how official the website might look. Reputable businesses will not inquire about your personal information in this manner.

It is very difficult, if not impossible, to catch identity thieves. Although you may not be liable, you still have to spend your time filing expensive legal affidavits, writing letters, and making telephone calls to clear your good name.

How to Minimize Identity Theft Risk

Criminals are very clever, and many are adept at using electronic means to steal your personal information. According to a variety of financial sources, there are a number of ways to avoid having your identity stolen:

▶ Carry only the ID and cards you need at any given time.

▶ Do not make Internet purchases from sites that are unsecured (check for a padlock icon to ensure safety).

▶ Do not write your PIN number, Social Security number, or passcode on any information that can be stolen or that you are discarding. Do not keep this information in your wallet or exposed in your living space.

▶ Try to memorize your passwords instead of recording them on paper or in the computer.

▶ Buy a shredder and use it.

iStockPhoto

How careful are you when it comes to protecting your financial and medical records?

▶ Avoid providing your Social Security number to any organization until you have verified its legitimacy.

▶ Check your credit file periodically by requesting a copy of your report.

▶ Do not complete credit card applications at displays set up on campus. This exposes your personal information to people you don't know.

▶ Use your home address as your permanent mailing address rather than a temporary address while in school.

▶ Do not provide personal information on a social network that can be accessed by an identity thief. You don't know these people!

▶ Carry your wallet in your front pocket instead of your back pocket.

▶ Place security freezes on your credit scores. This prevents anyone from looking at your credit report except the companies that already have a financial relationship with you. Lenders who can't pull your credit report are unlikely to grant new credit to someone else in your name.

▶ Opt out of preapproved credit offers, which are easy ways for identity thieves to steal your personal identity. This stops credit bureaus from selling your name to lenders. Go to the opt-out website at www.optoutprescreen.com or call 888-567-8688.

▶ Don't use obvious passwords like your birthday, your mother's maiden name, or the last four digits of your Social Security number. (Consumer Response Center brochure, *Identity Theft and Fraud*, 2003; *Consumer Reports, Money Advisor*, 2008; *The State*, August 31, 2008)

BATTLING THE BIG "IF"S

Do You Know What to Do When You Need Something?

You will find the following tips helpful for managing important financial decisions in your life and protecting yourself when things get tough.

IF YOU NEED TO PURCHASE A CAR

▶ Do not purchase a new car. We know it is tempting, but the value will plummet 20 to 40 percent the moment you drive off the lot. It is just not worth it! Purchase a two- to three-year old car from a reputable dealer.

▶ DON'T fall in love with a car before you know everything about it. Love is blind when it comes to people . . . and cars, too!

▶ Purchase an extended warranty, BUT read the terms carefully.

▶ Always ask for a "Car-fax" and a title search and ask the dealer to pay for them.

▶ Check to see if your state has a "Lemon Law" and if so, read it carefully.

▶ Don't be pressured into a sale by lines such as "This is our last one like this" or "I've got several people interested in this car." Let them have it!

▶ Make sure the car has passed the smog test if one is required in your state.

IF YOU NEED TO SAVE ON FUEL

▶ Consider carpooling.

▶ Make sure your car is in good running condition and that your tires are inflated properly. Get your car tuned up often.

▶ Drive slower and at a constant speed when possible. Driving 74 mph instead of 55 mph increases fuel consumption by as much as 20 percent.

▶ Check your car's air filter and fuel filter and replace them if they are dirty.

- Do not use "Jack Rabbit" starts. Accelerate easily after red lights and stop signs. "Flooring it" costs money.
- When stuck in traffic, try to drive at a steady pace and not stop and start. Watch how the large trucks do this—they seldom come to a complete stop.
- Plan your trips to maximize the number of right turns, thus saving time at lights. Also, combine your errands so that you can make fewer trips.
- Clean out your car. Carrying around just a few extra pounds in the trunk or backseat costs fuel.
- Stick with the wheels and tires that came with your car. Using larger wheels and tires than recommended creates more drag and weight on your car and costs you more fuel.
- Use the telephone. Often, many things can be accomplished without personal visits.

Do you work hard to control everyday and impulse spending?

IF YOU FEEL THE URGE TO MAKE AN IMPULSE PURCHASE

- Use the 72-hour rule. Wait 72 hours to make any purchase over $50.
- If you still feel the need to buy the item after 72 hours, consider your budget and how you are going to pay for the purchase.
- Consider waiting until you can pay cash for the item, or consider putting it on layaway. Do not charge it!
- Purchase the item later as a reward to yourself for getting all A's in your classes.
- Think about how purchasing this item will affect your family's budget.
- Make as few trips out shopping as possible to lower your temptation to purchase things you can't afford.

IF YOUR GROCERY BILL IS OUT OF CONTROL

- Shop with a calculator and enter each item as you place it into your cart. This will give you a great idea of what you're spending.
- Create a menu for each day of the week and shop only for the items on your list. Do not shop when you are in a hurry, tired, or after working all day.
- Consider purchasing generic brands—often they are the same product as brand-name items, just with a different label.
- Clip coupons. They actually work. Go online to your favorite product's website and print out their online coupons. Try to shop when stores double or triple coupons' value.
- Consider cooking in bulk and then freezing leftovers for later in the week.
- Look for placement of the product in the store. Items at chest level are the most expensive. Look up and down on the shelves to find less expensive items.
- Do not shop for convenience items such as premade meals, bakery items, or boneless chicken breasts. Purchase an entire chicken and cut it up. You'll save a lot of money this way.
- Buy in bulk at one of the major warehouse stores. Often this can save a lot of money if you are buying for a large family.

From Ordinary to *Extraordinary*

REAL PEOPLE | REAL LIVES | REAL CHANGE

LEO G. BORGES
Founder and Former CEO
Borges and Mahoney, San Francisco, California

Tulare, California, is still a farming community today, but in 1928 when I was born, it was totally agricultural and an exceptionally rural, detached part of the world. My parents had immigrated to California from the Azore Islands years earlier in search of a better life—the American dream. My father died when I was 3 years old and when I was 11, my mother passed away. Even though I lived with and was raised by my sisters, the feelings of aloneness and isolation were the two primary feelings I had growing up. We were orphans. We were poor. We were farm kids. We were Portuguese—not Americans. Every day, someone reminded us of these realities. One positive thing remained, however. My mother always told us that we could be anything or have anything if we believed in it and worked hard for it.

> *We were orphans. We were poor. We were farm kids. We were Portuguese— not Americans.*

I left home at 17 to attend a program in advertising in San Francisco. Later that year, I moved to Los Angeles and began working for a major advertising firm. From there I enlisted in the Coast Guard, and when my duty was over, I worked for an oil company and then a major leasing firm. In each position, I worked my way up the ladder, strove to do my very best, and proved that I was capable of doing anything regardless of my background.

When I was in my early forties, my best friend, Cliff, and I decided to start our own business. We were tired of working in "middle management" and knew that we could be successful if we worked hard. After much research and consulting with companies across the country, we determined that we would start a company in the water treatment business.

You may be asking yourself, "What experience did an advertising agency, an oil company, and a leasing firm give him to start a business in water treatment?" The answer is none. However, Cliff was an excellent accountant and I was an excellent salesman. We found a third partner who was one of the leading water treatment experts in the world and we were off. It was not easy and we had to eat beans for many meals, but Borges and Mahoney, Inc. was born.

Our first office was a small storefront in San Francisco. Through the development of our superior products, expert advice to clients, and outstanding customer service, we grew and grew, finally moving to our largest location in San Rafael, California. By the time we sold our business some 20 years later, we had 15 full-time employees and annual revenues in the millions of dollars.

To this day, I attribute my success to the fact that I was determined to show everyone—my sisters, cousins, aunts and uncles, former coworkers, friends and foes—that I would never let my past, my heritage, my economic background, or my history hold me back. I knew that I could be a success. Through hard work, determination, and surrounding myself with supportive, brilliant people, I proved that the American dream my parents sought years earlier is truly possible for anyone who works hard, believes in him- or herself, and doesn't give up. It is possible for you, too.

EXTRAORDINARY REFLECTION

Read the following statement and respond in your online journal or class notebook.

Mr. Borges states that through "hard work, determination, and surrounding himself with supportive, brilliant people," he and his partner, Cliff, were able to become very successful in business and beyond. Who can you call on in your life to offer you support and provide you with solid, smart advice? What questions do you need to ask them?

FIGURE

11.9   *Tracking Your Expenditures and Spending Habits Chart*

Over the course of the **next three days, write down EVERY CENT you spend,** including items such as fuel, food, bottled water, child care, newspapers, and so on. EVERY CENT. After three days, analyze your spending habits and determine at least five ways that you can cut expenses.

DAY 1	DAY 2	DAY 3

TOTAL FOR DAY 1

$ _____

TOTAL FOR DAY 2

$ _____

TOTAL FOR DAY 3

$ _____

What is the biggest lesson you have learned from tracking your money? What was the most shocking? Why?

_____

_____

_____

List five ways that you can cut your expenses.

1. _____
2. _____
3. _____
4. _____
5. _____

REFLECTIONS ON FINANCIAL RESPONSIBILITY

Although many young people fail in the management of their personal finances, there is no reason that you cannot manage your financial business well. You should think about personal finance and the management of money and investments as basic survival skills that are very important to you now, as well as for the rest of your life.

Since only 10 percent of high school students graduate from high school with any kind of instruction in personal finance, learning to budget your money, make wise investments, and avoid credit card debt are priority needs of all college students. As you move toward establishing yourself in a career, it is important to remember that a significant part of your success at getting what you want out of life will depend on your ability to make sound money decisions. We hope you will learn to make money work for you instead of your having to work hard for money because of poor decisions made early in life. En route to becoming a good money manager, the following tips will assist you:

- ▶ Don't get caught in the credit card trap.
- ▶ Know exactly how you are spending your money.
- ▶ Protect your credit rating by using wise money management strategies.
- ▶ Learn all you can about scholarships and grants.
- ▶ Understand the regulations about repaying student loans.
- ▶ Don't borrow any more money than you absolutely have to.
- ▶ Ask for your credit score at least once a year and be sure you have a good one.
- ▶ Use only one or two credit cards.
- ▶ Try to pay off your credit cards each month before any interest is charged.
- ▶ Write down your credit card numbers and keep them in a safe place in case your cards are lost or stolen.
- ▶ If you run into credit card trouble, get counseling.
- ▶ Learn everything you can about investments and retirement plans.

Learning to manage your money and protecting your credit rating will be as important to you as getting your degree. It is never too early to learn about money management. If you can do it when you have just a little money, it will be easier when you have more money.

"Never work just for money or for power. They won't save your soul or help you sleep at night."
—*Marian Wright Edelman*

CREATE SUCCESS
Your Journey to University, Career, and Life Beyond College

CONNECTING

Think about the people on your college campus. With whom can you make a connection to learn more about *protecting your FICO Score?* (Example: counselor, advisor, retention specialist, etc.) Why and how will this connection be important?

READING

Find one brief, relevant article (in print or online) relating to *managing debt wisely.* After you have read the article, write a brief summary of the additional facts you have learned.

E-LEARNING

Use the internet to research strategies for *reducing identity theft.* After finding at least five techniques, e-mail or text your findings to three friends who could use this information. List the five techniques here, too.

ANALYZING

Choose one main idea or topic from this chapter. After exploring and researching this idea further, determine how this information can help you succeed in other classes.

TRANSITIONING

How will you use the content found in this chapter to help you create a successful transition plan to your next semester and beyond?

EMPOWERING

Thinking about the entire spectrum of your life (college, family, friends, finances, career, etc.), how can you empower yourself to be more successful through the information found in this chapter?

SQ3R *Mastery* Study Sheet

EXAMPLE QUESTION *(from page 284)* What are four types of financial aid?	**ANSWER:**	
EXAMPLE QUESTION *(from page 284)* How does a grant differ from a loan?	**ANSWER:**	
AUTHOR QUESTION *(from page 285)* Discuss three steps in applying for financial aid.	**ANSWER:**	
AUTHOR QUESTION *(from page 287)* What have you learned about student loans that might help you make better decisions?	**ANSWER:**	
AUTHOR QUESTION *(from page 288)* Why is budgeting so important?	**ANSWER:**	
AUTHOR QUESTION *(from page 290)* What are some of the dangers of credit card debt?	**ANSWER:**	
AUTHOR QUESTION *(from page 294)* What practices will you employ to avoid becoming a victim of identity theft?	**ANSWER:**	
YOUR QUESTION *(from page ____)*	**ANSWER:**	
YOUR QUESTION *(from page ____)*	**ANSWER:**	
YOUR QUESTION *(from page ____)*	**ANSWER:**	
YOUR QUESTION *(from page ____)*	**ANSWER:**	
YOUR QUESTION *(from page ____)*	**ANSWER:**	

Finally, after answering these questions, recite this chapter's major points in your mind. Consider the following general questions to help you master this material.

▶ What was it about?
▶ What does it mean?
▶ What was the most important thing I learned? Why?
▶ What were the key points to remember?

CHAPTER 12
TRANSITION

PLANNING FOR YOUR FUTURE

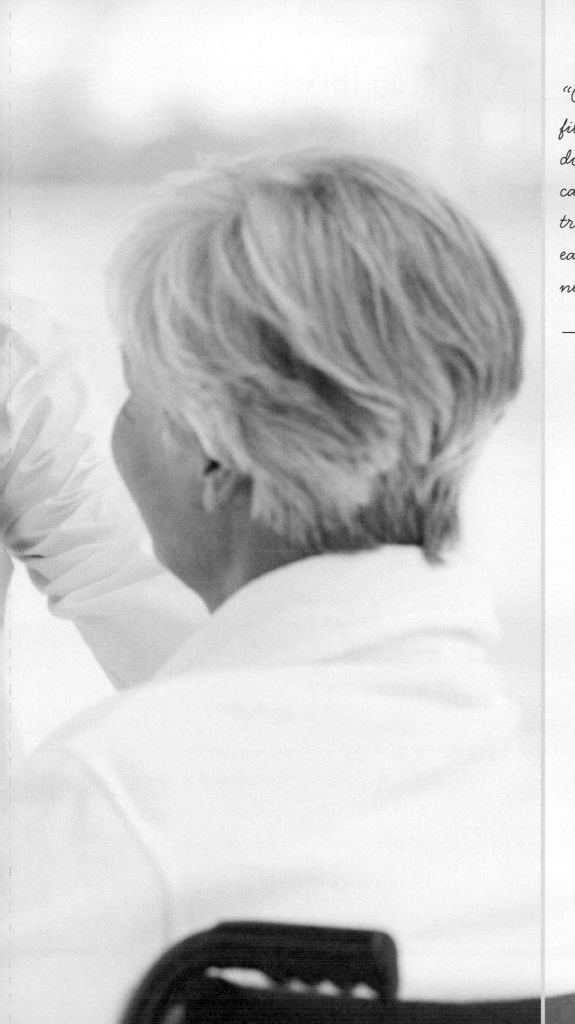

"Our lives are filled with doorways. We call them transitions. They each take us to new adventures."

—Mr. Prophet

PART THREE CHANGING YOUR LIFE

WHY READ THIS CHAPTER?

What's in it for me?

WHY do I need to worry about transitioning successfully to my sophomore year when I'm still worried about finishing this one? *WHY* is it important to start planning now for attending a four-year institution or university? *WHY* are transitions from college to the world of work important now? *WHY* will information on career planning help me at this stage of my college career?

Why? Because transitioning is definitely something you are going to do—you will either transition to a four-year setting or you will transition to the workforce. Successful transitions require forethought and the first step is to learn to think critically and prepare carefully. The world has changed dramatically over the past few years, making a great deal of previous information about college and careers obsolete. In fact, change has caused many jobs and careers that have long been staples of the U.S. economy to disappear. You have to take control of your life and your destiny. Many rules for success in college and entering the workforce have changed along with everything else. So you need to stay in touch with what is happening in the rest of the world, identify current and future job trends, and plan strategies to be prepared for a great career.

By carefully reading this chapter and taking the information provided seriously, you will be able to:

▶ Identify the 10 steps to preparing for the future.

▶ Design a four-year plan that covers your college career or college/work career.

▶ Develop a career self-study plan based on a series of personal questions.

▶ Write and sell yourself through an excellent cover letter.

▶ Use the DOCTOR system to write a powerful resumé.

CHAPTER 12 | TRANSITION

"In a time of drastic change, it is the learners who inherit the future. The learned usually find themselves equipped to live in a world that no longer exists."

—Eric Hoffer

QUENTON RICHARDSON
Graduate,
*Hawkeye Community
College, Waterloo, Iowa*

How my COMMUNITY COLLEGE *changed my life*

*An interview conducted and
written by*
CAROL HEDBERG
*College Counselor, Hawkeye
Community College*

"It hurt my heart when it became final—I knew I'd never go back!" These words reflect back on that painful day when Quenton Richardson made the life-changing decision to leave his family and friends in Chicago to begin a new life. Like many young African American men who stayed in the hood, he knew he could easily end up in prison or worse. At the age of 17, his best friend had been shot and killed. Surrounded by a culture of guns and drugs, he appraised the life of his peers. *"They think there is nothing beyond what they have. They learn to accept what they have because it's not easy to leave. What do you do—pack your bags? Where do you go when you leave?"*

But Quenton did have a place to go and so he got out. He returned to the safety of his grandmother's home, where he had spent many childhood summers. Once established, Quenton again appraised his options. Jobs were scarce without an education. And so with only a GED, Quenton enrolled in Hawkeye Community College.

"Hawkeye was a diving board—it launched me into life!" Quenton recalls. *"I needed to put my past behind me. I completely turned my life around."* But college culture was difficult for Quenton. *"It's tough to transition from out in the world to the structure, atmosphere, and rules of college. There were a lot of things I needed, but I sure didn't like them!"* Quenton chuckles. College was often frustrating and frightening for this young man seeking a new life. *"I didn't know what I was doing!"*

As a student, Quenton asked lots of questions, developing the support system he needed to persist. *"Part of my academic success was having a support system—someone who had my back!"*

Even with support, Quenton's first semester was less than stellar. *"I was trying to change my life!"* Yet mingled with the vulnerability he felt, Quenton knew Hawkeye was the key to that change. Ever so slowly, semester after semester, Quenton persisted. And as he persisted, he found his voice and discovered the meaning of his life.

After 11 years in higher education, Quenton is now a doctoral student at the University of Northern Iowa. He hopes his dissertation on poverty will illuminate the struggle he knew so well. Quenton still regularly visits his childhood friends in Chicago, and it deeply troubles him that they continue to exist as they did when he first left. He wants to make a difference, and so he speaks out, teaches classes, and encourages younger students.

In his rich, buttery voice, Quenton describes what he now calls his love affair with education: *"Hawkeye was like going out on a first date, but my love of education kept growing, and by the time I got to the university, it was like being married with kids! Learning is now the most important thing in life for me—it makes me realize what's important!"*

THINK ABOUT IT

1. Quenton had to leave his family and city to get a fresh start. What personal sacrifices have you had to make to ensure your own success in college?

2. Quenton states, *"It's tough to transition from out in the world to the structure, atmosphere, and rules of college."* What has been the hardest transition for you? Why? Who has "had your back" in adjusting to these transitions?

In the preface of this book (page xiv), you read about the **SQ3R study method.** Right now, take a few moments, **scan this chapter,** and on the SQ3R Mastery Study Sheet on page 331, write **five of your own questions** that you think will be important to your mastery of this material. In addition to the two questions below, you will find five questions from your authors on that study sheet. Use one of your **"Study for Quiz"** stickers to flag this page for easy reference.

EXAMPLES:

▶ How do I transition to my sophomore year? (from page 310)

▶ What does DOCTOR stand for? (from page 325)

MAKING AWESOME DECISIONS

What Am I Going to Do for the Rest of My Life?

"What am I going to do for the rest of my life?" is an overwhelming question for anyone, much less a beginning college student, especially in a dramatically changing global environment. What was true last year—and sometimes even last week—is no longer true. Current college students have a wonderful opportunity to be the first that truly function in a world economy; at the same time, you have the concern of having few guidelines to follow.

Although many concepts that worked for your parents and grandparents are still important and relevant today—ideas like ethics, integrity, hard work, education, honesty, and teamwork—many practices that were true in their time are no longer valid. Your grandfather may have gone to work for a company and stayed there all his life. Employers were loyal to employees, and employees were loyal to the company. Work stayed pretty much the same this year as it was the last. All that has changed. You will have many different jobs during your lifetime—you will most likely have three or four different careers, and what constitutes your work will be constantly changing. Because so much has changed over the past few years, it becomes especially important for you to plan for successful transitions from one stage of your life to the next.

Photodisc/Getty Images

What changes do you foresee coming in your chosen career field in the next five years?

STRATEGIES TO SUCCESSFULLY PREPARE FOR YOUR FUTURE

What Ten Baby Steps Will Become Giant Steps Tomorrow?

"The driving force of a career must come from the individual. Remember: Jobs are owned by the company; you own your career."
—Earl Nightingale, Author

You might consider what you are doing today and the rest of your college career as baby steps that will lead to giant steps in being prepared for the future. The following strategies (adapted from "Top Ten Career Strategies for Freshmen and Sophomores," Orndorff, 2008) will help you as you move toward your transition goals, whether they are moving to the sophomore class or to the world of work.

1. **Make good grades.** Grades do matter! Although not everyone can graduate with a 4.0, you need to be one of those who earns a respectable GPA. Not only do good grades show that you have gained knowledge in certain areas, they indicate a work ethic and a sense of responsibility that employers are seeking. Your grades can also affect your transition to a four-year institution.

2. **Come to grips with your abilities, interests, values, and personal characteristics.** You might be telling people you want to be a corporate attorney or a businesswoman. Do you really know what these careers entail? How many years of education are required? What kind of GPA does it take to get into a really good business school? Specifically, what do you want to do? Where will the jobs be? What kind of preparation does it take? Do you have the ability and perseverance to become what you dream about?

"A study has shown that first and second year students spend more time deciding on a movie to watch than on what they might want for a career, even though a movie lasts two hours and a career lasts a lifetime."
—*Bob Orndorff*

3. **Fine-tune your computer skills.** Most first-year students have good computer skills today, but these skills need to be very strong. Your skills need to include the ability to work with spreadsheets, databases, word processing systems, social media networks, and PowerPoint. Before you graduate, another new software program may become important. Learn to develop webpages, and create your own website that reflects a professional, career-oriented person.

4. **Hone your communication, speaking, and writing skills.** By now, you are tired of hearing this, but it's true. Enroll in classes that are writing and speaking intensive, even if you hate the thought of it. Many recruiters point out the weaknesses of applicants' writing and speaking skills. Good communications skills could be a major asset to you in a future job search.

5. **Actively engage in exploring career options.** Your career—and variations of it—will last a lifetime. Doesn't that fact make it evident that you need to spend some time "trying on" possibilities to see if one might be a good fit? Read about occupations in professional journals in your library, go to the career counseling center, talk to people who are in the field that interests you, and attend career fairs and job expos. Finding the "right" major and career require hard, intensive work.

6. **Get involved and stay active.** Job recruiters are looking for people who are leaders, who understand teamwork, who have shown by their involvement that they can manage time and make things happen. Select one or two activities or organizations and become actively engaged. Work your way to the top. You'll learn valuable skills, and it will look great on your resume! Go to job interviews with excellent career-related experiences to discuss.

What unique interests, skills, and talents do you possess to give you that "cutting edge" in today's workforce?

7. **Give back to your community.** Here again, recruiters consider service learning a great asset. Many times students look at community service as just another task, but after it's over, they realize what benefits they have derived from helping someone else. Many careers have been jump-started by an outstanding service learning project that showcased a person's talents. You'll get more than you give by participating in service learning.

8. **Spend your summers working in internships, preferably ones that carry college credit.** Once you have decided on a direction that interests you, explore the field by actually working in it. If you begin as a first-year student working for a company that interests you, perform well, and go back every summer, the chances are good that a job will be waiting for you. Many students transition from an internship to a career position.

Laima Druskis/PH College/Pearson

9. **Expand your cultural and international knowledge.** This is a great time to learn everything you can about people from different backgrounds. Make friends with international students, explore a variety of cultures, and learn to appreciate and celebrate diversity.

10. **Take advantage of your campus career center.** Few students really take full advantage of their career center. The counselors there may not have all the answers, but they can start you in the right direction by offering advice on trends, requirements, and changes in certain fields. Check out the center on your campus—and soon!

PLANNING FOR SOPHOMORE YEAR

What Do I Need to Do Now to Prepare for a Successful Transition?

"You are the way you are because that's the way you want to be. If you really want to be any different, you will be in the process of changing right now."
—Fred Smith

Because you are enrolled in this course, you already know that colleges and universities spend considerable amounts of time teaching you such things as how to improve your study habits, how to manage your time and money, and how to organize your work successfully when you are a first-year student. Rarely, however, will you be given much information about how to transition successfully into your **sophomore year** or how to navigate through this next step. You might say—and rightfully so—"I'm still trying to get through my first year. I don't have time to think about my sophomore year." But it is never too early to plan for the future, for your next step. It is advisable to set aside some time to think about what comes next and begin preparing to successfully take the steps to make this next venture a reality. Even if you begin your second year and are still classified as a first-year student, these steps can help you move toward your goals faster.

Who Do You Think You Are?

This may sound strange but the first step in successfully transitioning to anything, including your sophomore year, is to get your head straight. Just who do you think you are anyway? What makes you think you can make it through your sophomore year? Why do you deserve to take this step and then the next one and so on? Anytime you start to do something new, you are most likely plagued with childhood fears. You might start doubting yourself and second guessing your decisions. You might say to yourself, "I'm not smart enough to get a college degree." The antidote to these kinds of deep-seated fears that have been entrenched for a long time is to think of positive outcomes that are the opposite of the fears you are having. Instead of letting fears and doubts take over your subconscious, take control and say to yourself, "I am smart enough to be a college graduate; I deserve to have this degree, and I am going to get through this year and prepare for the next one." When doubts and fears creep into your mind, immediately combat this two-headed monster with a positive thought. Who do you think you are? You are a unique person who has special gifts and talents, and your time has come. Now, grab this opportunity; get ready to be successful, and plunge in without looking back. And remember, for every transition you face from now on, challenges may occur, but you have the capacity to succeed.

Can I Make It to My Second Year?

The following is a list of steps that will help you transition successfully to your sophomore year and beyond. Put them into practice and feel the power of knowing you are ready and prepared.

▶ **Begin with the end in mind.** Think about how happy you are going to be when you finish your sophomore year at community college and you are about to go on to a major university or getting ready to pursue a job that you really want. All the way through this venture—and any venture—work hard today but focus on the end result and enjoy the great opportunity that you have to learn and grow.

▶ **Formulate a clear vision about what you want your life to be.** This may not happen overnight or even for a few weeks or months, but you should begin embracing certain thoughts, ideas, and pictures of what you want your life to be. It may sound strange, but having a visual picture of what you want actually helps you move toward it. Each transition can be looked at as another step toward getting to this beautiful vision you have created in your head.

▶ **Begin now to explore options about career interests you would like to pursue.** Have you given much thought to what your purpose in life is or should be or what you want to do with your time on earth? Researchers are discovering that students really begin to zero in on how they want to spend their lives during the sophomore year (Reynolds, Gross, and Millard, 2005). Choosing a major requires that you have the ability to use decision-making skills, that you determine whether you have the ability and discipline to pursue certain majors and careers. Although you do not want to rush this important decision, it has been shown by researchers (Graunke & Woolsley, 2005) that sophomores with a high degree of certainty about their majors tend to perform better academically. Declaring a major is a hard decision, one that you may not get right the first time; nevertheless, you have to plunge in after thinking it through. We cannot put too much emphasis on the importance of exploring your interests and settling on a major that appeals to you and matches the vision you have for yourself.

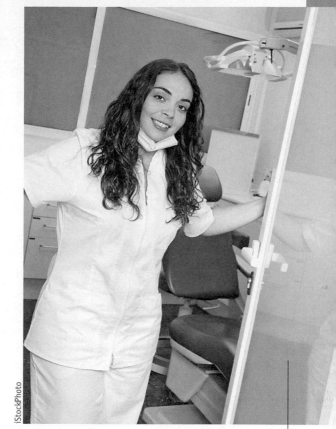

Do your interests and passion match your chosen major and/or career path?

▶ **Look inside yourself and get in touch with your inner feelings about school, work, family, and community.** You will most likely never have another time when you will be as free to focus on yourself as you are right now. Even if you have a family and children, you can consider your situation while you are in class and perhaps in between some classes. Because you are most likely a commuting student, you will have time to think about the next step in your life as you drive back and forth to school and work.

▶ **Beware of the "sophomore slump."** Although it is hard to pinpoint exactly what the "sophomore slump" really is, second-year students often find themselves confused about what they want to do; stressed because of hard decisions that need to be made; depressed because they are getting less attention in college than they did in high school; or simply tired from working, trying to spend time with family, and keeping good grades all at the same time. This condition might invade your space as early as the second semester of the first year, so be prepared to combat it. Some ways to deal with the "sophomore slump" include the following:

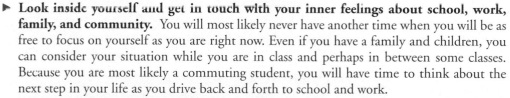

"Training teaches people what to do. Education teaches people what to be."
—Nido R. Qubein

▶ Interact with faculty and advisors and try to make a strong connection with at least one of them.

▶ Try to make connections with at least one or two fellow students with whom you have something in common.

▶ Realize that you may become less motivated and that finding a major and a purpose can help you get back on track.

▶ If you are not doing well in a particular subject, get help as quickly as you can. Talk to the professor, hire a tutor, start a study group, or connect with a study partner. Don't wait until it is too late!

From Ordinary to *Extraordinary*

REAL PEOPLE | REAL LIVES | REAL CHANGE

MARK JONES
Senior Customer Service Trainer,
SCANA, Columbia, South Carolina

My proudest moment? Finally coming to the realization that I am a functional member of a highly dysfunctional family. *I know. I know. Many people say they have a dysfunctional family,* but in my case, it is the raw, inescapable truth. My realization may not sound like much to an outsider, but when you finally realize that you do not have to be a victim of your family or your past, it is a proud moment! I can confidently say, ***"I am not like them."***

I don't have any memories of a time when my family was "normal." My mother, who has been clinically depressed my entire life, attempted suicide when I was four years old. I have never known a day when she was not heavily medicated. My father had the first of four heart attacks when I was six. My parents divorced when I was eleven and I remained with my father. My mother remarried when I was thirteen. When I was fifteen, my dad died, leaving us very little. Even the mobile home in which we lived was repossessed.

My new stepfather was legally blind and has never driven a car. My mother never drove either. They never wanted me to get my permit or drive and fought my attempts to do so for years. They thought walking everywhere was perfectly normal. My stepfather did not have any children of his own and did not have any parenting skills. I was treated more as a tenant than a son or stepson. As a matter of fact, I had to pay rent to live with him and my own mother. Due to my father's death, I drew a small Social Security check until I graduated from high school. Every month, much of that money had to be turned over to my stepfather. I even had to buy my own bed to sleep in. Of course, we had our share of good times, too. But I knew this situation was far from "normal"—whatever that was.

When I was in my early 20s I begged a dear friend, Stella, to let me use her car so I could try for my driver's license. I had practically no driving experience, but somehow, I passed the test. I paid $200 for my first car in two installments of $100 each. It was a 1973 Buick LeSabre that was wrecked down one entire side and had been used in demolition donut field races. But, it was much better than walking everywhere. This was a turning point in my life. I was in my early 20s and working in a local grocery store. I enrolled in the university right after high

> *I paid $200 for my first car... a 1973 Buick LeSabre that was wrecked down one entire side and had been used in demolition donut field races.*

school, but I had to drop out because I could not get a grant and did not make enough money to pay tuition. I later enrolled in the local community college but after one semester, I realized I could not afford this either.

Basically, I had to make a hard, life-altering decision. I did not want to live my life in debt as my father had done, so I made up my mind that I would have to take a few steps back to eventually go forward. I began to look for a job that offered educational benefits. I scanned the phone book for hospitals, utility companies, banks, and government agencies that offered this benefit. Every Monday night, their job lines would be updated and I would call, fill out an application, and wait. Nothing!

Finally, I learned how to properly fill out an application. I would call the job line many times and write down every word in their advertisement. Then, I would craft my application and letter based on *their needs,* not *my experiences.* I had to learn to apply for a job as if I already had it. After two years and many attempts to secure a suitable position, a utility company hired me—AND they had educational benefits. Finally, I could go back to school and get another car! I began working toward my degree and after six long, hard years, I graduated with a bachelor of science in business management. It was not easy, as I am sure you know. I had to take some courses online, and I was in class every Friday night for years and years.

During my time in college, I worked my way up in the company and today, 17 years later, I am a senior trainer for SCANA, an eleven-billion-dollar Fortune 500 utility holding company founded in 1846. I design training programs and development materials for new hires, system enhancements, and employee upgrades.

I look back on my childhood and early adulthood and I am proud of the fact that I did not let my past or my family dictate my future. I survived. I refused to succumb to their life. I knew that I had to have my own life with my own fate. You can have this too. Never let your past or your family tell you what you're capable of doing. Take chances. Take risks. And if you have to take a step backward to go forward, never be ashamed to do that too.

EXTRAORDINARY REFLECTION

Read the following statement and respond in your online journal or class notebook.

Mr. Jones came from a family that did not support him financially, emotionally, or educationally. What advice would you give to someone who might be experiencing the same type of environment? Does your family have to play a role in your life for you to be successful?

iStockPhoto

What campus services are available to help you transition to your sophomore year?

HELP! WHAT DO I DO NEXT?

Should I Continue My Education or Go to Work When I Complete My Certificate or Degree?

There is no simple, one-size-fits-all answer to the question, "Do I continue my education or go to work after my sophomore year?" It depends on the individual and one's personal interests, abilities, and desires. You have to make the right decision for you based on all the information you have to consider.

If you came to your community college with a specific associate degree program and career path in mind, entering the workforce may still be the best choice for you. You may have a burning desire to work in physical therapy, drafting, automotive technology, HVAC, or nursing. If your associate degree offers you the career opportunity you are seeking, by all means continue your plans. There are millions of people who hold associate degrees who have outstanding careers and limitless earning opportunities.

On the other hand, if you think you might like to be a nursing administrator, architect, or elementary school principal, you will want to consider pursuing a baccalaureate degree at some point. Your academic advisor may be able to offer you assistance in weighing this very important decision. Unless finances are an extreme problem for you, it is usually easier to continue your education while you are "in the groove."

Often, having a baccalaureate degree will assist you in moving into supervision and management much faster. Furthermore, you will give yourself more time to mature, to learn, and determine exactly what career you would like to pursue. When it comes to education, more is often better. But again, it depends on the individual and one's personal goals and career plans. Certainly, a baccalaureate degree is not for everyone, and there are many excellent, challenging career paths you can pursue with the right associate degree or certificate.

There are other circumstances in which your best choice would be to go to work if you can find a job that pays well and provides benefits, offers you a good career path, and is something you enjoy doing. If you are accumulating tremendous student loan debt, you might want to go to work and attend school part time. If you like school and are doing well, but you have no earthly idea what you want to do, you might find it helpful to work for a semester and try to focus on a career path that might interest you and then go back to school. The main question you need to consider is: What is right for me at this time in my life and career?

Making the Big Step Toward a Baccalaureate Degree

Leaving the comfort of your local community college and moving to another type of institution is indeed a big step, but a step well worth pursuing. Moving to another institution is a new beginning and will include new relationships, new buildings, new activities, new faculty members, and new experiences. Although it may be a little overwhelming at first, it should also be exciting. You have reached another milestone in your road to a rewarding career and life. You are preparing to make another transition.

Of course, you'll be a little nervous about making this commitment because you are again transitioning into the unknown. But you have made similar steps already and you have been successful. This is just one more step! It helps, however, if you prepare carefully, beginning NOW.

If you are relatively sure you want to continue your education after you complete your community college degree, consider the following ideas:

▶ **Decide where you want to transfer and go visit that campus if possible.** Find out everything you can about an institution before you make a decision to attend. The more you can learn about the different choices, the better prepared you are to make the right selection. Get familiar with the buildings where you will take classes. Find out about on-campus residential living quarters as well as off-campus possibilities. Learn where key offices are located, such as the financial aid office, career center, academic centers, the library, and others. Does this campus have a good "feel" to you? Does it appear to be a good match to your vision for yourself? Does it offer the major you are interested in pursuing? What are the costs involved with attending this institution? Can you afford it? Will you need loans and/or a job?

▶ **If you know someone who attends that institution, schedule a time for an interview to ask questions.** Is it a friendly campus? How is parking? What size are the classes? Is this person glad he or she made this choice? What recommendations does he or she have as you prepare to transfer later on? Does this person know anything about the major you plan to pursue? If the emphasis is on research, do major professors teach many of the classes?

▶ **If money is a problem, try to locate an in-state four-year institution close enough for you to live at home and pay in-state tuition.** This may not be what you want to do, but it is much smarter than accumulating large student loan debts. Another possibility that might make attending easier is to explore how many courses you can take online. Online courses greatly eliminate commuting expenses and by taking them, you might be able to work more hours and save money to help pay for school.

▶ **Consider external pressures that you will have to overcome in order to successfully transition to a four-year college or university.** You will, of course, have to deal with internal pressures of doubt, stress, depression, and frustration that impact everyone from time to time. In addition, you may have external pressures that have to be resolved before you transfer. How do your parents or spouse/partner feel about your continuing education? If you are a first-generation college student, others may not understand why this move is so important to you. What does your significant other think about this decision? How do your local friends feel about your moving to a different level if they aren't going with you? You will have to come to grips with these issues if they exist. The important thing is not to let anything or anyone stand in your way if you truly want a baccalaureate degree.

Do you know others who already attend your four-year college of choice?

THE SUCCESSFUL TRANSITION PLAN FOR FIRST-YEAR STUDENTS

How Can I Prepare for My Future?

If you are reasonably sure about continuing your education after completing studies at your two-year college, you need to create a four-year plan. Developing a four-year plan may be a little overwhelming at this stage of your college career, but it will pay big dividends in saved time, reduced frustrations, and well-designed career and educational objectives. Using the information in Chapter 1 about goal setting, you can actually develop long-range goals using this plan as a blueprint (see Figure 12.1).

Before you complete the activity of designing your four-year plan, explore several related websites to find ideas you might want to include in your plan and make a list of ideas that interest you. For example, you might review the website of a university in which you are interested. Your third-year list might include a statement about contacting them: "Write University of Success and seek information on their program in computer science."

On separate sheets of paper, design a transition plan based on your current objectives. If you plan to complete a baccalaureate degree, write your plan for that goal. If you plan to go to work after you complete your associate degree, write your plan for that goal. Remember, you can always change your plans and goals, but you will accomplish much more if you know where you are going.

DEVELOPING YOUR CAREER PLAN

What Do You Want to Be When You "Grow Up"?

More people than you can imagine have trouble deciding what they want to be when they "grow up." Studies indicate that more than 20 percent of all first-year college students do not know what their majors will be. That's all right for the time being, but before long you will need to make a decision, as this choice affects your selection of classes, co-curricular activities, and possible internships. If you delay selecting a major too long, you may lose credit hours and take unnecessary courses.

The questions that follow are designed to help you make the decision regarding what you want to do with the rest of your life—your career.

What Is Your Personality Type?

You can best answer this question by taking a personality inventory, such as the Myers-Briggs Type Indicator. (The PAP, an inventory based on the MBTI, is located in Chapter 7 of this book.) This question is important, because your personality may very well indicate the type of work in which you will be successful and happy. If you are a real people person, you probably will not be very happy, for example, in a job with minimal human contact and interaction.

Describe your personality type. _____

_____

How will your personality type affect your career path? _____

_____

What Are Your Interests?

Understanding your specific interests may help you decide on a career. If you love working on cars, you might consider becoming a mechanical engineer. If you love to draw or build things, you might be interested in architecture or sculpting.

What are your major interests? _____

_____

How can these interests be transferred to a career choice? _____

_____

FIGURE

12.1 *The Four-Year Plan*

FIRST YEAR

▶ Explore campus organizations and get involved in activities that interest you. If you already know your major, you can work in organizations that enhance your career options. Employers are interested in graduates who have been actively involved.

▶ Identify academic centers where you may get help in improving your grades. A solid GPA is important when you seek internships, part-time jobs, and full-time work later on. They are also important for scholarships and graduate school.

▶ Establish study groups for your courses and secure study partners for difficult courses.

▶ If you need developmental or remedial work, start it now.

▶ Develop a cover letter and resumé using the information found in this chapter. This will change as you grow and progress but it is good to have them on hand if needed.

▶ Establish relationships with advisors and professors who know your work firsthand and can be a personal reference for scholarships, internships, part-time employment, and so on.

▶ Become well acquainted with your professors and academic advisor because you will need employment references in the future.

▶ Begin now searching for a part-time position or a summer job. Competition is stiff during difficult economic times and many jobs are promised early.

▶ Attend job fairs even if you aren't looking for a job right now. Job fairs give you practice talking to people about work and allow you to meet people who might be able to tell you more about a career you are interested in.

▶ Try to identify a major that you like, that you can successfully pursue, and that meets your financial expectations.

▶ Visit the Career Center at your college.

▶ Take a personal finance course as an elective.

SECOND YEAR

▶ Don't let the "sophomore slump" impact your grades. Keep your GPA as high as possible.

▶ If you have not been working, try to find a part-time job that relates to your career interest. Don't work too many hours so work does not impact your grades.

▶ If you have determined a major and intend to transfer to a four-year college or university after you graduate from community college, establish a relationship with an advisor on that campus.

▶ Visit colleges and universities that interest you.

▶ Explore career options and interests in the library, at career fairs, and in Internet resources.

▶ Try to increase your range of responsibilities in campus activities to gain more leadership experience.

▶ Achieve exposure and experience through job shadowing and volunteering if you have time.

▶ Explore possible internships or cooperative programs in your field.

▶ Expand your relationships with professors who can serve as references.

▶ Update your resumé.

▶ Visit the college of your choice and speak with a transfer advisor.

THIRD YEAR

▶ Visit all the offices on campus that relate to your needs—financial aid, career counseling, academic enrichment center, and so on.

▶ Find a part-time job that relates to your major.

▶ Quickly build relationships with professors and advisors who can assist you and serve as references.

▶ Work hard to keep your GPA as high as possible as you get closer to the time to look for a job or pursue graduate school.

▶ If you want to attend graduate school, begin exploring options.

(continued)

12.1 *The Four-Year Plan (continued)*

▶ Find out the right place on campus that can help you with practice interviews.

▶ Attend all career fairs to practice your skills and to learn more about career options.

▶ Seek assistance from a major professor in getting an internship in your major to build your experience.

▶ Assemble new study groups and study partners.

▶ Update your resumé.

▶ Consider a study abroad program or international field study if you can afford it or if you can get a scholarship.

▶ Try to build an interviewing wardrobe of at least two suits and accessories.

▶ If you haven't had one yet, take a speech course.

FOURTH YEAR

▶ Get very serious about finding a career in your chosen profession NOW!

▶ Seek advice from a major professor relative to your resumé. How can you improve it? What is missing that you can do now?

▶ Participate in all job fairs and career fairs.

▶ Network with anyone and everyone you know who might be able to help you locate a good job in your field.

▶ Hone your online job search skills.

▶ Select a few companies and conduct a complete search about each one.

▶ If you get an interview, find out everything you can about the company.

▶ Make a list of questions that you want to ask an interviewer.

▶ Determine the areas that you are willing to move if asked to do so by an employer.

▶ If you plan to go to graduate school, find out what tests you need to take and begin taking practice tests to prepare. See whether there is a course you can enroll in to prepare for the test.

▶ Apply early for graduate school.

▶ Seek assistantships early!

Source: Adapted from the Career Center at the University of South Carolina. Retrieved January 18, 2010, from www.sc.edu.

Do You Enjoy Physical or Mental Work?

Many people would go crazy if they had to spend so much as one hour per day in an office. Others would be unhappy if they had to work in the sun all day or use a great deal of physical strength. The answer to this question will greatly narrow your list of potential career choices. For example, if you are an outdoor person who loves being outside in all kinds of weather, then you should probably avoid careers that are limited to indoor work. You should also consider whether you have any physical limitations that might affect your career choice.

Do you enjoy physical or mental work or both? Why? _____

_____

What does this mean to your career path? _____

_____

What Is Most Important: Money? Service? Independence? Or a Combination?

Most people, if asked "Why do you work?" would respond, "For the money." There is nothing wrong with wanting to make money in your profession, but not all professions, regardless of their worth, pay well. Some of the hardest and most rewarding work pays the least. You have to decide whether to go for the money or do something that is personally challenging and rewarding to you. Many times, you can find both!

Is your major goal in choosing a profession money or something else? What?

_____

_____

What does your goal mean to your career path? _____

_____

_____

Where Do You Want to Live?

Although this question may sound strange, many careers are limited by geography. If you are interested in oceanography, you would be hard-pressed to live in Iowa; if you love farming, New York City would be an improbable place for you to live. If you like small towns, you might not be happy in Atlanta. Some people simply prefer certain parts of the United States (or the world) to others. You need to ask yourself, "What climate do I really enjoy?" "Where would I be the happiest?" "Do I want to live near my family or away from them?"

Where do you eventually want to live? Why? _____

_____

What does your preference mean to your career path? _____

_____

Do You Want to Travel?

Some jobs require travel. Some people love to travel; some hate it. Ask yourself whether you want to be away from your home and family four nights per week, or whether you want a job that does not require any travel.

Do you enjoy travel? Do you want to do a lot of traveling? _____

_____

What does this mean to your career path? _____

_____

What Motivates You and What Do You Value?

Do you value relationships, possessions, money? Are you motivated by love, security, challenges, or power? Once you have identified what you value and what motivates you, you can identify careers that closely match your personal value system and eliminate careers that don't

HOT tips

TIPS FOR PERSONAL SUCCESS

Consider the following tips for preparing to be successful in your future career.

▶ Read about a variety of careers that interest you.

▶ Study several websites that provide information about career planning.

▶ Identify jobs and careers that appear to be "rising" and not "setting" (often known as sunrise and sunset jobs).

Now it is your turn. Create a list of three tips you would offer your fellow classmates about taking steps to prepare for the right career in the future.

1. _____

2. _____

3. _____

Would it bother you (or would you love it) to travel two to four days a week for your career?

iStockPhoto

motivate you. If you have to constantly compromise your values just to get a paycheck, you may be unhappy and motivation will be hard to find on a daily basis.

What do you truly value in your life and what motivates you? _____

_____

How might these factors affect your career decisions? _____

_____

What Are Your Skills?

Are you especially good at one or two things? Are you good with computers, a good manager of money, a good carpenter, a good communicator? Employers still stress the importance of three basic skills: writing, speaking, and listening. If you have these skills, you are ahead of the pack. If not, you need to enroll in a class that will help you to become better at all three.

What are your skills? What do you do well? _____

_____

*How could your strongest skills help you make a career decision?*_____

_____

Do You Like Routine?

The answer to this question will narrow down your choices tremendously. If you like routine, you will want a career that follows patterns and provides structure. If you do not like routine and enjoy doing different things each day, certain careers will be unrealistic for you.

Do you like routine or do you prefer variety? Why? _____

_____

How does this affect your career path? _____

_____

Your Dream Job

Using the answers you provided to the previous questions and a variety of additional resources such as websites, shadowing, and interviews, write a description for your dream job—the job you would have if you could do anything you would like to do.

_____

_____

_____

_____

_____

HELP ME: I'M UNDECLARED

Is It Awful That I Don't Know What I Want to Do?

No, it is not. And being undeclared is not a fatal disease. It is is not a disgrace or a weakness. It is a temporary state of mind, and the best way to deal with it is to stop and think. You should

SUCCESSFUL DECISIONS: An Activity for Critical Reflection

LaKeisha has been trying to plan for her future, but she really has no idea what she would like to do with her life. Her grades are excellent, and she loves college, but she doesn't have a clue what she wants to declare as a major. She has read her textbooks carefully, listened to her most forward-thinking professors, and talked to her parents, but so far she has come up with a blank slate. Her parents didn't go to college; Lakeisha is a first-generation college student so she can get very little guidance at home.

Lakeisha knows that she needs to declare a major—and that means she has to have some idea of what she wants to do with her life. Her biology professor, Dr. Margaret Palmer, has made quite an impression on her. In fact, she has suggested to LaKeisha that she should consider majoring in biology with plans of becoming a medical researcher or doctor. She said to LaKeisha, *"You are a very bright young woman. Students don't come along every day who can grasp science and math concepts*

like you can. I could help you apply for scholarships if you are interested."

LaKeisha would like to find out more from Dr. Palmer. She thinks she might love being a doctor or a researcher, but she believes that she needs to know more before going down that path. How can LaKeisha go about getting Dr. Palmer to become her mentor? How might she get Dr. Palmer to let her work with her as an assistant so she can get some hands-on experience?

_____

_____

What kinds of long-term plans does LaKeisha need to make if she decides to pursue a career as a doctor or medical researcher?

_____

_____

not declare a major because you are ashamed to be undeclared, and you shouldn't allow yourself to be pressured into declaring a major. Instead, you can take measures to work toward declaring a major and being satisfied with your decision. It is better to be undeclared than to spend several semesters in a field that is wrong for you, wasting hours that won't count toward a degree. On the other hand, the sooner you declare a major, the less likely you are to take courses that do not count toward your eventual decision. Although you need to take your time and make a good decision, you don't have forever!

Ten Steps to Career Decision Making

STEP 1: DREAM! If money were not a problem or concern, what would you do for the rest of your life? If you could do anything in the world, what would you do? Where would you do it? These are the types of questions you must ask yourself as you try to select a major and career. Go outside, lie on the grass, and look up at the sky; think silently for a little while. Let your mind wander, and let the sky be the limit. Write your dreams down. These dreams may be closer to reality than you think.

"Though no one can go back and make a brand new start, anyone can start from now and make a brand new ending."
—Carl Bard

STEP 2: GO WHERE THE PUCK IS GOING! Sound crazy? The great hockey champ Wayne Gretzky made the comment that *this ONE STEP* had been his key to success. What does it mean? He said that when he was playing hockey, he did not skate to where the puck was at the moment, he skated to where the puck was GOING. He anticipated the direction of where it was going to be hit, and when it came his way, he was already there—ready to play. Think of your career in this light. Go to where the future is bright, not necessarily areas that are bright at this moment. Look ahead and try to determine what is going to be "hot" in the future, not what is hot right now. Plan ahead. Look at trends. Read. Ask questions. Think in the future, not the moment.

STEP 3: TALK TO YOUR ADVISOR. Academic advisors are there to help you. But don't be surprised if their doors are sometimes closed. They teach, conduct research, perform community service, and sometimes advise hundreds of students. Always call in advance; make an appointment to see an advisor. When you have that appointment, make your advisor work for you. Take your college catalog and ask questions, hard questions. Your advisor will not make a career decision for you, but if you ask the proper questions, he or she can be of monumental help to you and your career decisions.

> "It's a sad day when you find out that it's not an accident—or time—or fortune, but just YOURSELF that kept things from you."
> —Lillian Hellman

Use students in your program as advisors, too. They will be invaluable to you as you work your way through the daily routine of college. Experienced students can assist you in making decisions about your classes, electives, and work-study programs. They can even help you join and become an active member of a preprofessional program.

STEP 4: USE ELECTIVES. The accreditation agency that works with your school requires that you be allowed at least one free elective in your degree program. Some programs allow many more. Use your electives wisely! Do not take courses just to get the hours. The wisest students use their electives to delve into new areas of interest or to take a block of courses in an area that might enhance their career opportunities.

STEP 5: GO TO THE CAREER CENTER. Even the smallest colleges have some type of career center or a career counselor. Use them! Campus career centers usually provide free services. The same types of services in the community could cost from $200 to $2,000. The professionals in the career center can provide information on a variety of careers and fields, and they can administer interest and personality inventories that can help you make career and other major decisions.

STEP 6: READ, READ, READ! Nothing will help you more than reading about careers and majors. Ask your advisor or counselor to help you locate information on your areas of interest. Gather information from colleges, agencies, associations, and places of employment. Then read it!

STEP 7: SHADOW. Shadowing describes the process of following someone around on the job. If you are wondering what engineers do on the job, try calling an engineering office to see whether you can sit with several of their engineers for a day over spring break. Shadowing is the very best way to get firsthand, honest information regarding a profession in which you might be interested.

STEP 8: JOIN PREPROFESSIONAL ORGANIZATIONS. One of the most important steps you can take as a college student is to become involved in campus organizations and clubs that offer educational opportunities, social interaction, and hands-on experience in your chosen field. Preprofessional organizations can open doors that will help you make a career decision, grow in your area of interest, meet professionals already working in your field, and, eventually, get a job.

STEP 9: GET A PART-TIME JOB. Work in an area that you may be interested in pursuing as a career. Get a part-time job while you are in school or work in a related job in the summer.

STEP 10: TRY TO GET A SUMMER PRACTICUM OR INTERNSHIP. Work in your field of interest to gain practical experience and see if it really suits you. Some programs require a practicum or internship, and this experience often leads to your first full-time job.

By working through this ten-step plan, you will come closer to finding what you really want and need in your life's work. Take your time, study, read, ask questions, shadow others, and, most importantly, make your own decision. Yes, you may change majors or even careers along the way, but that is a part of life's journey.

LANDING THE JOB

Is It Really Possible to Sell Yourself Through a Cover Letter and Resumé?

Remember the old saying, "You are what you eat"? When searching for a any position, you could change that to read, ***"You are what you write."*** Your resumé and cover letter are your first marketing tools and in many cases must stand alone when a recruiter is determining whether to interview you. Just as a well-designed and written resumé and cover letter can be a wonderful first step, a poorly designed and written resumé and cover letter can doom you before you ever leave your house. A good thing to remember is this: A resumé and cover letter get you the interview; the interview gets you the job.

A cover letter is basically an expansion of your resumé. A cover letter gives you the chance to link your resumé, skills, and experience together with your interest in ***a specific company's*** position and their advertising. You will need to write many cover letters to make this link work properly; in other words, you most likely need to write a cover letter designed for each position for which you apply. Your cover letter will often be the stepping-stone to get an employer to even look at your resumé. Consider it "a teaser," if you will, for all of your talents and experience. Just as you would never send someone a greeting card and not sign it, you would never send a resumé and not tell the person or committee *why* you sent it. Your cover letter tells why.

Writing a Powerful and Concise Cover Letter

The most important part of the job search process is the preparation that must be done ***prior to starting*** the interview process. A carefully crafted letter and resumé communicate your past history (education, skills, and experience) that makes you the ideal candidate for their position. They are the first marketing pieces a recruiter sees when determining whether to interview you. Consider the general tips outlined in Figure 12.2.

Figure 12.3 provides a sample cover letter and indicates the correct format and spacing to the left of the letter's content.

FIGURE

12.2 *General Tips for the Cover Letter and Resumé*

▶ Both your resumé and cover letter *MUST be typed*. There are no exceptions to this rule. Ever! Seriously, EVER!

▶ Your cover letter and resumé must be printed on the same *type and color* of *fine-quality paper*. Cheap paper sends the message that you don't care. This is not the place or time to pinch pennies; buy excellent quality, 100 percent cotton stock, resumé-quality paper.

▶ Check your printer and be sure that the print quality is impeccable. Never send a cover letter or resumé with smudges, ink smears, or poor print quality.

▶ When you print your cover letter and resumé, be certain that the watermark on the paper is turned in the correct direction. Hold it up to the light and you will see the watermark embedded in the paper. This may sound silly and picky, but people notice attention to detail.

▶ Do not fold your cover letter or resumé. Purchase a packet of 9 x 13 envelopes in which to send your materials.

▶ Do not handwrite the address on the envelope. Use a label or type the address directly on the envelope. Remember, first impressions are important.

▶ Never send a generic photocopy of a cover letter or resumé, even on the finest paper.

▶ Layout, design, font, spacing, and color must be considered in the building of your cover letter and resumé.

▶ Unless you are specifically asked to do so, NEVER discuss money or salary history in either your cover letter or resumé. This could work against you. When asked for a salary history, use ranges.

▶ Your resumé and cover letter MUST be error-free. That's right, not one single error is acceptable, including grammar, spelling, punctuation, layout/spacing, dates, or content.

▶ Each cover letter must be signed in black or blue ink.

FIGURE 12.3 *Sample Cover Letter with Formatting Information*

Your name and address. Your name should be larger and/or in a different font to call attention.	**CARSON SCOTT**
	1234 Lake Shadow Drive (123) 555-1234
	Maple City, PA 12345 Scott@bl.com
The date (then double space)	January 3, 2011
The specific person, title, and address to whom you are writing (then double space)	Mr. James Pixler, RN, CAN
	Director of Placement and Advancement
	Grace Care Center
	123 Sizemore Street, Suite 444
	Philadelphia, PA 12345
The formal salutation followed by a colon (then double space)	Dear Mr. Pixler:
Paragraph 1 (then double space)	Seven years ago, my mother was under the treatment of two incredible nurses at Grace Care Center in Philadelphia. My family and I agree that the care she was given was extraordinary. When I saw your ad in today's *Philadelphia Carrier*, I was extremely pleased to know that I now have the qualifications to be a part of the Grace Care Team as a Medical Assistant.
Paragraph 2 (then double space)	Next month, I will graduate with an Occupational Associate's Degree from Victory College of Health and Technology as a certified Medical Assistant. As my resumé indicates, I was fortunate to do my internship at Mercy Family Care Practice in Harrisburg. During this time, I was directly involved in patient care, records documentation, and family outreach.
Paragraph 3 (then double space)	As a part of my degree from Victory, I received a 4.0 in the following classes:

- Management Communications
- Microsoft Office (Word, Excel, Outlook, PowerPoint)
- Business Communications I, II, III
- Anatomy and Physiology I, II, III
- Medical Coding I, II
- Principles of Pharmacology
- Immunology I, II, III, IV
- Urinalysis and Body Fluids
- Clinical Practicum I, II, III

This, along with my past certificate in Medical Transcription and my immense respect for Grace Care Center, makes me the perfect candidate for your position.

Final paragraph or closing (then double space)	I have detailed all of my experience on the enclosed resumé. I will call you on Monday, January 24, at 11:30 a.m. to discuss how my education and experiences can help streamline operations and continue superior patient care at Grace. In the meantime, please feel free to contact me at the number above.
The complementary close (then four spaces)	Sincerely,
Your handwritten signature in black or blue ink within the four spaces	*Carson Scott*
Your typed name	CARSON SCOTT
Enclosure contents	Enclosure: Resumé

The Do's and Don'ts of Memorable Resumés

Eight seconds. That is all you have to gain the attention of your potential employer according to Susan Ireland, author and consultant (2003). *"In eight seconds, an employer scans your resumé and decides whether she will invest more time to consider you as a job candidate. The secret to passing the eight-second test is to make your resumé look inviting and quick to read"* (p. 14).

A resumé is the blueprint that details what you have accomplished regarding your education, experience, skills acquisition, workplace successes, and progressive responsibility and leadership. It is a painting (that YOU are able to "paint") of how your professional life looks. It is the ultimate advertisement of YOU! Your resumé must create interest and hopefully a *desire* to find out more about you! Just as your cover letter should be tailored to specific positions, your resumé should be too.

As you begin to build your resumé, remember to "call in the **DOCTOR**."

▶ *Design.* Visual design and format are imperative to a successful resumé. You need to think about the font that you plan to use; whether color is appropriate (usually, it is not); the use of bullets, lines, or shading; and where you are going to put information. You also need to pay attention to the text balance on the page (centered, left/right, top/bottom). The visual aspect of your resumé will be the first impression. "Make it pretty" (Britton-Whitcomb, 2003).

▶ *Objective.* Writing a clear and specific objective can help get your foot in the door. The reader, usually your potential employer, needs to be able to scan your resumé and gather the maximum detail as quickly as possible. A job-specific objective can help. Consider the following two objectives:

Before: **Objective:** To get a job as an elementary school teacher in the Dallas Area School District

After: **Objective:** To secure an elementary teaching position that will enable me to use my 14 years of creative teaching experience, curriculum development abilities, supervisory skills, and commitment to superior instruction in a team environment.

▶ *Clarity.* Clarity is of paramount importance, especially when including your past responsibilities, education, and job responsibilities. Be certain that you let the reader know exactly what you have done, what specific education you have gained, and what progress you have made. Being vague and unclear can cost you an interview.

▶ *Truth.* When writing your resumé, you may be tempted to fudge a little bit here and there to make your history look better. Perhaps you were out of work for a few months and you think it looks bad to have this gap in your chronological history. Avoid the urge to fudge. Telling the absolute truth on a resumé is essential. A lie, even a small one, can (and usually will) come back to haunt you.

▶ *Organization.* Before you begin your resumé, think about the organization of your data. You will be provided a model resumé in this chapter; however, there are several other formats you might select. It is most important that you present your information in an attractive, easy-to-read, comprehensive format.

▶ *Review.* Reviewing your resumé and cover letter is important, but having someone else review them for clarity, accuracy, spelling, grammar, placement, and overall content can be one of the best things you can do for your job search.

The following basic tips will help you as you begin building a dynamic resumé.

General Tips
▶ Do not date stamp or record the preparation date of your resumé in any place.
▶ Limit your resumé and cover letter to one page each (a two-page resumé is appropriate if you have more than 10 years of experience).

▶ Use standard resumé paper colors such as white, cream, gray, or beige.

▶ Use bullets (such as these) to help profile lists.

▶ Avoid fancy or hard to read fonts such as 𝒸𝓊𝓇𝓁𝓏 or Chiller.

▶ Use a standard font size between 10 and 14 points.

▶ Do not staple anything to your resumé (or cover letter).

▶ Try to avoid the use of *I, Me,* or *My* in your resumé (if you must use them, do so sparingly).

▶ Avoid contractions such as *don't* and do not use abbreviations.

▶ Use action verbs such as *designed, managed, created, recruited, simplified,* or *built.*

▶ Avoid the use of full sentences; fragments are fine on a resumé, but not in a cover letter.

▶ Use the correct verb tense. You will use past tense (such as *recruited*) except for your current job.

▶ Do not include irrelevant information that does not pertain to this particular job search.

▶ Choose a format that puts your "best foot" or greatest assets forward.

Remember that the job market is highly competitive. Your job is to write a resumé that is solid, appealing, comprehensive, and brief. The idea is to get someone to read it and want to know more about you.

There are different types of resumés, but primarily they can be classified as chronological, functional, or accomplishment centered formats, or a combination of each.

▶ A **chronological resumé** (Figure 12.4) organizes education and work experience in a reverse chronological order (your last or present job is listed first).

▶ A **functional resumé** organizes your work and experience around specific skills and duties.

▶ An **accomplishment resumé** allows you to place your past accomplishments into categories that are not necessarily associated with an employer but show your track record of "getting the job done."

The Interview: Making the Impression of a Lifetime

Remember the *"eight-second rule"* for making an impression. Consider this: During the interview process, you have even less. A judgment is made immediately about you: your dress, your grooming, your stance, your handshake, and your overall visual impression. Right or wrong, the interviewer will form an immediate first opinion of you—just as you will form an immediate first impression of your interviewer.

As you begin to prepare for your interview, consider the following mnemonic. If you confidently *carry* **REWARDS** with you to an interview, you will most likely *get* rewards after the interview, such as a job offer, benefits, and a career in which you can grow and prosper.

▶ *Rapport.* Rapport is basically your "relationship" (intended or unintended) with another person—the emotional alliance you establish with someone. Consider how you come across to others. Rapport involves your verbal and nonverbal communication efforts. You should strive to establish a positive relationship with potential employers and future colleagues.

▶ *Education and training.* Be confident about what you know and eloquently promote your abilities, skills, and talents to the interviewer. Remember, if you don't promote yourself, it is unlikely that anyone else will.

In the past, what preparations have served you best in getting ready for an interview?

Brand X/Jupiter Images

FIGURE **12.4** *Chronological Resumé*

CARSON SCOTT

1234 Lake Shadow Drive, Maple City, PA 12345   (123) 555-1234   Scott@bl.com

OBJECTIVE: To work as a medical assistant in an atmosphere that uses my organizational skills, compassion for people, desire to make a difference, and impeccable work ethic.

PROFESSIONAL EXPERIENCE:

January 2007–Present	Medical Assistant Intern Mercy Family Care Practice, Harrisburg, PA ▶ Responsible for completing patient charts ▶ Took patients' vitals ▶ Assisted with medical coding
February 2003–December 2006	Medical Transcriptionist The Office of Brenda Wilson, MD, Lancaster, PA ▶ Interpreted and typed medical reports ▶ Worked with insurance documentation ▶ Assisted with medical coding ▶ Served as Office Manager (1/05–12/06)
March 1998–February 2003	Ward Orderly Wallace Hospital, Lancaster, PA ▶ Assisted nurses with patient care ▶ Cleaned patient rooms ▶ Served patient meals
August 1995–March 1998	Administrative Assistant Ellen Abbot Nursing Care Facility ▶ Typed office reports ▶ Organized patient files

EDUCATION:

Occupational Associate's Degree—Medical Assistant
Victory Health Institute, Harrisburg, PA
May 2008 (with honors)

Certificate of Completion—Medical Transcription
Philadelphia Technical Institute
December 2002

Vocational High School Diploma—Health Sciences
Philadelphia Vocational High School
August 1995

▶ *Willingness.* Project a sense of willingness to learn new things, to become a team member, to assist the company with growth and new projects, and a willingness to keep up with advancements and changes in the modern world of work. Potential employers enjoy seeing an attitude of willingness and engagement.

▶ *Appearance.* Dress for success. Pay close attention to your grooming, your hygiene, your hair, your clothing, and, yes, even your shoes and socks (or hosiery). It all matters—and it is all noticed. Never make the mistake in thinking that appearance is not important.

▶ *Response.* Project positivity and optimism in your responses to the questions asked in the interview. Even if you have to talk about your weaknesses or past experiences of conflict and turmoil, put a positive spin on them. Let the interviewer know that you have learned from adversity.

▶ *Demeanor.* Cast a quality of confidence (not cockiness), intelligence, professionalism, and positivity. Carrying yourself with confidence during the interview will not go unnoticed. Pay attention to your handshake, your eye contact, your posture, mannerisms, and facial expressions.

▶ *Sincerity.* No one likes phony people, especially a potential employer. Be yourself and strive to be sincere in your answers, your emotions, and your passion.

Win, Lose, or Draw, Always Say "Thank You" in Writing

It is safe to say that failing to send a thank-you note is *"the most overlooked step in the entire job search process"* (Bolles, 2010). Yes, this is a mandatory step for every interview and it is necessary to send one to every person who interviewed you. Period. In today's world of high-tech and run, run, run, this one act will set you apart from the thousands who interview on a daily basis. And yes, you must send a thank-you letter even if you DO NOT get the job. "When do I send the thank-you note," you might ask? *Immediately after the interview.*

Sending a simple thank-you note does many things. It lets the employer know that you have good manners, that you respect other people's time and efforts, that you are considerate, that you really do care about the position, and that you have positive people and communication skills. Yes, all of that from a card and stamp that can cost less than $2.00.

In Figures 12.5 and 12.6 you will find examples of two thank-you notes. Review them and consider using them as templates to build your own notes.

FIGURE 12.5 *Thank-You Note: After the Interview*

CARSON SCOTT
1234 Lake Shadow Drive
Maple City, PA 12345
Scott@bl.com

January 20, 2011

Mr. James Pixler, RN, CAN
Director of Placement and Advancement
Grace Care Center
123 Sizemore Street, Suite 444
Philadelphia, PA 12345

Dear Mr. Pixler,

Thank you for the wonderful opportunity to meet with you and the team at Grace Care Center on Monday. Your facilities are amazing, and the new wing is going to be a remarkable addition to your center.

I enjoyed learning more about the new position in Medical Assisting, and I think that my qualifications and experiences have prepared me for this challenging opportunity. I would consider it an honor to answer any further questions that you might have or to meet with you again if you consider it necessary.

I look forward to hearing from you at your convenience. If you need any additional information, you can reach me at 123-555-1234.

Thank you,

Carson Scott

CARSON SCOTT

FIGURE 12.6 *Thank-You Note: After a Position Rejection*

CARSON SCOTT
1234 Lake Shadow Drive
Maple City, PA 12345
Scott@bl.com

January 20, 2011

Mr. James Pixler, RN, CAN
Director of Placement and Advancement
Grace Care Center
123 Sizemore Street, Suite 444
Philadelphia, PA 12345

Dear Mr. Pixler,

Thank you for the opportunity to meet with you and the team at Grace Care Center on Monday. I enjoyed learning more about your center and the planned addition.

While I was not offered the position, I did want to let you know that I appreciate your time and I would like for you to contact me if you have any future openings where you feel my qualifications and experiences would match your needs. Grace is an incredible facility, and I would consider it an honor to hold a position there.

If you need to contact me in the future, you can reach me at 123-555-1234.

Thank you for your time and assistance and good luck to you and your colleagues.

Sincerely,

Carson Scott

CARSON SCOTT

REFLECTIONS ON CAREER AND LIFE DEVELOPMENT

Making a decision about your major or career can be difficult, but, fortunately, you still have a few months before you have to make this choice. Use this time to explore all avenues that will expose you to different possibilities. This is a growing time for you and you might discover new interests and directions that you had never considered before. Follow your heart, and pursue your dreams. If there is something you have always wanted to do or be, chances are your desires will not change even after you study other options.

This is your one lifetime! You need to prepare to do something you love. No matter how much money you make, you won't be happy unless you are doing something that matters to you, something that allows you to keep learning and becoming, something that provides you opportunities to give back—perhaps the best gift of all.

As you reflect on this chapter, keep the following pointers in mind:

▶ Identify the assets you can offer a company.
▶ Learn to promote and sell yourself in an interview.
▶ Discover your personality type and make it work for you.
▶ Shadow and do volunteer work to learn as much as you can about the profession.
▶ Realize that life is *more* than money.
▶ Know your own *value* system and what motivates you.

"If you follow your bliss, doors will open for you that wouldn't have opened for anyone else."
—Joseph Campbell

CREATE SUCCESS
Your Journey to University, Career, and Life Beyond College

# Connecting Think about the people on your college campus. With whom can you make a connection to learn more about *transferring to a four-year institution?* (Example: counselor, advisor, retention specialist, etc.) Why and how will this connection be important?	
# Reading Find one brief, relevant article (in print or online) relating to *selecting a college major.* After you have read the article, write a brief summary of the additional facts you have learned.	
# E-Learning Using any search engine, find one piece of valid, reliable information about how to *prepare a resumé.* Briefly explain what you learned and why you think it is important.	
# Analyzing Choose one main idea or topic from this chapter. After *exploring and researching this idea* further, determine how this information can help you succeed in other classes.	
# Transitioning How will you use the content found in this chapter to help you *create a successful transition plan* to your next semester and beyond?	
# Empowering Thinking about the entire spectrum of your life (college, family, friends, finances, career, etc.), how can you *empower yourself to be more successful* through the information found in this chapter?	

SQ3R *Mastery* Study Sheet

EXAMPLE QUESTION *(from page 310)* How do I transition to my sophomore year?	ANSWER:
EXAMPLE QUESTION *(from page 325)* What does DOCTOR stand for?	ANSWER:
AUTHOR QUESTION *(from page 316)* Why does personality type matter when deciding on a major or job?	ANSWER:
AUTHOR QUESTION *(from page 317)* Why is it important to have a four-year plan?	ANSWER:
AUTHOR QUESTION *(from page 321)* Discuss three of the steps to career decision making.	ANSWER:
AUTHOR QUESTION *(from page 325)* Why is it important to write an excellent resumé?	ANSWER:
AUTHOR QUESTION *(from page 328)* Why do you need to write a thank-you note, even if you do not get the position?	ANSWER:
YOUR QUESTION *(from page ____)*	ANSWER:
YOUR QUESTION *(from page ____)*	ANSWER:
YOUR QUESTION *(from page ____)*	ANSWER:
YOUR QUESTION *(from page ____)*	ANSWER:
YOUR QUESTION *(from page ____)*	ANSWER:

Finally, after answering these questions, recite this chapter's major points in your mind. Consider the following general questions to help you master this material.

▶ What was it about?
▶ What does it mean?
▶ What was the most important thing I learned? Why?
▶ What were the key points to remember?

REFERENCES

Adler, R., Rosenfeld, L., & Towne, N. (2006). *Interplay. The Process of Interpersonal Communication* (2nd ed.). New York: Holt, Rinehart and Winston.

Altman, I., & Taylor, D. (1973). *Social Penetration: The Development of Interpersonal Relationships.* New York: Holt.

American Library Association. (1989). *Presidential Committee on Information Literacy. Final Report.* Chicago: American Library Association.

American Psychological Association. (2008). *For a Better Understanding of Sexual Orientation and Homosexuality.* Retrieved August 12, 2008, from www.apa.org/topics/orientation.html.

Anderson, L., & Bolt, S. (2008). *Professionalism: Real Skills for Workplace Success.* Upper Saddle River, NJ: Pearson Prentice Hall.

Association of American Colleges and Universities. (n.d.). *Top Ten Things Employers Look for in New College Graduates.* Retrieved April 14, 2010, from www.aacu.org/leap/students/employers topten.cfm.

Bach, D. (2003). *The Finish Rich Notebook.* New York: Broadway Books.

Bailey, T., Kienzl, G., & Marcotte, D. (August 2004). *Who Benefits from Postsecondary Occupational Education?* New York: Columbia University Teachers College, Community College Research Center.

Barrett, D. (2008). Average Student Loans Top $19,000. Retrieved September 2, 2008, from http://encarta.msn.com/encnet/departments/financialaid/?article=averagestudentloans.

Baxter, L. A. (1993). Conflict Management: An Episodic Approach. *Small Group Behavior, 13*(1), 23–42.

Beebe, S., Beebe, S., & Redmond, M. (2008). *Interpersonal Communication: Relating to Others* (5th ed.). Boston: Allyn and Bacon.

Block, S. (February 22, 2006). Students Suffocate under Tens of Thousands in Loans. *USA Today,* p. A1.

Bolles, R. N. (2010). *What Color Is Your Parachute? A Practical Manual for Job-Hunters and Career-Changers.* Berkeley, CA: Ten Speed Press.

Bosack, J. (1978). *Fallacies.* Dubuque, IA: Educulture Publishers.

Britton-Whitcomb, S. (2003). *Resume Magic: Trade Secrets of a Professional Resume Writer.* Indianapolis, IN: JIST Works Publishing.

Broderick, C. (2003). *Why Care about Your Credit Score?* InCharge Education Foundation.

Career Center, University of South Carolina. (n.d.). Four-Year Student Plan. Retrieved May 3, 2010, from www.sc.edu/career/studentplan.html.

Chronicle of Higher Education. (August 28, 2009). *Almanac Edition, 2008–2009, 55*(1), 18.

Chronicle of Higher Education. (January 29, 2010). From Community College to Ph.D. Retrieved February 1, 2010, from http://chronicle.com/article/Chart-From-Community-Colle/63712.

Cojonet (City of Jacksonville, FL). (2003). Consumer Affairs Gets New Tough Law on Car Title Businesses. Retrieved from www.coj.net/Departments/Regulatory+and+Environmental+Services/Consumer+Affairs/TITLE+LOANS.htm.

Collegeboard. (2008). College Prices Increase in Step with Inflation: Financial Aid Grows But Fewer Private Loans Even Before Credit Crisis. Retrieved from www.collegeboard.com/press/releases/201194.html.

Collins, J. (2001). *Good to Great.* New York: HarperBusiness.

Consumer Reports. (September 2008). Protect Yourself Online: The Biggest Threats and the Best Solutions.

Consumer Reports. Money Advisor. (September 2008). Protecting Your Identity.

Consumer Response Center. (2003). *Identity Theft and Fraud.*

Cooper, M. (2002). Alcohol Use and Risky Sexual Behavior among College Students and Youth. *Journal of Studies on Alcohol, 63*(2), S101.

Cooper-Arnold, A. L. (2006). *Credit Card Debt: A Survival Guide for Students.* Retrieved from www.youngmoney.com/credit_debt/credit_basics/050804-02.

Daly, J., & Engleberg, I. (2006). *Presentations in Everyday Life: Strategies for Effective Speaking.* Upper Saddle River, NJ: Allyn and Bacon.

DeVito, J. A. (2007). *Interpersonal Messages: Communication and Relationship Skills.* Boston: Pearson Education.

The Digerati Life. (2008). *Lost Money: How Money Drains Add Up to $175,000 in 10 Years.* Retrieved September 5, 2008, from www.thedigeratilife.com/blog.index.php/2008/07/31/lost-money-how-money-drains.

Domestic Violence Resource Center. (n.d.). Retrieved May 3, 2010, from www.dvrc-or.org /domestic /violence/resources/C61.

Donaldson, J. F., & Townsend, B. K. (2007). Higher Education Journals' Discourse about Adult Undergraduate Students. *Journal of Higher Education, 78,* 27–30.

Donatelle, R., & Davis, L. (2002). *Health: The Basics.* Upper Saddle River, NJ: Prentice Hall.

Dunn, R., & Griggs, S. (2000). *Practical Approaches to Using Learning Styles in Higher Education.* New York: Bergin & Garvey.

ERIC Digest. (2010). Retrieved April 3, 2010, from www.ericdigests.org/1992-3/college.htm.

Feagin, J. R., & Feagin, C. B. (2008). *Racial and Ethnic Relations.* Upper Saddle River, NJ: Pearson/Prentice Hall.

Forbes. (March 11, 2009). The World's Billionaires. Retrieved from www.forbes.com/lists/2009/10/billionaires-2009-richest-people_Warren-Buffett_C0R3.html.

Gamble, T., and Gamble, M. (1978). *Public Speaking in the Age of Diversity.* Upper Saddle River, NJ: Prentice Hall.

Gardner, H. (1983). *Frames of Mind: The Theory of Multiple Intelligences.* New York: Basic Books.

Get More Done. (2009). Retrieved January 3, 2009, from www.getmoredone.com.

Girdano, D., Dusek, D., & Everly, G. (2009). *Controlling Stress and Tension* (8th ed.). Boston: Benjamin Cummings.

Glenn, J. M. L. (October 2007). Generations at Work: The New Diversity. *Business Education Forum, 62*(1), 47–49.

The Goddess Path. (2009). *Mnemosyne, the Goddess of Memory.* Retrieved from www.goddessgift.com.

Goleman, D. (2006). *Emotional Intelligence: Why It Can Matter More than IQ* (10th Anniv. Ed.). New York: Bantam.

Gordon, E. E. (2005). *The 2010 Meltdown: Solving the Impending Jobs Crisis.* Westport, CT: Praeger.

Graunke, S. S., & Woosley, S. A. (2005). An Exploration of the Factors That Affect the Academic Success of College Sophomores. *College Student Journal, 39*(2), 367–376.

Hall, E. (1966). *The Hidden Dimension.* Garden City, NY: Doubleday.

HelpGuide.org. (n.d.). *Domestic Violence and Abuse: Signs of Abuse and Abusive Relationships.* Retrieved April 12, 2010, from www.helpguide.org.

Housden, R. (2007). Taking a Chance on Joy. *O's Guide to Life: The Best of the Oprah Magazine.* Birmingham, AL: Oxmoor House.

333

Ireland, S. (2003). *The Complete Idiot's Guide to the Perfect Resume*. Indianapolis, IN: Alpha Publishing Company.

Jung, C. (1921). Psychology Types. In *Collected Works of C.G. Jung* (Volume 6; R. Hull, Translator). Princeton, NJ: Princeton University Press, 1976.

Kallock, A. (April 16, 2009). Sunstein: Lack of Ideological Diversity Leads to Extremism. *The Harvard Law Review.*

Kennon, J. (n.d.). Warren Buffett Biography. *About.com.* Retrieved from http://beginnersinvest.about.com/cs/warrenbuffet/a/awarrenbio.htm.

Kiewra, K., & Fletcher, H. (1984). The Relationship Between Note Taking Variables and Achievement Measure. *Human Learning, 3,* 273–280.

Kirszner, L., & Mandell, S. (1995). *The Holt Handbook.* Orlando, FL: Harcourt Brace College Publishers.

Konowalow, S. (2003). *Planning Your Future: Keys to Financial Freedom.* Columbus, OH: Prentice Hall.

Lane, H. (1976). *The Wild Boy of Aveyron.* Cambridge, MA: Harvard University Press.

Lane, S. (2008). *Interpersonal Communication: Competence and Contexts.* Boston: Pearson/Allyn and Bacon.

Leinwood, D. (September 23, 2002). Ecstasy-Viagra Mix Alarms Doctors. *USA Today,* p. D4.

Light, R. (2001). *Making the Most of College: Students Speak Their Minds.* Cambridge, MA: Harvard University Press.

Maslow, A. (1943). A Theory of Human Motivation. *Psychological Review. 50,* 370–396.

McCornack, S. (2007). *Reflect and Relate: An Introduction to Interpersonal Communication.* Boston: Bedford-St. Martin's Press.

National Domestic Violence Hotline. (2010). Get Educated. Retrieved May 2, 2010, from www.ndvh.org/get-educated/?gclid=CM7Js-6MuaECFQVaagod9XIx_g.

National Institute on Drug Abuse. (n.d.). Drugs of Abuse. Retrieved from www.nida.nih.gov.

National Leadership Council for Liberal Education and America's Promise. (2008). *College Learning for the New Global Century.* Washington, DC.

Nellie Mae. (2005). *Credit Cards 101.* Wilkes-Barre, PA: Author.

Nelson, D., & Low, G. (2010). *Emotional Intelligence: Achieving Academic and Career Excellence.* Upper Saddle River, NJ: Prentice Hall.

Nobel Foundation. (1993). Nelson Mandela—Biography. Retrieved from http://nobelprize.org/nobel_prizes/peace/laureates.

1 on 1 Health. (2006). *You Can Stop Smoking: Tips to Help You Quit for Good.* GlaxoSmithKline Group. Retrieved from www.1on1health.com.

Ormondroyd, J., Engle, M., & Cosgrave, T. (2001). *How to Critically Analyze Information Sources.* Cornell University Libraries. Retrieved from www.library.cornell.edu.

Orndorff, Bob. (2008). *Top Ten Career Strategies for Freshmen and Sophomores.* Retrieved November 18, 2008, from www.jobweb.com/parents.aspx?id=50.

Pauk, W. (2007). *How to Study in College* (8th ed.). New York: Houghton Mifflin.

Paul, R., & Elder, L. (2006). *A Miniature Guide to Critical Thinking: Concepts and Tools.* Dillon Beach, CA: Foundation for Critical Thinking.

Payday Loan: Consumer Information. (2008). Retrieved February 12, 2009, from www.paydayloaninfo.org.

Personality Type Portraits. (n.d.). Retrieved December 2, 2008, from www.personalitypage.com.

Potter, J. (2005). *Becoming a Strategic Thinker: Developing Skills for Success.* Upper Saddle River, NJ: Pearson/Prentice.

Reynolds, P., Gross, J., & Millard, B. (2005). *Discovering Life Purpose: Retention Success in a Leadership Course at Indiana Wesleyan University.* Bloomington: Indiana Project on Academic Success, Smith Center for Research, Indiana University.

Rosato, D. (July 2008). Life Without Plastic. *Money,* pp. 91–95.

Russell, N. S. (2003). *Words, Words, Words.* Retrieved October 7, 2008, from www.careerknowhow.com/improvement/words.htm.

Sapir-Whorf Hypothesis. (1956). In Whorf, B., *Language, Thought, and Reality.* Cambridge, MA: MIT Press.

Schmalleger, R. (2006). *Criminal Justice: A Brief Introduction* (6th ed.). Upper Saddle River, NJ: Prentice Hall.

Seyler, D. (2003). *Steps to College Reading* (2nd ed.). Boston: Allyn & Bacon.

Shattuck, R. (1980). *The Forbidden Experiment: The Story of the Wild Boy of Aveyron.* New York: Farrar, Straus & Giroux.

Sherfield, R. (2004). *The Everything Self-Esteem Book.* Avon, MA: Adams Media.

Sherfield, R., & Moody, P. (2009). *Solving the Professional Development Puzzle: 101 Solutions for Career and Life Planning.* Upper Saddle River, NJ: Pearson.

Slavin, R. E. (2009). *Education Psychology: Theory and Practice.* Upper Saddle River, NJ: Pearson Education.

Smilksten, R. (2003). *We're Born to Learn: Using the Brain's Natural Learning Process to Create Today's Curriculum.* Thousand Oaks, CA: Corwin Press.

Smith, B. (2007). *Breaking Through: College Reading* (8th ed.). Upper Saddle River, NJ: Pearson Education.

Snyder, C. R. (2000). Hope Theory: Rainbows of the Mind. *Psychology Inquiry, 13,* 249–275.

Snyder, C. R., & Lopez, S. (2007). *Positive Psychology: The Scientific and Practical Explorations of Human Strength.* Thousand Oaks, CA: Sage Publications.

The State (Newspaper). (August 31, 2008). Protecting Your Identity, p. B12.

Steen, M. (2010). Essential Skills for College Grads. Retrieved September 21, 2010, from www.hotjobs.yahoo.com.

Steinke, R. (2007). Women on the Rocks. *O's Guide to Life: The Best of the Oprah Magazine.* Birmingham, AL: Oxmoor House.

Tarkovsky, S. (2006). Mind, Body, and Soul: The Key to Overall Wellness and Health. Ezine articles.com. Retrieved September 11, 2006, from http://ezinearticles.com/?Mind,-Body,-and-Soul---The-Key-To-Overall-Wellness-and-Health.

Texas A&M University. (n.d.). *Improve Your Memory.* Retrieved January 5, 2009, from www.scs.tamu.edu/selfhelp/elibrary/memory.asp.

Tidwell, L., & Walther, J. (July 2002). Computer-Mediated Communication Effects on Disclosure, Impressions, and Interpersonal Evaluations: Getting to Know One Another a Bit at a Time. *Human Communication Research, 28,* 317–348.

Tieger, P., & Barron-Tieger, B. (2007). *Do What You Are: Discover the Perfect Career for You Through the Secrets of Personality Type* (3rd ed.). Boston: Little, Brown.

TimMcGraw.com (n.d.). About Tim. Retrieved from www.timmcgraw.com/#about-tim.html.

Turnitin.com. (n.d.). Retrieved September 30, 2008, from www.turnitin.com/static/home.html.

21 Facts about the Internet. (2008). Retrieved January 24, 2009, from www.bizwaremagic.com/quick_internet_history.htm.

UC Berkeley—Teaching Library Internet Workshop. (2005). *Evaluating Web Pages: Techniques to Apply and Questions to Ask.* Retrieved from www.lib.berkeley.edu/TeachingLib/Guides/Internet/Evaluate.htm.

U.S. Bank. (2002). *Paying for College: A Guide to Financial Aid.* Minneapolis, MN: Author.

U.S. Bureau of the Census/U.S. Bureau of Labor Statistics. (2007). *Education and Training Pay.* Washington, DC: U.S. Government Printing Office.

U.S. Bureau of Labor Statistics. (2006). *How American Spend Time.* Washington, DC: Department of the Census. Retrieved February 9, 2009, from www.bls.gov.

U.S. Department of Education. (2008). *Newsblade.* Retrieved from http://newsblaze.com/story/2007091202000800001.mwir/topstory.html.

U.S. Department of Education. (2008–2009). *The Student Guide: Financial Aid.* Washington, DC: Author.

U.S. Department of Education/National Center for Education Statistics. (June 1998). *First-Generation Students: Undergraduates Whose Parents Never Enrolled in Postsecondary Education,* NCES 98-082. Washington, DC: Author.

U.S. Department of Justice. (July 2000). *Extent, Nature, and Consequences of Intimate Partner Violence: Findings from the National Violence Against Women Survey.* Retrieved May 10, 2010, from www.ncjrs.gov/pdffiles1/nij/181867.pdf.

U.S. Equal Opportunity Commission. (1990). *Americans with Disability Act of 1990,* Titles I and V. Retrieved from www.eeoc.gov/policy/ada.html.

Waitley, D. (1997). *Psychology of Success: Developing Your Self-Esteem.* Boston: Irwin Career Education Division.

Wallechinsky, D., & Wallace, A. (2005). *The New Book of Lists: The Original Compendium of Curious Information.* Edinburgh, Scotland: Conongate Books

Walther, J., & Burgoon, J. (1992). Relational Communication in Computer-Mediated Interaction. *Human Communication Research, 19,* 50–88.

Warner, J. (November 5, 2002). Celebratory Drinking Culture on Campus: Dangerous Drinking Style Popular among College Students. *Parenting and Pregnancy,* p. 37.

Webster's College Dictionary. (1995). New York: Random House.

Wechsler, H., & Wuethrich, B. (2002). *Dying to Drink: Confronting Binge Drinking on College Campuses.* New York: Rodale Press.

Wetmore, D. (2008). *Time Management Facts and Figures.* Retrieved December 1, 2008, from www.balancetime.com.

White House. (n.d.). Abraham Lincoln. Retrived from www.whitehouse.gov/about/presidents.

Wikipedia. (n.d.). Tim McGraw. Retrieved from www.wikipedia.org/wiki/Tim_McGraw.

Wikipedia. (n.d.). Warren Buffett. Retrieved from www.wikipedia.org/wiki/Warren_Buffett.

Williams, E. (June 26, 2008). Students Need Help Combating Credit Card Debt. Testimony before the House Financial Services Subcommittee on Financial Institutions and Consumer Credit. Retrieved September 2, 2008, from www.americanprogress.org/issues/2008/06/williams_testimony.html.

Woolfolk, A. (2006). *Educational Psychology* (10th ed.). Boston: Allyn and Bacon.

Yip, P. (August 31, 2008). College Campuses Are Ripe for the Picking. *The State* (newspaper), p. B22.

Zarefsky, D. (2001). *Public Speaking: Strategies for Success* (3rd ed.). Boston: Pearson/Allyn & Bacon.

Zen Habits. (2008). *Simple Living Manifesto: 72 Ways to Simplify Your Life.* Retrieved from http://zenhabits.net.